Tenacious Solidarity

Biblical Provocations on Race, Religion, Climate, and the Economy

WALTER BRUEGGEMANN

Edited and Introduced by
Davis Hankins

FORTRESS PRESS
MINNEAPOLIS

TENACIOUS SOLIDARITY
Biblical Provocations on Race, Religion, Climate, and the Economy

Cover image: Graffiti/Pixabay
Cover design: Laurie Ingram

Print ISBN: 978-1-5064-4770-4
eBook ISBN: 978-1-5064-4771-1

We gratefully acknowledge the following pieces included in the volume. All are reprinted by permission of the publishers for one-time use in this volume only.

Chapter 11: "Sabbath as Alternative," from *Word & World* 36, no. 3 (Summer 2016): 247–56.

Chapter 16: "Mentoring across Generations," published in *Mentoring: Biblical, Theological, and Practical Perspectives*, Cam Murchison and Dean Thompson, eds. (Grand Rapids: Eerdmans, 2018).

Chapter 19: "The Torah: Back to Basics, from Jesus to Moses," *Journal for Preachers* 41, no. 1 (Advent 2017): 11–20.

Appendix A: "Prophetic Studies," in *The Oxford Handbook of the Prophets*, ed. Carolyn J. Sharp (New York: Oxford University Press, 2016), 655–65.

Appendix B: "Biblical Theology: Testimony vs. Totalism"; first appeared as "Testimony that Breaks the Silence of Totalism," *Interpretation: A Journal of Bible and Theology* 70 (2016): 275–87.

Appendix C: "Biblical Interpretation," based on a version first printed as "Multitude of Moseses," *The Christian Century* 133, no. 21 (October 12, 2016).

The paper used in this publication meets the minimum requirements of American National Standard for Information Sciences — Permanence of Paper for Printed Library Materials, ANSI Z329.48-1984.

Manufactured in the U.S.A.

This book was produced using Pressbooks.com, and PDF rendering was done by PrinceXML.

Tenacious Solidarity

For
William Bellinger
Samuel Balentine
Terence Fretheim
Patrick D. Miller
Louis Stulman

Contents

ence is invited to mull over the story, to weave it into the deep fabrics of their lives, and to sit with it in "astonishment and thoughtfulness."[2] The recipient of information, however, is prompted to seek more facts that might verify, contextualize, or otherwise provide further information and greater explanation. Modern communication disseminates information without the authority that the storyteller's story possesses. The novel, for its part, is isolating, read in private, and fosters a sense of possessiveness, all of which sharply contrast with the public, communal, and shared experience of hearing a storyteller tell a story.

Benjamin's essay perceptively identifies trends that only accelerated in the postcolonial, late-capitalist environment that emerged during Brueggemann's lifetime. In these essays, Brueggemann consistently attempts to weave the biblical texts—vested as they are with the authority of a storyteller—into the deep contours of his readers' and listeners' experiences, in order to foster a tenacious solidarity that might overcome both the psychic numbness cultivated by a twenty-four-hour news cycle relentlessly disseminating information as well as the anxious possessiveness nurtured by so many privatized spiritualities.

Brueggemann introduces and deploys the concept of a "totalism" throughout these essays to name the complex, intersectional systems that function to crowd out any possibilities for the biblical ideal that he describes as "tenacious solidarity."[3] The Bible offers a series of testimonies attesting to various struggles with totalisms internal and external to the communities that created and transmitted its texts. For this reason the Bible provides rich resources for contemporary readers and interpreters wrestling with our own particular totalism. Like Benjamin's storyteller, Brueggemann enables and encourages his audience to allow the cadences of the biblical texts to sink into their lives. Through the craft of his interpretive practice, Brueggemann offers readers a point of entry to the biblical texts that is not available to other approaches. Traditional historical readings, for example, tend to want only to disseminate information, whereas any number of spiritual interpretations end in flat, private, or therapeutic interests that he here names "religious kitsch."[4] Brueggemann sometimes calls this practice that I am characterizing as storytelling "postcritical,"[5] but that phrase would be terribly misleading if it were taken to mean anything uncritical. It is indeed deeply critical, even of certain types of criticism.

Benjamin's distinctions between story, information, and novel are

2. Benjamin, "Storyteller," 90.
3. See chapter 17.
4. See pages 221–22, 387, 392.
5. See pages 422–23, 430.

instructive not only for our attempts to situate Brueggemann's interpretations against other types of reading practices; they are also, I think, deeply analogous to the recent effort by Cathleen Kaveny to distinguish prophetic from contemptuous rhetoric and moral deliberation.[6] According to Kaveny, whose work Brueggemann cites in chapter 18, prophetic rhetoric is always rooted in a sense of covenant or a social contract to which the prophet holds the community accountable. While prophecy can actually be corrosive and detrimental to communal bonds, it remains rooted in its sense of a bond to which a community should be obligated in ways that contemptuous rhetoric is not. Moral deliberation involves most of what we typically consider to be moral reasoning: debates about virtues, rights, what rules and goals should govern behavior in any particular circumstance, what constitutes human and nonhuman flourishing, and so on. Prophetic rhetoric, by contrast, involves moral indictment, calls for repentance, hopeful dreams for utopian futures, and so on. Kaveny suggests "that the rhetoric of prophetic indictment is best understood as a sort of *moral chemotherapy*, a reaction to a potentially life-threatening distortion in ordinary, day-to-day moral discussion."[7] Moral deliberation can become gravely distorted, and prophetic rhetoric is necessary to target the corruption and steer the community toward more healthy and sound moral deliberation.

Of course, Brueggemann does much more than utter indictments and call for repentance, yet I find that Kaveny's characterization of prophetic rhetoric provides an illuminating background for the form and content of his interpretations, as well as for his studious avoidance of the kinds of deliberations that characterize much biblical scholarship. Furthermore, while Brueggemann can be a fiery rhetorician, he also exemplifies humility by acknowledging his uncertainty and limitations about various claims, and he even expresses discomfort with the moniker of prophet.[8] All these characteristics, however, make him exemplary of the best use of prophetic rhetoric, both ethically and pragmatically. As Kaveny argues, contemporary prophetic rhetoric is most effective when it is spoken with humility. Brueggemann also exemplifies Kaveny's proposals for the best practices of prophetic speech because he speaks as a participant within rather than an external opponent of the totalizing systems that he critiques.[9] He not only criticizes but also laments the negative consequences of those systems; and he offers hope by articulating

6. Cathleen Kaveny, *Prophecy without Contempt: Religious Discourse in the Public Square* (Cambridge: Harvard University Press, 2016).

7. Kaveny, *Prophecy without Contempt*, 287.

8. See the discussion of Jeremiah and Baruch in chapter 18.

9. See chapter 10 in particular.

ways for the community to move beyond the problems that plague its social and political body so as to live into a deeper, more tenacious solidarity.

II. Synopsis of This Book

This book is organized into five parts, loosely corresponding to the shifting topical focuses of the chapters. As one would expect from essays written within a few years of each other, there is overlap among them in terms of their ideas, the secondary resources that they engage, and the biblical texts on which they pivot. But where the same concept is central to two chapters, such as the idea of a totalism in chapters 1 and 10, the primary biblical materials differ—in this case, Elijah and Elisha in chapter 1's treatment of Kings versus chapter 10's focus on the book of Job. And when one chapter considers a text treated in an earlier chapter, the interpretive upshot is never the same, which nicely illustrates Brueggemann's claim in Appendix A that the ancient words of the Bible perforce generate "transformative potential" whenever they are brought into contact with new contexts. For example, in chapter 15 the quotation of Ezekiel's lengthy condemnation of Tyre (Ezekiel 27) contributes to Brueggemann's larger point about how the social anxiety that arises at the end of unsustainably extractive regimes tends to end in violence targeting vulnerable groups such as children. He subsequently ties this situation to the lives of his audience with reference to the sacrifices of children in the United States to various forms of racial discrimination derivative from our "original sin" of slavery, the ongoing military arrangement of a volunteer army, our unsustainable dependence on fossil fuels that will come to a crisis point in the near future, and the present situation where millions of Americans are sacrificed in the dire circumstances of extreme poverty. The earlier quotation of the same passage (Ezekiel 27) in chapter 3, however, focuses rather on how the passage attests to a context in which all social relations have been reduced to their exchange value, which he calls commoditization. Here he weaves this passage into the lives of his audience through references to "the exposition of Ta-Nehisi Coates concerning the ways that whites have long dominated, owned, and abused black bodies,"[10] widespread sex trafficking, wage theft, and the symptomatic changes to the television program *Antiques Roadshow* when it immigrated from Europe, where it celebrated the craftsmanship of products of ancient labor, to the United States, where it aims to incite

10. Page 69.

an affective response to how much the market would value an object about which the owner typically knows little, if anything.[11]

Chapter 3 and the other chapters in the first part focus on the economy and society in ways that become thematic for the entire volume. In chapter 1, Brueggemann defines the key concept in the volume, "totalism," with reference to its origin in the psychological work of Robert Jay Lifton. Lifton's concept of totalism aims to account for the psychosocial effects of regimes that extend beyond the political-governmental capacities of totalitarian states. Brueggemann connects this idea to the work of the anthropologist James C. Scott on states that foster such governmental and extragovernmental totalisms. Brueggemann characteristically uses the work of these social scientists to move past some limitations that he identifies in the work of the theologian Jacques Ellul, a move that he accomplishes primarily through provocative readings of the narratives about Elijah and Elisha in the books of Kings. Chapter 2 considers the ideological role religion can play in legitimating economic regimes of extraction and shows how the Bible tends to be critical of such regimes and to advocate instead for economic regimes of sustainability that provide viable support for those who are exploited by extractive circumstances. Chapter 3 concentrates on the important role played by the notion of agency in the Bible's critiques of idols and its distinctions between them and God. Chapter 4 shares this focus on divine and human agency, which it relates to class antagonisms.

The chapters in part 2 reveal Brueggemann's insistent drive to analyze his contemporary circumstances through the transformative potential of biblical texts. The recent rise and emboldening of white supremacist movements is met here with a series of essays that trace such ideologies back through Christian and pre-Christian history—even unto Ezra's holy semen (see chapter 7). These chapters were written before the tragic events in Charlottesville, Virginia, on August 12, 2017. Brueggemann and I happened to be together that day in Cincinnati, discussing this book and other matters. As I noted then, these chapters clearly perceive, contextualize, and attempt to speak a way beyond the current climate of exceptionalism and dominance. Brueggemann addresses the church and does not shrink from articulating how Christianity has contributed to the white supremacism within the cultural and political roots of Western liberal democracies, even as he views churches as singular vehicles for living into an alternative future. He identifies four areas in particu-

11. One can find a program that celebrates craftsmanship in the United States, but it is tellingly available only through public television. *A Craftsman's Legacy* is directed by Kelly Davis, my colleague at Appalachian State University, and produced by Selena Lauterer, my neighbor in Boone, North Carolina.

lar that need urgent attention today: a new internationalism in place of old nationalisms, a new multiculturalism instead of racist, white domination, sustainable economic development to replace the destructive drive for constant growth, and finally a new ecumenism without the exclusionary beliefs and practices rooted in a sense of religious superiority.

Part 3 includes three chapters loosely connected by the attention that they pay to creation and the ecological crisis that our world currently faces. The upshot, with reference back to the programmatic essays in part 1, is that the ancient Hebrew scribes recognized a truth that the West has for some time denied but is now having to confront, namely, that the economy is not autonomous but rather is intimately connected to the environment. Brueggemann acknowledges that, although we do not believe that a God will magically "swoop in and punish" for environmental offenses, we are surely now exceptionally aware of the unavoidable ecological consequences of our economic choices—as I write this, many are still reeling from the death and destruction wrought by hurricane Harvey in the greater metropolitan area of Houston that has for so long prioritized unregulated economic growth.[12]

Part 4 contains five chapters on collective memory, the relationships among different generations, the healthy use and damaging abuse of communal traditions, and the great variety of styles and strategies of mentoring across generations. Again current social and political issues add a sense of urgency and relevance to these topics. As I write in the wake of Charlottesville, many in the United States are having debates about monuments honoring Confederate soldiers, among others. Such discussions raise significant questions about what a society needs to remember, what needs to be forgotten, what memories and people should be venerated, and what are the social functions of monuments and memorials. Here chapters 12 and 13 provide especially helpful, dialectical points about the twin dangers of amnesia and nostalgia as well as the paired requirements to remember some things and forget others. Brueggemann argues that nostalgia about the past is born from old wounds that cannot be healed and readily functions as a call to arms in ongoing social antagonisms. Likewise he claims that amnesia about the past breeds social indifference or "privatization" that must be overcome by robust public memories capable of generating deep social bonds grounded in economies that serve the common good. His attention to the complications that come with memories again illuminates current debates. So many Confederate statues erected in the south during Jim

---

12. See Manny Fernandez and Richard Fausset, "A Limitless City, Now Envisioning New Limitations," *New York Times*, August 31, 2017, A1.

Crow have functioned primarily not to preserve memory but to enable nostalgia and amnesia. They are nostalgic for Confederate valor that could be divorced from the cause of the Confederacy. Mississippi's declaration of secession proclaimed this cause unequivocally: "Our position is thoroughly identified with the institution of slavery." Yet our statues facilitate amnesia about this cause even as they consistently get used as icons to assist white supremacist movements. We need not only to erase the veneration of leaders of immoral causes but also to generate thicker memories, more faithful to our complicated and compromised pasts, which may even contribute to a more moral future. Such new memories would also supply us with a new, expanded list of ancestors to venerate including more of those who fought to hold us accountable to our ideals.

The final part includes three chapters that center on the three sections of the Hebrew Bible, the Torah, Prophets, and Writings. In terms of the prophetic tasks that Brueggemann famously distinguishes in his best known book, *The Prophetic Imagination*, each of these chapters is more focused on energizing an alternative consciousness than it is on criticizing the dominant consciousness.[13] In chapter 17 Brueggemann offers a fresh translation of the Hebrew term *ḥesed* as "tenacious solidarity," which I have used as the title for the volume. He characterizes such tenacious solidarity in the Psalms as "the deepest urge and hunger that is elemental to our humanness . . . the deepest need of the human heart, the deepest desire of the human community, and the deepest mark of the God who occupies this poetry." The Psalter, according to Brueggemann, provides a foundational script for living into the fullest and deepest realities of human existence.

In chapter 18 Brueggemann turns to the prophets and returns to his foundational concept of totalism. The prophets are those who did not subscribe to the totalizing efforts of the dominant ideologies but instead spoke from outside them, witnessing to an alternative way of life that undermines such totalizing efforts. Here Brueggemann defines prophetic preaching not simply as the use of prophetic rhetoric but as the subtle, careful work that takes prophetic rhetoric from the Bible and imaginatively interprets it in new circumstances such that the old text exceeds the horizons of its ancient context. Prophetic preaching thus participates in a process whereby texts exceed their capacities for meaning, a process that he shows to be already at work within the Bible itself.

Chapter 19 follows Jesus's cue to look to Deuteronomy and Leviticus

---

13. See Walter Brueggemann, *The Prophetic Imagination*, 40th anniv. ed. (Minneapolis: Fortress Press, 2018).

for the greatest commandments: love God and love neighbor. This chapter is again geared toward the task of preaching, but here too the content far exceeds the concerns of preachers alone. Brueggemann finds in Deuteronomy three primary characteristics of the God readers are commanded to love in Deuteronomy 6:5: forgiveness, hospitality, and generosity, all of which end in socioeconomic practices and ethical obligations that are not readily available in current circumstances. Leviticus commands readers to love neighbor in the midst of its excessive attention to holiness (Lev 19:18). Brueggemann shows that, while holiness builds walls of exclusion between insiders and outsiders, the trajectory of the tradition both within Leviticus and beyond reveals an ever-expanding zone that defines who counts as a neighbor. Already in the same chapter readers are told, "The alien who resides with you shall be to you as the citizen among you," and then commanded, "love the alien as yourself" (Lev 19:34). So even here "neighbor" clearly means something more than another member of the covenant community. And, as in Deuteronomy, such love in Leviticus involves vast social, ethical, and economic obligations. Leviticus 19 is concerned primarily with legislating practices that ensure that all one's neighbors, especially the poor and vulnerable, are not taken advantage of but rather are given what they need for a viable, sustainable life.

The three appendixes offer personal reflections from Brueggemann about current issues and future directions in biblical interpretation. The first identifies four areas of inquiry that he anticipates will remain fruitful in future work on prophetic literature. The second adds his foundational concept of totalism to the rubric of testimony developed in his 1997 tome *Theology of the Old Testament*.[14] He argues that the testimony of biblical literature characteristically counters totalisms by originating in and thus witnessing to a reality that the totalism is unable to silence or contain. He roots this capacity in his claim, following David Carr, that biblical literature emerges out of a series of traumatic events. The final appendix begins like an extended review of Theodore Ziolkowski's book on the rich and varied array of renderings of Moses in various cultural objects.[15] It becomes, however, an overview of the characteristics and limitations of the dominant interpretive approaches to the Bible as well as new reading practices that have emerged out of those limitations.

---

14. Walter Brueggemann, *Theology of the Old Testament: Testimony, Dispute, Advocacy* (Minneapolis: Fortress Press, 1997)

15. Theodore Ziolkowski, *Uses and Abuses of Moses: Literary Representations since the Enlightenment* (Notre Dame, IN: University of Notre Dame Press, 2016).

III. Conclusion: Social Totality against Antisocial Totalism

Despite his trenchant critiques in these essays of the totalizing hold that the market ideology of late capitalism has on us, it seems to me that one of Brueggemann's fundamental contributions is his insistent efforts to perceive and conceptualize what we can call totality so as to distinguish it from totalism. He proves consistently adept at describing social relations and cultural products in terms of their place and function within the complex interconnections of vast systems. At the core of these systems one finds the political economy and the antagonistic relationships of class. One can see this not only in his ability to diagnose the totalizing effects of market ideology, but also in his prescriptions regarding the common good as well as in his practices of reading across the canon of biblical literature. And after all, if the diagnosis of what he calls totalism is correct, it would seem necessary for the prescription to be no less totalizing. Otherwise, on offer would only be weak or reactionary gestures that may provide a sense of subjective freedom but ultimately serve to prolong the totalizing reach of the dominant ideology.

One of the symptoms that Brueggemann identifies of our current totalism is the automated fragmentation of social life such that we habitually and callously disregard our relations with others. Brueggemann finds in the suppressed content of the biblical past possibilities for renewing our sense of society as an intersectional totality, which may in turn enable us to live into a radically different future. The Bible and the God that emerges from it possess an agency upon which Brueggemann rightfully insists. His work shows how the Bible can cease being an inert object from the distant past and instead become an agent that calls our own form of social life into question. Through this dialectical move, our attempt to understand the Bible becomes a lesson from the Bible about ourselves. Therein may lie the ultimate power of Brueggemann's "storytelling," when he perceives and relates how the biblical text, in form and content, exposes who we are and invites us with what Ernst Bloch called a Utopian impulse to follow its lead into a radically transformed future.[16] The content of such a future is not clear, and in any case its arrival is surely not guaranteed. What is certain, however, is that its arrival will require a heavy dose of imaginative, gracious, even *tenacious solidarity*.

---

16. On Bloch and Utopia, see Fredric Jameson, *Marxism and Form: Twentieth-Century Dialectical Theories of Literature* (Princeton: Princeton University Press, 1971), 116–59.

Preface

As I near the end of my publishing work, I am overwhelmed with acres of amazement and thick waves of gratitude for the many ways in which I have been blessed. I am grateful for family, teachers, colleagues, publishers and editors, and students who have been for me ample gifts from God.

I am grateful to my family—Hilda my mother, August my father, and Edward my brother—who nurtured me in the tradition of German evangelical pietism, a tradition that is theologically innocent and ethically generous. It is happily my home from which I have not departed.

I am grateful to my teachers. In retrospect there is a clear line that flows from my first curmudgeonly college teacher, Th. W. Mueller, to my Doctor Father, James Muilenburg, a line that runs through my seminary teachers, the most venturesome of whom were Allen O. Miller and Lionel Whiston Jr. This sequence of teachers taught me not only a passion for good learning but the awareness that the world in front of us is a constructed world that can be differently constructed. Mueller led to into the mysteries of Durkheim, Weber, Veblin, Tonnes, Graham, and their company, and Muilenburg into the wonders of artful rhetoric. From beginning to end my teachers refused to absolutize our presumed world as a given world.

I am fortunate to have had good colleagues at both of my schools, Eden Theological Seminary and Columbia Theological Seminary, many beyond my two schools, many in my own discipline and many outside my discipline who made connections for me and pressed me to a better, more compelling connection of the dots of lived reality.

I am grateful for good pastoral colleagues who have valorized my work in practical ways and evoked from me more faithful discernment and more courageous interpretation. I am especially grateful for Roger Greene and Joe Phelps, who let the evangelical juice of their work spill over into my work and life with wisdom and passion, and who show me ways in which my work may connect to the reality of the church, both its treasure and responsibility. I am grateful for a host of editors and publishers, for the often unnamed, unacknowledged gremlins at Fortress Press who skillfully turn words into books, and for senior editors and book makers, a stalwart sequence that for me runs from Roland Sieboldt to Scott Tunseth and in between Norman Hjelm, Marshall Johnson, Michael West, and Neil Elliott. Among them is John Hollar who did so much for me as the most generative of them all and whose death I continue to grieve. I am most singularly grateful to Davis Hankins, who has labored mightily in editing this book. He is the *sine qua non* for its final appearance.

I am grateful for a host of good students, many of whom have become faithful, effective pastors, some of whom have joined me in the work of teaching and research, some of whom have gone well beyond me and have pressed me in new directions. That good teaching company of my former students is a point of singular pride for me.

To all of the above:

I can no other answer make,

but thanks, and thanks, and ever thanks (*Twelfth Night*)

Through the sweep of my years of teaching I have, along with my discipline, morphed from historical criticism to critical hermeneutics in a variety of forms. Had my discipline remained closely wedded to historical criticism, I would not have been able to do what I have done, because the illusion of objective descriptive work set a barrier to serious generative interpretation. As I articulated imagination, via Paul Ricoeur, as the key to my interpretive work, I have been able to engage in both the "suspicious" work of ideological criticism and indispensible work of "retrieval" that features alternative discernment, alternative thinking, and finally alternative policy. When I consider "how my mind has changed," I went through my "Secular City" phase as did many of us, and arrived at a sense of the urgency of church ministry and its vocation as a singular vehicle for courage, for keeping alive and for performing a "more excellent way" in the world. For all of the flaws and failures of the church it is still the case that it is the church that shows up first in justice questions, that by its very life attests to hospitality, generosity, and forgiveness as engines for a livable life for all creatures. Thus I have worked, quite beyond the permits of historical criticism, to evoke in pastors some lost courage for truthfulness and for hope, practices that are so urgent in our society that has lost its way in pretence and despair.

I make no great claim for my work but I have reflected on the gift and burden of being, a la Gramsci, an "organic intellectual," that is, one who invests energy toward the revolutionary cause. I believe that in the face of greed and fear, an ideology of scarcity, and willingness to act violently the gospel of emancipation is a revolutionary summons to counter-imagination and counter-performance of social reality. I am, moreover, glad when the church can find allies in other traditions for that urgent work.

I am glad to dedicate this book to my most long-standing colleagues who have been my steadfast companions in my scholarship. Bill Bellinger, whom I first met in a Psalms class, has been my continuing partner on the Psalms for many years. Sam Balentine has been variously my editor and wise counselor from whose work on Job I continue to learn. Terry Fretheim has been my constant counterpoint as we have together parsed the tricky issue of divine agency and human agency. Louis Stulman has been my go-to guy on Jeremiah studies with enough puckishness to keep us from crying too much with the prophet. Above all, Patrick Miller has been my faithful kinsman and a wise bridge for our discipline between historical and hermeneutical enterprises. He has expended great energy in the editing of much of my work.

Finally I mention Davis Hankins, wise young scholar that he is, for his thick engagement with my work, much to the distraction from his own research. In addition to his judicious editing of my work, he has taught me a great deal in spheres of interpretation that are very difficult for me. Since I believe in academic "apostolic succession," this is it with Davis for me to whom I am profoundly grateful.

Walter Brueggemann
September 13, 2017

PART I

Economics and Social Possibilities

and necessary by-product of economic progress. The destruction of mētis and its replacement by standardized formulas legible only from the center is virtually inscribed in the activities of both the state and large-scale bureaucratic capitalism.[6]

Examples of *metis,* some of which are mentioned by Scott include:

- The gift whereby a seasoned physician can do a diagnosis, but cannot quite tell us the basis of such knowledge.

- The awareness of a seasoned farmer who knows when it is time to plant potatoes or plow corn, knowledge that is not found in any agricultural manual.

- A good cook who uses no recipes but fully knows what to add when and for how long in order to have good outcomes.

- A competent teacher who can wisely depart at the right moment from the "lesson plan" for the sake of educational imagination.

Such *metis* is transmitted informally from generation to generation, mostly orally, passed on by observation and practice, in intimate local contact.[7] "Seeing like a state" is inimical to the valuing, practice, and transmission of *metis.* Indeed the state is likely to disregard and dismiss such artistry as folk magic or hokum in the interest of omniscience and uniformity. Thus, I propose in what follows that we consider the technical capacity of "the state" to quantify, produce, control, predict, maximize, and monetize as an exercise of totalism and the antithesis of neighborly *metis* that is hosted in local community in ways that generate abundance and that can foster health in human and nonhuman environments. The conflict and contrast between *techne* and *metis* are my entry point for a reconsideration of the narrative of the books of Kings in the Hebrew Bible, a narrative that Ellul has richly exposited in *The Politics of God and the Politics of Man.*

6. Scott, *Seeing like a State,* 177–78, 332, 317–18, 335. Scott reports that he appropriated the notion of *metis* from the work of Aleksandra Kollontay, Rosa Luxemburg, and Jane Jacobs.

7. Such transmission is most readily accomplished by one-on-one mentoring. See the forthcoming study of mentoring from Eerdmans Press edited by Cam Murchison and Dean Thompson.

II

In his book *The Politics of God and the Politics of Man,* Ellul has considered the prophetic narratives of Elijah and Elisha.[8] He has fully appreciated and called attention to the way in which these narratives present these two remarkable characters as embodiments of the "Word of God" that comes as transformative force into the history of Israel and into the history of the world. Ellul is of course a faithful reader and sees exactly the claim of the text. It is also the case, however, that Ellul did this work in the wake of National Socialism and under the impact of Karl Barth and his compelling "theology of the word," which is also reflected in the defining Old Testament scholarship of Gerhard von Rad. As a result, Ellul's reading of these narratives is, as it were, "from above," from the perspective of the transcendent God who freely intrudes into the affairs of human persons and human society. In his study of the Samuel narratives, von Rad has noticed that there is a propensity toward "Enlightenment sensibility" wherein the directness of God in the narrative recedes and human agents are increasingly left on their own.[9] This "progressive withdrawal" of God from human affairs is traced further by Jack Miles, who suggests that God readily disappears from the narrative of the Hebrew Bible, a judgment echoed by Richard Elliott Friedman.[10]

My interest is not in the disappearance of God; rather, I want to see what happens in the narratives when we read "from below" in the context of *techne* and *metis.* I suggest that Ellul in his exposition of the text did not linger long on the larger narrative intent of these prophetic tales. The prophetic narratives of Elijah (1 Kings 17–19; 21) and Elisha (2 Kings 2–10) are situated in the longer narrative recital of 1 Kings 1–22 and 2 Kings 1–25 that provide a time line and map of four hundred years of governance. The prophetic narratives, I suggest, can be understood only if they are seen to be a disruption of the royal totalizing tradition of Jerusalem and to a lesser extent Samaria. Read "from above" they attest the lively Word of God. Read "from below," they exhibit *metis* to which the kings had no access.

Thus we must begin our exposition of the prophetic narratives with a consideration of the royal recital that contains the prophetic narratives. The substance of the royal recital is the domination of the political economy by the urban elites who clustered around the throne. We must

8. See Jacques Ellul, *The Politics of God and the Politics of Man* (Grand Rapids: Eerdmans, 1972).

9. Gerhard von Rad, *Wisdom in Israel* (Nashville: Abingdon, 1972).

10. Jack Miles, *God: A Biography* (New York: Knopf, 1995); and Richard Elliott Friedman, *The Hidden Face of God* (San Francisco: HarperCollins, 1995).

surely identify King Solomon as the founder of that totalism that regulated political economic advantage that came to be exhibited in "magic" ways by his enormous building program that centered in the temple with its opulent display of gold.[11] That same exhibit of advantage is expressed in a lesser way in the extravagance of the royal entourage that ate very well indeed, with a menu of endless meat:

> Solomon's provision for one day was thirty measures of choice flour, and sixty measures of meal, ten fat oxen and sheep, besides deer, gazelles, roebucks, and fatted fowl. (1 Kgs 4:22–23)

There is no doubt that the temple and its royal liturgy functioned as legitimator for the regime; it gave a pious facade to raw usurpatious power, thus creating a hegemony that needed to host no question or critique.

The enormous wealth of the Solomonic system, we may judge from the recital, was made possible by three strategic initiatives. First, Solomon installed an orderly tax system wherein each of the twelve tribes was required to provide revenue for one month of the royal year. The tax districts are traced out in detail (1 Kgs 4:7–19). The administration of this system must have been lucrative, for two of Solomon's sons-in-law are administrators of district programs (1 Kgs 4:11, 15). It is a stunning mark of pre-Ellul or anti-Ellul historical criticism that scholars have used great energy detailing the boundaries of the tax districts but have never noticed that the entire system was predatory, and never saw reason to critique the tax system. It is a measure of the predatory quality of the tax system that, at Solomon's death, Rehoboam, his son and heir, had to renegotiate the tax rate. In that negotiation, his agent was stoned to death (1 Kgs 12:18), and the new king himself had to flee in his chariot for his life (1 Kgs 12:19).

Second, the opulence of the Jerusalem elite was made possible—as it always is—by cheap labor. In 1 Kings 5:13–18 it is reported that Solomon conscripted forced labor from "all Israel," as many as ten thousand in rotating shifts, seventy thousand laborers, ten thousand stonecutters, and thirty-three hundred supervisors. While the numbers seem inordinate, the point of the recital is to exhibit "seeing like a state," in large organized quantities. To be sure, in 1 Kings 9:22 it is insisted that Solomon conscripted only foreigners and non-Israelites. But the point is

---

11. See Walter Brueggemann, *Solomon: Israel's Ironic Icon of Human Achievement*, Studies on Personalities of the Old Testament (Columbia: University of South Carolina Press, 2005), chapters 5 and 7.

the same. The totalizing regime reduced human persons to functionaries in a predatory system.

Third, Solomon is portrayed as a global trader who dominated international exchange and profited greatly from it. This was not the normal profit from trade but rather tribute money (protection money) paid by lesser political powers who were dependent on Solomon. Thus the money poured into Jerusalem through its shrewd monetization of the global network (see 1 Kgs 10:14–25.).

Beyond that, Solomon was an arms dealer who functioned as middle-man trading horses and chariots:

> Solomon's import of horses was from Egypt and Kue, and the king's traders received them from Kue at a price. A chariot could be imported from Egypt for six hundred shekels of silver, and a horse for one hundred and fifty; so through the king's traders they were exported to all the kings of the Hittites and the kings of Aram. (1 Kgs 10:28–29)

James Risen, a contemporary journalist, has chronicled the profiteering that is inherent in the promotion of war and military armaments:

> Fear sells. Fear has convinced the White House and Congress to pour hundreds of billions of dollars—more money than anyone knows what to do with—into counterterrorism and homeland security programs, often with little management or oversight, and often to the detriment of the Americans they are supposed to protect. Fear is hard to question. It is central to the financial well-being of countless federal bureaucrats, contractors, subcontractors, consultants, analysts, and pundits. Fear generates funds. . . . They have built a cottage industry out of fear.[12]

Risen, moreover, identified one particular administrator of fear of terrorism, Steven Emerson:

> Emerson has been able to turn his anti-Muslim rhetoric and research into fundraising prowess. . . . Emerson's for-profit company, SAE Productions, received $3.39 million in 2008 to research connections between Muslims in the United States and foreign terrorism. . . . In his 2010 tax return, Emerson's nonprofit foundation reported paying more than $3.4 million to Emerson's SAE Productions for management services.[13]

Of course it is not clear that this can all be read back into our royal recital; but the royal account permits such a reading:

12. James Risen, *Pay Any Price: Greed, Power, and Endless War* (Boston: Houghton Mifflin Harcourt, 2014), 203, 220.
13. Risen, *Pay Any Price*, 221.

the *form* of the recital. Anyone who has read much in 1 and 2 Kings will have noticed that the royal report is formulaic in its boredom. Thus the report "sees like a state." The royal data offered consist in time of the beginning of the reign, the name of the mother of the king, the age of the king, the length of the reign, and a death report. Sometimes the formula encompasses a report of temple reform or war. It is spectacularly obvious that the kings, with few exceptions, have no narrative, because narrative is specific, detailed, and can be quixotic and subversive. Thus, to "see like a state" is to refuse the particularity of specific persons and to deal in summaries and statistics in resistance to narrative. Thus, for example, in 1982 Ronald Reagan sought to dismiss a specific narrative about job loss with the indignant dismissal:

> Is it news if some guy in South Succotash loses his job and gets interviewed?[14]

Reagan intended his question to have a negative answer: "No, it is not news." News comes in a memo. It is the case that Bill Clinton mastered the art of narrative and was able to respond to narrative specificity with, "I feel your pain." We are not, however, deceived by such phrasing. Thus I have suggested, following John O'Banion, that we may make a distinction and contrast between memo and poem.[15] O'Banion proposes "list and story," but that is the same contrast.[16] *Memos* are a vehicle for state strategy that need take no notice of human particularity. *Poetry and narrative*, by contrast, constitute acts of imagination that refuse the limits of totalism and dare to voice and construe alternative reality. In both poem and narrative, the quotidian specificity of human life is affirmed and appreciated, the very quotidian specificity that totalism means to disregard. It is for that reason that managers of the totalism characteristically conflict with poets and storytellers. In the Hebrew Bible, the poets and storytellers are called "prophets," those who call attention to the lived human reality that kings cannot afford to notice. In our world they are called "journalists" or "artists." As a result, the Reagan dismissal of the jobless guy in South Succotash has morphed into "fake news." Whatever quotidian specificity contradicts the totalism is dismissed as fake. The contrast is given summary expression 2 Kings 17:13–16:

14. William E. Smith, "Stumping in South Succotash," *Washington Post*, March 29, 1982, A1.

15. Walter Brueggemann, "Poems vs. Memos," in *Ice Axes for Frozen Seas: A Biblical Theology of Provocation*, ed. Davis Hankins (Waco, TX: Baylor University Press, 2014), 87–113.

16. John D. O'Banion, *Reorienting Rhetoric: The Dialectic of List and Story* (University Park: Pennsylvania State University Press, 1992).

Yet the Lord warned Israel and Judah by every prophet and every seer, saying, "Turn from your evil ways and keep my commandments and my statutes, in accordance with all the Torah that I commanded your ancestors and that I sent to you by my servants the prophets." They would not listen, but were stubborn, as their ancestors had been, who did not believe in the Lord their God. They despised his statutes, and his covenant. . . . They rejected all the commandments of the Lord their God and made for themselves cast images of two calves.

The prophets, regularly dismissed by the forces of totalism, summoned Israel back to covenantal reality. The refusal of the regime is slotted in this condemnation as the embrace of Baal, the god of production, with a glance at the "two calves," an allusion back to the "golden calf" of Aaron (Exodus 32). The combination of "golden" (that is, monetization) and "calf" (or "bull," that is, fertility production), summarizes the way of the regime and anticipates the Wall Street icon of the bull of gold. The kings are always "bullish" as they "see like a state." Thus, the royal recital anticipates the defining either/or of human history, the "either" of neighbor or the "or" of *techne* that is predatory and has reduced the specificity of human data to formula and memo.

III

This consideration of Lifton on totalism and Scott on *metis* is in order to articulate a context for the prophetic narratives that Ellul has so well exposited.[17] We may be astonished when we do the numbers. These two prophetic figures, Elijah and Elisha, occupy fully one-third of the "history" of four hundred years of the royal recital. It is as though the entire recital of 1 and 2 Kings is formulated precisely so that Elijah and Elisha can be front and center in an attempt to present Israelite history "from below," from an antitotalizing perspective. Indeed, I suggest that the structure of the narrative is intended to delegitimate the kings and to present them as dangerous irrelevances for covenantal history. If there is truth in this notion, then it is immensely radical for both Jews and Chris-

---

17. Of the four narratives I have discussed, Ellul (*The Politics of God & the Politics of Man*) discusses only the first two, the story of Naaman (2 Kgs 5:1–27) and the narrative of 2 Kings 6:24–7:17. For this second text Ellul notably uses as a title "Joram," the king who remains unnamed in the narrative. My judgment is that the king remaining unnamed is an intention[al] tactic for discounting and delegitimating royal power. Ellul's impulse is to discount hum[an] agency in the narrative. While the unnamed king surely lacks agency in the story, my i[nten]tence (against Ellul) is that the human agency of the prophetic figure is essential to the nar[rative], for it is the prophetic character who possesses the art of transformation, even as that po[wer of] transformation is given by YHWH.

tians, who together have counted a great deal on an anticipated Messiah who would arise from the royal line.

I shall propose that these prophetic narratives present these two characters as having abundant *metis*, the art and skill for the generation of life that is characteristically hosted in folk or peasant circumstance, an art and skill that are beyond precise articulation, but an art and skill that we know when we see it. It is of course affirmed in these narratives that that art and skill are given "by the word." But Ellul's reading "from above" seems to me more "supernatural" than the narrative requires, for these two figures, especially Elisha, are "of the people" and prefer the social reality of those below the radar of royal power among those who neither trust in nor benefit from the royal tradition. We may then consider these narratives "from below."

IV

In 2 Kings 4:1–7 Elisha is addressed by a desperate widow whose "creditor" threatens to seize her two children as slaves. In the parallel narrative of Elijah there is no mention of a creditor (1 Kgs 17:8–16). We have been told in 2 Kings 2:13–15 that the mantle and spirit of Elijah rest on Elisha. This signals to us that Elisha is possessed of a kind of folk authority, or *metis*, that is not subject to or verified by royal edict. He is the one to whom the economically bereft cry out in anguish and in hope. The other character is a widow with two children. She is exceedingly vulnerable. She is subject to a creditor who has laden her with debt. She has no stream of income but the creditor is calling in her debt. Since she cannot pay, the creditor proposes to take her two children as slaves, because most slaves in that economy are people working off unpayable debt. The widow is frantic and wants Elisha to intervene.

He does an intake interview. His initial question, "What shall I do for you?" is not answered (see Mark 10:51). But of course we know the answer: save the children! Fend off the creditor. The mention of a creditor evokes awareness of the predatory practices of the Jerusalem elite (or in the north the elite of Samaria for which King Ahab is a point person; see Amos 6:1–7). Following his unanswered question, Elisha quickly moves to a second question as he sets to do what the widow needs. What do you have? She has only a jar of olive oil, not nearly enough to pay her debt. His question anticipates the question of Jesus to the desperate crowd:

How many loaves have you? (Mark 6:20; 8:5)

Elisha knows what to do, now acting in bold imperatives.

> Go outside, borrow vessels from your all neighbors, empty vessels and not just a few. Then go in, and shut the door . . . and start pouring into all the vessels; when each is full, set it aside. (2 Kgs 4:3–4)

He commands her, "Go into the neighborhood . . . go into the house." Mobilize the neighborhood. Get resources from outside. On the inside watch for abundance. The work outside is with the neighbors. The term here means "residents," not the usual word for "neighbor." Ask for all the pots, pans, bowls, and pitchers that you can find. Don't ask for a few; ask for all of them, because the economy is about to be jump-started with *metis*.

She obeys this odd command. We get two participles for continuing action: They kept *bringing*; she kept *pouring*. She kept asking for more containers until there were no more. All were full! Only then did the olive oil stop. Notice, there is no explanation for the abundance. Indeed, Elisha did not even do anything that is reported to us, except to give her instruction. It is as though his presence and his confidence of themselves evoked an economic abundance that changed social reality.

The narrative concludes in verse 7; the widow reports the abundance to Elisha. He issues three more imperatives:

1. Sell the olive oil

2. Pay your debt

3. Live on the residue

It is all very terse.

This narrative provides a perfect map for neighborly economics. It begins in *a desperate cry* that is heard and taken seriously. It pivots on *an inexplicable abundance*, suggesting that there were in the neighborhood unrecognized resources. It concludes with *the elimination of debt* that fulfills the rule of Moses for the cancellation of debt. Notice, there is no mention of God. It is a neighborly act. And because it is was a neighborly act, the performance of abundance is outside the reach of the predatory system over which the king presides for which the creditor is a stand-in. Abundance happens outside the sphere of royal supervision, that is, outside conventional credit-loan arrangements.

When we compare this narrative with the parallel in Elijah (1 Kgs 17:8–16), we notice three things. First, in the Elijah version the creditor has disappeared, as though the narrator did not want to speak ill of the system. Second, the story with Elijah is dominated by the reality of God, whereas the Elisha version does not mention God. The Lord dispatched Elijah to the widow (v. 1). At the conclusion, it is "according to the word of the Lord" (v. 16). Third, there are no neighbors; there is only Elijah. On all three counts, I suggest, the Elisha version is closer to social reality . . . no direct divine intervention, the reality of the creditor, and the requirement of neighbors. The neighbors helped to contradict and nullify the power of the creditor. And this wonder-working uncredentialed man, I suggest, has *metis*. He knows what to do and how to do it, not unlike the folk I have seen effectively "witching water." The narrative is reticent, because such an act is beyond articulation, but it is clear that neighborly *metis* overcomes predatory efforts toward totalism.

In the second narrative of 2 Kings 4:8–37 (parallel to Elijah in 1 Kings 17:17–24), a wealthy woman has a son. Elisha has promised her a son:

> At this season in due time, you shall embrace a son. . . . The woman conceived and bore a son at that season, in due time, as Elisha had declared to her. (2 Kgs 4:16–17)

We may notice that it is simply the promise of Elisha—there is no mention of the word of the Lord. And then this wondrously given son is dead. Elisha prayed over the dead son and did mouth-to-mouth resuscitation:

> Then he got up on the bed and lay upon the child, putting his mouth upon his mouth, his eyes upon his eyes, and his hands upon his hands; and while he lay bent over him, the flesh of the child became warm. He got down, walked once to and fro in the room, then got up again and bent over him; the child sneezed seven times, and the child opened his eyes. (2 Kgs 4:34–35).

Elisha is identified as "a holy man" (v. 9); but that is all. He is a generator of new life. He knew what to do and how to do it. He has *metis*! It is a mark of the domestication of historical criticism that this narrative and the others like it have been dismissed as "folk legends." The critical guild has been inured to "seeing as a state."[18] In fact these narratives concern

18. I recall the oral report of Robert Coles, a Harvard psychiatrist, when he observed the courageous black children who integrated the Little Rock school. When Coles interviewed Ruby (one of those children) and her mother, he was astonished that Ruby's mother instructed her that she must forgive the rabid racists who harassed her as she entered the school. Coles

an alternative way of knowing; they attest that there is a path to life in the community that is not possessed by the state (or the corporation).

In 2 Kings 5:1–27 we have a narrative account of the dramatic healing of Naaman, a Syrian general, by Elisha. The general is frantic, as frantic as the widow; he has leprosy that will disqualify him for the exercise of his great political influence. The Israelite slave girl, a prisoner of war, sent him to Israel for healing. On the mistaken assumption that an occupant of the royal recital could heal, the general came with great pomp to the unnamed Israelite king. The king perforce refused to try to heal, acknowledging the limit of royal capacity:

> Am I God, to give death or life, that this man sends word to me to cure a man of his leprosy? (2 Kgs 5:7)

In a big comedown, the general came to Elisha for healing. It must have been humiliating to entertain the notion that healing could come from an uncredentialed nobody. Indeed, Elisha further insults the general by refusing to welcome him appropriately. Elisha's recommended treatment is sparse and simple, rooted in folk practice:

> Go, wash in the Jordan seven times, and your flesh shall be restored and you shall be clean [i.e., ritually acceptable]. (v. 10)

The general, with his loud large entourage, is indignant at the mode of healing proposed by Elisha. Eventually, after fierce resistance to such a simple procedure, the general received healing from this nobody. In a wonder of restoration, we are told:

> So he went down and immersed himself seven times in the Jordan, according to the word of the man of God; his flesh was restored like the flesh of a young boy and he was clean. (v. 14)

The healing is accomplished by a folk act that is contrary to Syrian totalism. There is between the two a clash of worldviews and modes of knowledge. Elisha follows an old remedy of Israel, so old that it surely antedated the Samarian royal regime. The clash between the two is continued in the ongoing narrative, even though we most often stop reading at the healing. The general, inured to the monetized healing system of his regime, wants to pay for his healing. He thinks in terms of insur-

---

reported that he and his wife were astonished by this response because it fit none of their preconceptions about the transaction. Coles said that he had no explanation; the only thing he and his wife could do was to go and "have a drink." The capacity of Ruby and her mother to forgive was grounded in a religious understanding that eluded the categories of social science.

ance, co-pays, and deductibles. He assumes that medical service must be monetized:

> Please accept a present from your servant. (v. 15)

But the holy healer refuses:

> As the Lord lives, whom I serve, I will accept nothing! (v. 16)

The general haggles some, but Elisha dismisses him and says, "Go in peace." It is all free. It is all a gift of God mediated through peasant acts. Nothing is explained. Nothing can be managed. Nothing can be replicated. This little exchange is a clash of two discernments of life, one that is set on money and so immediately introduces social stratification and distinction between those who can pay and those who cannot. The prophetic insistence otherwise asserts that neighborly healing is not subject to the norms of royal monetization.

What follows then in the narrative exposes the enduring force of monetization. Gehazi, Elisha's aide, secretly puts a hit on the general. His action in secret is not unlike the secret action of Senate Republicans in devising a more monetized health care plan:

> My master has sent me to say, "Two members of a company of prophets have just come to me from the hill country of Ephraim; please give me a talent of silver and two changes of clothing." (v. 22)

The general gladly complies:

> Please accept two talents. He urged him, and tied up two talents of silver in two bags, with two changes of clothing, and gave them to two of his servants. (v. 23)

The two, the general and the aide, collude against the prophet to monetize the healing. By the end of the tale, we see that such collusion can only serve to transfer the stigma of leprosy from the general to the aide, from the one who pays to the one who demands (v. 27). Both the general and the aide are so inured to the dominant economic system that they cannot understand, accept, or receive a free gift of restorative abundance. The narrative is cited by Jesus in his refusal of the notion that the goodness of God is only for those qualified in Israel.

> There were also many lepers in Israel in the time of the prophet Elisha, and none of them was cleansed except Naaman the Syrian. (Luke 4:27)

The thought that restoration was on offer to "outsiders" to the dominant system of the chosen evoked rage. It is offensive to distribute resources beyond the bounds of totalism.

In a third narrative, Syria is about to assault Elisha as a "leaker" of Syrian military intelligence (2 Kgs 6:8–23). But Elisha prays the Syrians blind:

> Elisha prayed to the Lord, and said, "Strike this people, please, with blindness." So he struck them with blindness as Elisha had asked. (v. 18)

Subsequently, when the Syrians had been captured and brought to Samaria, Elisha prays them back to sight:

> Elisha said, "O Lord, open the eyes of these men so that they may see." The Lord opened their eyes, and they saw that they were inside Samaria. (v. 20)

In the midst of this transaction the unnamed Israelite king, who has done nothing to protect his people, wants to kill the captured Syrians. Elisha, however, dismisses the Israelite king:

> No! Did you capture with your sword and your bow those whom you want to kill? (v. 22)

Elisha asserts to the king that he, Elisha, is in charge. He is the one who has acted. The king had had no part in the capture of the Syrians. And then, as a concluding master stroke, Elisha commands a feast:

> Set food and water before them so that they may eat and drink; and let them go to their master. (v. 22)

Elisha, in contrast to the king, knows "the things that make for peace" (see Luke 19:42). The king knows the things that make for war but has no clue about peace. Seeing like a state never results in peace. Elisha is presented as one gifted with skills to disrupt the violent posturing of the state, a skill before which his own king is helpless and impotent. Earlier in the narrative Elisha had reassured his frightened aide:

> Don't be afraid, for there are more with us than there are with them. (v. 16)

Elisha's peculiar arithmetic turned out to be correct. This odd character, with seemingly little effort, prevailed over both the king of Israel and the enemies of Israel. Elisha might have written these lines in Proverbs:

No wisdom, no understanding, no counsel,
can avail against the LORD.
The horse is made ready for the day of battle,
But the victory belongs to the LORD. (Prov 21:30–31)

The proverb and the narrative both attest that there is an inscrutability in the public process that is not answerable to the reductionism of *techne*. It is no wonder that the narrative ends, against every royal assumption, in a cessation of hostility evoked by a feast of generosity:

> And the Arameans no longer came raiding into the land of Israel. (2 Kgs 5:23)

After these episodes that concern in turn poverty (4:1–7), disease (5:1–22), and war (6:8–23), a further narrative concerns famine (6:24–7:20). It is remarkable that these four narratives in turn take up the big problems of public policy, the very matters that must most concern kings and states. It is even more remarkable that the sum of these four narratives is a sustained witness that this holy man, the bearer of *metis,* can manage and resolve these profound problems in a way that defies the usual explanations of establishment power.

In this fourth narrative of famine, two women are so desperate that they quarrel about whether the son of one of them will be eaten by the other woman. The narrative is framed with the insight accepted by later economists: famines are not about an absence of food but about scarcity that drives the price of food up so that it is unavailable to the poor:

> As the siege [of the Syrians against the capital city of Samaria] continued, famine in Samaria became so great that a donkey's head was sold for eighty shekels of silver and one-fourth of a cab of dove's dung for five shekels of silver. (2 Kgs 6:25)

That is much too much for a donkey head or a measure of dove dung!

When Elisha enters the narrative he declares that the current unbearable price of food will soon end:

> Tomorrow about this time a measure of choice meal shall be sold for a shekel, and two measures of barley for a shekel at the gate of Samaria. (7:1)

The prophet does not explain. His anticipation runs beyond royal management or imagination; not surprisingly, the royal officer resists the prophetic anticipation:

Then the captain on whose hand the king leans said to the man of God: "Even if the Lord were to make windows in the sky, could such a thing happen?" (7:2)

But Elisha insists. He does not explain, but he adds a twist of threat against the royal officer:

You shall see it with your own eyes, but you shall not eat from it. (7:2)

The stage is thus set for the life-or-death contest between royal *techne* that cannot produce food and the alternative of this peculiar man. Indeed, this unnamed king confesses his inability to manage the famine. He answers the two quarreling women:

No! Let the Lord help you. How can I help you? From the threshing floor or the wine press? (6:27)

The resolution of this conflict comes in a way not anticipated. The army camp of the dread Syrians was deserted. The army had run off in fear and left rich food supplies behind. And the reason for the abrupt departure of the frightened army?

For the Lord had caused the Aramean army to hear the sound of chariots, and of horses, the sound of a great army, so that they said to one another, "The king of Israel has hired the kings of the Hittites and the king of Egypt to fight against us." (7:6)

The narrative is elusive. The Syrians in their fearfulness had heard sounds like those of chariots, horses, and a mighty army. They fled because it seemed too ominous. The report does not say that there were horses, chariots, or army but only the sound of them. The report says further, "The Lord had caused . . ." Who knew? The cause was beyond the calculation of *Realpolitik* among those ranked in military planning. Maybe it was a great wind, but who knows about the wind? The scene exposes the limit of royal *techne* and the wonder of Agency beyond usual royal agency.

The rest of the narrative follows from the sound. Four lepers who were excluded from society and banished to garbage heaps "beyond the city gate" came upon the abandoned food of the Syrian army:

When the leprous men had come to the edge of the camp, they went into a tent, ate and drank, carried off silver, gold, and clothing, and went and hid them. Then they came back, entered another tent, carried off things from it, and went and hid them. . . . So they went after them as far as the Jordan; the whole way was littered with garments and equipment that the Arameans had thrown away in their haste. (7:8, 15)

The lepers (who had never relied on royal beneficence) were astonished at their good find. They felt an obligation to report their find to the king, and this is how they understood their find:

They said to one another, "What we are doing is wrong. This is a day of good news; if we are silent and wait until morning light, we will be found guilty; therefore let us go and tell the king's household. (7:9)

The lepers spoke of their "good news." The term they use is the common word for "message"; but the term also came to mean "good news, gospel." The matter is left open. "This is a day of good news . . . or this is a day for gospel news . . . or this is a day of news." This is a day of welcome surprise that is beyond royal planning or explanation.

Sure enough; the narrative concludes:

Then the people went out, and plundered the camp of the Arameans. So a measure of choice meal was sold for a shekel and two measures of barley for a shekel, according to the word of the Lord. (7:16)

The narrator remembers and reports in reiteration the prophetic response to the cynicism of the royal captain:

For when the man of God had said to the king, "Two measures of barley shall be sold for a shekel, and a measure of choice meal for a shekel, about this time tomorrow in the gate of Samaria," the captain had answered the man of God, "Even if the Lord were to make windows in the sky, could such a thing happen?" And he answered, "You shall see it with your own eyes, but you shall not eat from it." It did indeed happen to him; the people trampled him to death in the gate. (7:18–20)

The narrative artfully reiterates the previous interaction to underscore the prophetic defeat of royal cynicism. The royal officer is trampled to death by the hungry crowd that surged for food. The hungry crowd ate, by contrast, because food had abruptly become cheap and abundant. The narrative details an abrupt inscrutable historical reversal that is anticipated by Elisha and performed, so it is said, by the Lord, who caused the sound. The narrative identifies Elisha as a wise hoper; his capacity, however, depends on the divine agency for which the king had made no allowance. Nothing is explained; but when we hear the outcome, we may be amazed.

Critical scholarship has taken the royal chronicle as normative. You can find that royal time line in all the history books and in all church basements where people study ancient Israel. Here, however, the royal time line is dramatically interrupted for a very long pause in the midst of the Omri dynasty of northern Israel. "Chronicle" is disrupted by "narrative." Uniformity is exposed by amazement and wonder. Critical study has diminished and disregarded the narrative for the sake of the chronicle and has preferred explanation to amazement. It is not so only for the Bible, but elsewhere as well. In doing US history, we regularly focus on the sequence of presidents and their wars. In doing biblical history we rely on the royal sequence. From that insistent perspective it is possible that we would never guess that the real US history makers include Frederick Douglass, Susan B. Anthony, Eugene V. Debs, Martin Luther King Jr., Ida Tarbell, Howard Zinn, Daniel Berrigan, and dozens of others who have had no capacity for *techne* but who have embodied the available force of holiness that is operative in, with, and under royal time lines.[19]

V

Beyond these positive attestations that lie outside the totalism of royal recital, we may notice that the narratives in careful and understated ways are able to exhibit the impotence and ultimate irrelevance of those who occupy the royal time line.[20] For starters we notice that the kings in these narratives always remain unnamed, because once we have seen one king, we know about them all.

In 2 Kings 4:1–7 concerning the desperate widow, the king is not even mentioned. We get only a mention of a creditor and the payment of debt. That slight reference (which is absent from the parallel narrative of Elijah) is enough to indicate the looming presence of the predatory economy for which the king is the point person. Then as now, the imposition and management of debt are not an incidental phenomenon, but, as David Graeber has shown, it is a systemic arrangement designed to guarantee a dependent class that must settle for menial work and low wages.[21] Elisha not only provides food for the widow; he emancipates the helpless widow from the predatory economy for a new life of well-

19. See Walter Brueggemann, *Hope within History* (Atlanta: John Knox, 1987), 49–71, concerning history makers.

20. On the following, see Walter Brueggemann and Davis Hankins, "The Affirmation of Prophetic Power and Deconstruction of Royal Authority in the Elisha Narratives," *Catholic Biblical Quarterly* 76 (2014): 58–76.

21. David Graeber, *Debt: The First 5,000 Years* (New York: Melville House, 2011).

being. Such an emancipation, in the purview of Israel's faith, is an exodus *in nuce*, because the exodus writ large concerns the same emancipation from a predatory economy. Credit and debt, in the world of a neighborly peasant economy, is not a defining social reality.

In 2 Kings 5:1–27 the leprous Syrian general Naaman appeals to the unnamed Israelite king for healing. That unnamed king must, perforce, refuse the chance to heal:

> Am I a God, to give death or life? (5:7)

The king is not God! The king does not have healing power. The king lives within a tiny world of circumscribed capacity. That limit is not unlike the limit of Pharaoh's intelligence community that could not produce gnats! (Exod 8:18). But the narrative (and the destiny of the general) reaches beyond royal limitation to the healing accomplished by folk art. At the end of the narrative, Gehazi tried to monetize the healing. The effort is rejected by Elisha, but the encounter with Gehazi reflects the fact that Gehazi, for all his attentiveness to Elisha, is in fact hooked into a world of *techne* that believes the gifts of life can be commodified. Elisha generates a counter-world that completely eludes the general and even his own aide.

In the war story of 2 Kings 6:8–23, Elisha, by his threefold prayer, ended the hostility and brought peace. The Syrian king is rendered helpless by blindness and becomes a docile recipient of Elisha's work, reduced to a prisoner whom Elisha sent home in peace. The appearance of the unnamed Israelite king shows him to be irrelevant. The Israelite king wants to kill the Syrians, imagining that he is in charge. But Elisha must remind the king that he has no claim on the prisoners:

> No! Did you capture with your sword and your bow those whom you want to kill? (6:22)

The king did not capture them and therefore cannot kill them. It is Elisha, not the king, who must settle the matter.

In the narrative of famine, as we have seen the king recognizes his own limitation:

> No! Let the Lord help you. How can I help you? From the threshing floor or from the wine press? (6:27)

In sum:

1. In *the poverty narrative*, the drama of royal credit and debt is superseded (2 Kgs 4:7).

2. In *the disease narrative*, the king is not a God who can give life or death (5:7).

3. In *the war narrative*, the king is a bystander who has no right to the prisoners (6:22).

4. In *the famine narrative*, the king cannot provide food (6:27).

In poverty, in disease, in war, and in famine, the king is, before our very eyes and in our very ears, declared to be an irrelevance. The managers of *techne* have been reduced in stature as we readers are invited to recognize and savor that human agents of a very different ilk are the ones who know the arts by which to deal concretely with the realities of poverty, disease, war, and famine. When we line out these narratives that mock the royal time line that precedes and follows these narratives, we are more knowing readers. We are required to recognize that the outcomes of human possibility are in the hands of uncredentialed human agents who know and act otherwise. Ellul echoes this strange awareness:

> I try to do here the same thing I do in all my books: face, alone, this world I live in, try to understand it, and confront it with another realty I live in, but which is utterly unverifiable.[22]

The totalism is not nearly as total as it may imagine. "Seeing like a state" in the end is outflanked by uncompromising mystery that makes a way out of no way.

VI

I may add a coda concerning the Christian New Testament. Thomas Brodie and David Moessner have seen how the Jesus narrative, most particularly in Luke (and then in Acts) reiterates the Elijah-Elisha narrative.[23] Jesus, in his turn, is featured as a carrier of *metis* that contradicts

---

22. Jacques Ellul, *The Humiliation of the Word* (Grand Rapids: Eerdmans, 1985), 1.

23. Thomas L. Brodie, *The Crucial Bridge: The Elijah-Elisha Narrative as an Interpretive Synthesis of Genesis–Kings and a Literary Model for the Gospels* (Collegeville, MN: Liturgical Press, 2000); David P. Moessner, *Lord of the Banquet: The Literary and Theological Significance of the Lukan Travel Narrative* (Harrisburg, PA: Trinity Press International, 1989).

the *techne* of the Roman Empire and those of the Jews who colluded with Rome.

The explicit connection of Jesus to the old narratives is the fact that in his initial appearance at Nazareth, in the rendering of Luke, Jesus first quotes the jubilee reference from Isaiah 61:

> The Spirit of the Lord is upon me,
> because he has anointed me to bring good news to the poor.
> He has sent me to proclaim release to the captives
> and recovery of sight to the blind,
> to let the oppressed go free,
> to proclaim the year of the Lord's favor. (Luke 4:18–19)

Jesus cites the most subversive act of imagination offered in ancient Israel by alluding to the Jubilee Year. It is a reference that deeply contradicts royal totalism. Then, in response to hostility, he says:

> But the truth is, there were many widows in Israel in the time of Elijah, when the heaven was shut up three years and six months, and there was a severe famine over all the land; yet Elijah was sent to none of them except to a widow at Zarephath in Sidon. There were also many lepers in Israel in the time of the prophet Elisha, and none of them was cleansed except Naaman the Syrian. (Luke 4:25–27)

Jesus cites one narrative from Elijah and one from Elisha as justification for his own intention. Before this encounter at Nazareth, moreover, Luke at the outset has Mary articulate the theme for his longer narrative concerning the inversion of all social power:

> He has brought down the powerful from their thrones,
> and lifted up the lowly;
> He has filled the hungry with good things,
> And sent the rich away empty. (Luke 1:52–53)

And in Luke 3:1–2 Luke situates the narrative of Jesus amid the authorities:

> In the fifteenth year of the reign of Emperor Tiberius, when Pontius Pilate was governor of Judea and Herod was ruler of Galilee, and his brother Philip ruler of the region of Ituraea and Trachonitis and Lasanias ruler of Abilene, during the high priesthood of Ananias and Caiaphas, the word of God came to John, son of Zechariah in the wilderness.

That "wilderness" is not unlike the venue where Elijah first encountered the word (1 Kgs 17:1–7).

It turns out that Luke's narrative concerning Jesus is "a history of amazement" in response to this one who accommodated none of the royal arrangements.[24] After his embrace of inexplicable *metis,* we get this:

When his parents saw him, they were *astonished* (Luke 2:48).

They were all *amazed* and kept saying to one another, "What kind of utterance is this?" (Luke 4:36)

Amazement seized them all, and they glorified God and were filled with awe, saying, "We have seen strange things today." (Luke 5:26)

All were *astonished* at the greatness of God. (Luke 9:42)

The actions and words of Jesus defied explanation by the authorities who were inured to their technical limitations. Luke, moreover, continues that accent in Acts concerning the performance of the apostles:

Amazed and astonished, they asked, "Are not all these who are speaking Galileans?" (Acts 2:7)

Jesus of Nazareth, a man attested by you by God with deeds of power, *wonders,* and signs that God did through him among you, as you yourselves know. (Acts 2:22)

They were filled with *wonder and amazement* at what had happened to him. (Acts 3:10)

All who heard him [Ananias] were *amazed.* (Acts 9:21)

And of course in Luke's reading the Easter appearance of Jesus constitutes the ultimate defeat of imperial *techne.*

I have come to think and believe that this matter of amazement concerning *metis* carried by human agents (which is rooted in Israelite tradition, celebrated in Christian tradition, and shared in various forms in other religious traditions) is the clue to human survival, because the managers of *techne* (and we in their wake) have largely surrendered to

---

24. It is worth recalling that Martin Buber (*Moses: The Revelation and the Covenant* [Atlantic Highlands: Humanities Press International, 1946, 1958], 75) defines the starting point of "miracle" as "an abiding astonishment." The actions of Jesus and of the apostles, in the wake of Elisha, are acts that radiate just such abiding astonishment. It is understandable that those who refused "seeing like a state" preserved these narratives.

an ideology of death. The urgent question left from such a conclusion is whether there can be a new emancipatory ecumenism through which these several religious traditions can pool their capacity, or whether in sectarian defensiveness each tradition will attach its claim to a particular expression of *techne*. Amazement cannot be slotted on an organizational chart, packaged in an orthodoxy, or assigned to tribal myopia. It can, however, be distorted and robbed of transformative power when it is regarded as property, possession, or totem. It then loses its emancipatory capacity and leaves

- widows in the hands of creditors
- lepers in the grip of disease
- prisoners of war in the power of vengeful kings,
- hungry women at risk amid high priced food

All of this is common, ordinary, and normal. This tradition of *metis*, however, insists that it need not be so!

2.

Emancipation from Extraction

Portions of this chapter were initially delivered on September 17, 2016, in Charlottesville, Virginia, at an event sponsored by the Endowed Lectureship in Contemporary Theology at Westminster Presbyterian Church and cosponsored by the Virginia Center for the Study of Religion and the Institute for Advanced Studies in Culture at the University of Virginia.

I

I have recently written a book on the theme of "money and possessions in the Bible," and I want to report to you on my findings.[1] There can hardly be any doubt that the issue of the Bible and the economy is an urgent issue for those who take the Bible in some sense as a normative script. The matter is made more acute when we consider the fact that the established Western church has, for the most part, learned to read the Bible apart from, or even over against economics; thus we have been schooled, for a variety of reasons, to read the Bible in categories that are individualistic, privatistic, other-worldly, and "spiritual." We have learned to fend off any reading of the Bible that takes seriously the *relentless materiality* of the Bible that is expressed in the doxologies of creation, in the prophetic oracles of judgment and hope, and in the narrative of Jesus that grounds apostolic preaching concerning the resurrection of Jesus. It is easy to see the collision between the materialist claims of the Bible and our long-term reading habits against that materiality.

Without a doubt, the great breakthrough in critical interpretation of

---

1. Walter Brueggemann, *Money and Possessions* (Louisville: Westminster John Knox, 2016).

the Old Testament in recent decades has been a recovered awareness of its relentless materialism. While the sources of that recovery are diverse and complex, there can be no doubt that Norman Gottwald's book of 1979, *The Tribes of Yahweh*, put our study on a new level, a study that I identified in my SBL review of the book as much of a discipline-defining marker as that of Julius Wellhausen's *Prolegomena*.[2] A direct line runs from Gottwald to Roland Boer, whose recent important book, *The Sacred Economy of Ancient Israel*, is dedicated to Gottwald.[3] More broadly, in the same decade as Gottwald's book or just before, the liberation mantra of Central American Roman Catholic bishops, "God's Preferential Option for the Poor," indicated an awakening from dogmatic slumbers and a break with accommodationist and idealistic readings of Scripture.[4]

Boer's book is an immense achievement marked by attentiveness to a mass of detail, courageous critical analysis, and disciplined imagination. To be sure, the book could have benefitted from a good editing. It will no doubt be a defining marker for our work to come, for Boer has given us categories and vocabulary to rethink and reread. Surely Douglas Knight is correct in his editorial preface to say that "beneath it all pulses the tension between allocation and extraction."[5] Boer works that interface of allocation and extraction in a rich variety of riffs, showing how such practices are deeply rooted in concrete social relationships and how they amount, in both cases, to an identifiably coherent theoretical base, even if that theoretical base is unrecognized (in allocation) or deliberately kept hidden (in extraction). The measure of the effectiveness and significance of his book is surely the prospect that we will not again read texts as we have read them heretofore.

How did we learn to read so mistakenly? How did we miss the relentless materiality of the text? Of course there is a deep push toward an idealistic reading in "religious" circumstance, given the deeply mistaken notion of "religion" as spiritual enterprise, a mistaken notion now popularly voiced as "spiritual but not religious." But how was it that the academic community colluded in such an idealistic reading?

2. Norman K. Gottwald, *The Tribes of Yahweh: A Sociology of the Religion of Liberated Israel, 1250–1050 B.C.* (Maryknoll, NY: Orbis Books, 1979). See my review in "Theological Issues in *The Tribes of Yahweh* by N. K. Gottwald: Four Critical Reviews," *The Bible and Liberation: Political and Social Hermeneutics*, ed. Norman K. Gottwald, rev. ed. (Maryknoll, NY: Orbis Books, 1983), 173–81.

3. Roland Boer, *The Sacred Economy of Ancient Israel*, Library of Ancient Israel (Louisville: Westminster John Knox, 2015).

4. See Gustavo Gutiérrez, *A Theology of Liberation: History, Politics, and Salvation*, trans. and ed. Sister Caridad Inda and John Eagleson (Maryknoll, NY: Orbis Books, 1973).

5. Douglas A. Knight, "Foreword," in Boer, *Sacred Economy*, xii.

In the modern era I suggest that it was a decision, à la Johann Philipp Gabler, to take "history" as our primary cognate discipline, with a deep tilt toward Hegelian dynamism that has shaped our reading. "History" permitted us to be preoccupied with one-off questions about sources, dates, time lines, the personalities of dominant leaders, crises such as wars, all of this to reduce or disguise the reality of "system" as a "sequence" of time-identified realities without having to consider the constants of social relationships or the fabric of social power. We did not recognize that the preoccupation with "time lines" and all that they represent was itself an instrument of extraction, and, indeed, Boer notes the futility of trying to date texts with specificity, a favorite pastime of "historical" study.[6]

Indeed, even the Jesus Seminar, led by those who wanted to regard themselves as dangerous renegades, was preoccupied with historical questions, attentively dating texts with precision but with hardly any awareness of systemic social strategies in the power grid of contestation that surges through the texts. As a result, conservatives and fundamentalists have wanted to be sure that it all "happened," and progressives wanted, with equal passion, to be sure that most of it did not "happen."

Coupled with questions of historicity is the seemingly inescapable commitment to an evolutionary scheme as surely embedded in the documentary hypothesis. The evolutionary scheme of primitive to sophisticated, polytheistic to monotheistic, and magical to ethical permitted a surreptitious kind of supersessionism that concluded, as it assumed, that more recent claims are superior to earlier claims. I dare suggest that Boer's arrangement of "regimes" hints even yet at some evolutionary sequence, though he does not press the point.

An evolutionary grid that is widely assumed popularly and among scholars makes it possible to have a notion of how even materiality "developed." It avoids the thought that competing social visions and practices were operative at the same time and endlessly in contest with each other, so that interpretation involves entry into the contestation, as Boer so well models. Engagement in the contestation tells mightily against a posture of imagined objectivity and innocent adjudication.

But the evolutionary scheme does more than that. Davis Hankins and I have offered a riff on the critical work of Tomoko Masuzawa in her analysis of the rise of "world religions" as it pertains to the study of the Old Testament.[7] Masuzawa shows that the nineteenth-century grid of "world religions" (The Big Five) was not a generous recognition of "the

6. Boer, *Sacred Economy*, 168 n59.

7. Walter Brueggemann and Davis Hankins, "The Invention and Persistence of Wellhausen's World," *Catholic Biblical Quarterly* 75 (2012): 15–31. See Tomoki Masuzawa, *The Invention*

other" but was designed and effectively asserted the superiority of Christianity and particularly the inferiority of Semitic religions, Jewish and Muslim. There is no doubt, if we attend to the Hibbert Lectures of Abraham Kuenen, that there is a deep racism in this evolutionary scheme, a racism earlier voiced in Kant's taxonomy of ethnic groups.[8] That the linkage of racism and "evolution" has continued to serve white claims to superiority in Western and particularly in US Christian culture, racism that, without acknowledgment, legitimates white systems of extraction epitomized in slavery and now expressed as mass incarceration of dispensable people. The measure of the effectiveness of the scheme of *history-evolution-no-contestation-racist superiority* is attested by the fact that one can, in many churches, question the historicity of Scripture (as long as it is done cunningly and gently), but one cannot easily talk about the economic contestation present in the text. This scheme of interpretation has systematically obscured from consideration much of the real stuff in the world and in the normative faith tradition that characteristically concerns power, social control, and economic viability.

I may mention two indications of the distancing of the text from reality. First, a somewhat distant critical reference: the series of books connected with the name of S. H. Hooke was concerned with "Myth and Ritual and Kingship" as early as 1935.[9] These collections of essays focused on the great state myths that were performed regularly in the temple in ways that valorized royal or imperial power. Much was implied in these studies, but for the most part economic issues of exploitation and extraction were never voiced in any sustained way. As a result, even studies that were about power issues kept a distance from crucial issues of contested materiality.

Of course, these matters are made more urgent when we consider the economic crisis in which we are now enveloped. It is a crisis that features the growing gap between haves and have-nots, the violence that

---

of World Religions: Or, How European Universalism Was Preserved in the Language of Pluralism (Chicago: University of Chicago Press, 2005).

8. Abraham Kuenen, *National Religion and Universal Religions: Lectures Delivered at Oxford and in London in April and May, 1881*, The Hibbert Lectures (London: Williams & Norgate, 1882; repr., New York: AMS Press, 1979). For a full and critical exposition of the racist categories of Kant, see J. Kameron Carter, *Race: A Theological Account* (Oxford: Oxford University Press, 2008), 79–21. Carter's chapter on Kant is tellingly entitled, "The Great Drama of Religion: Modernity, Jews, and the Theopolitics of Race."

9. See S. H. Hooke, ed., *Myth and Ritual: Essays on the Myth and Ritual of the Hebrews in Relation to the Cultural Pattern of the Ancient East* (Oxford: Oxford University Press, 1933); Hooke, ed., *The Labyrinth: Further Studies in the Relation between Myth and Ritual in the Ancient World* (New York: Macmillan, 1934); Hooke, ed., *Myth, Ritual and Kingship: Essays on the Theory and Practice of Kingship in the Ancient Near East and in Israel* (Oxford: Clarendon Press, 1960).

finds people dispensable in the new technological economy, the exclusionary practices of globalism, and the readiness to savage the environment for the sake of more economic growth and productivity that serve the few. All of this has happened with the collusion and endorsement of the church that either wittingly or with witting timidity has remained silent as "neighborliness" has been squeezed out of a violent economy of commoditization in which everything and everyone has a price.

The analysis that I will present is very much parallel to and illuminated by Boer's book, although my research was far along before I had seen it. I am nonetheless glad that the primary accent points of my presentation resonate with his splendid study. The simple thesis that I will express consists in this:

1. Our current economy is an *economy of extraction.*

2. The Bible is relentless in its resistance to an economy of extraction and boldly confident in its articulation of an alternative *economy of restoration.*

I do not suggest that the Bible offers any simple resolution to our economic crisis. I have no doubt, however, that the Bible is a primary source for funding our imagination in ways that might lead to an alternative economy and that might generate the courage, freedom, and energy required to implement such an economy.

II

I will begin with a reflection on the context in which we, in the US church, read the Bible. My judgment is that we live in an economy of extraction. It is the term "extraction" that I want you to have at the end of your reading this. By "extraction," I mean policies and practices whereby wealth is extracted from vulnerable people and transferred to powerful people, so that that wealth can be incorporated into their surplus holdings. Such extraction, accomplished by the force of government and of corporations, is characteristically legal, even if it is destructive and I would say immoral. The provisions and procedures for extraction, moreover, are characteristically disguised and kept hidden from view by means of euphemism and the force of ideology that conceals reality.

In order to exposit the reality of extraction in our political economy, I will comment briefly on five recent books. These may not be the best five titles, but they are surely representative in their commentary on current extractive policy and practice.

1. Sven Beckert, *Empire of Cotton*, has traced the history of the production of cotton on a worldwide basis, even beyond the Old South of the United States.[10] He pays particular attention to the textile mills of Liverpool and Manchester, which had enormous appetites for more and more cotton. One result of that demand for more cotton was the escalation of cotton production by Southern planters in the United States, with increased pressure on the cotton-picking capacity of the slave community that was coerced to greater and more intense work. The conclusion that Beckert draws is that wherever cotton has been produced, there has come with production an escalation of violence. In our case in the United States, that violence took the form of cheap, exploited labor. Thus wealth was extracted from the slave community, to the profit of the textile mills and not incidentally to the Southern planters who reaped the benefit of cheap labor.

2. David Graeber, *Debt: The First 5000 Years*, is likely the most important of the books I will mention.[11] Graeber traces the way debt has long been an important tool of the powerful against the vulnerable. By a sustained process of the quantification of value, supported by a readiness to enact violence against the vulnerable, debt has served forever as a tool of social control, as a means of assuring cheap labor, and as a reinforcement of social class status.

Graeber notes, in response to such debt, that every social revolution has adhered to the same three goals:

- Cancel the debts that have become a permanent disablement.

- Burn the records that chronicle debt and credit.

- Redistribute the land that makes a debt-free life possible.[12]

Thus, debt is not simply a matter of bookkeeping. It is, rather, a vehicle for accumulation, social stratification, and the permanent supply of cheap labor. It is instructive that at the end of his book, Graeber suggests that the only way out of a debt-ridden social circumstance is the enactment of jubilee, the biblical provision for periodic debt cancellation.[13] It is surely telling that such an acute socioeconomic analysis must finally appeal to a biblical vision of debt cancellation. While readiness to cancel debts may be visionary, it is also quite practical, because the accumulated debt can never in any case be repaid. Such debt cancellation, in ancient

10. Sven Beckert, *Empire of Cotton: A Global History* (New York: Alfred A. Knopf, 2014).

11. David Graeber, *Debt: The First 5,000 Years* (New York: Melville House, 2011).

12. Graeber, *Debt*, 8, 82.

13. Graeber, *Debt*, 390–91.

vision or in contemporary practice, is clearly a decision to subordinate the hard realities of the economy to the nonnegotiable requirements of the social infrastructure.

3. James Risen, author of *Pay Any Price*, is a well-known journalist for the *New York Times*.[14] He has recently been in much litigation over his refusal to identify the sources of some of his reportage. In this book, Risen reports on the way in which "fear mongering" has brought wealth and power to those skillful at hyping the terrorist threat:

> Fear sells. Fear has convinced the White House and Congress to pour hundreds of billions of dollars—more money than anyone knows what to do with—into counterterrorism and homeland security programs, often with little management or oversight, and often to the detriment of the Americans they are supposed to protect. Fear is hard to question. It is central to the financial wellbeing of countless federal bureaucrats, contractors, subcontractors, consultants, analysts, and pundits. . . . Fear generates funds.[15]

Risen tells the remarkable tale of recent fear perpetrated upon the little town of Derby Love, Vermont, a town that straddled the US–Canadian border.[16] The residents of the town regularly passed across the border in the routines of daily life. But because of fear the Department of Homeland Security sealed the border between the two nations and so blocked the daily routines of the residents. One resident, Buzz Ray, eventually was arrested for entering the United States at an illegal point, even though as a US citizen he was following his daily routine.

Risen concludes that the media "has built a cottage industry out of fear."[17] That cottage industry moves back and forth between global terror and the daily diet of local violence that dominates local news. The result is a "terrorized" population that is willing to trade its civil rights for "security." The focus on "security" (for which we are mandated to yearn) leads to immense profit for the fear industry. Risen judges that we are in the end committed to perpetual war, because it is in the interest of the oligarchy to keep generating fear that generates wealth. We are thus on a permanent "war footing" and clearly have no exit strategy from conflict but can only keep the conflict expanding.

Beyond Risen, it may give us pause about (a) why the United States has more gun violence than any other developed nation and (b) why the United States is more preoccupied with "terror" in the Near East

14. James Risen, *Pay Any Price: Greed, Power, and Endless War* (Boston: Houghton, Mifflin, Harcourt, 2014).
15. Risen, *Pay Any Price*, 203.
16. Risen, *Pay Any Price*, 203–20.
17. Risen, *Pay Any Price*, 221.

than any of our allies. One may wonder, moreover, whether the epidemic of local violence and the funding of international wars are linked to each other. I note in passing that Firmin DeBrabander, with an appeal to Machiavelli, suggests that the governing authorities do nothing about gun control because letting people have guns causes them to cleave more loyally to the powers that be and to the fictitious narrative that sustains the oligarchy.[18] In a word, such "local" violence serves the interests of extraction.

4. Saskia Sassen, in *Expulsions,* has written of the way in which concentrated wealth is engaged in a long-term policy of expulsion of dispensable people by way of seizing their land and their water in a way that regards them as unwelcome inconveniences.[19] In her study, which is braced with extensive statistics, she observes that displacement of large populations is related to the confiscation and monopoly of land for the powerful few. As I write this, the *New York Times* reports that sixty million people are now on the move as refugees, fleeing the danger of violence in the service of extraction.[20] That "expulsion" is given specificity in my city of Cincinnati by a study written by Alice Skirtz entitled *Econocide,* a play on "Genocide."[21] The book traces the systematic way in which the city government and the Chamber of Commerce have over time slowly removed the poor from the city and confiscated their properties for up-scale "development." The play on "genocide" is telling indeed.

In terms of the appropriation of water rights, Sassen reiterates the infamous statement of Peter Brabeck-Letmathe, the former CEO of Nestlé:

> The one opinion, which I think is extreme, is represented by the NGOs, who bang on about declaring water a public right. That means that as a human being you should have a right to water. That's an extreme solution. The other view says that water is a foodstuff like any other, and like any other foodstuff it should have a market value.[22]

The quantification and commoditization of life-sustaining resources obviously makes the economically vulnerable accountable to the power-

---

18. Firmin DeBrabander, *Do Guns Make Us Free? Democracy and the Armed Society* (New Haven: Yale University Press, 2015).

19. Saskia Sassen, *Expulsions: Brutality and Complexity in the Global Economy* (Cambridge: The Belknap Press of Harvard University Press, 2014).

20. Sergio Pecanha and Timothy Wallace, "Around the Globe, a Desperate Flight from Turmoil," *New York Times,* June 21, 2015, 10.

21. Alice Skirtz, *Econocide: Elimination of the Urban Poor* (Washington, DC: NASW Press, 2012).

22. Sassen, *Expulsions,* 192.

ful, who administer what has been packaged for sale. The outcome is that the economically vulnerable have no social leverage and therefore no social possibility in a predatory economy. In a technologically advanced economy, moreover, increasing numbers of people have become dispensable. Sassen notes that expulsion in the United States economy takes the form of incarceration of great numbers of black people, on which of course see Michelle Alexander's study of mass incarceration.[23] One may imagine that such mass incarceration is generated by fear, but fear serves limited economic interests in the removal of dispensable people from participation in the political economy.

5. Matt Taibbi has written *The Divide*, which I regard as the most chilling of these several titles.[24] In alternative chapters Taibbi reports on *justice for the vulnerable poor* and *justice for the protected wealthy*. Among the poor, Taibbi chronicles the endless "police sweeps" in which the poor are treated to mass arrests without due process or evidence. Thus, the poor are arrested for standing on the sidewalk in front of their apartments for blocking traffic, or are arrested for standing on the grass in front of their apartments when they should have been standing on the sidewalk. Those taken in such sweeps are detained and then released, but they have been humiliated, inconvenienced, and handicapped in their work obligations, all without cause or apology. The alternative chapters of the book trace the manipulative policies and practices of big bankers and hedge fund investors, those who initiated bad loans and who evoked the recession of 2007. Taibbi observes, as has often been observed, that not a single such financial offender has been arrested or indicted for the high crimes of economic manipulation in the interest of extraction. Taibbi notes that Eric Holder, the attorney general, has taken no action against the offenders, precisely because Holder, the chief US justice officer, is in bed with Wall Street and its extractors.

The contrast between two modes of justice is a sad, alarming exposé of the ways that a justified policy and practice of extraction skew social relationships and social possibilities. I use the term "justified" to see that such an accepted, even if hidden, practice amounts to *a theodicy,* a theory of justice that, according to Peter Berger, may serve

> as legitimation *both* for the powerful *and* the powerless, for the privileged *and* for the deprived. For the latter, of course, they [that is, such theodicies] may serve as "opiates" to make their situation less intolerable, and by the

23. Michelle Alexander, *The New Jim Crow: Mass Incarceration in the Age of Colorblindness* (New York: New Press, 2012).

24. Matt Taibbi, *The Divide: American Injustice in the Age of the Wealth Gap*, rev. ed. (New York: Spiegel & Grau, 2014).

same token to prevent them from rebelling against it. For the former, however, they may serve as subjectively quite important justifications of their
enjoyment of the power and privilege of their social position.[25]

Berger observes:

> In both cases, the result is one of world-maintenance and, very concretely,
> of the maintenance of the particular institutional order. . . . there may be
> two theodicies established in the society—a theodicy of suffering for one
> group and a theodicy of happiness for the other.[26]

The sum of this evidence is to exhibit an economy of extraction whereby
wealth is regularly and substantively transferred from the vulnerable to
the powerful. Michael Lind has written of this arrangement:

> The American oligarchy spares no pains in promoting the belief that it does
> not exist, but the success of its disappearing act depends on the equally
> strenuous effort on the part of an American public anxious to believe in the
> egalitarian fictions and unwilling to see what is hidden in plain sight.[27]

None of these books alludes to the religious component of these practices. But we are bound to notice that the "egalitarian fictions" of the
US economy can be sustained only by religious legitimation that is
the mantra of God-given US exceptionalism. The concealed economic
practice could not be sustained without the religious fiction that legitimates it. For that reason, critical reflection on the religious fiction, sustained by a misreading of the Bible, summons us to reconsider the Bible
as a script for critical assessment of economic theory and economic practice.

III

We read the Bible, I propose, in the context of a brutalizing extraction
enterprise that is largely concealed from us by the domination of a *market
ideology* coupled with US *exceptionalism*. An alternative reading of the
Bible will make clear that the Bible, if actually read, is not answerable to
such a social construction. Thus I propose that the Bible is a script that
critiques an *economics of extraction* and that advocates, against such policy

25. Peter L. Berger, *The Sacred Canopy: Elements of a Sociological Theory of Religion* (Garden
City, NY: Doubleday, 1969), 59.
26. Berger, *Sacred Canopy*, 59.
27. Michael Lind, quoted in Jonathan P. Baird, "The Art of Hating the Poor," *Concord Mon-
itor,* June 3, 2015, B1.

and practice, an *economics of restoration* that aims to rehabilitate those who have been squeezed out by extraction. Here I will consider four examples of extraction in the biblical text, and then in turn I will consider the responses made to these four extractions in the biblical text.

Four Examples of Extraction

1. Pharaoh. There is no doubt that Pharaoh is the big extractor in the Bible. We do not know his name, because he is a recurring, predictable player in every economy. His story is endlessly reperformed in the drama of extraction. He has enough food to last forever; but he has nightmares about running out of food . . . seven bad cows eat seven good cows (Gen 41:1–7). Those with the most have the deepest anxiety about scarcity! It is imagined scarcity that propels confiscatory policy. Pharaoh organizes a food policy led by the Hebrew, Joseph. It turns out that Joseph has forgotten his identity—as we are wont to do—and has signed on to Pharaoh's policies of extraction. The narrative—that we never read in church—details the extraction (Gen 47:13–25). Pharaoh accumulates food until he has a monopoly.

In the first year of the famine Joseph sells the subsistence farmers food from the royal monopoly (Gen 47:14). He will not give them free food because that would make them lazy and dependent! In the second year of the famine, the subsistence farmers have no money, so Joseph trades them food for their cattle, their means of production (Gen 47:16). In the third year of the famine, when they still need food, they have no more resources at all, no money, no cattle. For the sake of food they give over their land (expulsion!) and their bodies (slavery) to Pharaoh (Gen 47:19). The system of extraction has reduced them to the helpless dependence of slavery. And because Pharaoh's mantra of entitlement is so powerful and compelling, the peasants-become-slaves say,

> You have saved our lives; may it please my lord, we will be slaves to Pharaoh. (Gen 47:25)

They are grateful for being inducted into slavery!

The final step in the report in Exodus 1:13–14 is that Pharaoh treated the slaves "ruthlessly." When we read the exodus story, we do not often ask how the Israelites became slaves. Now we know! They became slaves because the policies of extraction had placed them in a hopeless condition of debt that they could not pay, and they had no alternative. Pharaoh performs the drama of extraction perfectly:

Plenty—imagined scarcity—accumulation—monopoly—violence!

The narrative of extraction always ends in violence.

2. *Solomon*. The second example of extraction that I mention is the story of Solomon. It cannot be unimportant that Solomon is Pharaoh's son-in-law. I imagine Solomon and his wife went to Egypt often for Sunday dinner where his father-in-law could give him continuing lessons in extraction. And he learned them very well.

The narrative of Solomon reports his incredible affluence. We are told that the gold and silver, spices and clothes and all manner of exotic commodity poured into his realm. Indeed he built, we are told, an extravagant temple in Jerusalem so that he could exhibit the gold, all he said, to the glory of God. (But notice that Jesus, in Luke 12:21, observes that "not even Solomon in all his glory." "The glory of God . . . the glory of Solomon" . . . impossible to distinguish the two!) The opulence of Solomon is made clear, moreover, in verses that detail the food supply for one day in the royal household:

> Solomon's provision for one day was thirty measures of flour, and sixty measures of meal, ten fat oxen, and twenty pasture-fed cattle, one hundred sheep, besides deer, gazelles, roebucks, and fatted fowl. (1 Kgs 4:22–23)

They were lavish meat eaters amid an economy of subsistence.

We may ask how such extravagance was possible. We can identify three sources of such wealth:

a. Solomon, via military arrangement, *collected tribute*—protection money—from neighboring regimes.

b. Solomon had an effective *tax system*. Indeed, for the twelve tax districts, we are told that two of his sons-in-law, Benabinadab and Ahimaaz (4:11, 15), were the chief officials. These must have been lucrative posts, and the family enterprise was made secure by having relatives as extractors.

c. Solomon had a policy of *forced labor* (slavery, the draft) headed by Adoniram, Secretary of Forced Labor (1 Kgs 4:6). One text suggests that Solomon enslaved only foreigners, but elsewhere it is said even his own subject people were enslaved.

The combination of *tribute* from the outside, *tax* from the inside, and *cheap labor* made opulence possible. The opulence was so great that even the queen of Sheba, no slouch herself, came to be dazzled by Solomon:

She came to Jerusalem with a very great retinue, with camels bearing spices, and very much gold and precious stones. . . . When the Queen of Sheba had observed all the wisdom of Solomon, the house that he had built, the food of his table, the seating of his officials, and the attendance of his servants, their clothing, his valets, and his brunt offerings . . . there was no more spirit in her. (1 Kgs 10:2, 4–5)

He took her breath away! This is an extractor admiring an even more successful extractor. The world admires extractors (see Donald Trump!). Here is the conclusion:

The whole earth sought the presence of Solomon to hear his wisdom, which God had put into his mind. Every one of them brought a present, objects of silver and gold, garments, weaponry, spices, horses, and mules, so much year by year. (10:24-25)

3. Persian Empire. The third example of extraction I cite concerns the taxation policies of the Persian Empire under Artaxerxes. The Persian Empire has conventionally been regarded in Old Testament study in a relatively benign way. When one reads between the lines (or even reading the lines carefully), however, it is evident that the Persians acted the way empires act, that is, as a system of extraction from the colonies.

I will cite only one text, but the case there is quite clear. In Nehemiah 9, Ezra voices a long prayer that reviews the history of Israel, that acknowledges Israel's sin, and that gives thanks for God's mercy. At the end of the prayer Ezra voices a remarkable complaint:

Here we are, slaves to this day—slaves in the land that you gave to our ancestors to enjoy its fruit and its good gifts. Its rich yield goes to the kings whom you have set over us because of our sins; they have power also over our bodies and over our livestock at their pleasure, and we are in great distress. (Neh 9:36–37)

In his pathos, Ezra speaks of the good land that God had promised to the Jews; they were to enjoy its produce. But the circumstance of his community precisely contradicts that divine promise. Instead of enjoying the produce of the land as the divine promise had intended, its produce is extracted by foreign kings, that is, the Persian rulers. These rulers have power "over our bodies and over our livestock." That is, they have complete economic control. It requires no imagination to see that this characterization of a predatory imperial economy is an echo of the Pharaonic policies described in Genesis 47:13–25. In both cases the alien king came to oppress "bodies" (enslavement) and "cattle" (means of production). Or, conversely, it is plausible that the report on Pharaoh in Genesis 47 is in fact a backward projection from the Persian reality. Either way, Jews in the Persian period faced the same extractive reality as was remembered of the ancient Hebrews. The contrast voiced by Ezra concerns "their pleasure" and "our distress." The extraction system does indeed produce both "pleasure" and "distress," *pleasure* for the perpetrators who live well off their surplus, *distress* for those who are eventually squeezed into helplessness and slavery. The arrangement is so that the "producers" in the colony can feed and clothe the "nonproducers" who manage the empire and preside over the extraction system.[28]

In a second prayer, Ezra briefly alludes to "our slavery" and gladly acknowledges that God "may grant a little sustenance" (Ezra 9:8–9). It is instructive that in neither prayer does Ezra issue a petition. Even in his poignant summary in Nehemiah 9:36–37 he only describes the unbearable circumstance of his people, without asking for divine relief. The reason for an absence of petition may be that Ezra had colluded with Persian authorities and had received support for his reconstruction enterprise. In any case, the extractive force of Persia is evident; it contradicts any attempt to present the empire in a more benign mode.

4. Roman Empire. The fourth instance of extraction in the Bible that I cite is that of the Roman Empire, an extraction system that is the focus of the earliest Jesus movement. That extraction system has been well characterized by Douglas Oakman in his analysis *Jesus and the Peasants*, in which he understands Jesus as a patron of the overtaxed peasants in opposition to Roman predation.[29] Oakman nicely summarizes what we know about the Roman system wherein the ruling elites (including Jews who colluded with Rome) became creditors. Through a manipulation of taxes, loans, and rents the peasants gradually fell into debt. Given an inability to repay the debt on the basis of subsistence agriculture, the peasants lost their land.[30] Oakman pays particular attention to the elites who governed Jewish Palestine—Herod, priests, elders, scribes, and procurators who administered taxes and therefore debt, who slowly came to control the land and to reduce the landless peasants to helpless dependence.[31]

It is for this reason that the Gospel narrative portrays Jesus in the company of tax collectors (see Luke 3:12, 5:27–30, 7:29, 34, 15:1, 18:10–13). These were Jews who had signed on to collect taxes for Rome. It was

28. Boer, *Sacred Economy*, 202–3.

29. Douglas E. Oakman, *Jesus and the Peasants*, Matrix: The Bible in Mediterranean Context 4 (Eugene, OR: Cascade Books, 2008).

30. Oakman, *Jesus and the Peasants*, 140.

31. Oakman, *Jesus and the Peasants*, 143.

a "sweetheart" deal, as the collectors not only passed money along to Rome but were free to keep for themselves whatever they could collect beyond the requirements of Rome. Thus, as a "middleman," the tax collector functioned as an extractor for the imperial system.

The best known narrative of such a tax collector is that of Zacchaeus in Luke 19:1–10. In the narrative exchange, Jesus initiates the interaction:

> Zacchaeus, hurry and come down; for I must stay at your house today. (v. 5)

Zacchaeus is dubbed by the crowd "a sinner," one who has departed from the Torah tradition and has opted for an alternative way in the world that is inimical to covenantal identity (v. 7). Zacchaeus's response to the initiative of Jesus is that he will redress the extractive actions that have characterized his work. He will give half of his possessions to the poor, and he will repay those he has defrauded four times as much (v. 8). The narrative does not specify his wealth as an extractor. But surely he was rich. Perhaps in his service to the empire he has acquired such wealth that keeping half is more than enough. But he does make that decisive gesture, a gesture that is evoked by the presence of Jesus.

In response to the pledge of Zacchaeus, Jesus confirms to Zacchaeus his true identity:

> He also is a son of Abraham. (v. 9)

That is, he is a member of the neighborly community of covenant. It is as though for too much of his life Zacchaeus had forgotten his true identity and his true place of belonging (with its appropriate practices) and, like Joseph, had signed on with an alien regime to perform actions alien to his true identity. He had had such a lapse that we may take him to be "temporarily insane," that is, insane enough to sign on with the extractive regime. But now, "salvation has come to this house" (v. 9). "Salvation" is release from the extractive system and reengagement with a neighborly economy that has the poor in its horizon, an economy for which Jesus is an advocate.

When we consider the sum of these four instances of extraction that I have cited—*Pharaoh, Solomon, Persia, Rome*—we can see that they constitute or at least represent the defining time line of power for the sweep of Scripture. The community of faith—Israel, the Jesus movement, the church—is always "in the shadow of the empire," and the empire is regularly an extractive system.[32]

Given our own context amid an aggressive extractive enterprise, it is an urgent necessity, in my judgment, that we must read Scripture as an account of successive extractive regimes. It turns out that our obsessive preoccupation with (a) time lines, dating, and historicity, on the one hand, and (b) spiritual-religious preoccupation about "redemption," on the other hand, has caused us to miss the defining force of economic extraction that pervades the context and the text of Scripture. Fresh and informed attention to the recurring systems of extraction will permit us to read the Bible knowingly and responsibly, a reading that will be matched by a more knowing and responsible reading of our own economic circumstance.

III

The Bible lives amid various extraction systems. In its main contention, Scripture does more than live amid them. It responds to them in various forms of resistance; it refuses to accept the fiction that sustains them. Beyond that, it offers daring proposals for an alternative economy. Here I review the textual responses to each of the extractive instances that I have cited.

Responses to the Extractors

1. The paradigmatic extraction system of Pharaoh receives response in ancient Israel by its normative narrative of Exodus–Sinai. Imagine having a book of the Bible entitled "Exodus," or "exit." Israel's memory begins in a daring departure from Pharaoh's system of extraction in an embrace of an alternative existence. The exodus narrative is a paradigmatic proposal of withdrawal from an extraction system that in the Bible receives many subsequent performances. The main features of that narrative of departure are well known.

a. Departure requires an initial surreptitious resistance that here takes the form of the courage of the two midwives, Puah and Shiphrah, who defy Pharaoh by birthing Hebrew baby boys, the very babies proscribed by Pharaoh's edict (Exod 1:15–22). It is likely that the beginning of departure is in such a cunning act of subversion.

---

32. See *In the Shadow of Empire: Reclaiming the Bible as a History of Faithful Resistance*, ed. Richard A. Horsley (Louisville: Westminster John Knox, 2008).

b. Departure requires, beyond that, fierce confrontation with the extraction system. In this narrative, that confrontation consists in Moses' murder of an Egyptian foreman as Moses responds in indignation to the Egyptian abuse of a Hebrew slave (Exod 2:11–15). One of course prefers not to condone violence, but Moses does commit an act of violence that makes him persona non grata in the empire. His action is a response to the initial violence of Pharaoh toward the slaves, erstwhile subsistence farmers.

c. Departure requires the public processing of pain wherein the slaves groaned and cried out in their anguish (Exod 2:23–25). It turns out that their cry mobilized the power of YHWH on their behalf. Pharaoh of course does not mind if the slaves suffer in silence, or even groan privately in their huts. But out-loud protest is immediately dangerous for the regime, because pain publicly processed turns to bold, emancipatory energy.

d. Departure requires, in this narrative, the defining legitimacy of the holy God via the burning bush (Exod 3:1–6). The engagement of YHWH in the departure made the withdrawal from the extraction system a holy action that has cosmic implications. Imagine the holy God now allied with and committed to a company of slaves! This is indeed "God's preferential option for the poor," a decisive taking of sides with the slave community against the powers of extraction.

e. For all of YHWH's bombastic promises of deliverance for the slaves, the departure finally requires human agency. It is Moses (along with Aaron) who must go to Pharaoh (Exod 3:10; 5:1). It is Moses (not YHWH) who must run the risk of departure.

And so they leave. The exodus event is not about water, or even about geography. It is about a refusal of the extraction system. It is about a refusal to be cheap labor in a predatory system. It is a refusal to conform to the ideology of scarcity that propels Pharaoh to ever-intensified productivity in the interest of monopoly.

And so they left Egypt. They departed the fleshpots, albeit reluctantly. They entered the wilderness with great misgivings, a zone of reality outside the domain of Pharaoh's control, outside the reach of extraction. They departed the scarcity system of Pharaoh and half expected the wilderness to be a zone of death. It turned out, however, that the wilderness, beyond Pharaoh's extraction system, was an arena for life resources that they could not have imagined:

- meat from quail
- water from rock

- bread from heaven

Lots of it . . . enough for all! Who knew? Who knew that if they departed Pharaoh, they would arrive at abundance!

When they arrive at Sinai, the narrative becomes the launching pad for alternative political economy. They received Ten Nonnegotiable Guidelines for neighborliness from "the Lord your God who brought you out of the land of Egypt, out of the house of bondage" (Exod 20:2). This God of alternative prescribes a regular, holy day of work stoppage, a Sabbath (Exod 20:8–11). There had been no Sabbath in Egypt. There it was 24/7 production to meet the insatiable quotas of Pharaoh in his desperate pursuit of surplus. And now, rest from all such quotas! By the tenth commandment Israel is commanded: "Do not covet" (Exod 20:17). Do not imitate Pharaoh. Do not be greedy. Do not acquire. Do not confiscate what belongs to your neighbor. The tenth command sounds the word "neighbor" three times. There had been no neighbors in the extraction system, only slaves, rivals, threats, competitors. The Lord of Sinai proposes otherwise. The economy can be neighborly when it is conducted without acquisitive greed. In that economy, life-giving loaves abound. There is enough for all, but it must not be stored up. The story of faith in the Bible is the oft-reported reperformance of *departure* (exodus) from the extraction systems, the discovery of *abundant bread* in the wilderness outside the domain of Pharaoh, and the *charter of neighborliness* that defies and contradicts accumulation and monopoly.

2. The second example of extraction that I have cited, that of Solomon, receives a vigorous response in the Old Testament. Solomon is not simply a king; he is the icon of the entire dynasty, the metaphor for the predatory system of the Jerusalem elites who came to dominate the life and imagination of Israel.

The response made to Solomon may be traced in three ways.

a. In 1 Kings 11:29, Ahijah, a prophet from the old recalcitrant tradition of Shiloh, confronts Jeroboam in the parking lot and proposes that he lead a coup against the dynasty and the rule of Solomon. The rejection of the system of extraction is grounded in prophetic utterance that imagines that an alternative power arrangement is possible. This is indeed "prophetic imagination"!

b. In 1 Kings 12:1–19 the intrusion of prophetic imagination into the royal system is matched by concrete political action. The leaders of northern Israel negotiate with Rehoboam, Solomon's son and heir concerning tax policy in the new governance of the son. Rehoboam, advised by his cadre of young hedge-fund managers, believes there is no limit to their entitlement and urges higher taxes. The young king lacks all sense of proportion and is propelled only by avarice. Such an extractive system is unsustainable in the face of well-grounded neighborly existence that has a sense of its own legitimacy. The narrative concerns the rejection of such extraction by way of taxation of the produce of peasants who live a subsistence existence that benefits the oligarchy. We are told that the young king had to flee for his life; and his Secretary of Forced Labor, Adoram, was stoned to death. The king and his aggressive advisors had failed to reckon with dangerous resistance, because they imagined that the extraction system, legitimated by temple ideology, could contain and withstand all opposition. The tax resistance narrated in chapter 12 is of a piece with the exodus departure. Both departures declare the unsustainability of the extraction system. It cannot be sustained when there is resistance grounded in a deep sense of neighborly legitimacy. The negotiation of the peasants gives the lie to the fiction of the Jerusalem oligarchy.

c. But third, I think it is correct to conclude that the entire prophetic corpus from Amos to Jeremiah is one long resistance to the extraction system. It is time that we liberals recognize that prophets do not harp on this or that injustice. Rather they speak in poetic cadence about the system of extraction that is sustained by the religious ideology of piety and the liturgical myth. Amos's urgency about justice, Hosea's bid for mercy and not sacrifice, and Jeremiah's anticipation of dire judgment upon the city are all declarations that the extraction system of king and temple is unsustainable. The advocacy of justice is an insistence that the economy can be ordered differently. Indeed, it turns out that the reordering of the economy is the condition of social viability:

> Hate evil and love good,
> and establish justice in the gate;
> it may be that the Lord, the God of hosts,
> will be gracious to the remnant of Joseph. (Amos 5:15)

> Sow for yourselves righteousness;
> reap steadfast love;
> break up your fallow ground;
> for it is time to seek the Lord,
> that he may come and rain righteousness upon you. (Hos 10:12)

> For if you truly amend your ways and your doings, if you truly act justly with one another, if you do not oppress the alien, the orphan, and the widow, or shed innocent blood in this place, and if you do not go after other

gods to your own hurt, then I will dwell with you in this place, the land that I gave of old to your ancestors forever and ever. (Jer 7:5–7)

As you know, such texts can be endlessly multiplied, all of which declare the claim of the regime to be fiction. Concerning that fiction, the prophet Jeremiah regularly uses the term "falseness"![33]

3. Persian extraction was not done directly by Persian agents. Like every extractive regime, it identified local people, in this case Jews, who collaborated with the regime by being their agents of extraction. These Jewish "middlemen" were no doubt not greatly trusted by the Persian authorities and were surely resented by other Jews from whom they collected for the regime. Thus, the narrative encounter of Nehemiah in Nehemiah 5 may be taken as a form of Jewish resistance to Persian extraction and the proposal of an alternative Jewish economic practice.

The narrative begins with protests concerning the economic crisis caused by Persian extraction. It is reported:

> There were also those who said, "We are having to pledge our fields, our vineyards, and our houses in order to get grain during the famine." And there were those who said, "We are having to borrow money on our fields and vineyards to pay the king's tax. Now our flesh is the same as that of our kindred, our children the same as their children; and yet we are forcing our sons and daughters to be slaves, and some of our daughters have been ravished; we are powerless, and our fields and vineyards now belong to others." (Neh 5:3–5)

The crunch of hunger and taxation was forcing them into slavery.

Nehemiah, in great indignation, finds such extraction intolerable and severely reprimands that the tax-collecting, interest-levying Jews:

> "You are all taking interest from your own people." And I called a great assembly to deal with them, and said to them, "As far as we are able, we have bought back our Jewish kindred who had been sold to other nations; but now you are selling your own kin, who must then be bought back by us!" (vv. 7–8)

He issues an imperative of restoration:

> Restore them, this very day, their fields, their vineyards, and their olive orchards, and their houses, and the interest on money, grain, wine, and oil that you have been exacting from them. (v. 11)

---

33. See Thomas W. Overholt, *The Threat of Falsehood: A Study in the Theology of the Book of Jeremiah*, Studies in Biblical Theology 2/16 (Naperville: A. R. Allenson, 1970).

The outcome is that his urgent summons works. The extractors in the Jewish community do as Nehemiah urges and take an oath of solidarity whereby the disenfranchised are restored to viability:

> We will restore everything and demand nothing more from them. We will do as you say. (v. 12)

This was accomplished by Nehemiah, even though he was appointed governor by the Persians. In this instance, he opted out of the imperial exploitation for the sake of solidarity with his own people. He says that he managed food differently:

> Now that which was prepared for one day was an ox and six choice sheep, also fowls were prepared for me, and every ten days skins of wine in abundance; yet with all this I did not demand the food allowance of the governor, because of heavy burden of labor on the people. (v. 18)

This sounds not unlike an echo of the lavish food of Solomon; except that Nehemiah resisted it for the sake of his community. Systems of extraction characteristically impose a heavy burden of labor on the peasants. Yet it is possible, the narrative attests, for members of the oligarchy to act differently! Nehemiah brings relief.

4. In the face of the extractive system of Rome, the Jesus movement that was identified by the mantra "kingdom of God" opposed Roman extraction and in its place performed an economy of restoration that countered imperial predation. Thus, the Lord's Prayer petitions for the coming of "your kingdom" on earth as it is in heaven, and proceeds to focus on the cancellation of debts. It turns out that debt is the way in which the extractive system reduces those in subsistence to permanent dependence. It turns out further that the cancellation of debts is an antidote to subsistence that permits restorative relief. It would be an illuminating exercise in reading the Synoptic Gospels to test whether the repeated usage of "kingdom of God" means an alternative to the economic extraction of Rome. Such a usage resonates with the ancient Torah of Deuteronomy, in which Jesus is situated, that is preoccupied with issues of economic justice, debt cancellation, and neighborly restoration.

V

By way of exposition of this last point, I wish to consider in turn the testimony of Luke and of Paul.

1. It is remarkable that Luke (along with Acts) has been viewed as the most benign and accommodating toward Rome, when in fact the evangelist offers the most radical alternative to the rule of Rome. Five texts from Luke serve the point:

a. In Mary's Magnificat, she anticipates a radical economic reversal:

He has brought down the powerful from their thrones,
and lifted up the lowly;
he has filled hungry with good things,
and sent the rich away empty. (Luke 1:52–53)

b. In Luke 12:13–31, perhaps the most remarkable of these texts, Jesus critiques the greed system and proposes an alternative. The parable is framed by the petition of a man who wants Jesus to adjudicate a family real estate dispute. Jesus's first response to the man is a warning:

Take care! Be on your guard against all kinds of greed, for one's life does not consist in the abundance of possessions. (v. 15)

The term rendered "greed" (*pleonexias*) in the NRSV bespeaks an insatiable desire to have what belongs to another. The parable that follows concerns the successful, productive, rich farmer who had thought that he never had enough. He must accumulate more and store more, an act that recalls that in Exodus, the Hebrew slaves were building "storehouse cities" for Pharaoh, the great accumulator (Exod 1:11). In his success, the rich farmer proposes to celebrate his "good fortune." His successful acquisitiveness, however, is interrupted by God, who calls him a fool and demands his life. The parable, taken by itself, asserts that such greed is a nonstarter that cannot be sustained. Greed kills!

But Jesus instructs his disciples, utilizing the parable as a "critical incident" (Luke 12:22–31). He warns his disciples against being anxious, recognizing that endless acquisition evokes endless anxiety because, like the farmer, we never yet have enough. Never enough food, never enough clothing, never enough life; all such anxiety, however, cannot add "a single hour" to our life (12:25–26). He likens such avarice to the "glory of Solomon," who never yet had enough. He declares that such greed is out of sync with the reality of the generosity of God's creation. Such a teaching can be religiously reassuring if we think only of personal greed. But if taken in terms of political economy, it is a declaration that an economy of extraction has no future, and the fictitious ideology of acquisition that propels the dominant economy is in the end a way of death.

The alternative to such "striving" for more is to "strive" for God's kingdom, that is, for his rule of neighborly restoration (Luke 12:31). There is, Jesus asserts, an alternative to the greed system that is itself an anxiety system. We may usefully pause over the term "greed," (*pleonexias*), the insatiable desire for what belongs to another. A bit ago I read an article on Vladimir Putin in the *London Review of Books,* and there was the same Greek word, *pleonexia,* asserting that President Putin had an insatiable desire for what belongs to another.[34] It takes little imagination to see the same *pleonexia* at work in the accumulation-cum-monopoly of the oligarchy that now produces subsistence living in a debt economy among us for very many people.

c. In the parable of the banquet in Luke 14:16–24, Jesus tells how the vulnerable are indeed among those who will "eat bread in the kingdom of God":

> Go out at once into the streets and lanes of the town and bring in the poor, the crippled, the blind, and the lame. And the slave said, "Sir, what you have ordered has been done, and there is still room. Then the master said to the slave, "Go out into the roads and lanes and compel people to come in, so that my house may be filled. For I tell you, none of those who were invited will taste my dinner." (vv. 21–24)

d. In Luke 16:1–9 Jesus tells an enigmatic parable of the manager who cooked the books on behalf of the debtors. He concludes that the "wealth system" as it is officially arranged, does not need to be honored. He allows that the current wealth system cannot be sustained. And "when it is gone," you may be welcomed to eternal life (Luke 16:9). That testimony ends with this dictum:

> No slave can serve two masters; for a slave will either hate the one and love the other, or be devoted to the one and despise the other. You cannot serve God and wealth. (Luke 16:13)

There is a stark contrast between the wealth system and the economy of God, and we cannot have it both ways. The practice of "both/and" is an unsustainable illusion.

e. The final text I cite is the parable of the rich man and Lazarus (Luke 16:19–31). The outcome of the parable is that the rich man, along with

---

34. Tony Wood, "First Person," *London Review of Books,* February 5, 2015, 13–16.

his brothers, is left with nothing but "the law and the prophets" (vv. 29–31). Those ancient traditions that advocate neighborliness are to be heeded. When not heeded, the result is "torment" and the "agony of flames." Jesus can imagine an unbearable outcome for the practice of wealth that is exclusionary in an antineighborly way.

The sum of these Lucan texts amounts to an enormous critique of extraction that cannot be sustained. The summons of Jesus is to an alternative economy that regards the currently excluded as fully legitimate participants in the economy.

2. I have been surprised at the outcome when one poses economic questions to the letters of Paul.

a. I was led first to the "belated" letters of Paul, Ephesians and Colossians. In the instructional catalogues of these letters, "greed" (*pleonexia*) recurs:

In Ephesians 4:17–19, Paul speaks of "the gentiles," those who are not included in Gospel obedience who are "alienated from the life of God." He describes their self-destructive behavior, conduct of "the old self," that includes being greedy, the practice of every kind of impurity (*pleonexia*). He likens such greedy self-indulgence to impurity.

In Ephesians 5:3–5, Paul lists a series of behaviors that are not "proper" among the saints:

> But fornication and impurity of any kind, or greed [*pleonexia*], must not even be mentioned among you, as is proper among saints. Entirely out of place is obscene, silly, and vulgar talk; but instead, let there be thanksgiving. Be sure of this, that no fornicator or impure person, or one who is greedy (that is, an idolater) has any inheritance in the kingdom of Christ and of God.

Paul has in purview the new "kingdom." He equates greed with idolatry. Greed is acting out loyalty to an alternative God, the God mammon (capital).

The point is echoed in Colossians 3:5:

> Put to death, therefore, whatever in you is earthly; fornication, impurity, passion, evil desire, and greed [*pleonexian*] (which is idolatry).

This leads to his catalogue of deathly behavior, evidences of "the old self":

> But now you must get rid of all such things—anger, wrath, malice, slander, and abusive language from your mouth. Do not lie to one another, seeing that you have stripped off the old self with its practices. (3:8–9)

b. I was more surprised to find related matters in Paul's letter to the Galatians. In 5:19–21 Paul gives us an inventory of the "desires of the flesh":

> Now the works of the flesh are obvious: fornication, impurity, licentiousness, idolatry, sorcery, enmities, strife, jealousy, anger, quarrels, dissensions, factions, envy, drunkenness, carousing, and things like these.

He warns his readers:

> I am warning you, as I warned you before; those who do such things will not inherit the kingdom of God. (5:21)

Access to the coming kingdom of God is not on offer for those who live according to an extraction ethic that has no concern for the common good.

Now these counterlists are familiar to us. It is unfortunate that Paul uses the phrases "desires of the flesh" and "fruit of the spirit," because such usage has led to a misreading in terms of spirit–flesh dualism. A much more compelling reading is offered by Brigitte Kahl in her book *Galatians Re-Imagined*.[35] She contends, persuasively in my judgment, that "Galatia" is not a territory as is most often assumed. It is rather an attitude of dissent that resists the dominant values of the empire. It follows in her argument that "the law" that Paul castigates is not the Torah of Judaism; it is the "law of Rome" that revolves around greed, power, wealth, pride, and self-promotion.[36] To be "free of the law," then, means not to have one's life defined by the arrogant self-indulgence of the wealth culture that tramples over others to get ahead. It follows in Kahl's exposition that these destructive behaviors arise in an economy of extraction that is propelled by an endless need for more; all of these behaviors are marked by self-indulgence, self-promotion, and self-enhancement at the expense of the neighbor and at the expense of the neighborhood.

It requires no imagination to see that such a way of life depends on transposing everything into the pursuit of commodity that legitimates meanness, selfishness, and indifference to the neighbor. It is evident that we live according to the law of extraction, so that the media serve an antineighborly ethic of greed, and our laws are written to serve the insatiable greed of the powerful at the expense of the vulnerable.

---

35. Brigitte Kahl, *Galatians Re-Imagined: Reading with the Eyes of the Vanquished*, Paul in Critical Contexts (Minneapolis: Fortress Press, 2010).

36. Kahl, *Galatians Re-Imagined*, 257 and passim.

In the face of such predatory practice, Paul enumerates the fruit of the Spirit, all of which concern the neighborhood:

> By contrast, the fruit of the Spirit is love, joy, patience, kindness, generosity, faithfulness, gentleness, and self-control. There is no law against such things. (5:22–23)

In a pastoral way Paul articulates the either/or of social relationships and therefore of economics. Among us, as in ancient Rome, the law of extraction not only seems legitimate but is taken as normative. Among us, any critique of the extraction system is dismissed as an "assault on capitalism" without making any distinction concerning (a) a free market, (b) a rigged system that distorts that freedom, and (c) an attempt to offer market ideology as an adequate narrative for all of life.[37]

Paul is uncompromising in his insistence on a neighborly economy that flies in the face of extraction:

> For the whole law [that is, the law of Christ] is summed up in single commandment, "You shall love your neighbor as yourself." (Gal 5:14)

The whole law, the law of Christ, echoing the Torah of Judaism, is love of neighbor. It will not do to have abstract arguments about "capitalism and socialism" that are only smoke screens. What is important is the insistence, in the gospel tradition, that every economic theory and every economic system are focused on the neighbor.

Paul evidences his realism when he adds his negative warning.

> If, however, you bite and devour one another, take care that you are not consumed by one another. (5:15)

"Bite and devour" mean to treat every other economic player as a rival, a competitor, or a threat. It is worth notice that the Old Testament word for "interest" (nšk) has the connotation of "bite." It is a "bite" into the neighbor that will lead to a devouring of all in a debt-propelled economy. And then Paul adds tersely:

> Bear one another's burdens, and in this way you fulfill the law of Christ. (Gal 6:2)

The "law of Christ" contests the law of extraction in force in Rome; it means commitment to the neighborhood of burden sharing.

---

37. Gerald Berthoud, "Market," *The Development Dictionary: A Guide to Knowledge as Power*, ed. Wolfgang Sachs, 2nd ed. (New York: Zed Books, 2010), 74–94.

It is no wonder that the primary advocate and performer of the alternative economy had to be executed by those who operated and benefitted from the extraction system. The "desires of the flesh" are not simply base "natural habits." They are practices required in order to get ahead in the predatory economy of the empire. And the fruit of the spirit is not simply a practice of naive piety. They are rather the nonnegotiable requirements of a sustainable society.

VI

From this reading of the text I draw five conclusions:

1. We have learned and been carefully taught to misread the Bible. When we watch for it, we will see this issue of extraction/restoration everywhere in the text, even as we see it everywhere in our society. These categories of interpretation invite us to a fresh vigilance about the text.

2. Because of the totalizing impact of the extraction system that now dominates the government, the courts, the media, most of the universities, and surely corporations, there is no one left to do the work of critique and alternative except the church. Such work will require courage and honesty to reread this text faithfully, a rereading that as of now will be a great shock and affront to many of the baptized who have learned to misread.

3. None of this is easy. I suggest that, as we learn to read the text more faithfully, the primary work of the church will be to live in and with the deep tension between the gospel and the extraction system in which most of us have a deep stake. It turns out that neither liberals nor conservatives in the church have any high ground; all of us are plunged into this tension that cries out for honest acknowledgment.

4. This tension is a life-or-death either/or. The system of death recharacterizes human persons as competitors, threats, or rivals, or at least as a great inconvenience as dispensable persons who might be cheap labor. The power system of accumulation and monopoly has no patience with the vulnerable, who are cast as "nonproducers" without value. This system of death that commoditizes human persons, moreover, takes the environment as an endless resource to be plundered for the sake of an insatiable prosperity.

Alternatively the restoration system, termed by Jesus "the kingdom of God," situates human persons in an orbit of generosity, hospitality, and forgiveness, which constitutes the seedbed of restorative justice. Such an alternative views the environment as a fragile system of abundance that is to be honored, protected, and cared for.

5. The either/or of this life-or-death question issues in a legitimated, calculated *greed* (that is thinly disguised by euphemism) or, conversely, it issues in endless *thanks* for abundance to be shared. Imagine, the church is the only community that has a sacrament entitled "thanks," the Eucharist. It is bread given. It is bread given in abundance. It is bread shared. It is real bread that issues in real thanks. This bread contradicts the entire system of greed. It precludes the practice of coveting that is the way of the empire. Loaves abound! But not to be stored up; the surplus will get worms and become foul smelling and melt (Exod 16:20–21). We practice thanks for bread that is given daily! It is a fiction that bread that nourishes can be stored up in huge quantities. This is a fiction that we reject, because we know better.

3.

Political Agency against Idolatry and Commodity

God's covenant with God's people is singular and exclusive. The first commandment of Sinai precludes the worship of or trust in other gods; it proscribes any divided loyalty: "No other gods" (Exod 20:1)! Martin Noth speaks of the commandments of the Old Testament as safeguards of that exclusiveness:

> They are provisions which seek to ensure the exclusive nature of the relationship between God and people, between Yahweh and the Israelite tribes, or (in other words), which guard against a defection in any form from the sole God, who is thought of as the partner of the covenant.[1]

Jon Levenson notes that the utilization of the marital metaphor for the covenant assures a passionate jealousy on YHWH's part that allows no compromise

> The jealousy of the injured spouse and the anger of the person whose identity has been stolen are measures of the damage done. In the thinking that underlies the Decalogue, the "other gods" (Exod 20:3) of whom the Lord is jealous are impostors or counterfeits. . . . If we are to employ the term "monotheism," long used to describe Judaism, the only meaning the term can have within the specific context of covenant is in reference to this rigorous exclusivity of the relationship. The key issue in covenantal theology is not the number of gods; texts can easily be found in the Hebrew Bible that mention other deities without implying their nonexistence. The issue

1. Martin Noth, *The Laws in the Pentateuch and Other Studies* (Philadelphia: Fortress Press, 1967), 51.

is, as it were, political rather than philosophical. It has to do with loyalty and service, not with the nature of being.[2]

YHWH commanded exclusiveness; Israel assented to exclusiveness. The account of oath taking at Sinai, echoed in Deuteronomy, is exclusionary:

> This very day the Lord your God is commanding you to observe these statutes and ordinances; so observe them diligently with all your heart and with all your soul. Today you have obtained the Lord's agreement: to be your God; and for you to walk in his ways, to keep his statutes, his commandments, and his ordinances, and to obey him. Today the Lord has obtained your agreement: to be his treasured people as he promised you, and to keep his commandments; for him to set you high above all nations that he has made, in praise and in fame, and in honor; for you to be a people holy to the Lord our God, as he promised. (Deut 26:16–19)

Such exclusiveness belongs to the character of YHWH and to the origin of Israel.

Would that this singular God of exclusive loyalty were simply an articulation of universal, unconditional love as popular religion would wish it! From the outset, however, Israel knew better. This is a "God of love" . . . and of justice and righteousness and holiness, a God of sharp demand and rigorous sanction, a God who comes and goes in freedom and ofttimes in absence.

Israel, long before us, wished otherwise. The God who met Israel in the mystery of the burning bush uttered a mandate to depart (Exod 3:1–6), and the God who met Israel in the storm at Sinai imposed a destiny of obedience (Exod 19:16–25). This is, since the bush and the storm, a God who is not subject to explanation, about whose origin Israel knows nothing, a God who is simply there in the text, there in the life of Israel, there in the life of the world, speaking and acting and appearing on no schedule other than that of holy inscrutability. The historians may go on about the "origins of monotheism," but this God, present in the plot of covenant, is not subject to such explanatory commentary. From YHWH's side, any god who can be explained by historical emergence, derivation, or extrapolation is no god at all, for this God is indeed "wholly other."

In retrospect it is no great wonder that Israel discovered that this God is not useful, cannot be harnessed to "vain" purposes, cannot be recruited for pet projects (even noble ones!), will not serve our interests, and needs nothing we may offer as gift or sacrifice, as bribe or bargain (Exod 20:7).

2. Jon D. Levenson, *The Love of God: Divine Gift, Human Gratitude, and Mutual Faithfulness in Judaism*, Library of Jewish Ideas (Princeton: Princeton University Press, 2016), 11.

As a result, the wish for alternative in Israel is endless. This is a God who will be served . . . worshiped. They wanted a god useful, who adjusted divine purpose to human agenda. They readily blended together *loyalty* and *usefulness*. Augustine, later on, had it that we must *love God* and *use things*; but once the blending begins, *use* and *love* get confused. Israel found it easy enough to *use God* and *love things*. And so the abiding crisis of biblical faith is the readiness of God's people, partly in obtuseness and partly in willfulness, to mobilize God for purposes other than God's own godness.

I

The word for such religious accommodation is "idolatry." The objects of such religious accommodation are "idols." You can "make" idols. You can manufacture gods! So the prophets, in the wake of Sinai and with their sharp uncompromising irony, can playfully and polemically describe the "god-making" procedures that resulted in easier, more convenient authorities. The drama the prophets imagine is a contest between the God "who makes heaven and earth" and Israel who makes gods that would accommodate Israel's preferred historical reality.

Jeremiah can offer an overwrought (can it be overwrought?) contest between *the God who makes* and the *idols made by Israel*. God-making goes like this:

> For the customs of the peoples are false;
> a tree from the forest is cut down,
> and worked with an ax by the hands of an artisan;
> people deck it with silver and gold;
> they fasten it with hammer and nails
> so that it cannot move . . .
> Beaten silver is brought from Tarshish,
> and gold from Uphaz.
> They are the work of the artisans and of the hands of the goldsmith;
> their clothing is blue and purple;
> they are all the product of skilled workers. (Jer 10:3–4, 9)

They are objects of beauty, well crafted, and produced from the finest most precious materials. But the verdict on them is wholly negative:

> Their idols are like scarecrows in a cucumber field,
> and they cannot speak;
> and they have to be carried,

for they cannot walk.
Do not be afraid of them,
for they cannot do evil,
nor is it in them to do good . . .
For their images are false,
and there is no breath in them.
They are worthless, a work of delusion;
at the time of their punishment they shall perish. (Jer 10:5, 14–15)

The ultimate dismissive judgment on them is that they "have no breath" (Jer 10:14), no spirit, no governing capacity, no generative power. These so-called gods cannot act to do anything, evil or good. They are objects, not subjects; they cannot be the subject of an active verb.

Their impotence moreover, is matched by the falseness of those who make them. The verdict is that the idols themselves are "both stupid and foolish" (v. 8). Their makers are "stupid and without knowledge" (v. 14).

The poem of Jeremiah is designed for dramatic contrast so that testimony on behalf of YHWH, in the form of *doxology*, is interwoven into the *polemic* against the "made" gods. YHWH is in every way contrasted to the idols. YHWH is incomparable ("none like you"):

There is none like you, O Lord;
You are great, and your name is great in might;
Who would not fear you, O King of the nations?
For that is your due;
among all the wise ones of the nations
and in all their kingdoms
there is none like you . . .
But the Lord is the true God;
He is the living God and the everlasting King;
At his wrath the earth quakes,
and the nations cannot endure his indignation . . .
It is he who made the earth by his power,
who established the world by his wisdom,
and by his understanding stretched out the heavens.
When he utters his voice, there is a tumult of waters in the heavens,
and he makes the mist rise from the ends of the earth.
He makes lightnings for the rain,
and he brings out the wind from his storehouses. (Jer 10:6–7, 10, 12–13)

This is the creator God who has the power and the will to act on a cosmic basis in overwhelming power and with wisdom to match power, wisdom to order creation in proper life-giving ways.

The testimony of verse 12 gives us a series of three sets of three:

- Three powerful verbs: made, established, stretched out
- Three objects that together constitute all reality: earth, world, heavens
- Three characteristics of YHWH's capacity: power, wisdom, understanding

These three sets of three in the dramatic cadences of doxology could be arranged in a variety of configurations. The rhetorical sum of these three sets of three is to attest a God who in every way contrasts with the impotent idols. The idols cannot "make, establish, stretch out"; the idols do not create or govern "earth, world, or heaven"; the idols have no "power, wisdom, or understanding." The doxology yields in Israel game-set-match for the unrivaled creator God. This God, moreover, is the Lord of the covenant with Israel:

> Not like these is the LORD, the portion of Jacob,
> For he is the one who formed all things,
> and Israel is his inheritance;
> the LORD of Hosts is his name. (v. 16)

There can be no attachment of Israel to the idols, for YHWH has attached God's own self to Israel. YHWH is to be feared while the idols evoke no such emotional engagement. *Polemic* and *doxology* together bid to cause the imagination of Israel (and all in the wake of Israel) to focus on the exclusivity of covenant.

A second polemical articulation against god-making is in Isaiah 44:9–20. This extensive prose passage is in three parts. In verses 9–11, the prophet lays down the premise and conclusion of the argument. Idols are "nothing" (*tohu*). The term might suggest a zero of capacity, or it might suggest a chaotic force of negation. Either way, what follows is a mocked procedure for "fashioning a god" whose devotees are blind and sure to be terrified and shamed. The middle section of the passage describes in detail the god-making process, a description in high satire (vv. 12–17). The god is made with great artistic skill and from good material. Such god-making is absurd because in the end the god-makers imagine that their god-production will save.

The accent in verses 18–20 is no longer on the manufactured god but on those who produce, worship, and expect to be saved by such gods. Those who make and worship idols are so beguiled that they are without eyes to see, without minds to comprehend, without knowledge or discernment, and finally unable to figure out that such a god is a fraud.

The process is one of dumbing down to the zero of the god. This same rhetoric of willful obtuseness is elsewhere sounded by Isaiah:

> Keep listening, but do not comprehend;
> keep looking, but do not understand.
> Make the mind of this people dull,
> and stop their ears, and shut their eyes,
> so that they may not look with their eyes,
> and listen with their ears,
> and comprehend with their minds,
> and turn and be healed. (Isa 6:9–10)

This same rhetoric is utilized by Jesus in his reprimand of his obtuse disciples who do not comprehend his ministry of abundance:

> Do you still not perceive or understand? Are your hearts hardened? Do you have eyes, and fail to see? Do you have ears, and fail to hear? And do you not remember? (Mark 8:17–18)

Along with god-making comes the manufacture of a pretend world in which the powers of discernment and discretion have evaporated.

It will be noticed that in Isaiah 44:9–20, unlike in Jeremiah 10:1–16, there is no counterpoint of positive testimony for YHWH. It is noteworthy, however, that in Isaiah 44, the *prose* on idols (vv. 9–20) is followed by the *poetry* on YHWH (vv. 24–28) in which the generative power of YHWH is acknowledged and celebrated:

> I am the LORD, who made all things,
> who alone stretched out the heavens,
> who by myself spread out the earth;
> who frustrates the omens of liars,
> and makes fools of diviners;
> who turns back the wise,
> and makes their knowledge foolish;
> who confirms the word of his servant,
> and fulfills the prediction of his messengers;
> who says of Jerusalem, "It shall be inhabited,"
> and of the cities of Judah,
> "They shall be rebuilt,
> and I will raise up their ruins";
> who says to the deep, "Be dry—
> I will dry up your rivers";
> Who says of Cyrus, "He is my shepherd,
> and he shall carry out all my purposes";

and who says of Jerusalem, "It shall be rebuilt,"
and of the temple, "Your foundation shall be laid." (Isa 44:24–28)

This series of participles attests YHWH's generative power. It is perhaps not unimportant that the idols get only prose, but YHWH evokes doxological poetry. The "living God" (see Jer 10:10) requires dynamic rhetoric in contrast to the idols that can be fully contained in one-dimensional (lifeless) prose. The sum of the rhetoric in Jeremiah 10:1–16 and Isaiah 44:9–20 is to call attention to the sheer folly of god-making, which not only offends YHWH and violates covenant but reduces the makers/worshipers of idols to their own impotence and helplessness. In prophetic purview one must be primordially stupid to depart covenant for such a lifeless hopeless alternative.

II

It turns out that Israel was that stupid, willful, or wayward. The core narrative of Sinai ends in Exodus 24:18 with the report that Moses "was on the mountain forty days and forty nights." That narrative continues directly in Exodus 32:1:

> When the people saw that Moses delayed to come down from the moun-
> tain, the people gathered around Aaron, and said to him, "Come, make gods
> for us; as for this Moses, the man who brought us out of the land of Egypt,
> we do not know what has become of him."

Israel could not wait. They found the absence of Moses (which is matched by the elusiveness of YHWH) to be unbearable. In response to that absence (and that elusiveness), Israel promptly resorted to god-making. The processes of god-making so mockingly reported in Jeremiah 10 and Isaiah 44 were now implemented by Aaron in order to meet Israel's immediate need. As in prophetic poetry, this god was manufactured from precious material, gold. In the narrative, Israel did not petition this god for deliverance as in Isaiah 44:17; but Israel did credit this manu-factured god with the remembered deliverance from Sinai (Exod 32:4). In their self-deceiving illusion, they imagined a god made from precious metal that could have saved. Karl Barth sees this act of god-making out of gold (precious metal) in the form of a calf (bull) as an expression of vir-ile self-sufficiency. This was an act of autonomy as though Israel could manage without the God of the exodus:

> Israel itself was this bull, defiantly standing on its short thick thighs and feet, tossing its horns and thrusting its tail. . . . [The bull is] the picture of their own vital and creative power as a people when left to themselves and controlling their own life.[3]

The combination of *gold* and *bull* yields a "golden bull," the ultimate icon of self-possessiveness, self-control, and self-sufficiency, the very icon of that temple of self-possessiveness, Wall Street and its Stock Exchange. It is no wonder that this act of illusionary defiance evoked the anger of YHWH and belatedly the indignation of Moses.

It is plausible to judge that Psalm 115 is a reflection on the god-making narrative of Exodus 32 with its reiteration of themes from Jeremiah 10 and Isaiah 44. The psalm begins by pointing "glory" away from Israel toward YHWH:

> Not to us . . . not to us. (v. 1)

The alternative to self-praise is glory to YHWH, the God of covenant who (a) "does whatever he pleases" (v. 3) (b) in "steadfast love" and "faithfulness" (v. 1). The phrasing of verses 1–3 connects the power of YHWH with the fidelity of YHWH, so that YHWH is recognized as an agent with transformative capacity. That agency is expressed in the threefold "help" in verses 9–11, and in the fourfold "bless" in verses 12–13, the latter a reference to the blessing of creation, reinforced by "give increase" in verse 14. The doxology is all about agency that has a capacity, as Claus Westermann has seen, both to *bless creation* and to *transform history*.[4] The wonder of YHWH is effective agency!

That doxological affirmation is set in bold contrast to the idols of verses 4–7. The idols are "made" ("the work of human hands") of precious metals (gold and silver). The key feature of the idols is that they do not live and cannot give life. But the psalm voices no such abstraction as that. It provides, rather, a specific bodily inventory of the idols, bodily in the sense that they resemble YHWH, who also has identifiable bodily members: hands, mouth, eyes, ears, nose, feet, "throat," even though YHWH's appearance is, unlike that of the idols, verbal and not visual.[5] But the body parts of the idols can only malfunction. In function the body parts of the idols are quite unlike those of YHWH, whose body

---

3. Karl Barth, *Church Dogmatics IV.1* (Edinburgh: T&T Clark, 1956), 427–31.

4. Claus Westermann, *What Does the Old Testament Say about God?* (Atlanta: John Knox, 1979).

5. On the "body of God," see Benjamin D. Sommer, *The Bodies of God and the World of Ancient Israel* (Cambridge: Cambridge University Press, 2009).

parts function coherently to do what the creator God pleases. As Aubrey Johnson has persuasively argued concerning the human person, the body parts of YHWH function synecdochically, each and every part as an expression and enactment of the whole.[6] The hostile characterization of the idols will allow for no such coherence of body parts for the idols, for they have no organic identity; they are constructed of parts, one part at a time! Thus the idols have,

- mouths that do not speak
- eyes that do not see
- ears that do not hear
- noses that do not smell
- hands that do not feel
- feet that do not walk
- "throats" that do no sound

The intent and effect of this detailed rhetoric are cumulative. The dismissive mocking builds to a conclusion. They have no agency. They cannot act to bless as creator. They cannot act to deliver as savior. The absence of agency follows from being "made," gods who are "without spirit," lifeless, unable to live and unable to give life. They are only treasured commodity, an object of worship, adoration, and admiration, but not subject. That is what Aaron produced. Only an extremely anxious Israelite community could imagine such nonagents could be implicated in a remembered exodus or any anticipated transformation or rescue.

The practical payout of this rhetoric is in the verse that follows this negative portrayal of the idols:

> Those who make them are like them;
> So are all those who trust in them. (Ps 115:8)

The real issue is not the worship of commodities made from precious metals; the real issue is what happens to those who engage in such worship. They become like the commodities they worship. The made-gods of precious metals have no agency. Those who worship such made-gods eventually have no agency, cannot walk, talk, see, hear, and so on,

---

6. Aubrey R. Johnson, *The Vitality of the Individual in the Thought of Ancient Israel* (Cardiff: University of Wales Press, 1964).

because they are contained within and defined by a world of lifeless no-gods who have no life and cannot give life.

In his famous exposition of the first commandment of Sinai, Martin Luther declared, "Whatever your heart clings to and relies upon, that is properly your God." Thus verse 8 employs the term "trust," that is, reliance upon. Trust in such lifeless nonagents is contrasted with the threefold "trust in the Lord" that follows in verses 9–11. Thus, the narrative of Exodus 32, thematized in Psalm 115, becomes a *doxology* for YHWH set over against a *polemic* against those who do such practice and become "dead" and "silent," that is, opt out of responsible historical existence:

> The *dead* do not praise the Lord,
> nor do any that go down into silence. (v. 17)

The recognition that we become like that which we worship is reiterated in Psalm 135, again with the word "trust":

> The idols of the nations are silver and gold,
> the work of human hands.
> They have mouths, but they do not speak;
> they have eyes, but they do not see;
> they have ears, but they do not hear,
> and there is no breath in their mouths.
> Those who make them
> and all who trust them
> shall become like them. (Ps 135:15–18)

The phrase "no breath" is "no *ruah*," no generative spirit. And those who worship them are also eventually without generative capacity. The contrast in the Psalms between exuberant *doxology for YHWH* and the countertheme of *dismissal of the idols* is elemental in Israel's articulation of covenantal faith.

The ante is upped in prophetic utterance:

> But they came to Baal-peor,
> and consecrated themselves to a thing of shame,
> and became detestable like the thing they loved. (Hos 9:10)

Now the false gods are "detestable." And Israel, by its worship of them, has become likewise detestable, so unlike YHWH, so unacceptable to YHWH, so lacking in the vitality of covenantal engagement because life is reduced to control, security, and self-sufficiency, without any possibility of dynamic engagement, because the idols are incapable of such engagement. Alas, in the end the worshipers are likewise incapable of such engagement.

III

Here then is my first thesis: *Idolatry consists in the reduction of all of life to the pursuit of and trust in commodity (originally an object made in an artistic way from precious metals) as both the goal of life and the means of living.* It is not a sleight of hand to transpose "idols" without agency to "commodities," because in the rhetoric of psalms and prophets the idols are from silver, gold, and wood, commodity objects before which the "stupid" bow down and upon which they rely. It is clear that the worship of idols is no narrow religious concern but has immense pertinence to issues of political economy. To put it in more contemporary terms, when "religion" is monetized, something catastrophic happens to the participating community and the social possibilities that can be enacted in the community. It is my judgment that in our contemporary culture the process of such commoditization is now well advanced with enormous momentum, so that everything and everyone is reduced to a commodity. Everyone and everything has a price, can be bought and sold, used and traded, as we are taught and so we imagine that such a process will make us safe and make us happy. The accent I make of this process is that such a way of living causes and expects the loss of agency; it results in an ersatz notion of well-being.

Three texts occur to me concerning the loss of agency and reduction of life to commodity:

• In Ezekiel 27, a prophetic invective concerning the city-state of Tyre, the polemic is addressed against the "merchants" and their "merchandise" because everything in Tyre had become a tradable commodity. In her fine exposition of this text, Ellen Davis speaks of "commerce as fornication":

> Tyre was the essential agent in the emergence of a new kind of economic system, a mercantile economy based on the circulation of precious metals (silver and gold), which gradually replaced a simpler more subsistence-oriented system in which goods were bartered.[7]

---

7. Ellen F. Davis, *Biblical Prophecy: Perspectives for Christian Theology, Discipleship, and Ministry*, Interpretation (Louisville: Westminster John Knox, 2014), 120.

Most telling is the dreary prose inventory of mercantile commodities in Ezekiel 27:12–25:

> Tarshish did business with you out of the abundance of your great wealth; silver, iron, tin, and lead they exchanged for your wares. Javan, Tubal, and Meshech traded with you; they exchanged *human beings* and vessels of bronze for your merchandise. Beth-togarmah exchanged for your wares horses, war horses, and mules. The Rhodians traded with you; many coastlands were your own special markets; they brought you in payment ivory tusks and ebony. Edom did business with you because of your abundant goods; they exchanged for your wares turquoise, purple, embroidered work, fine linen, coral, and rubies. Judah and the land of Israel traded with you; they exchanged for your merchandise wheat from Minnith, millet, honey, oil, and balm. Damascus traded with you for your abundant goods because of your great wealth of every kind—wine of Helbon, and white wool. Vedan and Javan from Uzal entered into trade for your wares; wrought iron, cassia, and sweet cane were bartered for your merchandise. Dedan traded with you in saddlecloths for riding. Arabia and all the princes of Kedar were your favorite dealers in lambs, rams, and goats; in these they did business with you. The merchants of Sheba and Raamah traded with you; they exchanged for your wares the best of all kinds of spices, and all precious stones, and gold. Haran, Canneh, Eden, the merchants of Sheba, Asshur, and Chilmad traded with you. These traded with you in choice garments, in clothes of blue and embroidered work, and in carpets of colored material, bound with cords and made secure; in these they traded with you. The ships of Tarshish traveled for you in your trade.

Ezekiel's list is so long for the sake of its cumulative effect (and I replicate it for the same reason). The list is long so as to be comprehensive; there is nothing outside of it! The almost inexhaustible inventory points to an economic culture in which everything is bought and sold. The test case is in verse 13 wherein "human beings," that is, slaves, are "exchanged with vessels of bronze" and all other tradable commodities. Human persons are given monetary value. And when human persons are given monetary value, some are worth more than others, and some are worth nothing and are dispensable and disposable. The "merchants" are castigated by the prophet because traffic in commodities has come to constitute the whole of their existence, their raison d'être. Thus, the inventory is dominated by the repeated use of the term *rkl*, variously translated as "did business," "traded," and "exchanged." It is all a commodity transaction in precious goods that gives no life. We can imagine that the life of the traders and those who were sustained by them became increasingly like the commodities they traded, in which they trusted, and by which they measured their lives . . . with no agency beyond the sphere of commerce. They existed to buy and sell and so to possess.

• As Davis has seen, the inventory of Ezekiel 27 with reference to Tyre is replicated in Revelation 18 with reference to Rome under the guise of Babylon:

> And the merchants of the earth weep and mourn for her [Babylon], since no one buys their cargo anymore, cargo of gold, silver, jewels, and pearls, fine linen, purple, silk and scarlet, all kinds of scented wood, all articles of ivory, all articles of costly wood, bronze, iron, and marble, cinnamon, spices, incense, myrrh, frankincense, wine, olive oil, choice flour and wheat, cattle and sheep, horses and chariots, slaves—and human lives [*psychas anthrōpōn*]. (Rev 18:11–13)

The more extended text in this chapter is all about "merchants," and this list ends, yet again with "human lives" that are assigned an undistinguished place among other commodities. Davis comments:

> The cargo list of twenty-eight items offers a thumbnail sketch of Roman society, where the superrich might spend the equivalent of five or six million U.S. dollars on one citron-wood wine table. . . . It also highlights political and military power (horses and chariots) as well as the stuff of ordinary life: wine, oil, and grain were the dietary staples for everyone. Probably few Romans would have considered the final item on the list to be a luxury. Slave labor was the essential energy supply for the Roman economy; it fueled agriculture, mining, and every other form of industry, as well as every household. Slaves, called *somata* ("bodies") in the market "were treated much like livestock." . . . That status befits their placement here, beside the domestic animals owned by ordinary people as well as the horses and chariots belonging to the rich.[8]

The reference to "bodies" calls to mind the exposition of Ta-Nehisi Coates concerning the ways that whites have long dominated, owned, and abused black bodies.[9] Davis sees that in the critique of both Ezekiel and Revelation, the text contradicts the dominant economic system:

> On the one hand, there is the unrighteous and godless economy of Empire, the "little economy" that is already doomed, however powerful it may appear to be. On the other hand, there is "the Great Economy of a world created and healed by God, which alone guarantees long-term flourishing. Such flourishing is possible only when land and people and nonhuman creatures flourish together, in intricate systems of interaction. The contrast

8. Davis, *Biblical Prophecy*, 129. Davis cites David E. Aune, *Revelation 17–22*, WBC 52C (Nashville: Thomas Nelson, 1998).

9. Ta-Nehisi Coates, *Between the World and Me* (New York: Spiegel & Grau, 2015).

between the two underscores the modern, prophetically informed insight: "The Earth is sufficient for everyone's needs but not for everyone's greed."[10]

• In a third, very different sort of text, the issue of commoditization of human persons and the loss of agency is treated with high irony. Ahasuerus, king of Persia, had great wealth:

> There were white cotton curtains and blue hangings tied with cords of fine linen and purple to silver rings and marble pillars. There were couches of gold and silver on a mosaic pavement of porphyry, marble, mother-of-pearl, and colored stones. Drinks were served in golden goblets, goblets of different kinds, and the royal wine was lavished according to the bounty of the king. (Esth 1:6-7)

This is indeed "conspicuous consumption"! The king's table is a venue for extraordinary opulence that of course led to self-indulgence: "Drinking was by flagons, without restraint" (Esth 1:8). It is easy enough to conclude that Vashti, the queen, was a part of the furniture of commoditization in her role as a deferential trophy wife. She is without agency in that environment and is expected to be happily without agency in the context of exquisite commodities.

The story turns, however, on her refusal to be without agency and on her abrupt and inexplicable exercise of agency, which causes a narrative-producing upheaval in the palace. The report is terse:

> But Queen Vashti refused to come at the king's command conveyed by the eunuchs. (v. 12)

The royal response to her refusal is prompt and equally terse:

> At this the king was enraged, and his anger burned within him. (v. 12)

Vashti's inexplicable action created an enormous crisis and placed the entire power arrangement of the regime in jeopardy. The king is enraged; but the more general worry is that her defiant act of agency will become contagious among the other royal women. Power arrangements based on commoditization are always placed in jeopardy by such emancipated agency, and so Vashti must be banished from the royal presence. She is expendable in order that the system of commoditization may be maintained. Vashti plays no great role in the narrative, but she

---

10. Davis, *Biblical Prophecy*, 126. The final quotation is from Leonardo Boff, *Cry of the Earth, Cry of the Poor*, trans. Phillip Berryman (Maryknoll, NY: Orbis Books, 1997), 2, paraphrasing Mahatma Gandhi.

already performs a choice for historical agency that will be reperformed by Esther, her successor.[11]

Subsequently Esther is made queen and embraces the role as trophy wife, at least until the crisis on which the narrative turns. With a plot initiated by Haman, all Jews in the kingdom are immediately at risk. Given the emergency for Jews, Mordecai warns Esther against her conformist self-protection:

> Do not think that in the king's palace you will escape any more than all the other Jews. For if you keep silence at such a time as this, relief and deliverance will rise for the Jews from another quarter, but you and your father's family will perish. (4:13–14)

And then he summons her to take an active role in the crisis:

> Who knows? Perhaps you have come to royal dignity for just such a time as this. (v. 14)

In response to this challenge, Esther is ready to run great risks that break the royal protocols.

> After that I will go to the king, though it is against the law; and if I perish, I perish. (v. 16)

The transformation of Esther from *passive commodity* to *active agent*, it turns out, makes the rescue from a certain death for the Jews in the kingdom possible. She refuses to be cast any longer as a commodity on exhibit for the king; she acts her role in making history. Esther seems to anticipate the modern bumper sticker "Nice women do not make history." She is transformed into a history maker!

In considering the narrative of Esther, we have come a long way from the narrative of Aaron and his god-making. Her courage notwithstanding, trust in lifeless commodities (calf, trophy wife) is devastating for the Persian king, just as it was for Aaron and his impatient people.

IV

Out of this cluster of texts, it is not a far reach to see that in our contemporary culture we face a like crisis of the reduction of all of life to the

11. On the structural importance of Vashti in the narrative and for the other characters, especially Esther and Mordecai, see Timothy K. Beal, *The Book of Hiding: Gender, Ethnicity, Annihilation, and Esther*, Biblical Limits (New York: Routledge, 1997).

pursuit and overvaluing (worship!) of commodities. Writ large we can see that market ideology now has established a totalism in which nothing is imaginable in public life beyond the accumulation of commodities that we are taught will make us safe and happy. Thus, the "market" is no longer a public place of exchange but has become "a principle for regulating social relationships":[12]

> This normative representation of social regulation is increasingly reinforced by technological innovations in key sectors like information, telecommunications and biogenetics. The clearest result of this process is market dynamism, giving the impression that commoditization has no limits whatsoever. "Can *everything* be bought and sold?" is a moral question which has been progressively emptied of all meaning.[13]

A "particular place" has been transposed into a "generalized principle." Gerald Berthoud has traced the practical consequence of such an enterprise:

> Schematically three categories of people result from such forced development. First, a small class of ultra-rich, who can accumulate much wealth while spending ostentatiously. Second, a varying number of people in an intermediary position. They represent the middle classes, those who balance production and consumption. Finally, there are the poor, excluded from the sharing of wealth, and preoccupied by problems of mere survival.[14]

Given this large rubric, one may detail many instances of its performance:

• The popular television show *Antiques Roadshow* began in Britain with its exhibit of treasured crafted old objects. The show featured artistic assessment and appreciation of the craftsmanship of the objects. When the program immigrated to the United States, however, such artistic assessment and appreciation almost completely disappeared. Now, in the United States, on the program, antiques are rated only to state a dollar worth of the object with the predictably required "gasp" of amazement. Treasured crafted objects of beauty have been reduced to market commodities.

• In an infamous statement, the CEO of Nestle products, with a commitment to "bottled water," can characterize water as a commodity that must be priced, sold and bought.

---

12. Gerald Berthoud, "Market," *The Development Dictionary: A Guide to Knowledge as Power*, ed. Wolfgang Sachs, 2nd ed. (New York: Zed Books, 2010), 79.
13. Berthoud, "Market," 75.
14. Berthoud, "Market," 87.

The one opinion which I think is extreme, is represented by the NGOs, who bang about declaring water a public right. That means that human beings should have a right to water. That's an extreme solution. The other view says that water is a foodstuff like any other, and like any other foodstuff it should have a market value.[15]

Thus, a "natural resource" is commoditized so that it inevitably becomes the right and property of only those with resources to purchase. The CEO does not reflect on the fate of those without resources to purchase. And of course the mantra of privatization is reiterated with the privatization of everything imaginable, so that anything of social value is assigned exclusively to the "more fortunate."

• The worship of commodity and the reduction of human persons to zombies have more pernicious consequences. Thus, widespread "sex traffic" is the outcome of the reduction of children and women to tradable, usable objects.

• Wage theft is a widespread practice in which vulnerable workers are systematically cheated out of their just earnings by the bookkeeping management class (on which see Deut 24:14–15 and Jer 22:13). Isabel Wilkerson has narrated the wage theft that was a part of the tenant farmer arrangement in the Old South after the emancipation of the slaves in which the owner managed the books to the disadvantage of the farmer:

> The planter pulled out his books. "Well, John," the planter began. "Boy, we had a good year, John."
> "Yes, sir, Mr. Reshard. I'm sure glad to hear that."
> "We broke even. You don't owe me nothing. And I don't owe you nothing."
> The grandfather had nothing to show for a year's hard toiling in the field.
> "This is all he ends up, 'We broke even.'" George would say years later. "He has no money, no nothing for his family. And now he's ready to start a new year in the master's debt. He'll start all over again. Next year, they went through the same thing—"We broke even.'"
> The following year, the grandfather went to the big house and got the same news from Reshard.
> "Well, by God, John, we did it again. We had another good year. We broke even. I don't owe you nothin, and you don't owe me nothin."
> George's grandfather got up from the table. "Mr. Reshard, I'm sho' glad to hear that. Cause now I can go and take that bale of cotton I hid behind the barn and take it into town and get some money to buy my kids some clothes and some shoes."

15. Peter Brabeck-Letmathe, is quoted by Saskia Sassen, *Expulsions: Brutality and Complexity in the Global Economy* (Cambridge: The Belknap Press of Harvard University Press, 2014), 192.

The planter jumped up. "Ah, hell, John. Now you see what, now I got to go all over these books again."

"And when he go over these books again," George said long afterward, "he'll find out where he owed that bale. He gonna take that bale of cotton away from him, too."[16]

The experience of George's grandfather, the tenant farmer, is many times replicated, right up until today.

• The sum of commoditization—in the concentration of wealth and power in the hands of the few, the mad scramble of the rat-race to get ahead or to stay ahead, and the reduction of life to mean-spirited competition via privatization—is sustained by an elaborate system of "bread and circuses" in which professional sports and entertainment function as an opiate for the maintenance of a system that precludes covenantal questions of justice. That enterprise of "bread and circuses" features an endless exhibit of money, power, celebrity, and sex. As a corollary to our thesis of commoditization as idol worship, we may add this judgment: *the process of commoditization ends in violence because every "other" is a potential threat or a useful tool.* In professional sports the violence is (more or less) contained by rules. In the market, there are no such rules.

V

My second thesis is this: *As critique of and alternative to commoditization as idolatry, the Bible attests to the possibility of dialogic interaction in which the "other" is seen to be not object, but partner.* It follows that the more life is reduced to commodity, the more the possessor and owner of commodity can assume a posture of absolutism, as with the "owner" of the tenant farmer. When the "other" is no longer commodity but partner, however, the would-be "owner" is drawn into interaction that subverts absolutism and requires responsiveness, that is, responsibility to the other who may no longer be counted on or dismissed as object.

In the narrative in Exodus that follows the episode of Aaron's "Bull of Gold," we can see dramatically played out the transposition from *divine absolutism* to *dialogic engagement*. The first response of YHWH to the commoditization of worship by Aaron is unstrained, unmitigated anger. In order that YHWH may be left unrestrained, YHWH says to Moses:

16. Isabel Wilkerson, *The Warmth of Other Suns: The Epic Story of America's Great Migration* (New York: Vintage Books, 2011), 53.

> Now let me alone, so that my wrath may burn hot against them and I may
> consume them. (Exod 32:10)

This remarkable statement is a recognition by YHWH that, in the presence of Moses, YHWH is restrained and is not free to emote in destructive ways. YHWH wants for now to be unencumbered, in order to give
full vent to rage. YHWH imagines that YHWH can be absolute in rage
and not held accountable beyond justified anger.

But of course the narrative does not end and cannot end there with
the proposed dismissal of Moses, because Moses persists. Moses will
not leave YHWH free in YHWH's emotive absolutism. At great risk,
Moses reminds YHWH that YHWH cannot be so unencumbered, both
because YHWH is bound to old promises made to the ancestors in Genesis and because YHWH must live in the presence of other peoples and
other gods (Exod 2:11–13). The force of old promises and of the presence of other witnesses inescapably encroaches on YHWH's absolute
freedom to wallow in anger. But the force of these realities depends
on the fierce courage of Moses, who refuses to permit YHWH such
unchecked freedom.

What follows in Exodus 32–34 is a complex negotiation between
YHWH and Moses that is conducted face to face (Exod 33:11). The
import of the narrative account is that YHWH is not free to treat Aaron
as an object of destruction or to treat Israel—the Israel of Aaron—as an
object to be scuttled. That awareness that transposes the absolutism of
YHWH to dialogic engagement is made possible by the presence of
Moses, who insists on being YHWH's partner and who refuses, for that
reason, to let YHWH be "alone" in emotional extremity.

To be sure, the matter is not simple. Moses at first comes to share
YHWH's anger and colludes with YHWH in meting out punishment
against the perpetrators of god-making (Exod 32:25-29). It is, however,
the presence of Moses that forces YHWH to think about the future
beyond this moment of emotional extremity alongside a residue of anger
that lingers:

> But now, go lead the people to the place about which I have spoken to you;
> see, my angel shall go in front of you. Nevertheless, when the day comes for
> punishment, I will punish them for their sin. (32:34)

That statement exhibits YHWH's resolve to "blot out" in unchecked
absolutism but to provide for the future as well.

In the on-going dialogic exchange of Exodus 33:12–22, Moses makes
demand of YHWH:

If your presence will not go, do not carry us up from here. (33:15)

YHWH concedes the main point to Moses, a concession that modifies YHWH's previous absolutism. The tone of communication is altered. One can only conclude that it is the insistent presence of Moses that requires YHWH to "move on." To be sure, YHWH will not give in on all points and, finally, will assert divine freedom:

> I will be gracious to whom I will be gracious, and I will show mercy on whom I will show mercy. . . . You cannot see my face; for no one shall see me and live. (33:19–20)

In the subsequent text YHWH, in a self-declaration, manages to articulate both the *absolutism* of "visiting iniquity" and *the covenantal alternative of fidelity*:

> The Lord, the Lord,
> a God merciful and gracious,
> slow to anger,
> abounding in steadfast love and faithfulness,
> keeping steadfast love for the thousandth generation,
> forgiving iniquity and transgression and sin,
> yet by no means clearing the guilty,
> but visiting the iniquity of the parents upon the children
> and the children's children,
> to the third and the fourth generations. (Exod 34:6–7)

The culmination of the exchange is in the final decision making of Exodus 34:8–10. Moses fully acknowledges YHWH's sovereignty and readily yields to that sovereignty in worship and confession:

> If now, I have found favor in your sight, O Lord, I pray, let the Lord go with us. Although this is a stiff-necked people, pardon our iniquity and our sin, and take us for your inheritance. (34:8–9)

And YHWH, in response, pledges new covenant (v. 10). It is possible to judge that the exchange, in the scope of the narrative, has deeply altered YHWH's disposition. Beyond emotive extremity, YHWH, in dialogic interaction, is required by the exchange itself to act in responsible and alternative ways, ways that push beyond YHWH's desire to be "left alone."

In a much more modest narrative exchange, we have an account of the way in which a nameless woman who had lost her property makes vigorous protest and petition to the king (2 Kgs 8:1–6). We are told nothing about the nameless king. But we know that he was a royal son of Ahab; for that reason it is not unlikely that he was committed to an economic absolutism, reflected in the Ahab narrative of 1 Kings 21, whereby he readily dealt in commodity accumulation. At the moment the nameless king is enthralled by "the great things that Elisha has done" (v. 4). That royal preoccupation, however, is interrupted by the nameless woman who brings her case before the king and insists on her rights. This inter-ruption of royal attention, forced by the nameless woman, results in a royal decree for restoration of her property. Given the narrative of Naboth's vineyard, it is remarkable that a son of Ahab would make such a ruling. This is yet another episode in which *dialogic engagement* alters *settled power*. The woman refuses to be a silent pawn in the rough-and-tumble of "normal" economics over which the king presides.

It is highly probable that this modest narrative in Kings became the source of a teaching of Jesus on the boldness of prayer.[17] In Luke 18:1–8, Jesus offers a parable about how to pray and why to pray. In the parable a nameless widow kept assertively insisting on justice from an indifferent judge. Finally the judge yields to the petition of the woman because she has worn him out:

> Though I have no fear of god and no respect for anyone, yet because this widow keeps bothering me, I will grant her justice, so that she may not wear me out by continually coming. (v. 5)

The inference to be drawn from the parable is that persistent petition to God will draw God into an attentive relationship that could not happen without such persistence. Thus, as Moses *refused to leave YHWH alone* in YHWH's absolutism, and as the woman *refused to leave the king alone* until her petition is taken seriously and processed, so the woman in the parable *refused to leave the judge alone*. The sum of Jesus's testimony in this parable is that the God to whom Jesus attests is not a warm fuzzy but is a "chilly divinity . . . not given the warmth of a human face."[18] It is the task and possibility of the petitioner to draw this chilly deity into attentiveness. In all three cases—Moses, the woman before the king, and the woman in the parable—the key agent refuses a passive role before *the absolute God, the preoccupied king,* or *the indifferent judge.* Or, in our con-

---

17. On the linkage of these two texts, see Walter Brueggemann, "A Royal Miracle and Its *Nachleben*," in *The Economy of Salvation: Essays in Honor of M. Douglas Meeks*, ed. Jürgen Molt-mann, Timothy R. Eberhart, and Matthew W. Charlton (Eugene, OR: Cascade Books, 2015), 9–22.

18. Richard Lischer, *Reading the Parables*, Interpretation (Louisville: Westminster John Knox, 2014), 115.

text, the petitioner refuses to be a usable commodity and boldly exercises agency that summons God to attentive engagement. The outcome in each case is not what we might have expected:

- God grants renewed covenant to Moses (Exod 34:10).
- The king grants restoration to the woman (2 Kgs 8:6).
- The judge grants justice to the woman (Luke 18:5).

In each case, the figure of authority is compelled to act differently. Thus, if we return to the Moses narrative, this God of steadfast love and mercy is perfectly unlike the gods who cannot smell or hear or see or walk. So it is with the adherents to YHWH. They are wholly unlike the worshipers of idols. They may indeed become like the God they worship, capable of agency and freedom, capable of insisting on steadfast love and restorative justice. The made-gods of Jeremiah have "no *ruaḥ*" (Jer 10:14). Nor do their worshipers! Thus, the either/or of commoditization or dialogic engagement is a huge theological question concerning a God with or without *ruaḥ*. But the practical matter that concerns public life is the political-economic potential of the adherents of one God or another. The adherents to commoditization eventually are incapable of agency. They are narcoticized for a life void of transformative energy. Conversely the adherents to YHWH are agents and actors in the political economy, generating future historical possibilities that require sustained investment. They are, in the end, a dramatic contrast to Aaron, who could only add one more commodity to an enterprise devoid of covenantal potential.

VI

It is the outcome of *worship of YHWH* as a covenantal transaction that holds the prospect of *recovering and maintaining human agency*. The Psalms celebrate YHWH as the one who "does what he pleases." As we become like the idols we worship (without agency), so worship of YHWH as a covenantal transaction permits us to become like YHWH, able to act in free and generative freedom. The transfer of worship from *lifeless idols* to *life-giving YHWH* has important implications for human life and for the political economy, because it bespeaks emancipated life-filled people who may function in the political economy with vitality, intentionality, and wisdom.

I suggest, in the context of the alternative worship in Psalm 115 dis-

cussed above, that Psalms is a script for the practice of dialogical emancipation, for engagement with this "other" who sees, hears, smells, walks,
talks, and saves, who may awaken and sustain human agency. Practice
of the Psalter both requires and evokes agency, for it consists in valuing and trusting YHWH—the creator of heaven and earth, the savior of
Israel who does what he pleases. Here I will mention only four aspects
of that Psalter practice of dialogical engagement that requires and evokes
human agency.

1. There can be dialogic engagement with this lively holy one only if
the human subject can act in self-announcement, that is, can say "I" or
"we" with some boldness. The worshipers of idols soon lose agency and
cannot engage in self-announcement but become as dumb as the idols
they worship. By contrast the narrative of Israel with YHWH features
self-announcement as an exercise of human agency. Thus, in the Exodus
narrative, it is the self-announcement of the suffering slaves in Pharaoh's
regime that evokes engagement with YHWH:

> After a long time the king of Egypt died. The Israelites groaned under their
> slavery, and cried out. Out of the slavery their cry for help arose up to God.
> God heard [unlike the unhearing idols] their groaning, and God remem-
> bered his covenant with Abraham, Isaac, and Jacob. God looked upon the
> Israelites [unlike the unseeing idols], and God took notice of them [unlike
> the unnoticing idols]. (Exod 2:23–25)

The God of Genesis would not have heard or noticed unless the slaves
had announced themselves. YHWH had not been engaged in the narrative until Israel's self-announcement. As James Plastaras has seen, the
Exodus narrative, from 2:23–25 to 15:20–21 is shaped and patterned
according to the dramatic movement of the lament psalms.[19] Thus,
in Psalms we may see that lament-complaint is the primary mode in
which Israel breaks defeated or deferential silence and announces self to
YHWH. In Psalm 30, for example, the dismayed speaker initiates a new
interaction with YHWH by self-announcement that pleads for intervention:

> To you, O Lord, I cried,
> and to the Lord I made supplication. (v. 8)

What follows is a daring challenge to YHWH (v. 9), and an imperative
address that recruits YWWH to care about "me" and to be "my" helper
(v. 10). Self-announcement evokes YHWH's engagement (vv. 11-12).

19. James Plastaras, *The God of Exodus: The Theology of the Exodus Narratives* (Milwaukee,
WI: Bruce, 1966).

In Psalm 115, the psalm begins in deference, "Not to us, O Lord, not to us" (v. 1). But by verse 16 those who engage YHWH (and not the idols) are able to assert that "the earth he has given to human beings." From that the speakers who have gained voice (and freedom and courage) are able to assert, "We will bless the Lord" (v. 18). This is an astonishing self-assertion, for it assumes that it is in the gift of the worshipers to magnify or enhance "the Lord." Such self-assertion derives from self-announcement that begins in lament-complaint. Such boldness is in contrast to the worship of idols that invite or authorize no such self-announcement, and surely no notion that the worshipers could further enhance the gods of precious metals. Interaction with YHWH is one of emancipated dialogic engagement, an act not possible with idols that cannot speak or hear or see or save. The lament-complaint is bid on such dialogic engagement.

2. But of course the psalms of lament-complaint do not characteristically remain in a posture of need and dismay. Characteristically such pleadings turn to resolution, well-being, and eventually to praise. In the Exodus narrative, it is a long tense route from the initial complaint to the doxology of Miriam, but it is a route that was traveled in the memory and imagination of Israel and often reiterated in liturgic performance. The "I" or the "we" of dismay and need is regularly transformed into the glad "I, we" of doxology. As the lament-complaint is a matter of claiming self and the legitimacy of one's need, so doxology is the glad act of ceding one's self over to the wonder of YHWH. The move from lament-complaint to doxology is a process of *claiming and asserting self* in order to have a self that can be gladly *ceded over*. Thus, praise by a self that has not been fully claimed and asserted is feeble praise, as we may imagine the praise of idols to be, for it is praise offered by selves that have not been fully and vigorously claimed.

Thus, in Psalm 30, in anticipation of the narrative report of verses 6–12, the speaker begins in exuberant doxology. The self is asserted, as verses 1–3 are filled with first-person pronouns by a speaker who is fully confident of self before God. But this joyously asserted self is readily ceded over to the "Lord," for the threefold reference to "the Lord" dominates these lines, further filled out by affirmation of "you." Thus, the "I" is fully on exhibit in glad submissiveness to "you" who has "drawn me up, helped me, healed me, brought up my soul, and restored me." The Lord is worshiped as the worshiper arrives in a state of well-being. Neither side of this equation is possible in a transaction with an idol *without agency* by a worshiper *without agency*. If we want to understand why so much worship among we "privileged" (those with ample "precious metals") is anemic, it is because worshipers without agency address idols without agency. In such an empty transaction, joy, energy, and courage are not possible.

In Psalm 115, the "we" that speaks is from the outset preoccupied with and confident of "your steadfast love and your faithfulness" (v. 1). Such confidence evokes "trust" (vv. 9–11) and assurance of generative "blessing" that will cause creation to flourish (vv. 12–14). The vocabulary of this doxology—steadfast love and faithfulness, trust, blessing, and the flourishing of creation—is in contrast to the idols who are not capable of steadfast love or faithfulness, who have no power to bless, and who are not to be trusted. The dialogic transaction of praise concerns a "we" who engages a "you" (thou) who sees, hears, and saves.[20]

3. A third dimension of the covenantal transaction that features a fully claimed, fully ceded self in engagement with YHWH who sees, hears, and saves is the recognition that the script for engagement is the Torah. The Torah is an authorization from Sinai that includes an extensive, dynamic, pluralistic legacy of interpretation. All of that is subsumed under the rubric of "Torah." The Psalter is framed, from the outset, by the Torah in Psalm 1.[21] This introduction suggests that all that follows in the Psalter is under the aegis of Torah, which sets the practitioners of "Torah on the way to glad, obedient, righteousness. Two other psalms are readily cited as "Torah Psalms."[22] In Psalm 19, the Torah is celebrated as a salvific force that "revives the soul" (v. 7). That phrase is more familiar to us in Psalm 23:1, where it is YHWH as shepherd who "restores my life." While we appreciate the somewhat "softer," more personal imagery of Psalm 23, in the Psalter and in the horizon of Israel, it is exactly Torah that restores the self.

In the more extended acrostic Psalm 119, it is the Torah that creates a venue for life. Contrary to some Christian caricatures that understand the psalm as a simple *quid pro quo* tradition (obedience guarantees life), it is clear in the psalm that it is the Lord of Torah who guarantees and freely gives life:

20. On the "we" of faith that moves from Israel to humanity and back to Israel, see Franz Rosenzweig, *The Star of Redemption* (Notre Dame, IN: University of Notre Dame Press, 1970), 236, 325, and passim; and Walter Brueggemann, "The 'Us' of Psalm 67," in *Palabra, Prodigio, Poesía: In Memoriam P. Luis Alonso Schökel, S.J.,* ed. Vicente Collado Bertomeu, Analecta Biblica 151 (Rome: Pontifical Biblical Institute, 2003), 233–42.

21. See Patrick D. Miller, *Israelite Religion and Biblical Theology: Collected Essays,* Journal for the Study of the Old Testament: Supplement Series 267 (Sheffield: Sheffield Academic Press, 2000), 318–36.

22. See James Luther Mays, "The Place of the Torah-Psalms in the Psalter," *Journal of Biblical Literature* 106 (1987): 3–12.

I am severely afflicted;
Give me life, O Lord, according to your word. (v. 107)
Uphold me according to your promise, that I may live,
and let me not be put to shame in my hope. (v. 116)
In your steadfast love hear my voice;
O Lord, in your justice preserve my life. (v. 149)
Great is your mercy, O Lord;
give me life according to your justice. (v. 156)

Torah is the practice of those who are able to make petition to YHWH. In the arena of Torah, there is opportunity for Israel to "listen" (*shema'*), to be instructed, to have life shaped for glad response to YHWH. *The listening of Israel* to Torah instruction is a specific counterpoint to the *listening that YHWH does* to the cries of Israel. Thus, the dialogic listening is one of mutual listening, of attending to the voice of the other. This mutual listening is quite in contrast to the nonlistening in the worship of idols. The idols cannot hear, so there is no listening from that side. And because the idols cannot speak, idol worshipers have no reason to listen. In the world of commodity transactions, neither serious speech nor attentive listening is possible. The mutual listening of YHWH and Israel is itself a sharp act of resistance against the nonengaged life of commodity. One can notice in our contemporary world that serious mutual listening is emphatically trumped by image, as the visual defeats the auditory. Thus, transaction in and with lifeless objects regularly overrides the mutual subjectivity of listening that calls both parties to new life.

4. A fourth articulation of dialogic engagement with YHWH is found in the "wisdom psalms," the principal one of which is Psalm 37.[23] In these psalms we have the slow, steady observation of creation, how the world works, what the givens and limits of viable conduct are, and what choices generate good futures. The practice of wisdom concerns good judgment, but such judgments are rooted in careful observation of the reality of the world, which gives expression to the will and intent of the creator. That is, wisdom begins in *noticing*.

In Psalm 37, the wisdom teachers have noticed the kinds of conduct and perspective that generate safety and well-being in the land. Five times in the psalm it is observed that loyal covenantal conduct (waiting for the Lord, meekness, being blessed by YHWH, righteousness, and

---

23. See J. Kenneth Kuntz, "The Canonical Wisdom Psalms of Ancient Israel: Their Rhetorical, Thematic, and Formal Dimensions," in *Rhetorical Criticism: Essays in Honor of James Muilenburg*, ed. Jared J. Jackson and Martin Kessler, Pittsburgh Theological Monograph Series 1 (Pittsburgh: Pickwick, 1974), 186–222.

keeping to "his way") lead to secure land inheritance (vv. 9, 11, 22, 29, 34). The clearly implied negative counterpoint is that conduct that does not take YHWH into serious account results in being "cut off" from the land, that is, displaced. Thus, the "notice" of wisdom is a dialogic response to the generativity of creation willed by the creator. It is a response that understands the givenness of creation that cannot be mocked or disregarded with impunity.

In Psalm 115 we have only an allusion to ordered creation in verse 14, but that allusion concerns the whole of generative creation:

> May the Lord give you increase,
> both you and your children. (v. 14)

The term "increase" (add) suggests the fruitfulness of creation and specifically human creation. That anticipation of "increase" echoes the creator as voiced in Genesis 1:28, where the fruitfulness of humanity is mandated. It requires no imagination at all to see that wisdom concerns "care for the earth," protection of the environment that permits it to be endlessly flourishing and productive.[24] Conversely, "foolishness" (indifference to the ordered will of the creator) leads to loss of land, displacement, and among us an environmental crisis of lethal proportion. It is anticipated that the creator of heaven and earth will continue to bless the earth and its inhabitants, those who are not "sinners" who violate creation (Ps 104:35), those who are not "wicked" in their abuse of creation (Ps 145:20). When the dots are connected, it becomes clear that the *foolish* are those *without agency*, who have neither the will nor the capacity to care for the earth in ways that will produce generative futures. The loss of agency leads to small-time self-care, but not sufficient will or energy to attend to creation as the creator has ordered it.

VII

The people of God are always choosing: between commoditization and covenantal engagement.

- So Moses:

    See, I set before you today life and prosperity, death and adversity. . . . Choose life so that you and your descendants may live,

---

24. On creation and care of the earth, see Ellen F. Davis, *Scripture, Culture, and Agriculture: An Agrarian Reading of the Bible* (Cambridge: Cambridge University Press, 2009).

loving the Lord your God, and obeying him, and holding fast to him. (Deut 30:15, 19)

- So Joshua:

  Now if you are unwilling to serve the Lord, choose this day whom you will serve . . . but as for me and my household, we will serve the Lord. (Josh 24:15)

- So Elijah:

  How long will you go limping with two different opinions? If the Lord is God, follow him; but if Baal, then follow him. (1 Kgs 18:21)

- So Jesus:

  Enter through the narrow gate; for the gate is wide and the road is easy that leads to destruction, and there are many who take it. For the gate is narrow and the road is hard that leads to life, and there are few who find it. (Matt 7:13–14)

- So the church:

  I wish that you were either cold or hot. So, because you are luke-warm, and neither cold nor hot, I am about to spit you out of my mouth. (Rev 3:15–16)

For our purposes it is not unimportant that this text goes on to talk about being rich, and counsels "you to buy from me gold refined by the fine so that you may be rich" (vv. 17–18).

I suggest that in Paul's epistles, this urgent choosing is made specific and concrete. In his letter to the Galatians, Paul traces out the practical implications of the law of the empire that is the law of commoditization.[25] The actions appropriate to the "law of the empire" lead to "the desires of the flesh," the insatiable craving that precludes neighborliness:

Now the works of the flesh are obvious: fornication, impurity, licentious-ness, idolatry, sorcery, enmities, strife, jealousy, anger, quarrels, dissensions, factions, envy, drunkenness, carousing, and things like these. (Gal 5:19–21)

25. On this reading of Paul's either/or, see Brigitte Kahl, *Galatians Re-Imagined: Reading with the Eyes of the Vanquished*, Paul in Critical Contexts (Minneapolis: Fortress Press, 2010), 269–73.

Included in the catalogue is "idolatry." These are not innate evil habits. They are rather the outcomes of adherences to a social system in which covenantal engagement is disregarded. Conversely, the practical outcome of a life in covenantal engagement is the fruit of the spirit:

> By contrast, the fruit of the Spirit is love, joy, peace, patience, kindness, generosity, faithfulness, gentleness and self-control. (5:22)

It is no wonder that Paul can declare:

> For the whole law is summed up in a single commandment, "You shall love your neighbor as yourself." (5:14)

And then he adds a warning against the destructive power of greed for commodity:

> If, however, you bite and devour one another, take care that you are not consumed by one another. (5:15)

In derivative textual tradition, Paul images "the fruit of the light" (Eph 5:9) and commends the avoidance of a list of actions not unlike those in Galatians 5:19–21:

> But fornication and impurity of any kind, or *greed,* must not even be mentioned among you, as is proper among the saints. Entirely out of place is obscene, silly, and vulgar talk; but instead, let there be thanksgiving. Be sure of this, that no fornicator or impure person, or one who is *greedy (that is, an idolater)* has any inheritance in the kingdom of Christ and of God. (Eph 5:3–5)

Note especially the judgment that "greed is idolatry" and so excludes from the kingdom. So also in Colossians, the writer commends elimination of deathly practices:

> Put to death, therefore, whatever in you is earthly: fornication, impurity, passion, evil desire, and *greed (which is idolatry).* (Col 3:5)

Again we have the phrase, "greed which is idolatry." "Greed" in this usage refers to an insatiable desire to have what belongs to another, a perfect rendition of the unrestrained pursuit and accumulation of commodities that are to be overvalued (worshiped) at the expense of the vulnerable.

The early church, in these letters, is urged to choose. That church lived, as do we, in a culture that was seduced by commodity. The church, in the horizon of these epistles, is to choose otherwise, to opt for neighborly engagement. The epistles see clearly that a priority of commodity ("greed as idolatry") leads to the diminishment of the neighbor and of the neighborhood. Covenantal engagement results in neighborliness and the valuing of the neighbor. In a context of endless "selfies," the option of dialogic engagement, as scripted in the psalms and practiced *by Moses, by the nameless woman in 2 Kings,* and *by the widow in the parable,* is a matter of urgency. The absolutizing propensity to be "left alone" in a world of commodities is a replication of the god-making of Aaron. It is only the agency of Moses that permits otherwise!

4.

The Joker amid Class Warfare

An earlier version of this chapter was presented at the Festival of Homiletics in May 2018.

"Standing up for justice" is a different deal in a world where the gospel of God is in play. In what follows I will enumerate eight theses, consider two texts, and draw five conclusions. So if you are tracking it, it is a sequence of "8-2-5."

I. Eight Theses Concerning Class Warfare

You can see that "justice" is an adjudication, negotiation, dispute, and conflict between classes, a contest between haves and have-nots, between the powerful and the vulnerable. At its most honest, that adjudication, negotiation, dispute, and conflict are a class war of competing claims and interests.

1. The justice agenda is inescapably participation in class warfare that requires imagination and movement beyond our comfort zone.

2. Class warfare is characteristically waged "from above" by the powerful haves. It is conducted by interest rates, tax arrangements, mortgage rates, loan and credit stipulations, and low wages, all of which are legal because the golden rule specifies that the ones with the gold make the rules.

3. Many people in mainline congregations share a sympathy for

class warfare waged "from above." We have, moreover, largely learned to read the Bible so that the justice issues of class warfare voiced therein are mostly not noticed and certainly not highlighted.

4. Combatants in class warfare "from above" mostly do not want class warfare noticed or talked about. Indeed, if the issue is identified or raised "from below," the predictable reaction is that those "below" are the ones waging class warfare. When class warfare is unrecognized and unacknowledged, it amounts to an assurance that the status quo economic settlements can remain in place without disturbance or disruption.

5. Much of the Bible is preoccupied with class warfare. This is the issue in the paradigmatic conflict between Moses and Pharaoh; Pharaoh's response to Mosaic protest is to "make more bricks." This is the recurring conflict between kings who preside over the urban surplus and prophets in ancient Israel who speak from outside the royal domain. Thus, for example, Elijah versus Ahab and Jezebel (see Naboth), Amos and Amaziah, Jeremiah and Jehoiakim. The royal strategy in each case is to silence the prophetic voice "from below." It is not different in the New Testament, wherein Jesus, among other things a representative of Galilean subsistence peasants, finally must go to Jerusalem to confront the exploitative power of the urban elites who have colluded with the tax-collecting force of Rome. The mode of conflict conducted by Jesus is cagey and deliberately ambiguous; but clearly he was not executed for being a nice man.

6. The church, energized by such Scripture, is an apt arena for the conduct of class warfare. That of course contradicts the predictable preference of "religion" to make nice and construe matters as "spiritual." But the relentless materiality of the Bible will not permit such illusion. The church as an arena for this effort does not require abrasive confrontation, but it does require alert interpretation and intentional pedagogy concerning the conflict of interests.

7. Class warfare, as a component of the struggle for justice in both the Bible and in contemporary society, always features two combatants, the powerful and the vulnerable, the haves and the have-nots. The conflict is characteristically unequal because the interest of the vulnerable have-nots is most often not made explicit, not well organized or mobilized, and not regarded as

a legitimate force. But without that explicit voicing, organization, and mobilization, there can be no effective struggle for justice. By contrast, the interest "from above" is characteristically well articulated, well organized, readily mobilized, and easily regarded as legitimate.

8. The news, the good news, in the gospel narrative is that there is a third participant in the dispute about justice, namely, the God of the exodus, the father of our Lord Jesus Christ whom we name as Father, Son, and Spirit. The testimony of Scripture is that this particular, peculiar God is not neutral or indifferent, but has decisively taken sides in the struggle for justice. Thus, as early as the Song of Moses, YHWH is celebrated as a "man of war" (*'ish milhamah*) who has entered the enduring justice dispute on behalf of the Hebrew slaves against the dominating power of Pharaoh (Exod 15:3). (Note that our more benign translations have it less offensively "a warrior.")

These eight theses, I propose, provide a map of justice that is textually informed, theologically rooted, and practically compelling. The map is an insistence that without the investment of YHWH in the struggle for justice, there will be no legitimate sustained struggle. This map helps us to see why most local congregations much prefer missions of charity to the dangerous work of justice ministry. I state the matter this baldly because in a society that is increasingly governed by a monopoly of power, wealth, and technology, there is almost no ground for mounting and sustaining an effective advocacy for justice unless it is grounded outside the monopoly in holy reality that has not been co-opted by that monopoly of power, wealth, and technology. That holy reality that provides ground for justice has been peculiarly (not exclusively but peculiarly) entrusted to the church, and it is pastors who have the privilege and burden of interpreting and enlivening these ancient texts that constitute a way in which holy resolve enters the arena of adjudication, negotiation, dispute, and conflict.

II. Psalm 10 as a Case Study

In order to explicate these theses, I have selected two texts that are fairly obvious but also fairly typical. Psalm 10 is a map of justice advocacy.[1]

1. See Walter Brueggemann, "Psalms 9–10: A Counter to Conventional Social Reality," in *The Bible and the Politics of Exegesis: Essays in Honor of Norman K. Gottwald on His Sixty-Fifth*

The psalm clearly is on the tongue of those "from below" who have been left behind and left out. And the reason for being left behind and left out is that YHWH—their great advocate—has been missing, standing afar off, and hiding (v. 1). And when YHWH is disengaged, there is lots of room in which "the wicked" can take advantage of the poor (v. 2).

Because YHWH has been disengaged and far off, it is necessary for these advocates "from below" to line out for YHWH the social reality of injustice and exploitation. Thus, in verses 3–11 we get a characterization of "the wicked" processed through the filter of the left behind. Such a characterization of course is not neutral or disinterested but is voiced with urgent passion.

The wicked are greedy in their unrestrained aggressiveness. In their tacit utterance, they simply dismiss YHWH as a serious reality:

God will not seek it out . . .
There is no God. (Ps 10:4)

When YHWH is dismissed, so YHWH's commandments are dismissed; and when the commandments are dismissed one is free to covet one's neighbor's house and anything that is one's neighbor's.

As a result of this dismissal of God, the God of Exodus and of the commands of Sinai, the wicked are free to manipulate the economy and so can "prosper at all times" and treat their opponents with dismissiveness as folk who really do not matter (v. 5). Because of such endless prosperity, unlimited power, and economic growth, they can readily imagine:

We shall not be moved;
Throughout all generations we shall not meet adversity. (v. 6)

No wonder the advertising mantra can assert "Life is good." Life is very good for those in the ownership class who dismiss YHWH and are free to manage the neighborhood to their own advantage.

The wicked—as experienced by these advocates "from below"—are in fact deliberately predatory. Once in a while, in extreme cases, we get some e-mails that expose such predation, as in the cases of Enron and Wells Fargo. Most of the time, however, the predation is not so bald; but it is surely operative. There is money to be made at the expense of the vulnerable. Such work, so verse 7, requires deceit, oppression, mischief, iniquity—cunning exploitation—which amounts to nothing less than an ambush in which the predatory powers prey upon the unsus-

Birthday, ed. David Jobling, Peggy L. Day, and Gerald T. Sheppard (Cleveland: Pilgrim, 1991), 3–15.

pecting through interest rates, mortgage and credit arrangements, and regressive tax laws that take the vulnerable by surprise.

In order to help YHWH to see what is really going on, verses 8–10 appeal to dangerous imagery:

> They sit in ambush in the villages;
> in hiding places they murder the innocent.
> Their eyes stealthily watch for the helpless;
> they lurk in secret like a lion in its covert;
> they lurk that they may seize the poor;
> they seize the poor and drag them off in their net.
> They stoop and crouch,
> and the helpless fall by their might.

In verse 8 they are like hunters. Now they are more like a lion. This hungry ruthless lion lurks in secret, lurks and then leaps, grabbing the poor in its teeth, dragging them off for a big dinner of loud chewing and bone crushing and deep sighs of satisfaction and then long naps in the comfortable shade. The lions of predation stoop, crush, hide, coil, and leap. Game over!

In verse 11 the speaker remembers that YHWH is being addressed and returns to the theme of verse 4, namely, the dismissal of YHWH as a player. They think:

> God has forgotten,
> he has hidden his face, he will never see it.

There are only two of us, the predator and the delicious supper constituted by the vulnerable poor. The purpose of such a statement is to get YHWH's attention, to say to YHWH, "Do you notice? They do not take you seriously. They are dissing you. They think you are an ancient memory that has no role to play in 'modern life.'" Oh, they do not do this mocking overtly. It is all unvoiced. But anyone who cares can see the *dismissal of the poor* as a legitimate neighbor constitutes the *dismissal of YHWH*, the guarantor of the neighborhood. Thus the Proverb can assert:

> Those who mock the poor insult their Maker.
> Those who are glad at calamity will not go unpunished. (Prov 17:5)

Israel has always known that YHWH and the poor are intimately connected, that what is done to "the least" is done to YHWH (Matt 25:40). One could expect that this exposé of dismissal would evoke YHWH to interest, engagement, and action, and that clearly is the intent of verses 4–11. It is all lined out for YHWH to witness. Thus the claim of Proverbs 17:5 is echoed elsewhere by the wise:

> Those who oppress the poor insult their maker;
> and those who are kind to the needy honor him. (Prov 14:31)
> Do not rob the poor because they are poor,
> or crush the afflicted at the gate,
> for the Lord pleads their cause
> and despoils of life those who despoil them. (Prov 22:22–23)

Verses 4–11 are designed to ready YHWH for engagement. In verse 12 then, the psalm shifts gears dramatically. Now there is no more description. Now there is direct address. This voice from below assumes it can speak directly to YHWH and that YHWH will listen. This is such a contrast to the wicked. The wicked are confident that YHWH is an inanimate object, does not see, does not care, has forgotten, will not act. By contrast, this speaker from below counts directly upon YHWH who can and will act. The theological, epistemological contrast is not unlike the contrast of theological progressives who think YHWH is at best a placeholder from whom nothing can be expected in contrast to the urgent evangelical rhetoric of the poor and needy who naively make appeal to YHWH because they have no other court of appeal. My judgment is that as long as the pastors of the church are embarrassed by this urgent language to God and assume in our Enlightenment model that such rhetoric has no actual force, we will not get very far in the struggle for justice.

This voice from below is unembarrassed. It does not speak politely, asking little because not expecting much. It baldly addresses YHWH with a big urgent imperative: Rise up! Get moving! Get engaged. End your sleepiness. Lift up your drowsy head. Take action. Remember us. Remember me. Notice us. Do not forget. Because you have been mocked as noted in verses 4–11; your honor is at stake. In verse 13 the speaker returns to the opening question of verse 1: Why?

> Why, O Lord, do you stand far off?
> Why do you hide yourself in time of trouble? (Ps 10:1)
>   Why do the wicked renounce God,
> and say in their hearts "You will not call us to account." (v. 13)

Why do the wicked get away with such dismissive mockery? The wicked answer, "Because God has been so disengaged that there are no risks in mocking God." The wicked boldly count on holy irrelevance.

The speaker, however, refuses the judgment of the wicked and calls YHWH to account:

But you do see! (v. 14)

I know you do! You notice trouble and grief and oppression and suffering. And when you notice, you act. You take it into your hands. The NRSV translates verse 14, "The helpless commit themselves to you." It is more directly rendered, "The abandoned go to you." The speaker voices the claim of the abandoned, those abandoned by the powerful, by the prosperous, by those who have resources to help. When the powerful do not do their neighborly duty, there is recourse to the ultimate neighbor. The reason to go to YHWH is that YHWH is already known to be an advocate for the desperate poor. In a patriarchal society one has to count on one's father as advocate. And when one's father defaults, the only source of help is YHWH, who takes orphans along with widows and immigrants as a special concern. Thus, the urgent petition of verse 12, "Rise up," is a bid that YHWH should act according to YHWH's true self as an advocate. That is who YHWH is. And now we summon YHWH to YHWH's proper role in the world. It is a big demand: Rise up! Be the Easter God! "Easter" is not about the resuscitation of a dead man. It is about the rising up of the advocate of widows and orphans and immigrants who have no other help. So in another place, another psalmist can make the same appeal:

If my father and mother forsake me,
The LORD will take me up. (Ps 27:10)

Or with John Calvin:

When other helpers fail and comforts flee,
Help of the helpless, O abide with me.[2]

This is the help of the helpless, and none is more helpless than an orphan . . . or an immigrant.

In verse 15 the imperative continues. In verse 12 it is "Rise up." Now a second petition:

Shatter the arm of the wicked and evildoers. (Ps 10:15)

Notice the physical reality. The "arm" of the wicked refers to the capac-

2. Henry Francis Lyte, "Abide with Me" (1847), in *Glory to God: The Presbyterian Hymnal* (Louisville: Westminster John Knox, 2013), 836.

ity of "those above" to do real harm. So we may speak of the Fed as an "arm" of the governing class. But this "arm" is countered by the hand of YHWH:

> Lift up your hand. (v. 12)
> Take it into your hands. (v. 14)

Let *your hand* break *their arm*. This is violent stuff. The violent rhetoric is in response to experienced violence. The violence anticipated here, moreover, is that of YHWH, not the speaker. The speaker is helpless, has no capacity against the arm of the wicked. But YHWH does!

In verse 15 the speaker could not and need not restrain the rage felt toward the crouching lion of the predator. But then in verse 16 it is as though the liturgy committee moved in on the courageous psalmist and kicked the rhetoric upstairs into a safer register:

> The Lord is king forever and ever. (v. 16)

YHWH is strong and powerful. YHWH will govern. The dismissal by the wicked will not work. YHWH will not be dismissed but will govern forever and ever. "For thine is the kingdom and the power and the glory forever and ever." That is the end of our best prayer. But the prayer begins, as you know, with the petition, "Let your rule come on earth as it is in heaven." In that rule, there is no predation. Let your kingdom come into the land.

The point I want to assert is that the wicked as presented here and the needy petitioners are operating in two very different systems of rhetoric. The wicked practice a rhetoric of autonomy in which a summons to the agency of God is treated as absurd. By contrast, the speaker from below counts on and is confident of direct address to YHWH that will mobilize YHWH to act. I believe we are in a time of crisis when we may rethink the rhetoric in which we operate. The cool language of reasonableness, reflective of the Enlightenment and cherished by progressives, assumes that the world is in reality closed in on two combatants, only two. In that cool world there is no appeal to holy agency, no accountability to holy agency, no expectation of holy agency, and no fear of holy agency.

By contrast, the idiom of the psalm refuses that rhetoric because it knows that that rhetoric ends in despair. That rhetoric insists that there is no real advocate beyond the predator. I got this about rhetoric in conversation with a hospital chaplain supervisor. One of the chaplains had been asked by a Jehovah's Witness to pray for a miracle for a very sick child. The chaplain refused and said, "I don't pray for miracles." The parents said, "Send us a different chaplain who will without hesitation or embarrassment pray for help from beyond, pray to the one who works when 'other helpers fail and comforts flee.'" Such urgent petition for a child is in contrast to our usual pleas for social justice, which are not real summons but only pro forma gestures.

The matter is, I judge, an urgent one in the struggle for justice. It is urgent for facile evangelicals who have got God reduced to a safe package. It is urgent for progressives who only for the sake of niceness appeal to God at all. Because the question is whether the justice issue is staged in a world with a very low ceiling managed by crouching lions, or whether the world is open so that the creator God can be mobilized to dote especially on the poor and powerless.

I have, in my title, used the term *joker* for this third participant in the struggle for justice. The joker is a wild card that may be played at any time, that may trump any other claim for truth. The joker God changes the calculus of the justice dispute. Now that justice question is not simply adjudication, negotiation, dispute, and conflict between the *imperially powerful* and the *desperately abandoned*. Now a third party is in play, summoned by the poor who have no other advocate. And what happens in this summoning of the joker is that the map of injustice is radically altered. Now the world is open to a holy resolve that cannot be dismissed by greedy, cynical people. It is an insistence that the world is other than the predators have imagined. And our faith and our ministry are staked on the conviction that the world is other than the powerful take it to be.

This revised world reality is on dramatic exhibit in the trial of Jesus before Pilate in the Fourth Gospel. In their exchange, it turns out that Pilate and the Roman authority that he embodies are in fact on trial. And Pilate's final question, "What is truth?" indicates the bamboozlement of Rome—and of all imperial authority—that thought they could manage the world. It turns out that the Roman governor was living by what Kellyanne Conway calls "alternative facts" that are not true. So Paul Lehmann can conclude:

> The point and purpose of the presence of Jesus *in the world*, and now before Pilate, are to bear witness to the truth, that is, "to make effective room for the reality of God over against the world in the great trial between God and the world."[3]

The purpose of Jesus is to make effective room for the reality of God in the world! What a mandate for ministry. The psalmist is making room

3. Paul Lehmann, *The Transfiguration of Politics* (New York: Harper & Row, 1985), 53. In his statement Lehmann quotes Rudolf Bultmann.

for God in the world by refusing the dismissive rhetoric of the wicked who want the justice issue to be between only two combatants. No, insists the psalmist, there is a third, a joker who refuses to conform to the will of the powerful. Jesus turned out to be the Easter joker amid the Roman Empire. And even before Jesus, the psalmist could host Easter possibility: "Rise up!" The dismissive wicked had assumed there was no one to "rise up," because their monopoly of power would not allow it. Their rhetoric contains all possibilities, they had thought. Imagine that the church meets to shatter such a limited dismissive notion of the world. Because the justice struggle is lost if there are only two combatants.

But the psalmist knows otherwise. For that reason, the psalm concludes in confidence:

O YHWH, you (v. 17) (direct address):

You will hear;
You will strengthen;
You will incline.

The God who hears, strengthens, and inclines is the God who bolsters the meek who are victimized by injustice. The speaker who readily participates in that alternative rhetoric does not doubt. The work of YHWH is not explained; but it is not doubted!

To do justice for the orphan and the oppressed,
so that those from the earth may strike terror no more. (v. 18)

Imagine that: justice for the orphan and the oppressed, those without an advocate. It is justice that the orphan cannot secure for herself. It is justice that the oppressed cannot manage and will not receive in a two-party combat. Thus, the work is to summon this third player, the joker whom the wicked little suspect. The outcome is that the orphan and the oppressed need no longer be terrorized by low wages and high interest rates and eviction notices and denial of health care.

It is a lot to expect from this third party. That expectation, however, has been fully voiced in the intense imperative "Rise up!" If God is not raised up to do justice, there will be none. If Christ has not been raised, our ministry is in vain (1 Cor 15:14). But God can be raised by such psalmists who summon. Christ has been raised:

Therefore, my beloved, be steadfast, immovable, always excelling in the work of the Lord, because you know that in the Lord your labor is not in vain. (1 Cor 15:58)

III. Luke 18:1–8 as a Case Study

My second text is the parable of Jesus in Luke 18:1–8. In the parable Jesus mobilized the entire protest tradition of ancient Israel and Psalms. His followers want to pray the way he would pray. Maybe they never knew how to pray. Maybe they were talked out of good strident Jewish prayer because they were infected with the polite holiness of the empire in which one did not ask because one would not receive. Or maybe they were inured to the long set prayers of frozen Judaism. Or maybe they anticipated the polite high-church prayers of the liturgical church that are long on rhetoric but short on passionate asking. Not asking so as not to be disappointed. Or maybe they had fallen into the easy mantras of one-dimensional simplicity: "Father, we just want . . . father." Or maybe their request to Jesus about prayer was acutely serious. They wanted to know!

So Jesus told them a parable about the need to pray always and not to lose heart (18:1). He does not promise that we get what we want. He says only "not to lose heart," not to succumb to despair and resignation. Timid, deferential, meek prayers are already a sign of losing heart.

You know the story. There was a judge who neither feared God nor respected people (v. 2). He sounds like the "wicked" in Psalm 10 who did not fear God. He had already decided that there are only two of us, and no third party to whom he had to answer. He lived in disregard of the wisdom proverbs that asserted that when we abuse the poor we mock God. He did not mind doing both, mocking God whom he did not fear and abusing the vulnerable poor whom he did not respect.

Alongside the cynical confident judge who had a cushy life of tenure, there was a widow. She was a nobody with no male advocate. She belonged to the hopeless triad of "widow, orphan, immigrant." For reasons we are not told, however, she "kept coming" to the judge, showing up in court every day. She persists. She insisted on getting a hearing. She had this deep nonnegotiable conviction that she was entitled to justice. She is popularly termed "importunate," a fancy word for "irksome, annoying." She nagged the judge to death, because she would not relinquish her sense of dignity, legitimacy, and entitlement. Justice requires loud insistent petition!

The judge was unmoved by her incessant plea. He had arranged his life so as to be deaf and unnoticing of injustice. He admits, in his practice, that the narrative has it right: he in fact does not fear God because he lives in a world where God is a dismissed irrelevance. And he does not respect anyone. He has long since ceased to be a participant in the neighborhood. He probably was chauffeured regularly from the court to the club to his gated home. He saw no evil, he heard no evil, he knew nothing about evil.

But what an annoyance she is! She showed up every day. He was hollered at as he got into his limo to go to the club. She stood outside the gate to his home. Not only was he irritated; his wealthy neighbors were getting impatient with all the inconvenience. To get rid of her he gave her justice.

But it is a parable. The judge, in the story, plays the role of God. God is indifferent; God is silent or absent, a nonparticipant. God does not notice the injustice, too busy hosting angels with their heavenly practices. But this God, like the judge, is penetrable. He has been since the exodus; there it is reported that, when the Hebrew slaves groaned and cried out, God heard:

> Out of their slavery their cry for help rose up to God. God heard their groaning, and God remembered. . . . God looked upon the Israelites, and God took notice of them. (Exod 2:23–24)

God heard, God saw, God knew, God remembered, God came down. God was summoned. It is as though the slaves prayed, "Rise up, break the arm of Pharaoh." It is as though this nameless widow petitioned the court; "Rise up, do justice!" It is as though the world can be forced open and God mobilized.

And then, at the end of this little study, Jesus said, "Pay attention to what the judge just said in the story." The judge is unjust; that is, God to whom we pray is not overly committed to justice, just as the judge is not. But cry out day and night. Utter big petitions. Shun excessive deference. Open the world for a future. And Jesus asked his astonished students, "Do you think God will delay justice long if you cry out day and night?" And he answers his own question: "God will quickly grant justice." But it requires a resolved rhetoric. And Jesus adds almost as a throwaway line in verse 8: I wonder when Messiah comes if there will be people capable of such prayer. I wonder if there will be people who have not been talked out of dialogic prayer and dialogic life. I wonder if the legacy of dismissal, so rational, will finally prevail so that justice is flattened to only two parties. I wonder if there will be the capacity to summon the joker. The parable ends with a question. It is left unanswered. It is left for us to answer. Faith is the resolve not to give in to a low-ceiling world from which holy resolve has been eliminated.

Now you may think it odd, or even silly, that I use my time with you to talk about justice in this way. You may wonder, as do I sometimes, if this insistence on the rhetoric of the holy joker is a nice church game without substance. I ponder with you. But consider. Consider what might happen over time in a congregation if the dangerous, foolish rhetoric of the insistent abrasive psalmist or the insistent abrasive widow were taken as normative for our faith. My impression is that many congregations:

- consist in people who have never thought about class warfare and what happens when God weighs in

- consist in people who are bottled up in despair that is part anger and part grief, but without prospect of serious relief

- consist in people who know only the options of authoritarian evangelicalism or progressive coolness without energy

- consist in people who have learned that prayer consists in deference and meekness, partly out of politeness and partly out of an inability to dare for more

In such a congregation the practice of summoning the joker may open the world to let folk see that our faith is committed, in the most relentless way, to a world in which *the agency of God* matters decisively, but that agency must be summoned. Gerald Sheppard takes a social-scientific approach to the Psalms. He asks, in addition to an authentic appeal to God, is there a more "horizontal" function to the Psalms.[4] And his answer is that these prayers, in their early use and since, are intended to be "overheard" in ways that address actual social power. The "overhearing" summons the despairing to greater courage. And the overhearing amounts to a refusal to collude any longer in silence that is a vote for the status quo. Thus, if we think of Dr. King in Selma kneeling in prayer before Sheriff Jim Clark, Dr. King's prayer was no doubt authentically addressed to God as a prayer for justice. But King was a wise, cunning man. He knew as well that the prayer was addressed to the media in a way that would evoke sympathy and support. The prayer was addressed to the sheriff and his deputies to shame them into self-awareness. And the prayer was addressed to the thugs all around to call them to account before the holy God.

We may imagine then, I propose, that Psalm 10 is indeed addressed to God to summon God to "rise up." But the psalm may also have been a strategic pedagogical device to communicate an evangelical map of

---

4. Gerald T. Sheppard, "'Enemies' and the Politics of Prayer in the Book of Psalms," in Jobling et al., *Bible and the Politics of Exegesis*, 61–82.

injustice both to shame the congregation and to win support for those engaged in the struggle. Thus, in the life of a congregation, these psalms and such prayers are authentic acts of faith and piety. But they are also powerful advocacies that function to reorder the map of injustice and to rearticulate the prospect of justice. They are an insistence that the map of injustice includes the holy joker who can indeed be summoned to the crisis. And when the joker enters the fray, albeit through the rhetoric of those "below," all parties are impacted. Those "below" are invited to imagine. Those "above" are put on notice but also are invited to recalibrate their sense of faithfulness. It requires almost no faith to pray within the approved confines of the low ceiling of the empire. It takes great faith in the reality of God to pray in ways that refuse and subvert imperial limits. It is no wonder that Jesus's lesson in prayer ends with the unanswered question about faith. The speaker in Psalm 10 was a person of great faith who refused the dismissive mocking world of the wicked. It takes great faith to utter bold insistent imperatives to the holy joker who conforms to none of our usual practices. Indeed faith is the daring, risky, intentional refusal of such practices that serve to keep the lid on justice questions. The practices of those alongside the joker are very different. They would have us walk into social reality and tell the truth, the truth about historical pain and historical possibility that are not fully acknowledged by the rulers of this age.

IV. Five Conclusions

In reflecting on my reading of these two texts, a psalm and a parable, I draw these five conclusions:

1. In a good creation everything works for good because YHWH, the creator, wills the haves and have-nots together in an engaged neighborliness. We have a clear sketch of that well-working creation in Psalm 145:

> The LORD upholds all who are falling,
> and raises up all who are bowed down.
> The eyes of all look to you,
> and you give them their food in due season.
> You open your hand,
> satisfying the desire of every living thing.
> The LORD is just in all his ways,
> and kind in all his doings.
> The LORD is near to all who call on him,
> to all who call on him in truth.

> He fulfills the desire of all who fear him;
> he also hears their cry, and saves them.
> The LORD watches over all who love him. (vv. 14–20a)

One is struck by the repeated use of "all," thus those "above" and those "below." This doxological affirmation is echoed by Paul's doxological verdict:

> We know that all things work together for good for those who love God, who are called according to his purpose. (Rom 8:28)

In a faithful creation, pigeons and hippos and butterflies and cantaloupes all work together for good because they all love the creator. Psalm 145, moreover, adds a sober warning to the disrupter of good creation:

> But all the wicked he will destroy. (v. 20b)

These wicked are surely an echo of those in Psalm 10 who neither fear God nor respect persons.

2. When the creator God is silent or asleep or indifferent (we know not why), the powerful are free to occupy the space of creation in predatory ways that prey upon the vulnerable. Good creation depends on the sustaining attentiveness of the creator, and when that attentiveness by the creator wanes for an instant, wickedness takes on destructive authority. We have a sketch of creation gone amok in Psalm 14, wherein foolishness prevails, foolishness that Gerhard von Rad has termed "practical atheism":[5]

> Fools say in their hearts, "There is no God." (v. 1a)

And where there is no God, corruption follows:

> They are corrupt, they do abominable deeds;
> There is no one who does good. (v. 1b)

The psalmist (and the creator) together wonder:

> Have they no knowledge, all the evildoers
> who eat up my people as they eat bread,
> and do not call upon the Lord? (v. 4)

The verdict of the psalm anticipates Dostoyevsky:

5. Gerhard von Rad, *Wisdom in Israel*, trans. James D. Martin (Nashville: Abingdon, 1972), 65.

Without God everything is permitted.

What is permitted (that eventually becomes normative) is the capacity to eat up my people as they eat bread, devouring the vulnerable with an insatiable appetite to consume everything and everyone. The psalm goes on to say that such perversity "confounds the plans of the poor" (v. 6).

3. The poor dared summon God back unto the transaction of creation, confident that when God can be mobilized creation can be restored to fruitful function. The capacity to summon God is reflected in the great imagination of the Psalter. Thus, in Psalm 44 the God who has failed and betrayed Israel is accused and chastised:

> You have made us the taunt of our neighbors,
> the derision and scorn of those around us.
> You have made us a byword among the nations,
> a laughingstock among the peoples.
> All day long my disgrace is before me,
> and shame has covered my face
> at the words of the taunters and revilers
> at the sight of the enemy and the avenger. (vv. 13–16)

But these troubled folk are able to reverse field; they now address this failed God with urgent imperatives, confident that if God can be made to answer, all will be well. Imagine the *chutzpah* of such a summons after such an aggressive accusation:

> Rouse yourself! Why do you sleep, O Lord?
> Awake, do not cast us off forever!
> Why do you hide your face?
> Why do you forget our affliction and oppression?
> For we sink down to the dust;
> our bodies cling to the ground.
> Rise up, come to our help.
> Redeem us for the sake of your steadfast love. (vv. 23–26)

These verses voice four urgent imperatives: "rise, awake, rise up, redeem." The imperatives are intertwined with accusatory questions to God:

- Why do you sleep?

- Why do you hide your face?

- Why do you forget our affliction?

The questions are followed in verse 25 with a complaint to be sure that God gets the point of extreme need:

> We sink down to the dust;
> Our bodies cling to the ground.

But the accent is on the petitions that are finally reinforced by this uncompromising reminder to God:

> For the sake of your steadfast love. (v. 26)

Or better:

> For the sake of your tenacious solidarity.

It is as though God had forgotten God's self and needed to be reminded.

Does it astonish you that we do not use this psalm in the church or any like it? It is too violent, too daring, too bald, too insistent, too much of an affront to conventional church piety. As long as such demanding insistence is too much of an affront, God will never be summoned back into the justice struggle. But such summons is exactly the point of petition. It is the compelling interest of intercessory prayer. It is to file a grievance on behalf of another, a grievance about the miscarriage of justice, a grievance against predatory neighbors or against the God who seems to have colluded with predatory neighbors. Thus:

> Rouse yourself . . . pay attention!
> Awake . . . you sleepy head!
> Rise up, you Easter God who has waited much too long.
> Redeem us . . . get us out of hock.

Do that, because tenacious solidarity (ḥesed) is your brand and we count on it.

4. It is the work of the church and its ministers to pray without ceasing, to be an engaged friend of the court, to file complaints on behalf of others, to issue urgent petitions, uncompromising intercessions, and unaccommodating imperatives, all of which intend to summon the creator God back into the world that suffers from divine disregard.

The most difficult psalm is Psalm 88, because there is no response from God. The remarkable thing about Psalm 88 is that the address to God is relentless, even though the addresses to God are among accusations against God:

O LORD, God of my salvation,
when, at night, I cry out in your presence,
let my prayer come before you;
incline your ear to my cry . . .
Every day I call on you, O LORD;
I spread out my hands to you . . .
But I, O LORD, cry out to you;
In the morning my prayer comes before you. (vv. 1–2, 9, 13)

The mood is one of desperation. But it is desperation accompanied by unwavering resolve. The faithful know they have no alternative, because there is no alternative to the creator God who is able to right creation. Thus, with John Calvin:

Our hope is in no other, save in you alone.[6]

General H. R. McMaster, the former national security advisor to President Trump, has written a book about the Vietnam War entitled *Dereliction of Duty*.[7] His book explores the failure of US policy in Vietnam due to confusion and deception in which the true state of affairs was kept hidden from policy makers. McMasters's thesis is that it was the duty of civilian and military officers to tell the truth as a basis for policy; but those officials were "derelict of duty" because they did not tell the truth.

I take McMasters's title *Dereliction of Duty* to reflect on how the church has abdicated its responsibility to be truth tellers before God and before the human community concerning the sorry state of creation. It turns out that it is the poor, needy, and vulnerable who bear the brunt of such failure to tell the truth. But the poor, needy, and vulnerable have allies in the Psalter and in the church. These allies do not hesitate to participate in the class war that brutalizes the vulnerable. When we are not derelict in our duty, we will be truth tellers before God to insist that God return to just governance. And as God is summoned, so God's people are summoned by truth telling. And, when God's people are summoned, they, like the awakened creator God, insist on justice beyond charity. Thus, Psalm 112 provides a profile of such an engaged ally of the vulnerable, identified as "righteous":

They [the righteous] rise in the darkness as a light for the upright;
They are gracious, merciful, and righteous.
It is well with those who deal generously and lend,

6. John Calvin, "I Greet Thee, Who My Sure Redeemer Art" (1545), in *Glory to God*, 624.
7. H. R. McMaster, *Dereliction of Duty: Lyndon Johnson, Robert McNamara, the Joint Chiefs of Staff, and the Lies that Led to Vietnam* (New York: HarperCollins, 1997).

Who conduct their affairs with justice . . .
They have distributed freely,
they have given to the poor;
their righteousness endures forever;
their horn is exalted in honor. (vv. 4–5, 9)

5. When God is summoned back into play, neighbors can be together
in shared common well-being that is the hallmark of evangelical justice.
Thus, Psalm 133:

How very good and pleasant it is
when kindred live together in unity!
It is like the precious oil on the head,
running down on the beard,
on the beard of Aaron,
running down over the collar of his robes.
It is like the dew of Hermon
which falls on the mountains of Zion. (vv. 1-3a)

How wondrous when neighbors live together in unity, when the neighbors "from above" are well connected with the lives of neighbors
"below." Two terms are used to characterize the glorious wonder of
authentic neighborliness:

- How pleasant, that is, how lovely, how delightful.

- How good!

These two terms sound like the creation narrative. God saw it was "very
good," very beautiful, very harmonious, very fruitful. And the mark of
restored neighborliness when God is summoned back to do creation is
the rush of abundance given in two images:

- precious oil, olive oil, as the ointment of unity, as the sacramental sign of living well together;

- dew, that is, the surprise of morning water in an arid climate.

Good neighborliness, restored by the good creator, yields abundance.
That abundance is in sharp contrast to the misery of scarcity produced
by predation, in which the haves never have enough and the have-nots
must do without. Imagine that precious olive oil and precious water,
both in abundance, are given in, with, and under good neighborliness!

Now it may strike you as a fantasy to summon the joker into the class
war when we have urgent issues like health care and poverty and street

violence. These issues, however, cannot and will not be addressed in a sustained way unless they are seen to be theological issues that require the summoning of the creator God into action. It is our work, I propose, to reclassify justice with respect to the creator God who actively cares when summoned with insistence. And if it strikes you that this seems remote from the real world, consider the verdict of Robert Jenson:

> As pop scientists urge over and over, the tale told by Scripture and creeds finds no comfortable place within modernity's metanarrative. It is time for the church simply to reply: this is certainly the case, and the reason it is the case is that the tale told by Scripture is too comprehensive to find place within so drastically curtailed a version of the facts. Indeed, the gospel story cannot fit within *any* other would-be metanarrative because it is itself the only true metanarrative—or it is altogether false.[8]

It is that singular metanarrative about the God of justice willingly recruited into the class war that is entrusted to us!

---

8. Robert W. Jenson, *Canon and Creed*, Interpretation (Louisville: Westminster John Knox, 2010), 120.

PART II

Relinquishing Ethnocentric Ideologies for Sustainable Societies

5.

Relinquishing White Supremacism

Christian extremism, aka "white extremism," is widespread in our society. It comes in two forms. On the one hand, white Christian extremism is of the thuggish popular variety that tilts toward and is tempted by violence (with the rhetoric of anger and hate). On the other hand, it is of a legal variety that operates by regressive measures concerning voting rights and immigration policy (with the rhetoric of "The Constitution"). Both forms of Christian extremism aim at protecting white Christian privilege and excluding nonwhites (non-Christians) by circumscribing rights, privileges, and entitlements of US citizenship. Both forms of Christian white extremism have long depended on white supremacy that requires exclusion by legal means and by means of thuggish intimidation.[1] It happens that such Christian white extremism is currently aimed at Islam ("radical Islam"), but it is the same force and energy that have been directed toward other populations that constitute a threat of "the other." The combination of thuggish and legal action has served to protect and maintain or recover white Christian monopoly. It is my judgment that we cannot fully understand white Christian extremism if we do not consider white Christian supremacy, that is, white Christian superiority. Here I will consider three important historical moments in the long-term emergence of superiority and supremacy that regularly issues in extremism.

1. See James Cone, *The Cross and the Lynching Tree* (Maryknoll, NY: Orbis Books, 2011); and the astonishing work of Ida B. Wells in Paula J. Giddings, *Ida: A Sword among Lions: Ida B. Wells and the Campaign against Lynching* (New York: Amistad, 2008).

I

At the outset, the early Christian movement was a Jewish sect within Judaism. The early, highly contested decision to open the Christian community to gentiles opened the way for growth and expansion beyond the confines of a Jewish sect (Acts 15). The transport of Christian faith and Christian community west from Jerusalem to Rome is laid out in the career and epistles of the apostle Paul, in the book of the Acts of the Apostles (see Acts 28:11–14), and in the legends of St. Peter. It was inevitable that this early movement would be transposed into a gentile phenomenon.

Even given the rapid expansion and growth of the movement, the Christian church remained an illicit, subversive movement in the Roman Empire that was subject to abuse by imperial authorities.[2] All of that was changed by the Edict of Milan in 313 CE. The exact details of that historical turn are unclear; what is clear is that in these years Emperor Constantine encouraged a policy and practice of toleration toward the Christian movement that was confirmed and sealed by Licinius, emperor in the East. While the grant of Milan in 313 was a general confirmation of religious freedom, its clear intent was to make space for the Christian movement to which Emperor Constantine became an adherent.

While the Edict of Milan only gave "toleration" for the freedom of the Christian movement, it did not of itself confirm Christianity as the religion of the empire. But it did not, on the other hand, preclude the political effect whereby the "religion of the emperor Constantine" became "the religion of the empire." That is, making space for its *legitimacy* promptly led to the *establishment* of Christianity as the imperial religion. Thus, a ready case can be made that this moment of legitimation established Christian domination, which took a long while to implement in practice. The effect was to join *power* to *chosenness*, this replicating the practice of ancient Israel, which joined chosenness to power in the Davidic-Solomonic dynasty, a joining that was terminated only by the end of the dynasty with the destruction of Jerusalem. From the outset the Christian movement understood itself as "the chosen of God," but that chosenness did not until now convert to power (see John 15:16; 1 Cor 1:27–28; 1 Pet 2:9–10). When chosenness is linked to power, however, it is predictable that a sense of superiority and supremacy will soon

2. See Rodney Stark: *The Triumph of Christianity: How the Jesus Movement became the World's Largest Religion* (New York: HarperOne, 2011).

follow.[3] Christians (white Christians in the west) were on their way to being both supreme and superior.

II

The long-term development of the new Christian West solidified into the domination of the Roman Church through the authority of the pope, coupled with the establishment of a variety of "Christian princes." While the relationship between and interaction among the Vatican and these several princes were complex and endlessly contested, the growing assumption of dominant Christian tradition, Christian authority, and Christian power was settled, established, and unquestioned. The tacit assumption is that these established powers (church and states) by right and by obligation should extend their authority to the entire known world so that Christendom should be conterminous with the known world. The ground for such a claim is that Christian truth was without challenge or rival, and that truth could be extended and expanded by Christian governance.

It was of course inevitable that such universal claims would collide with other theo-political claims, notably those of Islam in the East. At the end of the eleventh century, Alexius, emperor in Constantinople, appealed to Rome for assistance and relief from Islamic political pressure. In 1095, Pope Urban II responded to that urgent appeal for help by proclaiming a crusade that would mobilize a political military force of Christian powers in the West against Muslim power in the East, and specifically in the context of Jerusalem:

> Urban now proclaimed the Crusade in an appeal of almost unexampled consequence. The enterprise had magnified in his conception from that of aid to the hard-pressed Alexius to a general rescue of the holy places from Moslem hands. . . . The real work of the First Crusade was accomplished by the feudal nobility of Europe. . . . The complete defeat of an Egyptian relieving army near Ascalon on August 12, 1099, crowned the success of the Crusade.[4]

Thus, the barbaric assignment of the First Crusade consisted in a military assault on Muslims in the East propelled by the religious authorization of

3. Peter Brown, *Through the Eye of a Needle: Wealth, the Fall of Rome, and the Making of Christianity in the West, 350–550 AD* (Princeton: Princeton University Press, 2012) has traced the dramatic altering of Christianity in the fourth and fifth centuries CE when wealthy persons joined and came to dominate the church.

4. Williston Walker, *A History of the Christian Church*, rev. ed. (New York: Charles Scribner's Sons, 1959), 220–21.

the pope as the final authority of Christendom. While the venture played out in political military ways, it implied at every step the duty and obligation of Christendom to extend its reach to the East and the right to eliminate Islamic power. It is highly ironic that Saladin, the Islamic ruler in Syria and Egypt, a primary adversary of the Crusaders, conducted himself with generosity that was in sharp contrast to the ruthlessness of the Christian crusaders.

For our purpose it is sufficient to notice that the pope and the Christian princes simply assumed the legitimacy of Christian military force to extend the presence, influence, and political power of Christendom to the East. Those who opposed the crusaders on religious grounds were dismissed as illegitimate agents who were rightly eliminated by whatever means necessary. Thus, the superiority of the Christian West, the primacy of Christian theological claims, and the propriety of Christian power were all treated as settled legitimacies.

Remarkably, the great historian Williston Walker can celebrate the gains of the Crusades as contributing to the "highest theological development," yielding "great popular religious movements," and evoking "great artistic development," that for him allow the verdict:

> Admitting that the Crusades were but one factor in this result, they were worth all their cost.[5]

Such a remarkably myopic verdict is fully contained within the rights and privileges of white Western Christians without any notice of the blatant dismissal of the claims of Islam, or the residue of resentment that would continue to fester for foreseeable futures. That verdict is an example of the sheer disregard of "the other" when evaluating and appreciating the gains made for the "superior" historical reality of Christendom.

The Crusades performed white Western Christian superiority toward the external "other" of Islam. Within a century of the proclamation of the First Crusade (1095) the same performance of superiority was offered toward the internal "other" by the Synod of Toulouse in 1229. That Synod initiated an investigative Inquisition into a variety of "heterodoxies" that departed from the teaching of the Catholic Church and that challenged the monopoly of faith taught by the Roman Church. Thus, the Inquisition can be seen as the internal expression of the same impulse to which the Crusades gave external expression. Both externally in the Crusades and internally in the Inquisition, the unquestioned authority of the church provided the warrant for aggressive action. In order to main-

5. Walker, *History of the Christian Church*, 224.

tain that unchallenged authority, the church via the Inquisition did not hesitate to enact harsh violent measures against heterodox tendencies.

The history of the Crusades and the Inquisition is, to be sure, enormously complicated. It is not complicated, however, to discern the singular claim that is championed through all of the complexity, namely, that Christian faith of a particular kind, codified in a particular form, deserves to be dominant and justifies the use of violence to enforce and maintain that claim. We have here come a very long way from the Edict of Milan in 313. That edict only allowed Christian faith; it did not establish it. From the first, however, that "toleration" was tied to the power of the empire. As a result what was allowed at Milan was de facto established and soon placed beyond question or challenge. When tied to power as it was in the horizon of the Christian princes, it was an easy step toward exclusive legitimacy that would not and could not tolerate "the other," not "the other" of Islam and not "the other" of heterodox Christian teaching.

III

The modern world arrived with the theological revolution of Martin Luther and the scientific reasoning of René Descartes. In the same moment, with the work of Columbus, Balboa, Magellan, Pizarro, de Soto, and Cortés, the princes of the Christian empire readily "deserved" the whole new world of the Western hemisphere that was filled with both compelling resources and a population of "the other" who fit none of the categories of imperial Christendom. That "discovery" of the New World by these daring explorers, backed by the rights and legitimacy of nation-states, led to enormous energy in the claim and occupation of western lands and, not surprisingly, to intense competition for control among the European powers.

In order to adjudicate such competing claims and in order to assert the authoritative reach of Christendom into "the new lands," the Vatican in 1493 issued its decree "The Doctrine of Discovery."[6] It is impossible to overstate the importance and long-term impact of this edict. It declared, in tight and comprehensive legal reasoning, the right and duty of the Spanish king to control and administer vast lands in "the new world," the freedom to occupy the land, to possess its rich resources, and to con-

6. For a contemporary critical assessment of the Doctrine of Discovery (the papal bull *Inter Caetera*), see *Yours, Mine, Ours: Unravelling the Doctrine of Discovery*, a special issue of *Intotemak* edited by Cheryl Woelk and Steve Heinrichs, published by the Mennonite Church Canada (2016).

vert its populations. While the decree was to the immense advantage of the Spanish state, which was closely allied with the papacy, we should not miss the astonishing assumption of authority by the pope and the high-handed reasoning that the "new lands" are waiting to be "discovered," occupied, and exploited by European princes. The entire project smacks of an assumption of cultural-political superiority and of religious supremacy.

The Doctrine of Discovery served to dispossess native peoples of their lands and resources and was especially important in the colonial practices of the English-speaking world. The doctrine illuminates our theme of superiority and supremacy, for, as Robert Miller (et al.) can assert:

> The Doctrine of Discovery has its origin in the notion of superiority. The Doctrine is built upon this largely racialized philosophy: those who were superior had superior rights to those who were inferior. "Infidel" inferiority was predicated upon notions of correspondence with the imperialist defined notions of humanity. Finding the basis in religious theology, the Old World was understood to exist by virtue of the theology which defined colonizing nation inhabitants as possessing direct relationship to the Supreme Power through His representatives on earth. Those who were unrelated to the representatives were understood to be opposed to and conflicting with the authority. They were also understood to possess lesser humanity. This understanding led, further, to the supremacist understanding that those who did not share imperialist religious beliefs and who did not act in accordance with those beliefs, were lesser humans. Lesser humans had, as well, lesser rights: to liberty, to property, to life. This list of infidels included Indigenous peoples within the "New World."[7]

As we draw our attentions closer to the superiority and supremacy in the United States, we are able to see how the Doctrine of Discovery has come to serve white supremacy. Thus, Lindsay Robertson has traced the way in which the Doctrine was incorporated into US law by Chief Justice John Marshall, and how the Doctrine became the basis for Andrew Jackson's displacement of the Cherokee Indians in order that whites in Georgia could secure the land as their own.[8] Thus, the land is claimed not by conquest but by "discovery."

A recent echo of possession "by discovery" is narrated by Patrick Phillips, *Blood at the Root,* who reports on the way in which African

7. Robert J. Miller et al., *Discovering Indigenous Lands: The Doctrine of Discovery in the English Colonies* (Oxford: Oxford University Press, 2010), 94.

8. See Lindsay G. Robertson, *Conquest by Law: How the Discovery of America Dispossessed Indigenous Peoples of Their Lands* (Oxford: Oxford University Press, 2005); and Steven T. Newcomb, *Pagans in the Promised Land: Decoding the Doctrine of Christian Discovery* (Golden, CO: Fulcrum, 2008).

Americans were forcibly dispatched out of Forsyth County Georgia in the twentieth century.[9] The displacement of the black population of the county featured a combination of white extremism in both thuggish and legal types. The thuggish way consists in forcibly removing all blacks under pain of death. The legal aspect was that, when blacks had abandoned their homes and property in fear, whites paid tax on the property for seven years and thereby became the new owners. The dramatic expulsion from Forsyth County is only a recent example of the long-term enactment of Christian white superiority and supremacy that eventuates in extremism in both thuggish and legal modes. It takes no imagination at all to see the linkage between this displacement and the ancient displacement of the Canaanites by the chosen who were entitled to the land.

We come now, in the wake of Donald Trump, to the mantra "Make America Great Again." The phrase is shot through with racist nostalgia for the occupation of the land by those who are superior and supreme. I am bound to conclude that President Trump himself is only the point person and means of expression of that misguided sense of supremacy and superiority. That sense of superiority now receives legal expression in immigration restrictions, voter repression, and the militarization of police authority, all of which aim to delegitimize "the other," which embodies threat and alternative to white domination. Thus, the adrenalin behind the mantra is yet another expression of a superiority and supremacy that are deep and long-standing in white Western Christendom.

IV

The matter is much more complex than this simple enumeration. I suggest, however, that when we read backward, we are able to see the long line of development that has eventuated in Christian white extremism. The most recent articulation of such extremism, of course, is the current anti-Muslim fad that concerns both a new "crusade" against Islam and an exclusion of Muslims from the United States on religious grounds. That anti-Muslim white extremism is of a piece with long-term, anti-black extremism that yields harsh reaction against any black gain in politics or economics.[10]

9. Patrick Phillips, *Blood at the Root: A Racial Cleansing in America* (New York: Norton, 2016).

10. See Carol Anderson, *White Rage: The Unspoken Truth of Our Racial Divide* (New York: Bloomsbury, 2016).

But behind that extremism toward blacks and toward Muslims (or toward any other challenging group) is deeply rooted in the Doctrine of Discovery, which assumes the legitimacy of white Western European control over native peoples who are incapable of self-governance. The action of "discovery" has given ground for endless land appropriation. But that "doctrine" would not have been possible had not the authority of the church and its administration of all Christendom been articulated and performed in the Crusades and the Inquisition. That enormous assumption of authority, in turn, would not have been possible without the toleration and the legitimation of the establishment of Christian faith as the true religion of imperial Europe and of the entire known world. The thuggish and legal means of extremism are possible only because of the long-term claim of supremacy and superiority that has no capacity for positive engagement with "the other."

I may add a coda that will indicate that such extremism is not simply the work of thuggery but in fact is a compelling conviction of much of the intellectual class as well. Refer, for example, to Walker's verdict on the Crusades cited above. Tomoko Masuzawa has detailed the way in which "world religions" developed as a nineteenth-century project in Europe.[11] While the project was concerned with the five world religions (Judaism, Christianity, Islam, Hinduism, Buddhism), the hidden but powerful agenda was to exhibit the superiority of Western Christianity. Masuzawa shows that, for all of its urbane scholarship, in fact "world religions" was shot through with racist assumptions. Davis Hankins and I, moreover, have shown how this assertion of white European superiority was bootlegged into our discipline of Old Testament study in the form of the "Documentary Hypothesis," which purported to trace "religious evolution" in the Bible from "primitive Semitism" to the sophistication that culminated in Western categories of faith.[12]

I cite this remarkable insight from Masuzawa to indicate how racist proclivity has permeated the domain of critical scholarship that makes a pretense of objectivity. The current fruit of this long-term trajectory of racial superiority is the war on "radical Islam," which is readily taken to be characteristic of all Islam. This articulation of cultural reality has been given classic and effective formulation by Samuel Huntington in *The Clash of Civilizations*.[13] That model of cultural reality now appeals

11. Tomoko Masuzawa, *The Invention of World Religions: Or, How European Universalism Was Preserved in the Language of Pluralism* (Chicago: University of Chicago Press, 2005).
12. Walter Brueggemann and Davis Hankins, "The Invention and Persistence of Wellhausen's World," *Catholic Biblical Quarterly* 75 (2013): 15–31.
13. Samuel P. Huntington, *The Clash of Civilizations and the Remaking of World Order* (New York: Simon & Schuster, 2011).

with great weight not only in popular US opinion but in the high councils of learned experts. It is clear enough, in my judgment, that his current preoccupation with "radical Islam" is simply another manifestation of Western white supremacy that has shown up in opposition to Muslims in the Crusades and more broadly in the Doctrine of Discovery.

It is of immense importance that Huntington's well-known thesis has been effectively answered by Martha Nussbaum, who has shown that it is the inability to honor "the other" that is the key issue in Huntington's formulation and in the Doctrine of Discovery.[14] (Nussbaum offers a close reading of the Hindu–Muslim conflict in India as a case study for her compelling thesis.) It is clear that "the other"—non-Christian, non-white, non-Westerner—does not need to be honored if and when Christian white Westerners are in all cases and circumstances superior. The entire trajectory of superiority serves to diminish and dismiss "the other" as an important and defining presence in the world.[15] Nussbaum has proposed, to the contrary, that the "clash" of which Huntington writes is in fact a "clash within." She sees that in each of us there is a clash between fear of "the other" and welcome of "the other." And how we work out that clash is decisive for our common human future. Because the clash is "within," it is clear that pastors have important and quite distinctive work to do in making that clash available to our own awareness and then providing processes and venues in which the clash can be appropriately dealt with. Without such processing it is no wonder that demagogues find it easy to mobilize that great fear of "the other" in popular, violent, and dangerous ways. It is not likely that there is much thuggish supremacy among our church constituency. But it is for sure that there is much legal, polite white supremacy within the confines of the church. For that reason this is an urgent task for pastors. We will do well to let people in on this long-term history of supremacy and how we ourselves are on the receiving end of that trajectory, much to the betrayal of evangelical faith.

14. Martha C. Nussbaum, *The Clash Within: Democracy, Religious Violence, and India's Future* (Cambridge: Belknap Press of Harvard University Press, 2007).

15. Even in the Edict of Milan, the language was only the rhetoric of "tolerance" that regularly turns out to be patronizing and condescending. Significant honoring of "the other" requires much more engagement than what is indicated by "tolerance."

6.

Choosing against Chosenness

Portions of this chapter were initially delivered on September 17, 2016, in Charlottesville, Virginia, at an event sponsored by the Endowed Lectureship in Contemporary Theology at Westminster Presbyterian Church and cosponsored by the Virginia Center for the Study of Religion and the Institute for Advanced Studies in Culture at the University of Virginia.

There is no doubt that the Bible, in both Testaments, is preoccupied with a "chosen people," a particular historical community that is elected and designated by God for special status and destiny in the world.[1] There is no doubt, moreover, that Western Euro-American culture and history (which take the Bible as their normative script) are haunted by that same claim. That claim of exceptionalism is sometimes stated in secular terms. Even in its secular articulation, however, the claim is never far removed from a religious undercurrent, for good or for ill. In this presentation I want to probe the theme of chosenness and consider the future of such claims in light of present circumstance and in light of a mixed historical tradition.

I

The fundamental claim of chosenness can be considered, I suggest, in four dimensions.

---

1. This theme and its problematic have been opened for me by Todd Gitlin and Liel Leibovitz, *Chosen Peoples: America, Israel, and the Ordeals of Divine Election* (New York: Simon & Schuster, 2010). I am glad to commend this book as a starting point.

A. *The Bible in its inception presents a God who readily enters into historical engagement in a quite particular way.* If we take Genesis 1–11 as a framing narrative, we can see that God's engagement with Abraham and Sarah is the beginning of the core narrative of the Bible. God's address to and engagement with them is completely inexplicable and depends solely upon God's initiative. It is God's decision to take sides and choose a favorite in history to be God's partner.[2] The Abraham narrative continues to return to this divine initiative. In Genesis 12, Abraham is promised a name, a land, a great nation, and to be a carrier of blessing:

> Go from your country and your kindred and your father's house to the land that I will show you. I will make of you a great nation, and I will bless you, and make your name great, so that you will be a blessing. I will bless those who bless you, and the one who curses you I will curse; and in you all the families of the earth shall be blessed. (12:2–3)

In Genesis 15 Abraham is promised "great possessions"; he will be the possessor of "this land," a land that consists, in contemporary rhetoric of "Greater Israel":

> To your descendants I will give this land, from the river of Egypt to the great river, the Euphrates, the land of the Kenites, the Kenizzites, the Kadmonites, the Hittites, the Perizzites, the Rephaim, the Amorites, the Canaanites, the Girgashites, and the Jebusites. (15:18–21)

And in Genesis 17 the covenant between God and Abraham is guaranteed "throughout their generations, for an everlasting covenant":

> As for me, this is my covenant with you: you shall be the ancestor of a multitude of nations. No longer shall your name be Abram, but your name shall be Abraham, for I have made you the ancestor of a multitude of nations. I will make you exceeding fruitful; and I will make nations of you, and kings shall come from you. I will establish my covenant between me and you, and your offspring after you throughout their generations, for an everlasting covenant, to be God to you and to your offspring after you. And I will give to you, and to your offspring after you, the land where you are now an alien, all the land of Canaan, for a perpetual holding, and I will be their God. (17:4–9)

It is easy enough to see that the sum of chapters 12, 15, and 17 is an unconditional, unilateral act on God's part that assures Abraham a future,

2. Joel S. Kaminsky has fully and carefully explored the biblical texts concerning the divine election of Israel (*Yet I Loved Jacob: Reclaiming the Biblical Concept of Election* [Nashville: Abingdon, 2007]).

in which God will be attentively engaged on his behalf. This unconditional unilateral assurance turns out to be crucially important in the
sixth-century exile. When all historical props have failed Israel, the Abraham tradition became a fallback assurance of the survival and future well-
being of Israel.

The matter is very different in the Moses tradition. To be sure, the
theme of chosenness for Israel is very strong here as well. The texture
of the divine initiative, however, is very different because here the relationship is conditional. At Sinai, Moses declares a huge "if" over the
covenant:

> If you obey my voice and keep my covenant, you shall be my possession out
> of all the peoples. Indeed the whole earth is mine, but you shall be for me a
> priestly kingdom and a holy nation. (Exod 19:5–6)

This conditionality is echoed in the verses leading to the oaths of fidelity
that follow the Decalogue:

> But if you listen attentively to his voice and do all that I say, then I will be
> an enemy to your enemies and a foe to your foes. (23:22)

There is no doubt that the "if" is reflective of the rhetoric and assumptions of Deuteronomy, which bases the covenant on Israel's capacity to
obey the Torah.[3] The rhetorical structure of covenant is all "if-then,"
and "then" will be a blessing or a curse according to Israel's obedience or disobedience. It is this conditional quality that makes space for
the prophetic tradition to follow. The dominant rhetorical form of the
prophets, a speech of judgment with indictments and sentences, is a reiteration of the "if-then" of Sinai.[4]

Thus, we are able to see the deep tension in the tradition between
the memories of Abraham and Moses. That tension permitted the subsequent tradition to have ample interpretive maneuverability; it also leaves
unresolved the question of the durability of the status of the chosen people. In response to the question, many exilic texts attest the durability of
the Abraham covenant; see Leviticus 24:8, 2 Samuel 23:5, Psalm 105:10,
Isaiah 55:3, 61:8, Ezekiel 16:60, 37:26. So powerful and persuasive is the

---

3. On that qualifying "if," see Walter Brueggemann, *Solomon: Israel's Ironic Icon of Human Achievement*, Studies on Personalities of the Old Testament (Columbia: University of South Carolina Press, 2005), 139–59.

4. On this rhetorical pattern, see Claus Westermann, *Basic Forms of Prophetic Speech* (Philadelphia: Westminster, 1967).

sixth-century claim that some suggest that the Abraham tradition in fact emerged only in the sixth century.[5]

Even that collage of affirmative texts, however, is not without challenge. Thus, Jeremiah in prophetic judgment can liken Israel and Jerusalem to a broken pot beyond repair:

> So I will break this people and city as one breaks a potter's vessel, so that it cannot be mended. (Jer 19:11)

And in the enigmatic conclusion to the grief songs of Lamentations, the matter is left open:

> unless you have utterly rejected us,
> and are angry with us beyond measure. (Lam 5:22)

Tod Linafelt persuasively proposes that the verse is "a conditional statement that is left trailing off":

> I have chosen to translate the line as a conditional statement that is left trailing off, leaving a protasis without an apodosis, or an "if" without a "then." The book is left opening out into the emptiness of God's nonresponse. By leaving a conditional statement dangling, the final verse leaves open the future of the ones lamenting. It is hardly a hopeful ending, for the missing but implied apodosis is surely negative, yet it does nevertheless defer that apodosis. And by arresting the movement from an "if" to a "then" the incomplete clause allows the reader, for a moment, to imagine the possibility of a different "then," and therefore a different future.[6]

On this reading, Israel does not know about its future and cannot say. Many other texts know more. This text, however, makes clear that some in sixth-century Israel hoped, but also wondered, because they knew of the unsettled play between Abraham and Moses. That question came to occupy Israel in the sixth century and of course many times since.

B. *There cannot be any doubt that in the New Testament we have reverberations of the theme of chosenness from the tradition of ancient Israel.* The replay of that theme of course opens the way for supersessionism, that "this chosen people," which we can call the church even if that term is not present in all the texts, displaces the older chosen people, Israel. But the matter need not be resolved in supersessionism. The tortured argument of Paul in Romans 9–11 indicates an acute sensibility to the matter,

5. See John Van Seters, *Abraham in History and Tradition* (New Haven: Yale University Press, 1975).

6. Tod Linafelt, *Surviving Lamentations: Catastrophe, Lament, and Protest in the Afterlife of a Biblical Book* (Chicago: University of Chicago Press, 2000), 60–61.

and we may simply notice the subject of the church as "chosen," while leaving open the vexed issue of Israel vis-à-vis the church.

There is no doubt that Jesus chose disciples to form a community of companions that would share his teaching and his way in the world. There is no doubt, moreover, that the New Testament epistles play on the theme of chosenness. Thus Paul can declare about the early church:

> But God chose what is foolish in the world to shame the wise; God chose what is weak in the world to shame the strong; God chose what is low and despised in the world, things that are not, to reduce to nothing things that are, so that no one might boast in the presence of God. (1 Cor 1:27–29)

Paul will speak, moreover, of the church as "the Israel of God" (Gal 6:16). And "Peter," in an echo from Sinai, can use the cadences of Deuteronomy and Hosea to identify the church as the people of God who have received mercy (1 Pet 2:9–10). There is no doubt, moreover, that the great triumphal hymns of the subsequent church readily appropriate the language of chosenness for the church:

> Ye chosen seed of Israel's race,
> `Ye ransomed from the fall,
> Hail him who saved you by his grace,
> and crown him Lord of all.[7]

That hymn, without hesitation, uses the language of election and claims that the church is the carrier of Israel's genes of chosenness.

C. We are, however, not finished with a sketch of chosenness when we mention Israel and the church. *A third trajectory of "chosenness" has to do with American self-understanding that is the defining tradition of the United States.* There is no doubt that the rhetoric of chosenness pervades US history and culture. Sacvan Bercovitch has traced the way in which the early articulators of US identity recast biblical chosenness for the sake of US destiny.[8] Thus, for example, John Winthrop, the initial governor of the Massachusetts Bay colony, identified Cotton Mather as "America's Nehemiah," that is, as the governor of the chosen people. And Bruce Feiler has traced the way in which the rhetoric of Moses has pervaded political discourse in the United States from the earliest time until now:

---

7. "All Hail the Power of Jesus' Name!" in *Glory to God: The Presbyterian Hymnal* (Louisville: Westminster John Knox Press, 2013), 263.

8. Sacvan Bercovitch, *The Puritan Origins of the American Self* (New Haven: Yale University Press, 1975).

The American elevation of Moses grew out of an extraordinary collusion of trends—geographical, religious, and technological. For waves of believers who left the civilized world, crossed a forbidding sea, and arrived in untamed territory, the New World could plausibly be considered a wilderness. . . . "The rising of the sea was very favorable to me," he [Christopher Columbus] recorded in his journal, "as it happened formerly to Moses when he led the Jews from Egypt." On a later voyage Columbus claimed that God had treated him like Moses and David, adding, "What more did he do for the people of Israel when he brought them out of Egypt?"[9]

Feiler shows the way in which there is a fairly direct line from the early formulation of the Monroe Doctrine with its uncompromising claim of territory to the expansionist "Manifest Destiny" of an emerging empire to Harry Truman's readiness to be "the leader of the free world." This exceptionalism is deeply present in American public rhetoric and every political leader must subscribe to it. Moreover, appeal to this exceptionalism as God's chosen people can cover a multitude of sins, for example, economic injustice and political oligarchy, all in the name of chosenness.[10]

D. *The interplay of Jewish, Christian, and American chosenness is our theme.* To be sure, attention is best focused in the deep intertwining of Christian and American election, but all of that depends on appeal to the initial Jewish claim to chosenness. It is most likely the case, moreover, that the intense political attachment of the United States to the contemporary state of Israel in important ways is fed by the link of all of these varied accents upon chosenness.

To these, however, I must add a coda. It is this. The rather inchoate but pervasive appeal to chosenness in the public rhetoric of the United States has within it an unexpressed but powerful element of white chosenness, so that the theme of "chosenness" can also be a placeholder for racism. There is no doubt that American chosenness derives especially from European antecedents, so that the "real Americans" who are chosen are those with European rootage. Much of the rhetoric of US chosenness is also marked by a hostility to "foreigners" (nonwhites) who, it is said, diminish chosenness, and by the "Christian" rhetoric of "taking back our country" from the foreigners and restoring it to it proper order and management. Much of the great triumphal language of the church eas-

---

9. Bruce Feiler, *America's Prophet: Moses and the American Story* (New York: HarperCollins, 2009), 21.

10. Thomas Frank has explored the way in which the ideology of chosenness, coupled with the dreams of capitalism, has caused voters to vote on behalf of that ideology against their own vested interest and the evident reality on the ground (*What's the Matter with Kansas? How Conservatives Won the Heart of America* [New York: Henry Holt, 2005]).

ily imagined white missionaries carrying the gospel to benighted non-whites. That missionary zeal, moreover, is evident ("manifest"!) in US foreign policy. Thus, in the 1840s William Fall Giles could say of US expansionism:

> We must march from ocean to ocean . . . straight to the Pacific Ocean, and be bounded only by its roaring waves. . . . It is the destiny of the white race, it is the destiny of the Anglo-Saxon race.[11]

Or John Calhoun in the same period:

> We have never dreamt of incorporating into our Union any but the Caucasian race. . . . Ours, sir, is the Government of a white race.[12]

Of course white supremacism is not an exclusively American or even European ideology. Bradley traces the way in which the Japanese, at the turn of the twentieth century, presented themselves as "different Asians" who could thereby be accepted by the United States as "honorary Aryans."[13] Teddy Roosevelt's favorite Japanese, Baron Kaneko, supported an "Aryan ideology" in order to connect with the United States. He found solidarity between the United States and Japan in this assertion: The Himalaya Mountains were

> The fountain head of the two great waves of human energy [which created] all our enlightened modern civilization. From the western slopes there began . . . that Aryan march which established its dominion over the whole of Europe and flowered into Occidental civilization. From the mountain's eastern sides there flowed that slower but no less profound tide which we know as orientalism.

> Kaneko explained that just as England, off the coast of Europe, had become the highest receptacle of Anglo-Saxonism, Japan, off Asia's coast, was the highest repository of Orientalism.[14]

The matter persists as General Arthur MacArthur, US military governor of the Philippines could say:

> As to why the United States was in the Philippines, the broad actuating laws which underlie all these wonderful phenomena are still operating with relentless vigor and have recently forced one of the currents of this magnif-

11. James Bradley, *The Imperial Cruise: A Secret History of Empire and War* (New York: Little, Brown, 2009), 63.

12. Bradley, *Imperial Cruise*, 64.

13. Bradley, *Imperial Cruise*, 183–84.

14. Bradley, *Imperial Cruise*, 220–21.

icent Aryan people across the Pacific—that is to say, back almost to the cradle of the race—thus initiating a stage of progressive social evolution which may reasonably be expected to result in substantial contributions on behalf of the unity of the race and brotherhood of man.[15]

The matter could be extended with reference to more recent US experience in Southeast Asia or in Southwest Asia vis-à-vis Persians, Arabs, and others. Closer to home, white supremacy continues to be a defining subtext for economic policy and practice. All of this is enough to suggest that chosenness is at best problematic. It is for good reason that Abraham Lincoln could refer to the Union as "the almost chosen people."[16] The "almost" signals a conscious awareness of the problematic of the claim. To this problematic we may now turn.

II

I will trace the problematic of chosenness—as concerns Israel, the church, the United States, and whites—through four theses that I acknowledge may be presented with varying degrees of certitude. I intend to suggest a taxonomy of chosenness and so will speak in a somewhat schematic way. We can then assess how fully the actual claims fit such a taxonomy.

A. *Chosenness issues in entitlement.*

1. There can be no doubt that Israel, via chosenness, received the land as a perpetual possession through divine promise. The Deuteronomic "if" that pervades prophetic teaching finds it thinkable that the land could be lost through disobedience. In the midst of "land loss" in the sixth-century deportation, the traditions of promise were recalled to bear witness against the facts on the ground. It is likely, moreover, that the purchase of land as a burial ground for Sarah (Genesis 23) and the purchase of land by Jeremiah with an accent on legal formalities (Jer 32:1-15) are representative statements of land possession as a legal and inalienable right.

That entitlement to land is now a primary claim of contemporary Zionism, which appeals to these old traditions of promise. Thus, David Novak purports to offer "a new theory" amid the current Israeli–Palestinian crisis, but in the end his "new theory" is simply a reiteration of the oldest, largest claims of Israel to the land. He

15. Bradley, *Imperial Cruise*, 105.

16. Abraham Lincoln, "Address to the New Jersey Senate, Trenton, New Jersey," *Speeches and Writings 1859–1865* (New York: Library of America, 1989), 209.

speaks of Israel's covenant as "the best choice God could have made under the circumstances." He judges that

> God's desire to elect a people is in God's best interest.[17]

The legal legitimacy of the land is underscored by Novak in his comment about Palestinian rights in the land:

> At least according to Maimonides [a teacher that in this case Novak takes at face value], non-Jews do not have full political autonomy because they do not have full legal autonomy.[18]

2. Chosenness means that Israel, Jews, and then Christians are entitled to an intentional friendship with God. Abraham already is said to be "friend of God," wherein "friendship" is taken as a parallel to chosenness:

> But you, Israel, my servant,
> Jacob, whom I have *chosen,*
> the offspring of Abraham, my *friend.* (Isa 41:8)

In Genesis 18:17, moreover, the intimate connection Abraham has with God means that Abraham is "in on the secret" of what God will do. This usage suggests an easy intimacy that shares all kinds of confidences.

This imagery of friendship is operative in the Fourth Gospel account of Jesus teaching his disciples. Again "friendship" is linked to chosenness:

> You are my friends if you do what I command you. I do not call you servants any longer, because the servant does not know what the master is doing; but I have called you *friends,* because I have made known to you everything that I have heard from my Father. You did not choose me but I *chose* you. And I appointed you to go and bear fruit, fruit that will last, so that the Father will give you whatever you ask in my name. I am giving you these commands so that you may love one another. (John 15:14–17)

As with Abraham, such friendship lets the disciples know what "the master is doing." "Friends" are contrasted to "servants," who are not chosen, who do not enjoy intimacy, and who are not privy to the

---

17. David Novak, *Zionism and Judaism: A New Theory* (Cambridge: Cambridge University Press, 2015), 127.
18. Novak, *Zionism and Judaism,* 221–22.

master's intention. Thus, it is given to the church to "know the mind of Christ." This intimacy becomes, among other things, the ground for prayer. As Moses could speak with God face-to-face (Exod 33:11), so Christian prayer is an exercise of such intimacy. That special intimacy is, at the same time, a summons to obedience, so that entitlement means to be fully in sync with Christ and with his Father.

3. The United States, as God's (almost) chosen people, knows itself to be fully entitled to limitless land, to rich natural resources, and to unfettered freedom without coercion.[19] There are two real "national anthems" of US celebration that embody us with special privilege. Irving Berlin, in "God Bless America," celebrated the wonder of this land of mountains, prairies, and oceans in rhetoric reminiscent of "the good land" characterized in Deuteronomy 6:10–11 and 8:7–10. And "America the Beautiful" matches abundance with talk of brotherhood, mercy, and self-control, all echoes of the Deuteronomic condition for keeping the land.

That sense of US entitlement was originally fed by the sense of open space and natural resources; it very soon, however, morphed into aggressive and ambitious foreign policy in which Americans could imagine they were entitled, as well, to oil and natural resources from elsewhere. At bottom it is all about being entitled!

4. We need only add that white chosenness of course assumed entitlement that would disadvantage all "lesser people" and mete out to them only very limited portions of the vast material entitlement, whether housing, schools, health care, or any of the other features of a prosperous society. Clearly such entitlement carries with it an unspoken sense that the others are "not entitled."

B. *Chosenness leads to exclusion.* It figures: if the chosen are peculiarly entitled, others are not!

1. Ancient Israel ordered itself as an exclusionary society. It did so through purity codes that drew sharp lines between insiders and outsiders. The accent was on being "a holy people to YHWH" that required intentional and visible disciplines of distinction. Thus, in Deuteronomy 14:1–2, holiness is linked to physical appearance:

19. On the thickness of the notion of American exceptionalism, see Tom Wolfe, "The Future of the American Idea," *The Atlantic*, November 2007, 13–62; and Mark Danner, "After September 11: Our State of Exception," *New York Review*, October 13, 2011, 44–48.

You are the children of the Lord your God. You must not lacerate yourselves or shave your forelocks for the dead. For you are a people holy to the Lord your God; it is you the Lord has chosen out of all the peoples on earth to be his people, his treasured possession. (Deut 14:1–2)

The most programmatic statement on exclusion is in Deuteronomy 23:1–6, which concerns both ethnic exclusion based on specific historical memories and exclusion in terms of physical "disorder" reflective of social deviance:

No one whose testicles are crushed or whose penis is cut off shall be admitted to the assembly of the Lord. Those born of an illicit union shall not be admitted to the assembly of the Lord. Even to the tenth generation, none of their descendants shall be admitted to the assembly of the Lord. No Ammonite or Moabite shall be admitted to the assembly of the Lord. Even to the tenth generation none of their descendants shall be admitted to the assembly of the Lord, because they did not meet you with food and water on your journey out of Egypt, and because they hired against you Balaam son of Beor, from Pethor of Mesopotamia, to curse you. . . . You shall never promote their welfare or their prosperity as long as you live. (Deut 23:1–6)

The most direct ground for such exclusion concerns the purity of "holy seed," which requires "separation" from other peoples:

The people of Israel, the priests, and the Levites have not separated themselves from the peoples of the lands with their abominations, from the Canaanites, the Hittites, the Perizzites, the Jebusites, the Ammonites, the Moabites, the Egyptians, and the Amorites. For they have taken some of their daughters as wives for themselves and for their sons. Thus the holy seed has mixed itself with the peoples of the lands, and in this faithlessness the officials and leaders have led the way. (Ezra 9:1–2)

A legacy of this tradition is the fact that in contemporary Israel there continue to be vigorous debates about the identity of "real Jews," an identity that excludes many would-be Jews. Beyond the internal question of Judaism, it is clear that contemporary Zionism (not to be equated with Judaism) draws rigorous distinctions against the legitimacy of Palestinians, so that the wall built to exclude Palestinians as a "security measure" is a visible articulation of exclusion.

2. The early church in the New Testament worked to maintain a distinct identity that would mark it off from its social environment.

Thus, Paul can urge resistance to "conformity to this world" (Rom 12:2), and "Peter" can assert that the church is "a chosen race, a royal priesthood, a holy nation" (1 Pet 2:9). A more vigorous distinctiveness is articulated in 2 Corinthians 6:14–7:1:

> Do not be mismatched with unbelievers. For what partnership is there between righteousness and lawlessness? Or what fellowship is there between light and darkness? What agreement does Christ have with Beliar? Or what does a believer share with an unbeliever? What agreement has the temple of God with idols?. . . .

> Since we have these promises, beloved, let us cleanse ourselves from every defilement of body and spirit, making holiness perfect in the fear of God.

This rhetoric of "holiness and defilement" sounds the accents of Israel's old purity codes. The status of this text as Pauline is much in dispute. Mitzi Minor regards the text as a "scribal gloss."[20] The text may well be an intrusion into Paul's statement, for it is clearly against the grain of Pauline rhetoric. Its presence nonetheless attests a trajectory of exclusionary separateness that was operative in the early church, whether, Paul's, Pauline, or not.

And of course in the long history of the church, exclusionary practices have flourished. The pressure for conformity to "orthodoxy" was vigorously expressed in the Inquisition, and the Roman Catholic Church long taught that "error has not the same right as truth."[21] Garry Wills can remark, "The real wonder is that the church did not exclude itself out of existence."[22] In the contemporary church, we know about the exclusion of groups and denied people, all those who have not met certain rigorous norms of either belief or conduct. That exclusionary practice is dramatically evident in the capacity of the church to "silence" those who have thought or said "otherwise." While the capacity for exclusion in the Roman Catholic Church is more visible and characteristic, the same exclu-

---

20. On the critical issues related to this difficult text, see Mitzi L. Minor, *2 Corinthians*, Smyth & Helwys Bible Commentary (Macon, GA: Smyth & Helwys, 2009), 129–35.

21. The papal bull *Inter Caetera* (Alexander VI), May 4, 1493. On the way in which the "Doctrine of Discovery" has been bootlegged into US law and practice based on white supremacy, see Robert Miller et al., *Discovering Indigenous Lands: The Doctrine of Discovery in the English Colonies* (Oxford: Oxford University Press, 2010); Steven T. Newcomb, *Pagans in the Promised Land: Decoding the Doctrine of Christian Discovery* (Golden, CO: Fulcrum, 2008); and Lindsay G. Robertson, *Conquest by Law: How the Discovery of America Dispossessed Indigenous Peoples of Their Lands* (Oxford: Oxford University Press, 2005).

22. Garry Wills, *The Future of the Catholic Church with Pope Francis* (New York: Viking Press, 2015), 22.

sionary practices are operative in many forms of Protestantism as well.

3. The exceptionalism of the United States is given inclusive expression in the lyrical welcome of the Statute of Liberty, portraying the United States as a welcoming alternative for those excluded elsewhere. In practice, however, that exceptionalism has quite effectively functioned as a kind of nativism that wants to protect our society for those "like us" to the exclusion of all others. The current heated debate about immigration and the widespread practice of deportation evidence the continuing power of exclusivism as a way to enforce and insist on a certain kind of chosenness.

4. From exclusionary exceptionalism in the United States, it is easy enough to segue to white exclusionary practice so that US chosenness really pertains to whites of European rootage. The long-standing practice of racial segregation and the illusion of "separate but equal" have served white advantage. And even with more recent legislation (voter rights) and court rulings (*Brown v. Board of Education*), the actual practice of racial segregation continues to be an exclusionary force through which nonwhites are denied access to the privileges and advantages of "the chosen."

C. *Chosenness issues in extraction by coercion.* That is, wealth is extracted from the vulnerable nonchosen and is transferred to the "chosen," who turn out to be the powerful who manage the processes of socioeconomic distribution.

1. The dramatic case against the chosenness of Israel is that it violently appropriated the land of the Canaanites, and it did so, says the tradition, at the behest of and with the legitimating power of YHWH. The Book of Joshua is replete with narratives of the barbaric dispatch of the indigenous population, and with attestation of divine sanction for such actions.

And of course that ancient tradition continues to be fully operative in contemporary Zionism, which is uncompromising in its claim to the total land of promise that is grounded in the old tradition, and that is unrestrained in its occupation of that land. The displacement of Palestinians from the land is simply a reiteration of the ancient displacement of the Canaanites. Quite clearly the ideological force of Zionism has no interest in or inclination for compromise about the land and fully intends to claim in concrete ways all of "Greater Israel," all in the name of chosenness.

2. The church historically has been an extracting enterprise. The most distinctive instance is the papal bull of Alexander VI (*Inter Caetera*) in 1493, often termed "The Doctrine of Discovery." This statement, immediately following Christopher Columbus in 1492, sought to bring order to the competition among European colonial powers in the "New World." Its effect was to legitimate occupation, domination, and extraction from the New World to serve the benefit of old European powers. The scope of the authorization is sweeping indeed:

> We . . . give, grant, and assign to you and your heirs and successors, kings of Castile and Leon, forever, together with all their dominions, cities, camps, places, and villages, all rights, jurisdictions, and appurtenances, all islands and mainlands found and to be found, discovered and to be discovered toward the west and south.[23]

The rest of course is history, as the colonial powers, notably Spain, were free to plunder and extract at will, a process that brought enormous wealth to the colonial powers. The legitimacy given to the extraction process by the pope attests to the power of chosenness, for the pope recognized the European powers as legitimately authorized in their chosenness as God's agents:

> We exhort you very earnestly in the Lord and by your reception of holy baptism, whereby you are bound to our apostolic commands, and by the bowels of the mercy of our Lord Jesus Christ, enjoin strictly, that inasmuch as with eager zeal for the true faith you design to equip and dispatch this expedition, you purpose also, as is your duty, to lead the peoples dwelling in those islands and countries to embrace the Christian religion. . . . Let no one, therefore, infringe, or with rash boldness contravene, this our recommendation, exhortation, requisition, gift, grant, assignment, constitution, deputation, decree, mandate, prohibition, and will.[24]

It is the old and recurring missionary story of evangelism coupled with extraction. It may be noted that in 1992 the United Confed-

23. *Inter Caetera*, Papal Bull issued by Pope Alexander VI, May 4, 1493.
24. *Inter Caetera*, Papal Bull issued by Pope Alexander VI, May 4, 1493.

eration of Taino People took the first steps to have the papal bull revoked.[25]

3. The United States, according to its very old sense of chosenness as "a city set on a hill," found it legitimate to appropriate the lands of the native population. It did so, moreover, while deliberately echoing the old cadences of Israel's ancient conquest of the land of Canaan.

There is undoubtedly a direct line from the extraction practiced by that ancient exceptionalism to contemporary US status as the last superpower that gives the United States the capacity and the legitimacy to extract revenues from elsewhere, not least the extraction of "our oil" from other economies in the service of "globalization," which is an extractive exploitative enterprise.

4. It follows easily and readily that white chosenness has legitimated extraction of goods and services from nonwhites. The obvious case is the "peculiar institution" of slavery that was a source of cheap labor that brought great wealth to the ownership class. There is no doubt that the long-standing arrangement of "separate but equal" served (and was designed to maintain) a supply of cheap labor by denying access and education that would permit nonwhites to participate fully in the prosperity of the dominant economy. In contemporary practice, Matt Taibbi has narrated the widespread practice of "police sweeps," whereby police are free to confiscate what the police want from the vulnerable.[26] Indeed, Taibbi makes clear that the very norms of justice (injustice!) operate among the disenfranchised vulnerable. "Police sweeps" constitute only a contemporary form of extraction that is long-standing and legitimates the exercise of chosenness. Or a small, recurring sort of item: the *New York Times* reported recently that Honda in a Department of Justice settlement agreed to pay $24 million to minority car buyers who were "past victims of discriminatory lending and cap the interest rates dealers can charge."[27] Who knew?

It is impossible to imagine these several practices of extraction without some sense of chosenness:

25. See "Revoking the Bull 'Inter Caetera' of 1493," at The Manataka American Indian Council, https://tinyurl.com/ycdlseay.

26. Matt Taibbi, *The Divide: American Injustice in the Age of the Wealth Gap* (New York: Spiegel & Grau, 2014).

27. "Honda Settles Discrimination Claims with Justice Department," *New York Times*, July 14, 2015.

- Israel was *chosen to possess* the land of Canaan.
- The church was *chosen to evangelize* alongside colonial powers in the New World and thereby to usurp wealth.
- The United States was *chosen to extract* land and resources from the vulnerable native population.
- Whites are *chosen to manage and benefit* from cheap labor in coercive modes.

The chosen characteristically manage to cast the vulnerable unchosen as "hewers of wood and drawers of water" (Josh 9:21). The matter of such chosenness is readily and succinctly stated by Jana Riess in her comment on Joshua 12–13:

> Nanny, nanny, boo, boo. List of 31 kings we disgraced and tribes we destroyed. This land is our land, it is not your land . . . . G gave Josh 2 jobs: First, kill Canaanites and grab land. Check! Second, divide land equally among 12 tribes. Hmmm, harder than it seems.[28]

D. *Chosenness issues in entitlement, exclusion, and extraction.* From that it follows that *chosenness characteristically issues in violence.*

1. In ancient Israel it is violence against the indigenous Canaanites—so narrates the book of Joshua.[29] In contemporary Israel, it is violence against the Palestinians, all in the name of "security."

2. It cannot be doubted that the church continues to be a "wounding" institution. Its long practice of authoritarian absolutism, reinforced by the sanctions of "hellfire and damnation" or the more concrete readiness to "excommunicate," has left a scorched-earth policy of fear and anger in too many quarters. It is telling that the church—whether Roman Catholic or the evangelical right—comes to care about "religious freedom" only when it is in the minority.[30] When it is in the majority, it has no interest in "religious freedom" for those who deviate from specific and nonnegotiable norms. Chosenness has given the church something like a blank check in its capacity for abuse. Of late the Canadian Truth and Reconciliation Commission has concluded that the church committed "cultural genocide" against aboriginal children.[31] In his recent visit to

28. Jana Riess, *The Twible: All the Chapters of the Bible in 140 Characters or Less* (Published by Jana Riess, 2013), 47.

29. On these vexed texts, see Jerome F. D. Creach, *Violence in Scripture*, Interpretation (Louisville: Westminster John Knox, 2012), 97–124.

30. See Emily Bazelon, "The God Clause," *New York Times Magazine*, July 12, 2015, 13–15.

31. Thomas King, "No Justice for Canada's First Peoples," *New York Times*, June 12, 2015,

South America, moreover, Pope Francis explicitly apologized for "crimes committed against native peoples during the so-called conquest of America."[32]

3. There can hardly be doubt that the United States, with its bravado militarism and its clandestine manipulation of dependent regimes, has overseen a perpetuation of immense violence, all in the service of "the free world." In contemporary practice, the readiness for violence in the name of democracy and excessively punitive treatment for deviation, together attest to a defense of a certain kind of moral ordering of "freedom," but it is freedom for some at the expense of others.

4. White violence committed against blacks is self-evident and requires no extended comment. The collusion of legal segregation until recently, the legitimacy of police violence, and the vigilante justice of the Klan, together with the gun lobby, have created a society of violence. Fox Butterfield has chronicled the legacy of violence by noting that whites historically have been "above the law" and blacks have been "outside the law" and outside any credible protection.[33] James Cone shows that the legacy of lynching makes unavoidable the culture of violence that has permeated white privilege.[34]

On all these counts, chosenness turns out to be immensely problematic. The issue is made more urgent and more acute by the fact that, for the most part, the beneficiaries of chosenness are unable and unwilling to recognize its problematic character. Consequently, they are unwilling and unable to acknowledge the toxic implications of such chosenness. This chosenness—in the cases of Israel, the church, the United States, and white hegemony—takes on an ideological force that is unquestioned in its legitimacy and, for the most part, unrestrained in its practice. Chosenness is simply taken for granted with a kind of self-satisfied innocence that refuses any self-critical awareness.

23; and Ian Austen, "Report Details 'Cultural Genocide' at Schools for Aboriginal Canadians," *New York Times*, June 3, 2015, A7.

32. Jim Yardley and William Neuman, "In Bolivia, Pope Apologizes for Church's 'grave sins,'" *New York Times*, July 10, 2015, A4.

33. Fox Butterfield, *All God's Children: The Bosket Family and the American Tradition of Violence* (New York: Vintage Books, 2008).

34. James H. Cone, *The Cross and the Lynching Tree* (Maryknoll, NY: Orbis Books, 2011).

III

Given such a reality, it is important, I would insist, that the church in its critical theological reflection should face the deeply problematic character of chosenness and invite a broader awareness of the uneasiness that is appropriate to the subject of chosenness. In what follows, I will consider evidence that already in the Bible among the chosen, there is an awareness of the problematic character of chosenness. The texts to which I will point are not many and they may exist only at the edge of the tradition. But they are there and merit close attention. I will mention five texts and then two post-text references that deserve consideration.

1. Amos 9:7.[35] The prophet Amos exposes the chosenness of Israel as a risky business. It is clear in his historical context that the political, economic leadership of northern Israel had assumed that its chosenness gave the powerful warrant for exploitative practices and policies of extraction from the vulnerable (see 8:4-6). In 3:2 Amos acknowledges the chosenness of Israel, and then asserts that chosenness becomes ground for divine judgment:

> You only have I known
> of all the families of the earth;
> therefore I will punish you for all your iniquities.

The verb "know" here functions as "choose." Only Israel is chosen! Amos acknowledges that peculiar status, or at least recognizes that his listeners assume it. His rhetorical surprise is that the "therefore" that is the threat of divine judgment arises exactly from chosenness. It is as though being chosen evokes God's special scrutiny of Israel, and that divine scrutiny will find Israel deeply at fault.

More remarkable, however, is Amos's rhetoric in 9:7:

> Are you not like the Ethiopians to me
> O people of Israel? says the LORD.
> Did I not bring Israel up from the land of Egypt,
> and the Philistines from Caphtor
> and the Arameans from Kir?

---

35. See Walter Brueggemann, "'Exodus' in the Plural (Amos 9:7)," in *Many Voices, One God: Being Faithful in a Pluralistic World; In Honor of Shirley Guthrie*, ed. Walter Brueggemann and George Stroup (Louisville: Westminster John Knox, 1998), 15–34; reprinted in Walter Brueggemann, *The Role of Old Testament Theology in Old Testament Interpretation and Other Essays*, ed. K. C. Hanson (Eugene, OR: Cascade Books, 2015), 142–62.

The initial question in this text would likely evoke a response of no from Amos's listeners. No, we are not like the Ethiopians because we are chosen. But Amos intends a yes. Yes, Israel is like the Ethiopians, thereby subverting the claim of chosenness. Amos answers the question by a second question in three parts. The first part acknowledges Israel's peculiar historical memory of the exodus from Egypt. Yes, Israel can remember and celebrate that exodus, a clear claim attached to being God's own chosen. But then there is reference to the divine deliverance of the Syrians and the Philistines alongside Israel. The three deliverances are affirmed in one question, so that only one answer is permitted. The question in the first line requires a yes, so that the answer to the whole is yes.

- Yes, God "brought up" Israel from Egypt;
- Yes, God "brought up" the Philistines from Caphtor;
- Yes, God "brought up" the Syrians from Kir.

Amos names Israel's two most immediate traditional enemies, the Philistines and the Arameans (Syrians). The language of "brought up" is reminiscent of the exodus. God has caused an exodus for the enemies of Israel just as God has caused an exodus for Israel. Israel is regarded by God just like the other peoples, just like the others in dependence upon YHWH. This terse statement thus deabsolutizes Israel's claim of exceptionalism. Or perhaps better, Amos asserts that God has many chosen peoples, including Israel's adversaries. Whereas 3:2 accents Israel's peculiar chosenness as a ground for divine judgment, in 9:7 Amos problematizes that claim of chosenness. Israel is not so distinctly and impressively chosen if the others are chosen as well.

2. Micah 4:1–5. In Isaiah 2:2–4 the prophet offers an anticipatory vision of a coming drama in Jerusalem. In the vision "all nations" and "many peoples" will come to Jerusalem to be instructed in YHWH's Torah. Jerusalem will be a place for the assemblage of many nations, so that the temple precinct will no longer be the distinct venue of Israel. There the nations will receive justice from the God of all justice, and they will learn and practice disarmament. The verses suggest that the Jerusalem temple is no longer a place for Israelite worship of an Israelite God. Now it is a place where all nations will worship the God of all nations. Isaiah here has subtly eroded Israel's peculiar claim on the temple and its status as chosen.

The same poetic unit is reiterated in Micah 4:1–3; the reiteration suggests that the poetry was well known and free-floating so that it could be utilized in a variety of ways. Remarkably, Micah adds verses 4 and 5 to the lines from Isaiah. In Micah 4:4 Micah adds a line concerning peasant existence:

> But they shall all sit under their own vines and under their own fig trees,
> and no one shall make them afraid;
> for the mouth of the LORD of hosts has spoken.

Whereas Isaiah was a city guy, Micah knew about small subsistence farmers who lived a modest life with only a vine and a fig tree. Perhaps he understands that the disarmament anticipated in verse 3 will require a lower, more modest standard of living.

It is verse 5, however, that is stunning. The poet picks up on the imagery of all nations in procession to Jerusalem to learn about peace and justice. In this verse, the poet characterizes that procession as constituted by many peoples with many different faith affirmations. He allows that each people in the procession will have its own faith commitment and be motivated by "its God," who is not the God of Israel. He insists that Israel will remain loyal to "the Lord our God." Joining the procession of peace and justice to Jerusalem does not compromise Israel's Yahwistic faith. On the other hand, however, the poet does not insist that other peoples should convert to Yahwism. That is, Yahwism has no monopoly on the pilgrimage of peace. Other peoples with other gods can join the parade of peace. Such an act of imagination completely contradicts the "only YHWH" passion of exceptionalism that wants to insist on "only YHWH" and "only Israel." Peace requires an embrace that is more expansive. Micah calls his listeners out of their tribal primitivism to a very large world of generous faith.

3. Isaiah 19:24–25. In this passage Isaiah imagines a new map of the Near East. As you know, the geopolitics of the area always situates the small state of Israel between two larger powers that threaten it, just now Egypt and Iran. Isaiah, however, imagines an alternative to that longstanding threatening history. In time to come there will be free passage between the several nations and shared worship between Assyria, the northern power, and Egypt, the southern power (v. 23).

Then, in verses 24–25 the prophet goes further and imagines God constructing a new regime of chosenness:

> On that day Israel will be the third with Egypt and Assyria, a blessing in the midst of the earth, whom the Lord of hosts has blessed, saying, "Blessed be Egypt my people, and Assyria the work of my hands, and Israel my heritage."

This divine utterance takes up three names that are regularly used for Israel as God's chosen people, "my people," "the work of my hands," and "my heritage." The recurring first-person pronoun in all three phrases shows God's intimate engagement with the peoples named. But now the text takes these three pet names for chosen Israel, and generously distributes them across the Near East to include Israel's long-standing adversaries. The outcome, quite remarkably, is that God has many chosen peoples, including Israel's erstwhile enemies. "Many chosen peoples" means that Israel, as a chosen people, has no monopoly on that claim. The God given voice here is no tribal God who is confined to the tribes of Israel. This God operates on a large scale and engages many peoples as chosen. Just as Amos has named the Syrians and Philistines as recipients of God's generous deliverance, so now Isaiah names Assyria and Egypt as chosen in a way that shatters any sense of peculiar entitlement claimed by Israel.

4. Acts 10:9–16, 28, 44–48. In the New Testament, the admission of gentiles into the fellowship of the church was the decisive shattering of old Jewish notions of chosenness. Because the gentiles constituted an excluded "other" in the community of the circumcised, this act of acceptance was not easy in the early church. The entire narrative of Acts 10–11 portrays the crisis of Peter and the movement of the early church beyond its traditional notion of chosenness, a notion protected by purity codes. This move entailed, in the apostolic decision of Acts 15, acceptance of uncircumcised gentiles as members of the church community.

The narrative in chapters 10–11 pivots on Peter's trance/vision in which he was commanded to eat reptiles and birds: "Get up, Peter, kill and eat." It was a trance, an experience beyond Peter's rationality, that functioned to break all conventional assumptions. Peter resists the command:

> By no means, Lord; for I have never eaten anything that is profane or unclean. (10:14)

Peter is a child of the old purity laws, the very laws that were designed to maintain Israel's holiness and so to assert Israel's chosenness. The purity laws were to fend off defilements that would violate holiness. But the commanding voice is insistent, speaking three imperatives and issuing the defining verdict:

> What God has made clean, you must not call profane. (v. 15)

God has defied the purity laws! In doing so the God of the trance has violated Israel's definition of chosenness. All of the old certitudes about chosenness are coming unglued. There is no distinction between pure and impure, clean and unclean. So is there no distinction any longer between chosen and unchosen?

The trance is concerned singularly with purity laws about food. But when Peter is called to report on his experience to gentiles (Cornelius and "his relatives and close friends," v. 24). Peter has already made the decisive interpretive move. He understands that his vision of snakes and birds is not about snakes and birds. His explanatory statement is in two parts. First, he summarizes what everybody knows and what everybody takes for granted:

> You yourselves know that it is unlawful for a Jew to associate with to visit a Gentile. (v. 28)

The summary is followed by the defining adversative, "but":

> But God has shown me that I should not call anyone profane or unclean. (v. 28)

"God showed me" in a trance that contradicted what I have always known; whatever the status of snakes and birds as clean or unclean, the takeaway is that gentiles are not "unclean." God has made clear that gentiles, those most unlike us, are legitimate and acceptable, so that the old borders of chosenness are powerfully overridden. The narrative is at great pains to show that Peter came to this conviction through no ordinary reasoning. Such a radical contradiction of chosenness required a "supernatural" happening that shattered his entire known, trusted world. And from this follows the entire evangelical history that undermines all patterns of exclusionary privilege. What follows is that the Jews of purity have no privileged claim on God's spirit. Inclusion of gentiles in the community means for Peter the end of Jewish exceptionalism!

What Peter knows now becomes operational:

> While Peter was still speaking, the Holy Spirit fell on all who heard the word. . . . Then Peter said, "Can anyone withhold the water for baptizing these people who have received the Holy Spirit just as we have?" So he ordered them to be baptized in the name of Christ. (vv. 44–48)

Peter declared in this sermon:

> I truly understand that God shows no partiality. (v. 34)

No partiality toward the chosen! No privilege, no entitlement! No exclusion and certainly no extractive violence. The new ordering is attended by the surge of God's spirit. It is no wonder that "circumcised believers" were astonished that the Holy Spirit would not stay safely among them, but would be poured out on gentiles. The Spirit is not domesticated by our doctrines of chosenness! Baptism and full membership cannot be withheld from those whom God has declared clean.

5. Romans 15:8–13. It remained for Paul to give formal articulation to this miracle whereby old chosenness was reshaped to admit and include the unchosen. It is not remarkable, I suppose, that Paul could welcome gentiles, given his experience of shattering (en route to Damascus) alongside that of Peter. It is remarkable, however, that, given his new awareness, he is able to find in the old traditions of Israel's exceptionalism the affirmation of welcome to the unchosen. In this passage he quotes from the Old Testament and finds in each of four quotations a claim for the gentiles in the tradition of promise.[36]

- In verse 9 he quotes Psalm 18:49:

  Therefore I will confess you among the gentiles,
  and sing praises to your name.

"Nations" becomes "gentiles" in Paul's rendering.

- In verse 10 he quotes Deuteronomy 32:43:

  Rejoice, O gentiles, with his people.

- In verse 11 he quotes Psalm 117:1:

  Praise the LORD, all you gentiles,
  and let all peoples praise him.

"Nations and gentiles" become "gentiles and peoples."

- In verse 12 he quotes Isaiah 11:1:

  The root of Jesse shall come,
  the one who rises to rule the gentiles.

---

36. Paul's quotations from the Old Testament are evidently from the Greek translation. See the helpful discussion of N. T. Wright, "The Letter to the Romans: Introduction, Commentary, and Reflections," in *The New Interpreter's Bible*, ed. Leander E. Keck (Nashville: Abingdon, 2002), 10:746–49.

In all these cases, Paul finds convincing textual support for the apostolic decision to move beyond Jewish chosenness. It turns out, in Paul's hands, that the entire Jewish Scripture has in fact made such an advocacy that tells against any narrow chosenness. In Paul's account of Scripture, there is ample room for the other who is welcomed into the midst of chosenness. It is a welcome that places in jeopardy all easy or reductionist notions of chosenness. Garry Wills provides a fitting conclusion to this consideration of New Testament texts: "All that Paul and Luke are saying is that choosing one people does not exclude others."[37]

6. Beyond the Bible itself I call attention to a remarkable statement on chosenness by Vladimir Putin. Before the Ukrainian crisis, the president of Russia must have chafed at the condescending US exceptionalism that pervades US foreign policy with its enduring sense of Manifest Destiny. In response to such a claim, tacit if not explicit, Putin undertakes the tasks of critiquing such a sense of chosenness as is embodied in much US self-presentation:

> I carefully studied his [Obama's] address to his nation on Tuesday. And I would rather disagree with a case he made on American exceptionalism, stating that the United States' policy is "what makes America different. It's what makes us exceptional." It is extremely dangerous to encourage people to see themselves as exceptional, whatever the motivation. There are big countries and small countries, rich and poor, those with long democratic traditions and those still finding their way to democracy. Their policies differ, too. We are all different, but when we ask for the Lord's blessing, we must not forget that God created us equal.[38]

Putin is surely correct, as Amos saw before him, that claims of exceptionalism are "extremely dangerous." They invite an undue sense of self-importance and self-righteousness, and a readiness to forgo restraints in acts of self-assertion that arise from God-given entitlement. Putin, moreover, is surely correct to see that all kinds of nation-states—big and small, rich and poor—have a legitimacy and a due sense of their own importance. That sense of importance in such states may be overlooked or disregarded by an entitled superpower, but it is this sense nonetheless that evokes passion and drives policies in ways that are not to be disregarded. Putin's conclusion would seem to echo the vision of Isaiah 19:24–25: there are many nations, all of which imagine, in their own frame of reference, that they are appropriate recipients of divine blessing, and so have an equal claim as God's creature. This is a quite remarkable

37. Wills, *Future of the Catholic Church*, 41.

38. Vladimir V. Putin, "A Plea for Caution from Russia," *New York Times*, September 11, 2013.

statement from the Russian president; it is, however, congruent with the prophetic tradition that intends to destabilize claims of chosenness.

7. Many of the hymns of the church are blatantly triumphalist, especially when they provide travel music for Western capitalism. The hymn "This Is My Song" was written by Lloyd Stone in 1934, in a moment of peace after World War I when the nations were engaged in peacemaking and disarmament before the resumption of hostility with World War II:[39]

> This is my song, O God of all the nations,
> a song of peace for lands afar and mine.
> This is my home, the country where my heart is;
> Here are my hopes, my dreams, my holy shrine;
> but other hearts in other lands are beating
> with hopes and dreams as true and high as mine.
>
> My country's skies are bluer than the ocean,
> and sunlight beams on cloverleaf and pine.
> But other lands have sunlight too, and clover,
> and skies are everywhere as blue a mine.
> So hear my song, O God of all the nations,
> a song of peace for their land and for mine.

The third verse was added later by Georgia Harkness, a great ecumenical teacher, to assure a specifically Christian reference to the song.

> This is my prayer, O Lord of all earth's kingdoms;
> thy kingdom come; on earth thy will be done.
> Let Christ be lifted up till all shall serve him,
> and hearts united learn to live as one.
> So hear my prayer, O God of all the nations;
> myself I give thee; let thy will be done.

It is to be noted that the first two verses are generic. The third verse by Harkness is explicitly Christian and for that reason explicitly absolutist about the rule of Christ.

The hymn begins with an affirmation of "my home, my heart, my hopes, my dreams, my holy shrine." It makes all the sounds of glad exceptionalism. But then it reaches the adversative, "but" at the end of verse 1, an adversative that echoes the "but" of Peter in Acts 10:28 that contradicts all the preceding. The God addressed is "the God of all nations." The hymn recognizes the legitimacy of the others to stand

---

39. Lloyd Stone, "This Is My Song," in *Glory to God*, 340.

alongside "me." By this rhetorical move, the absolute claims of chosenness are subverted, and room is made for others. Their chosenness alongside my own, exactly the truth uttered by Amos!

These several texts do not negate chosenness. But they do, in every case, deabsolutize it and so reject every absolutizing claim of exceptionalism.

IV

In my conclusion I wish to probe two points. First, it is evident to any attentive observer that we have arrived at a time in our society when the old exceptionalisms no longer carry conviction. Absolute chosenness is at an end, and otherness will not go away.

- The Zionist absolutist claims to the land of promise rooted in old traditions of chosenness are unsustainable. Peace will not come in the Holy Land until Israel's leaders acknowledge and act from an awareness that its claims of exceptionalism are deeply problematic. Room must be made for the "unchosen Palestinians."

- The church's claim that the Christian gospel is the only absolute truth is unsustainable, given what is known of the legitimacy of Islam and Judaism, without even speaking of the so-called Eastern religions. Tomoko Masuzawa has shown how much urbane Western scholarship has been designed to establish the superiority of Christianity and with it the superiority of Western "Christian" culture.[40] Such absolutizing of faith is unsustainable and flies in the face of the gospel itself. Such absolutizing has taken confessional statements and turned them into insistent universals.

- The peculiar chosenness of the United States with its mantras of entitlement has come to an end, a reality that makes us nervous indeed. But such anxiety does not keep it from being true. The rise of China and the finding of voice by long-silenced peoples means that the United States as the last practitioner of colonialism cannot, by its compromised moral authority or its massive and unrivaled military capacity, any longer have its unfettered way in the world.

40. Tomoko Masuzawa, *The Invention of World Religions: Or, How European Universalism Was Preserved in the Language of Pluralism* (Chicago: University of Chicago Press, 2005).

- The chosenness of whites is over. Even given the continuing energy of racism as a political-economic force, the rise of non-whites to power and leverage is underway in a process that may be slowed, but it cannot be stopped.

All of these absolutizing exceptionalisms are now fully at risk. The matter is not simply an observation of geopolitical reality, though that is not unimportant. We are now able to see, beyond that, that such absolutism is an idolatry, whether of race or class or nation or faith.   On the grand scale of policy enactment, the end of chosenness is of great importance. Closer home, however, the issues play themselves out in quotidian ways. Thus, it can hardly be doubted that the Tea Party movement, the venturesome gun lobby, or zeal for the Confederate flag constitutes a rear-guard action seeking to maintain old traditional power arrangements and economic benefits. The adherents to such movements, moreover, know at least in inchoate ways that the old order cannot be sustained, even as we, all of us I suspect, are very uneasy about what comes after the old arrangements of exceptionalism. The end of chosenness, however we articulate it, evokes huge anxiety for us all. It is an anxiety felt acutely in the church as we ponder the disappearance of leverage and advantage, as we worry about numbers and dollars, as we imagine the evaporation of our established status and position in the world. All of those exceptionalisms have lost their force among us. And rear-guard actions performed in anxiety will not change any of that.

My second conclusion is this: it is the pastoral task of the church to help and guide people to engage in and process the reality of the end of exceptionalism. That task is not easy, partly because exceptionalism, powerful as it is, is mostly unacknowledged except in the case of national posturing. We do not usually think of Christian or white as exceptional status, even though we count on it. Relinquishment of such claims is a process of allowing for the legitimacy of nonwhite, nonstraight, nonmale, non-Western, non-Christian neighbors as first-class citizens in the common good. It is exceedingly difficult for some to make this allowance, and it surely cannot be done if it is not talked about honestly and frontally. All of us who benefit from the old exceptionalisms, liberal and conservative, have assumed our chosenness without recognizing it. We recognize it only when it slips through our fingers, and that recognition evokes anxiety and anger and the need to control, dominate, and demonize.

The evangelical response to such anger, anxiety, and need to control, dominate, and demonize, of course, is that we are saved by grace. This is Paul's argument in the Letter to the Romans as he ponders how Jewish Christians and gentile Christians will live well together in the church. In our chosenness we have not much had to rely on God's grace, because we had virtue, entitlement, or cultural leverage enough to make it on our own. We chosen do not think of ourselves as chosen. But we operate so. We extract what is needed from the vulnerable in many ways, some overt.

And now such practices become increasingly unacceptable:

- In the place of *entitlement,* there is *neighborliness.*

- In the place of *exclusion*, there is *inclusion.*

- In the place of *extraction*, there is *the common good.*

- In the place *violence*, there is *justice and compassion.*

These new realities to which we are invited must have been what Jesus meant in his talk about "the kingdom of God." It is an alternative that has been entrusted to us, to ponder and to act, for talk and for walk. The work of the pastor is not easy:

- It is a tall order for Jews to yield on the absoluteness of the land.

- It is a tall order for Americans to yield on being God's best people in the world.

- It is a tall order for Christians to allow that those in other faith traditions have in hand something of the truth of God.

- It is tall order for whites to yield their sense of supremacy and entitlement.

But that is now our moment in the gospel. It is our moment in pastoral responsibility. In this moment we may be haunted by these questions:

- Are claims of chosenness intrinsic to gospel faith? Must there be some who are chosen?

- If such claims are intrinsic to the gospel, are they inherently violent in their implementation?

- If chosenness is not intrinsic to gospel faith, how should those old claims of chosenness now be articulated? How shall we sing other than in triumphalist cadences?

- Who are the other chosen peoples alongside us? Philistines and Syrians with Amos? Egyptians and Assyrians with Isaiah? Gentiles with Peter and Paul? All brothers and sisters, all neighbors?

7.

American Pharaoh's Last Race

An earlier version of this chapter was delivered at a convocation on race at Eden Seminary in St. Louis, March 29–30, 2016. The title of the Spring Convocation was "Forward from Ferguson: Prophetic & Pastoral Visions."

I was glad when Dean Krause invited me to this convocation, and I am proud to claim her as my student.[1] When she wrote me that the subject for this meeting, in the wake of Ferguson and now Charleston, was race, I knew of course that I have no special expertise about race and know only what we all know, which is more than we mostly acknowledge. So I wrote her and said that I could not deal with race but could only do texts. She answered, "Then come and do texts." So I am glad to do some texts, which I hope will be of interest and of value.

Before I begin with some texts, I want you to notice the clever title of my presentation, "American Pharaoh's Last Race." You might think this is about that great horse and his winning of the Belmont.[2] If you look closely, however, you will see that it is not about that horse, for the horse's name, "Pharoah," is spelled with an "*oa*," while the king of Egypt is spelled with an "*ao*." (It took me awhile to get that). If we remove the adjective "American," that leaves "Pharaoh," the Egyptian king who was an embodiment of rapacious greed, brutalizing exploitation, and unrestrained violence. If we add the adjective "American," that is, "American Pharaoh," we get the huge concentration of wealth and power in the US economy that is propelled by rapacious greed, maybe brutaliz-

---

1. Dr. Deborah Krause is academic dean and professor of New Testament at Eden Seminary in St. Louis.

2. With the victory at the 2015 Belmont Stakes, the Thoroughbred racehorse American Pharoah became the twelfth horse to win the American Triple Crown.

ing exploitation, and is regularly tempted to unrestrained violence in the manipulation of the political economy for the sake of the few to the disadvantage of the many. If we ask what is the last, ultimate race of American Pharaoh, we answer, it is not the Belmont; it is *white*. "White" is the last case of privilege, entitlement, and chosenness that both gives warrant to and benefits from rapacious greed, brutalizing exploitation, and unrestrained violence. My topic is "American Pharaoh's Last Race." That will be the subtext of what I have to say through this review of texts.

I

My title gives me warrant to begin with Pharaoh. We know him to be a historical memory in Israel but also a metaphor for the monopoly of land and food, the exploiter of cheap labor who in his brutality finally drove the God of emancipation to perform the exodus deliverance. But before we get to Exodus, we know the story of Joseph, who was sold into slavery, who came to the attention of Pharaoh as a dream interpreter, and who brought his desperate brothers to Egypt to get food, as well as to host his father Jacob. When his brothers arrived in Egypt, it was a happy time of celebration with the prospect of a lavish meal of welcome.

But then we are jolted with the report in Genesis 43:32:

> They served him [Joseph] by himself, and them [the brothers] by themselves, because the Egyptians could not eat with the Hebrews, for that is an abomination to the Egyptians.

The Egyptians could not eat with the Hebrews! The report here recalls the lunch counters of not long ago that "reserved the right to refuse service." It recalls for me the arrangement in the little town of Blackburn, Missouri, where whites and blacks ate from the same restaurant kitchen, but next door to each other in separate buildings, separate but equal!! And the reason Egyptians could not eat with the Hebrews is that it was an "abomination." The word rings and shatters and echoes: Abomination! *Toevah*! Say it with me: "*Toevah*." It would have been an abhorrent contamination. The term evokes all the purity laws that separate insiders from outsiders; they already had those laws in Egypt, long before the book of Leviticus. It had been decreed and accepted that food shared with Hebrews would defile Egyptians. Those purity rules had no doubt been devised by Egyptian priests who presided over such matters. The priests were in the employ of Pharaoh. They would make rules that would justify hierarchy, stratification, and exclusion. It is always Pharaoh who decrees what is pure and impure, clean and unclean. It is people at the top of the pyramid who decide such matters. It is a system designed to assert and protect rank, privilege, and entitlement, based on the most elemental response of what disgusts us. What disgusts us are Hebrews; they turn our stomach and spoil our meal.

Mary Douglas has famously concluded that the issue of impure and unclean concerns what is "out of place" or in the wrong place.[3] And of course Pharaoh is the one who determines what the proper place is. Trouble comes when those assigned to a place do not stay in their assigned place. Elsewhere they are an abomination. So Donald Trump, one voice of American Pharaoh, can declare that Mexicans are rapists, and they should stay in their assigned place, that is, in Mexico, and not jeopardize the order of the "last race" in the United States.

Richard Beck, in his study entitled *Unclean*, has catalogued the things that predictably evoke disgust.[4] He concludes that conservatives have a bigger list of disgusting items than do liberals, but the shared list would include the following:

- the oral activity of taking food
- bodily products such as feces and vomit
- animals (rats) and insects
- sexual behaviors (incest)
- contact with the dead (corpses)
- violation of the envelope of the body (deformity)
- poor hygiene
- interpersonal contamination (contact with unsavory persons)
- moral offenses[5]

All of that comes with the term "abomination." The Hebrews were carriers of all of that. And now in Genesis, they have not stayed in their place. Occasionally such contaminating persons have been able to "pass." So Joseph was able to "pass" and act like an Egyptian and serve Egyptian interests of exploitation and confiscation. But he is at best the exception.

The affront of Hebrew existence dominates Egyptian perception. For

3. Mary Douglas, *Purity and Danger: An Analysis of Concepts of Pollution and Taboo* (1966; repr., London: Routledge, 2003).

4. Richard Beck, *Unclean: Meditations on Purity, Hospitality, and Mortality* (Eugene, OR: Cascade Books, 2011).

5. Beck, *Unclean*, 143.

that reason we get two more uses of "abomination" (*toevah*) in this narrative. In Genesis 46:34 Joseph gives his brothers and father instructions on how to conduct themselves in the presence of Pharaoh. They are, says the text, "shepherds" who have brought their "flocks and herds" with them to Egypt. But he says,

> When Pharaoh calls you and says, "What is your occupation?" you shall say, "Your servants have been keepers of livestock from our youth even until now, both we and our ancestor—in order that you may settle in the land of Goshen, because all shepherds are abhorrent [*toevah*] to the Egyptians. (Gen 46:33–34)

Being a shepherd is an abomination (*toevah*) to Pharaoh. We are not told why. Maybe they are dirty and uncultured. Maybe they range over the pastureland in a way that fails to respect ownership rights. In any case, when you come to Pharaoh, lie and say you do cattle, not sheep. Cattle must rank higher on the purity quotient. The point is that *purity* pushes into *economics*. It is not simply ritual exclusion. It is economic stratification. How you make your living, how you produce, determines your acceptability.

We are not surprised when we read in Genesis that Pharaoh, via the heavy hand of Joseph, had no reservation about confiscating the money and the livestock and eventually the land of subsistence people, reducing them to slavery (Gen 47:13–25). The condition of slavery in Exodus is accomplished in Genesis by a skewed economic arrangement in which the abominable shepherds no longer have any means of production and are reduced to hopeless debt.

By the time we reach Exodus 1, it is clear that the ritually unacceptable landless Hebrews have become cheap labor for Pharaoh's enterprise of surplus accumulation. The move is from *ritual* to *economics,* and now the move is from *economics* to *violence*:

> The Egyptians became ruthless in imposing tasks on the Israelites, and made their lives bitter with hard service in mortar and bricks, and in every kind of field labor. They were ruthless in all the tasks that they imposed on them. (Exod 1:13–14)

You would not treat neighbors so violently. But these are not neighbors. They are very low-class people who have been ritually diminished and economically exploited. They have no rights, no social leverage, no production value, so that by Exodus 5, the great production manager can exclaim:

You are lazy, lazy; that is why you say, "Let us go and sacrifice to the Lord." Go now, and work; for no straw will be given you, but you shall still deliver the same number of bricks. (Exod 5:17–18)

They only want to go to "church" because they are lazy. Laziness comes with ritual contamination.

We are offered a third use of "abomination" (*toevah*):

Then Pharaoh summoned Moses and Aaron, and said, "Go, sacrifice to your God within the land." But Moses said, "It would not be right to do so; for the sacrifices that we offer to the Lord our God are offensive [*toevah*] to the Egyptians. If we offer in the sight of the Egyptians sacrifices that are offensive to them, will they not stone us?" (Exod 8:25–26; Hebrew vv. 21–22)

Moses is making an excuse about why the Hebrews must worship outside the land of Egypt. In Egypt, worship of YHWH would be an abomination. It is just an excuse. It is, however, a telling excuse. Worship of YHWH, sacrifice to YHWH, is an abomination to Egyptians. Perhaps it is offensive because it is too emotional for royal style. Perhaps they whooped instead of reasoning. Or maybe they engaged in call and response instead of pious silence. Implied of course is that it is worship of the God of emancipation that Pharaoh cannot tolerate.

So we have three uses of "abomination" (*toevah*):

- In Genesis 43:32 as food
- In Genesis 46:34 as economic occupation
- In Exodus 8:26 as worship

Food, work, and worship, the great triad of human existence. If we cluster these three uses together, we can see that what is an abomination (*toevah*) is the very existence of the Hebrew slaves. Their very existence constitutes an inconvenience, or an interruption, or an exposé and a threat to the ersatz authority of Pharaoh. Pharaoh had established the last, ultimate race. And now here were these nobodies insisting otherwise. The rule of abomination is to assure that all the right folk with the right food and the right work and the right worship are just like us. Anyone or anything to the contrary is unbearable.

The narrative exhibits the defining power of Pharaoh to reduce some to ritual contamination, economic dependence, and function as cheap labor. That privileged arrangement of Pharaoh's last race, however, is abruptly interrupted:

Let my people go. (Exod 5:1)

The Lord of the burning bush, who turns out to be the God of Abraham, has taken the slaves as "my people"; more than that, this is "my firstborn son" (Exod 4:22). The narrative refuses the social arrangements of Pharaoh by articulating an alternative arrangement that is revolutionary. In Exodus 8:22–23, YHWH asserts:

> But on that day I will set apart the land of Goshen where my people live, so that no swarms of flies shall be there, that you may know that I the LORD am in this land. Thus I will make a *distinction* between my people and your people.

There is a distinction. It is, however, a counterdistinction. The distinction made by Pharaoh's priests is *a distinction by contamination* that sets the "races" apart. Now it is *a distinction by the decree of the emancipatory God.* The excluded have become the precious insiders. The last have become first; the humbled will be exalted!

That verdict by the emancipatory God that means the termination of old sociopolitical arrangements is given social embodiment in Exodus 12:38:

> A mixed crowd also went up with them, and livestock in great numbers, both flocks and herds.

The departing company is a mixed multitude, an amorphous riff-raff without pedigree. This is the wave of the future that defies the stratification imposed by Pharaoh. This phrase is what Hardt and Negri term "the multitude," the swarm that can overwhelm empire.[6] The ones who had been excluded are on their way to wilderness abundance, led by the God of all provisions. It is no wonder that they sang as they departed:

> We are marching in the light of God.
> We are marching in the light of God.
> We are marching in the light of God.[7]

We are told in the next verse:

> They had baked unleavened cakes of the dough that they had brought out of Egypt; it was not leavened, because they were driven out of Egypt and

6. Michael Hardt and Antonio Negri, *Multitude: War and Democracy in the Age of Empire* (New York: Penguin Books, 2005).

7. *Glory to God: The Presbyterian Hymnal* (Louisville: Westminster John Knox, 2013), #853.

could not wait. Nor had they prepared any provisions for themselves. (Exod 12:39)

They could not wait! They could not bear the status of abomination one nanosecond longer. They left, not having prepared any provisions. They left and soon came to a place where loaves abound, out of reach of Pharaoh . . . OK to be Hebrews, OK to be shepherds, OK to be at worship, OK with YHWH. The narrative obliterates the force of the purity laws of Egypt. If they are barred from Pharaoh's table because they would contaminate, they are now with YHWH, who prepares a table for them in the presence of their enemies. The narrative begins with a table prepared for Pharaoh's last race; it ends otherwise, because Pharaoh's last race turned out to be stunningly penultimate, not "last."

II

The vexed multitude of Hebrew slaves, barred from Pharaoh's table, became the firstborn son of the emancipatory God. It is an act of socio-economic transubstantiation! Israel worked hard to articulate this newly given status as a holy people that would not be barred any longer from the table of well-being.

- At Sinai they were invited to become "my treasured possession out of all peoples" (Exod 19:5).

- In the testimony of Deuteronomy, it was affirmed:

> For you are a people holy to the Lord your God; the Lord your God has chosen you out of all the peoples of the earth to be his people, his treasured possession. (Deut 7:6)

Both of these promises carry with them the big "if" of obedience.

- With David the "if" of condition disappears:

> But I will not take my steadfast love from him, as I took it from Saul whom I put away from before you. Your house and your kingdom shall be made sure forever before me; your throne shall be established forever. (2 Sam 7:15–16)

- Solomon played the promise back to God:

> Therefore, O Lord, God of Israel, keep for your servant my
> father David that which you promised him, saying, "There shall
> never fail you a successor before me to sit on the throne of Israel
> ... if" ... (1 Kgs 8:25)

The "if" has reemerged, but Solomon did not linger over it. So we get a
holy people, a holy city, a holy dynasty. The vagaries of history caused
the loss of Jerusalem and the deportation of leading members of the community. The claim, however, is continually resilient, and will not be
defeated:

> They shall be my people, and I will be their God. (Jer 24:7 and numerous
> times in Jeremiah and Ezekiel)

All exilic texts! All defiant insistences and all assurances on God's lips that
the emancipated slaves, now morphed into self-assurance, will continue
to be the chosen of God.

But just to be sure of that status, the priests sorted things out by purity
code. They created an inventory of abominations (*toevah*) that could
jeopardize Israel. Indeed, Ezekiel can scold the priests for neglecting such
distinctions in a way that endangered the community:

> Its priests have done violence to my teaching and have profaned my holy
> things; they have made no distinction between the holy and the common;
> neither have they taught the difference between the unclean and the clean,
> and they have disregarded my Sabbath, so that I am profaned among them.
> (Ezek 22:26)

They neglected holiness in a way that permitted all kinds of "abhorrence" (*toevah*) concerning sexuality (Lev 18:22–29), weights and measures (Deut 25:13–16), and imitation of the nations (Deut 18:9). The
priests intended an ordered community with everyone and everything in
its proper place. Clearly they had forgotten, from their experience with
Pharaoh, that such precision in holiness and such control of all possibilities would eventuate in absolutism that would be expressed in violent
ways.

So finally, the tradition arrives at Ezra and the promulgation of Torah
that would guide and instruct this holy people that had been rescued
from Pharaoh. Ezra is dismayed at the careless indifference of Israel that
did not treasure and perform its peculiar identity in the world. It is

reported to Ezra by "the officials" that the responsible leaders have not been responsible:

> After these things had been done the officials approached me and said, "The people of Israel, the priests and the Levites have not separated themselves from the peoples of the lands with their abominations, from the Canaanites, the Hittites, the Perizzites, the Jebusites, the Ammonites, the Moabites, the Egyptians, and the Amorites. For they have taken some of their daughters as wives for themselves and for their sons. Thus the *holy seed* has mixed itself with the peoples of the lands, and in this faithlessness the officials and leaders have led the way." (Ezra 9:1–2)

These officials are anxious about the status of Israel. Their report pivots on four terms that cluster here as nowhere else in Scripture:

- The lead theme is *holy seed*, or, as Robin might say, "Holy semen, Batman." Interpreters are wont to explain away the "racial" conceit in the phrase, but there it is. Through the long interpretive process the "mixed multitude" of Moses has been transposed into a racially pure, theologically identified community that must guard its purity by not linking its holy semen to disqualified persons. The officials clearly understand that the community is a tribal community of pure blood lines and sexual relations. Of course it takes little imagination to translate this in our time to the claim of "white supremacy" that fears "racial mixing," that sees black semen into white women as mongrelization, and that is obsessed with purity.

- The second term is *separated*. It bespeaks a clear order that separates Israel from the peoples (see Num 16:9). The term in the creation narrative separates land from earth and day from night. All these uses, in different ways, bespeak a proper, reliable order. But here it is an indictment: have not separated, and so have skewed a given order.

- The third term is its counterpoint, *mixed*, to have fellowship with, to share, to commingle. The indictment is that holy seed—holy semen—has been mixed with other peoples.

- Predictably the fourth term is *abomination*; when holy seed is mixed and not separated, Israel will participate in the abominations of other peoples. This is the very thing about which Moses had warned them in Deuteronomy 7:25–26:

The images of their gods you shall burn with fire. Do not covet the silver or the gold that is on them and take it for yourself, because you could be ensnared by it; it is abhorrent [*toevah*] to the LORD your God. Do not bring an abhorrent [*toevah*] thing into your house.

In Ezra the abominations are not specified; they are generic, because Israel is not to engage in any way with other peoples. Such engagement will distort. Pure race, pure tribe, pure sect! All a product of a community anxious about its survival.

Ezra's response to the report on holy semen, separation, mixing, and abomination is passionate:

> When I heard this, I tore my garment and my mantle, and pulled hair from my head and beard, and was appalled. Then all who trembled at the words of the God of Israel, because of the faithlessness of the returned exiles, gathered around me while I sat appalled until the evening sacrifice. (Ezra 9:3)

Ezra is twice "appalled," that is, devastated and horrified, that Israel could have failed to maintain its purity. The community was in acute jeopardy. It is the same sense of jeopardy that frightened people have brought in their resistance to same-sex marriage. It is the same felt jeopardy that some have brought forever to the defense of white supremacy, and white advantage by way of white purity.

Ezra must institute reforms to protect the purity of the tribe. As you know, Ezra and Nehemiah took steps to protect by purging the community of foreigners:

> On that day they read from the book of Moses in the hearing of the people and in it was found written that no Ammonite or Moabite should enter the assembly of God, because they did not meet the Israelites with bread and water, but hired Balaam against them to curse them; yet our God turned the curse into a blessing. When the people heard the law, they separated from Israel all those of foreign descent. (Neh 13:1-3)

They found the right reference in Deuteronomy 23:3-7:

> No Ammonite or Moabite shall be admitted to the assembly of the Lord. . . . You shall never promote their welfare or their prosperity as long as you live.

In Nehemiah 13:23-27, they go even further in the purification by sending home married women "from Ashdod, Moab, and Ammon." The appeal is to Solomon who lost his way because he loved many foreign women (v. 27). Those who had married foreign women are accused of acting "treacherously" (v. 27). The account of breaking up marriages for the sake of purity values is an *essentialism* of Jewish blood over against relationships that we assume were kept in fidelity. It is certain that when *an imagined essentialism* is prized over *relationships of fidelity,* notions of purity have hardened into ideology that is removed from the actual realities of lived life. (So likewise is breaking up marriages in order to deport an "undocumented worker.") But then, anxiety has a way of propelling such illusionary essentialism. It is an easy analogue to see among us white essentialism, refusing to recognize "race" as a construct. It is an essentialism that teaches notions of ritual abomination and economic advantage that readily issues in violence, all in order to maintain an imagined essence.

Fortunately that rigorous holiness of Ezra's holy semen did not go unanswered in emerging Judaism. There is no doubt that Third Isaiah, Isaiah 56–66, voices a very different notion of the identity and destiny of Israel. Specifically, in Isaiah 56 the poet take up the exclusionary temptation that must have been urgent in his midst. This poetry is commonly dated before Ezra, but surely this alternative sentiment and conviction were in play in the time of Ezra and always in Judaism. Here the poet considers the status of foreigners and eunuchs. In turn they fear exclusion from the community:

> Do not let the foreigner joined to the LORD say,
> "The LORD will surely separate me from his people";
> and do not let the eunuch say,
> "I am just a dry tree."

First the poet responds to *the eunuchs* who fear exclusion:

> For thus says the LORD:
> To the eunuchs who keep my Sabbaths,
> who choose the things that please me
> and hold fast my covenant,
> I will give in my house and within my walls,
> a monument and a name
> better than sons and daughters;
> I will give them an everlasting name
> that shall not be cut off. (Isa 56:4–5)

They will be included in the community. They will be treasured, valued, and remembered, even though they have no children to remember them. They are required only to keep covenant and to observe Sabbath. Sabbath is the visible acknowledgment that life is not defined by commoditization. Covenant is a practice that is allied with YHWH in resistance to Pharaonic seductions. Fred Gaiser, in what now seems another era, has well argued that this text can be read as an inclusion of gays, as a challenge to the old law of Moses concerning those with "disabled genitals" (Deut 23:1).[8]

Second, the poet says the same about foreigners concerning the prohibitions of Deuteronomy 23. It is noted by Herbert Donner that this is the only clear instance in which subsequent teaching directly contradicts the teaching of Torah.[9] Imagine, old Torah tacks in a defensive posture about maintaining old community order, old discriminations, and old exclusions. And then comes new poetry that declares old teaching as false. "New occasions teach new duties; time makes ancient good uncouth."[10] It was now uncouth to keep out eunuchs and foreigners. It has become, it turns out, uncouth to keep out gays. It has become deeply uncouth to shut black people out of economic possibility. The poetry of Isaiah 56 recognized new occasion and voiced new duty:

> And the foreigners who join themselves to the LORD,
> to minister to him, to love the name of the LORD
> and to be his servants,
> all who keep Sabbath and do not profane it,
> And hold fast my covenant—
> these I will bring to my holy mountain,
> and make them joyful in my house of prayer.
> their burnt offerings and their sacrifices
> will be accepted on my altar. (vv. 6–7a)

They are welcome in the holy precincts. They are at home in the worship of Israel. It is no wonder that blacks in the United Church of Christ call the eucharistic table the "welcome table." Third Isaiah already knew that. And then the poet utters the most awesome affirmation, having God say:

> My house shall be called a house of prayer for all peoples. (v. 7b)

---

8. Frederick Gaiser, "A New Word on Homosexuality? Isaiah 56:1–8 as Case Study," *Word & World* 14 (1994): 280–93.

9. Herbert Donner, "Jesaja lvi 1–7: Ein Abrogationsfall innerhalb des Kanons—Implikationen und Konsequenzen," in *Congress Volume: Salamanca 1983*, ed. J. A. Emerton, Supplements to Vetus Testamentum 36 (Leiden: Brill, 1985), 81–95.

10. These lines are from the poem of James Russell Lowell used in the well-known hymn, "Once to Every Man and Nation." The lines were first published in the *Boston Courier* on December 11, 1845, in protest against the Mexican-American War.

All peoples! All eunuchs with their "odd" sexuality. All foreigners who lack holy semen. All are welcome. Listen to this riff on the "all" of God:

> The LORD is faithful in all his words,
> and gracious in all his deeds.
> The LORD upholds all who are falling,
> and raises up all who are bowed down.
> The eyes of all look to you,
> and you give them their food in due season.
> You open your hand,
> satisfying the desire of all living things.
> The LORD is just in all his ways,
> and kind in all his doings.
> The LORD is near to all who call on him,
> to all who call on him in truth.
> He fulfills the desire of all who fear him;
> he also hears their cry, and saves them.
> The LORD watches over all who love him. (Ps 145:10–20a)

And the poet of Isaiah 56 adds a concluding line with an eye on all Jews displaced in diaspora:

> Thus says the LORD God,
> who gathers the outcasts of Israel,
> I will gather others to them besides those already gathered. (Isa 56:8)

Three times "gather," three times inclusion! The term "outcast" concerns those "driven away," those forced out. The outsiders are made insiders. The claim is the very antithesis of Ezra, who is busy excluding, separating, and driving out those who are carriers of abomination. Ezra has given voice to an exclusivism that closely echoes the old practice of Pharaoh. The good news is that this posture did not contain all of emerging Judaism. The poet of Isaiah 56 asserts otherwise!

III

The issue of "holy seed" and abomination is alive and well in the narrative of Jesus as it is given us in Mark. The evangelist juxtaposes two remarkable texts. In Mark 7:1–23 (Matt 15:1–20), Jesus engages the Pharisees in a discussion of defilement. He argues that what "defiles" is not what goes in but what comes out. Jesus is in the line of the prophets in his argument that human speech and human conduct are what defiles, that is, what skews and distorts neighborly relations:

> For it is from within, from the human heart, that evil intentions come:
> fornication, theft, murder, adultery, avarice, envy, slander, pride, folly. All
> these evil things come from within, and they defile a person. (Mark 7:21–23)

The point is a deep challenge to conventional notions of pollution and
impurity, focusing on relationships and not on "essence." We may note,
however, that Jesus continues to be preoccupied with issues of purity
and defilement. He may disagree profoundly with the tradition of the
Pharisees; but he takes the issue seriously and is concerned with obedient
Israel that is "undefiled" as the holy people of God.

Given this continuing concern for a holy people, albeit with a very
different intent, we are scarcely prepared for the narrative that follows
in verses 24–30 concerning Jesus's engagement with the gentile (Greek)
woman of "Syrophoenician" origin. The woman takes the initiative and
comes to Jesus with an urgent need for her daughter. The daughter has
"an unclean spirit," thus keeping us linked to issues of purity and pollution. As a non-Jew she comes to him expectantly, likely having heard,
in the Marcan narrative, of his previous transformative healings for gentiles. She begs him to cast out the demon.

Jesus does not respond immediately to her request for healing but
instead remonstrates with her about her status:

> Let the children be fed first, for it is not fair to take the children's food and
> throw it to the dogs. (Mark 7:27)

The proverbial imagery to which he refers contrasts "children" with
"dogs," which, in context, concerns Jews with gentiles. We have seen
in 7:1–23 just above that Jesus continues to be concerned for the holy
people Israel. Now in this engagement with the woman, he still gives
priority to Jews. In the Marcan narrative he says, "Let the children be
fed first." The parallel in Matthew does not have "first," suggesting it is
only the children, that is, Jews who will be fed. In her crisis, the addition
of "first" allowing for a subsequent offer to gentiles helps her not at all,
because the matter is urgently immediate; she cannot wait for "all deliberate speed." In the Matthew narrative the point is made explicit:

> I was sent only to the lost sheep of the house of Israel. (Matt 15:24)

There it is, out loud! God cares for the house of Israel. Jesus's horizon is
the people of Israel. His self-perception is contained within the orbit of
Israel. He is indeed a son of the Torah; he is an heir to Ezra who is concerned about the holy people of God. He has been nurtured in a small

world of chosenness and has no reach beyond it. Such a small horizon fits with our theme. He need not notice "the others." He need not attend to the others because they are not in fact his responsibility. So it is with "the last race," the ultimate race, whether Egyptians with Pharaoh, Jews with Ezra, or whites with us. The others merit nothing and can, in terms of attitude, action, and policy, remain unnoticed.

We may judge, if we stay inside the narrative, that this encounter with the gentile woman was a formative moment in the ongoing education of Jesus as he learned more about his vocation from the woman. The woman, whom Alan Culpepper terms "witty," will not let him settle in a traditional horizon. She is not only witty; she is courageous. She is like someone who will not let a racist slur or a racist joke or a racist dismissiveness go unanswered. In fact she calls him to account by asserting that she will not accept such a provincial view of reality. It may be she is a feminist, as Elisabeth Schüssler Fiorenza has so well shown, for her insistent "But she said."[11] This is in fact an insistence on human reality, in this case her daughter's urgent need that will and must triumph over and override our conventional and convenient hedges of uncleanness.

She will not argue with his demeaning imagery of children and dogs, perhaps a bad and conventional racist joke. She lets that go and will play the role of the dog in the presence of the children. But, she insists, dogs need to eat too, even if crumbs. The bread of bounty cannot all be kept for Jewish children. Remarkably, he does not comment on her argument. He only grants her what she asks, a demon-free daughter. The narrator adds:

> So she went home, found the child lying on the bed, and the demon had gone. (Mark 7:30)

But I wonder; maybe along with the demon that left the child, maybe the demon of tribalism left Jesus. We are not told what he thought or how he reacted to her bold insistence. He had said:

> It is not fair take the children's food and throw it to the dogs. (Matt 15:26)

But she would not leave it at that. She summons him; she instructs him. She calls him out. We are like that in our tribal thinking. We do think tribal . . . our whiteness, our domination, and at best the United States of America with our religion of exceptionalism. She stands before him as

---

11. Elisabeth Schüssler Fiorenza, *But She Said: Feminist Practices of Biblical Interpretation* (Boston: Beacon Press, 1992).

an "other" who subverts his precious chosenness. She might be imagined saying to him:

> My country's skies are bluer than the ocean,
> and sunlight beams on cloverleaf and pine.
> But other lands have sunlight too and clover,
> and skies are everywhere as blue as mine.[12]

Other lands, other skies, other peoples . . . and he is educated, perhaps converted!

Culpepper notes (and I would have missed this), that Jesus in the Marcan order departs for the Decapolis, that is, gentile territory. And there, in the next chapter, he feeds four thousand. His encounter with the woman in chapter 7 is placed between the feeding of five thousand Jews in 6:31–44 and of four thousand in gentile territory in 8:1–10. Culpepper nicely notices:

> This experience may have been a turning point for Jesus' ministry. Whereas he had worked only among the Jews before this incident . . . this courageous and witty Gentile woman may have convinced Jesus that God's mercy could not be limited to the Jews only. This time the feeding takes place on the other side of the Sea of Galilee, in a Gentile area. What Jesus had done for the Jewish crowd [in chapter 6], he now did for the Gentile crowd—he gave them bread.[13]

Bread for the gentiles, crumbs for the dogs, and care for the other constitutes a crisis even for Jesus. The other is always a crisis that calls us beyond old settlements, old certitudes, and old tribal advantage.

IV

In Acts we have narrated the transformative education of Peter, the head of the apostles. What strikes us first about the narrative is that it readily utilizes language of the extraordinary. This is no common event that conforms to our explanatory categories. Thus, Cornelius, a gentile, at the outset has a "vision" in which he clearly saw an "angel of God" (Acts 10:3). Peter's experience is said to be a "trance" (10:10) that he subsequently terms a "vision" (10:17, 19). In thinking about the vision, "the Spirit said to him" (10:19). In a reprise, it is remembered that Cornelius was "directed by a holy angel" (10:22). He reports that suddenly "a man

12. Lloyd Stone, "This Is My Song," in *Glory to God*, #340 verse 2.
13. R. Alan Culpepper, *Mark*, Smyth & Helwys Bible Commentary (Macon, GA: Smyth & Helwys, 2007), 242.

in dazzling clothes stood before me" (10:30). After Peter preaches, we are told that "the gift of the Holy Spirit" was poured out on gentiles (10:45). When Peter reports on his experience, he said, "in a trance I saw a vision" (11:5). The narrative concludes with "the Spirit told me to go with them" (11:12), and "the Holy Spirit fell upon them" (11:15).

This is a remarkable cluster of terms that defy explanation: "trance, vision, angel, Spirit, man in dazzling clothes." This is no ordinary happening. When we are ordinary, we stay with our comfortable tribal selves, not noticing the others. Pharaoh in his ordinary venue thought that the Hebrews were carriers of abomination. Ezra in his ordinary venue thought gentile wives must be sent away. Jesus in ordinary venue had no gifts for gentile dogs. And Peter, in his ordinary venue, had no opening beyond purity laws . . . until he was faced with a sheet of snakes. The narrative does not admit of ordinary explanation. We can recognize, moreover, that a move beyond our tribalism never happens in the ordinary. It takes a miracle, or a jolt, or a gift, or killing (as in Charleston) to awaken us from our tribal numbness, to see and act afresh. We have, in this narrative in Acts 10–11, nothing less than the evangelical education of the head apostle.

The narrative turns on the trance/vision of Peter. In the trance, the heavens were opened enough to allow a sheet filled with snakes and birds into the room with the apostle. A voice speaks . . . you know how it is in a dream. You cannot remember the next morning who it was. This is an imperative voice addressed to Peter: "Get up, kill, and eat!" Terse insistence that Peter do what he had never done. He had never eaten a snake. It had to be a trance. That voice would never have been permitted to speak while he was "conscious."

Peter refuses. He is a child of the Torah, an heir of Ezra. He has the inventory at his fingertip:

> For you are a people holy to the LORD your God; it is you the Lord has chosen out of all the peoples on earth to be his people, his treasured possession. You shall not eat any abhorrent thing. But these are the ones that you shall not eat: the eagle, the vulture, the osprey, the buzzard, the kite, of any kind; every raven of any kind; the ostrich, the nighthawk, the sea gull, the hawk, of any kind; the little owl and the great owl, the water hen and the desert owl, the carrion vulture, and the cormorant, the stork, the heron, of any kind, the hoopoe and the bat. (Deut 4:2–18)

Long list; big holiness! Rules to maintain holiness! Guidance to preserve certitude:

> By no means, LORD, for I have never eaten anything that is profane or unclean. (Acts 10:14)

You must be well schooled to resist such a voice in a trance. But the voice is relentless. Shut up and eat!

> What God has made clean, you must not call profane. (Acts 10:15)

This happened three times, good pedagogy.

With the arrival of Cornelius, a gentile, Peter reiterates his learning that he has not yet processed:

> You yourselves know that it is unlawful for a Jew to associate with or to visit a gentile; but God has shown me that I should not call anyone profane or unclean. (Acts 10:28)

His statement is in two parts. First, what we all know and have known since Pharaoh ate alone. But second, introduced by an adversative, God showed me what does not fit, what we have all known. Nobody is profane or unclean. Nobody can be discounted. Nobody is second-class. Nobody is subject to dismissal. Nobody should be cheap labor. Nobody should suffer systems of violence. Old living is contradicted by the truth of the Spirit. The superstition of superiority is broken. The old distinction of chosenness is placed in question.

From that, Peter will preach:

> I truly understand that God shows no partiality. (Acts 10:34)

He concludes:

> All the prophets testify about him that everyone who believes in him receives forgiveness of sins through his name. (Acts 10:43)

Everybody advances to go! In the old administration of justice some—those like us—went free while the others were detained. Some—those like us—had hard drugs that were considered not as dangerous as the drugs the other used. The justice meted out by the holy people to the "lesser people" is now upset. Now . . . no partiality, pardon for all.

And then, while still speaking, the Holy Spirit made an entrance:

> The circumcised believers who had come with Peter were astounded that the gift of the Holy Spirit had been poured out even on the gentiles. (Acts 10:45)

Who knew? Who knew that the Lord of life would rest on the uncircumcised, the unchosen, the inferior? They were astonished at the indiscriminate rush of the spirit. When this text came up in the lectionary last year, I said in my sermon:

> We *liberals* would not want our daughters to marry a conservative,
> but we may be amazed that the Holy Spirit may be poured out on a *conservative*.
> You *conservatives* would not want your daughter to marry a liberal,
> but you may be amazed that the Holy Spirit may be poured out on a *liberal*.

No respecter of persons . . . of piety, of ideology, of race, no partiality!

Chapter 10 is rich and complex. But then Luke adds chapter 11 so that we are sure to get it. In this subsequent chapter, Peter goes to the circumcised believers in Jerusalem who interrogate him:

> Why did you go to the uncircumcised men and eat with them? (11:3)

He explains his reasons "step by step . . . a trance, a vision, an angel." His core dream is reiterated:

> The voice said, "Get up and eat snakes and birds!"
> I answered, "By no means."
> By no means, Lord, for nothing profane or unclean has ever entered my mouth (11:8).
> The insistent voice in the vision said:
> What God has made clean, you must not call profane. (11:9)

This chapter ends with a torrent of action by the Spirit, who respects none of our protective givens:

> The Holy Spirit fell on them just as it had on us at the beginning. . . . If then God gave them the same gift that he gave us when we believed in the Lord Jesus Christ, who was I that I could hinder God? (11:15, 17)

Who was I to hinder? Who am I to resist the spirit's will to have one humanity? Who am I to guard old entitlements when the gospel tells otherwise? Peter is insistent and uncompromising with the circumcised who had been dismissive of the uncircumcised. They are persuaded by his singular witness:

> When they heard this, they were silenced. And they praised God, saying, "Then God has given even to the gentiles the repentance that leads to life." (11:18)

What a conclusion: even to the gentiles! Even to the poor, even to blacks, even to the devalued and the unproductive!

As you know, none of this was easy in the early church. The admission of gentiles into the community is the hardest point in the New Testament. As you know, none of this is easy in the church, with the coming end of privilege, entitlement, certitude, and superiority. We have no doubt that we are in a moment when the spirit of God is making new. The spirit blows against our passion for privilege in the same way it blew against the army of Pharaoh with his last race.

V

The fifth text I consider after Pharaoh, Ezra, Jesus, and Peter, is the script being written among us. That script, since the first white colonialists, is a script largely written by American Pharaohs, the concentration of wealth and power of property owners who did not, over time, hesitate, as required, to engage in rapacious greed, brutalizing exploitation, and unrestrained violence. One might object that these three modifiers—rapacious, brutalizing, unrestrained—are too strong, and do not take into account the human counterpoint that has always run through US (white-European) history. Perhaps so. But perhaps not. Because the script narrated by American Pharaoh has always been about the "last race," about the ultimate white race.

Thus the "Founding Fathers" clearly assumed a white republic and wrote it into the Constitution. That assumption was the cause of the Civil War with an outcome, among other things, of race-baiting Confederate flags. That was the impetus for the sorry state of Reconstruction and for the more recent "New Jim Crow," wherein plantation "drivers" have morphed into police who are charged with the maintenance of unbearable justice.[14] (It is a side issue, but not unimportant that the same twisted anxiety led to the wholesale internment of Japanese Americans.) That same passion for "the last race" produced "Separate but Equal," enshrined as law with *Plessey v. Ferguson*, which has very slowly, with "all deliberate speed," been countered by *Brown v. Topeka*.

That narrative of the "last race" was legislated and sustained by its linkage to religious exceptionalism, the conviction that the United States has a God-given destiny that came to be expressed as the Manifest Destiny of the last race, with its huge military competence and its reliance on cannon fodder from those otherwise excluded from the economy. Of course

14. Michelle Alexander, *The New Jim Crow: Mass Incarceration in the Age of Colorblindness* (New York: New Press, 2012).

that narrative of "the last race" by American Pharaoh had a gentler, more inclusive side, as we sing:

O beautiful for patriot dream that sees beyond the years
thine alabaster cities gleam, undimmed by human tears!
America! America! May God thy gold refine
till all success be nobleness and every gain divine![15]

It is perhaps telling that we envision "alabaster cities," an adjective that has as its first meaning, "a dense translucent white gypsum," so that even our dreams are white. We sing, moreover, of our gold, even if refined, our gold.

The big story became for many of us whites a personal, intimate, daily story of white exceptionalism. So this still-being-written text asks, How did you come to this story? How did you come to this story of "the last race"? I came to it in Saline County, Missouri:

- I remember my teacher in our small school telling us that blacks much preferred to live in unpainted houses.

- I remember my teacher in our small school telling us that blacks were offended if you addressed them as "Mister" or "Mrs.," and much preferred to be called by their first names. I think it likely that she believed this.

- I remember that the "Black Grade School" was three hundred yards down the hill from the school in Blackburn. My dad had arranged that my brother and I would be the custodians at that school, which we did morning and evening. But it was still "the black school," with its shabby furnishings.

- As I remember it, right here in Webster Groves when my sons were young, the city council chose to close the swimming pool in the heat of summer rather than be integrated, because for whites to swim with blacks would have been an abomination.[16]

For many of us whites, of course, there was the counterstory of Jesus and his love and dignity for all. Thank God for that! That counterstory was carried by Sunday School teachers, the missionary hymns of the church, and the generous compassion of local congregations. My memory, however, is that this counternarrative was kept modest and timid,

15. Katharine Lee Bates, "O Beautiful for Spacious Skies," in *Glory to God*, #338 verse 3.

16. Swimming ranks right up with eating (see Pharaoh) among the most intimate activities where contamination is seen as the greatest risk.

safely within the confines of the stronger narrative of "the last race." Indeed, white privilege, entitlement, and advantage were so assured that the counternarrative never really impinged upon these limits. The counternarrative was confined to generous charity that has resulted in the church's good works of compassion with soup kitchens, tutoring programs, and work camps but never a question of structural power arrangements that sound, on the face of it, too dangerous. Thank God for the counterstory that also surges through the narrative of exceptionalism, that knows better, that the "last race" is the human race.

It surely may be a time when the script entrusted to the church should be performed in ways that interrupt the narrative of "the last race":

- In the face of Pharaonic abuse, there is,

    "Let my people go."

- In the face of holy semen that protects the last race, there is

    "My house shall be a house of prayer for all peoples."

- In the face of feeding the children of the chosen fist, there is

    Crumb for the dogs, introduced by the adversative, "But."

- In the face of "I have never eaten anything profane or unclean," there is,

    "What God has called clean, you must not call profane."

I have no doubt that direct action arises directly from this counternarrative, all the way from exodus departure to the admission of gentiles. But alongside action, there is the teaching function. It is an urgent time for the church to teach, to teach directly and unambiguously that the truth of our faith has in purview a very different "last race." It is time for the faithful to see what our script teaches. All the worried lament about millennials who are absent from the church opens an opportunity for honesty about our narrative that many younger folk will find compelling. It is time for inviting folk out of lazy complacency to the hard work of interpretation. It is time to sound the sounds of alternative so that the public face of the church does not consist in the fear-mongers who defend privilege and entitlement with evangelical euphemisms. It is hard, but it is time.

The course of Peter's sermon in Acts 10:34–43 is remarkable for its sequence in three parts:

- At the outset Peter asserts what we were taught in homiletics to call "the thesis sentence":

  I truly understand that God shows no partiality.

Peter does not tell his listeners how hard it was for him to learn that truth. He grew up with Jewish particularity. But in a flash he had his certitude overthrown by the interrupting voice of alternative.

- His sermon moves, second, to his favorite affirmation:

  But God raised him on the third day and allowed him to appear (10:40)

He speaks a truth that defies Pharaoh or Caesar or any ideology that aims only to protect privilege in an Easter-negating way.

- He arrives at his conclusion that all may be forgiven:

  All the prophets testify about him that everyone who believes in him receives forgiveness of sins through his name. (10:43)

The sequence is enough for us: *No partiality . . . Easter wonder . . . Forgiveness* that permits new creation and new social possibility.

Too many coercions of failed teaching serve the same purpose, to assure sameness:

- The abomination of eating with Hebrews maintains the *sameness* of Egyptian hegemony.

- The treasuring of holy semen serves the *sameness* of Jewish control.

- The entitlement of bread for the children of privilege maintains the "separate but equal" exclusion in the interest of privilege.

- The refusal to eat what we thought was unclean assures a purity system that keeps everyone *in his or her place.*

There is a fearful hunger for sameness among us. The more anxious we are, moreover, the more we hunger for sameness. Sameness for rules against odd family configurations, sameness expressed for straight folks against gays and lesbians, sameness expressed as Christian hostility against Muslims, sameness expressed as white citizenship against Mexicans who are in any case rapists, sameness expressed against blacks who now insist on medical coverage, sameness among the prosperous to keep the poor invisible and in debt, and so on and so on. Sameness permits a conviction about being chosen or "almost chosen."

But the Tower of Babel and Pentecost together show the way in which God puts the other in front of us, the other as companion and neighbor, not as threat or competitor, but as neighbor. Martha Nussbaum, in her study of ethnic tension in India, has concluded that the deep tension there is not between Hindus and Muslims. In an answer to Samuel Huntington and his thesis of "The Clash of Civilizations," Nussbaum identifies a different clash:

> The clash between the proponents of ethnoreligious homogeneity and proponents of a more inclusive and pluralistic type of citizenship is a clash between two types of people within a single society. At the same time this clash expresses tendencies that are present, at some level, within most human beings: the tendency to seek domination as a form of self-protection, versus the ability to respect others who are different, and to see in difference a nation's richness rather than a threat to its purity.[17]

It sounds familiar, does it not? Domination as a form of self-protection! But then in her final paragraph, Nussbaum draws a remarkable conclusion:

> The real "clash of civilizations" is not "out there," between admirable Westerners and Muslim zealots. It is here, within each person, as we oscillate uneasily between self-protective aggression and the ability to live in the world with others.[18]

The clash is within each person. It is a clash between "self-protective aggression and the ability to live in the world with others." It is the otherness that God has put in front of us:

- For Pharaoh, *the otherness* of Hebrew shepherds
- For Ezra, *the otherness* of foreign women
- For Jesus, *the otherness* of the Syrophoenician woman and the dogs

---

17. Martha Nussbaum, *The Clash Within: Democracy, Religious Violence, and India's Future* (Cambridge: Harvard University Press, 2007), 15.
18. Nussbaum, *Clash Within*, 337.

- For Peter, *the otherness* of gentiles who are no longer unclean

The pastoral task is to help all of us, each of us, manage that "clash within" in generative, gospel ways; that can only happen when it is talked about. Pharaoh had it wrong. The American Pharaoh has it wrong. The good news is that we may yet again depart the regime of Pharaoh, the regime of the American Pharaoh with its "last race."

> Therefore, since we are surrounded by so great a cloud of witnesses, let us lay aside every weight and the sin that clings so closely, and let us run with perseverance *the race* that is set before us, looking to Jesus the pioneer and perfecter of our faith. (Heb 12:1–2)

What a race! The writer does not refer to the Belmont!

As I write this, Pope Francis is in Ecuador. The *New York Times* says this of yesterday:

He asked for people to pray, so that Christ "can take even what might seem to us impure," scandalous, or threatening and turn it "into a miracle."[19] The last race is a miracle of the gospel and we are carriers of it!

---

19. Jim Yardley and William Neuman, "Pope Focuses on Family in Ecuador Mass for Hundreds of Thousands," *New York Times*, July 7, 2015, A6.

8.

Relinquishment and Reception

Portions of this chapter were delivered at the Festival of Homiletics on May 16, 2017, in Washington, DC.

When Jesus summoned people to discipleship, he said tersely, "Follow me" (Luke 5:27). He summoned them to receive a wholly different life that he termed, enigmatically, "the kingdom of God." The response of those he summoned is equally terse: they "left everything and followed him" (Luke 5:28). Indeed, he had said to the hesitant:

> No one who puts a hand to the plow and looks back is fit for the kingdom of God. (Luke 9:62)

The process of signing on with Jesus consists in *relinquishing* what is old and treasured and *receiving* what is promised in the goodness of God. Those whom he summoned could not have it both ways. If they did not relinquish, they would not receive. If they relinquished what was old and treasured, the newness of God embodied in Jesus of Nazareth could be received by them.

I want to think with you about the twin themes of *relinquishing and receiving* because, I propose, these two themes may provide structure and shape for the ministry to which we are now called. The two themes, relinquishment and reception, permit a multilayered, complex interpretation. I will explore some specific dimensions of that ministry and do so through

- *Seven theses* that characterize our context of ministry;
- *Two biblical texts* that offer specificity, and
- *Four case studies* before I finish.

I

Seven theses concerning the context of our ministry:

1. *We are at a fissure—a splitting apart—of historic proportion in our culture.* We are aware of some of the dramatic symptoms of radical displacement, but we might usefully reflect on the larger project. This fissure signifies nothing less than a crisis in modernity and the jeopardy of Enlightenment rationality, that is, a dispute over what we know and how we know it.

The crisis of modernity means increasing skepticism about individual autonomous reason that was championed by René Descartes, the assumption that the individual human person could reason to certitude and therefore arrive at universal truths. That crisis calls into question the certitudes of John Locke concerning the absolute sanctity of private property and the absolute claims of the nation-state. That crisis, moreover, places in doubt any scientism with its claim to arrive at absolute certitudes. All of this was adjudicated in Einstein's theory of relativity, which has been of late confirmed, the hypothesis that the character of an element of reality is relative to any other element of reality and that all are in process and in relationship to.[1] The practical consequence of such "relativity" is the undermining of every absolute authority, whether of state, church, or academy, a relativity perhaps signaled by Stephen Colbert's notion of "truthiness," a mode of knowing further abused by President Trump and the fostering of "fake news" or "alternative facts." This judgment on the old normative claims of René Descartes and John Locke are deeply felt by many who have never heard of Descartes or Locke.

2. *This fissure that jeopardizes all old absolutes and that questions all old certitudes evokes a rough and raw season of anxiety, fear, and anger.* It evokes a sense of being in free fall without any secure reference point, a sense of loss, and thus a conviction that someone has taken from us that on which we counted and to which we have long been entitled. That amorphous anxiety of free fall readily conjures equally amorphous fears that lead to conspiracy theories that hypothesize about the forces of evil that are out to destroy us. It results in anger and wanting to lash out at those who

---

1. See Steven Gimbel, *Einstein's Jewish Science: Physics at the Intersection of Politics and Religion* (Baltimore: Johns Hopkins University Press, 2012).

have taken away from us old absolutes and trusted certitudes that guaranteed entitlements.

For some, those who have long been excluded and left behind by old arrangements, the collapse of old certitudes and absolutes may yield a sense of relief and emancipation. Thus, for those who have felt the relentless pressure of white, Western domination, the failure of those forces may be welcome. That, however, is not for the most part those with whom we minister. For the most part, folks at this sort of conference minister among those who manage and benefit from those certitudes that function to guarantee entitlement and privilege. Thus, our "natural" church constituency consists in those who feel the free fall most acutely and who are for that reason candidates for anxiety, fear, and anger. The overt expression of anger tends to surface more powerfully among those who term themselves "conservatives" or "far right," those who are unencumbered by "political correctness" and who feel most acutely the loss of what is gone or fading. I suggest, however, that the depth of anxiety is as acute among self-styled "liberals" and "progressives," even if it is managed in more political or politic ways. Thus, I propose that the fissure of failed authorities and dissolved certitudes that together constitute a loss of control is a widespread reality in the culture where God has called us to ministry.

3. This fissure is experienced as a heavy-duty assault on major social institutions that have had a stake in an ordered political economy. For that reason, it is not a surprise that *this deep fissure impacts the church as it does every settled social institution,* because the church has come to have deep commitments to modernity with its habits of absolute truth claims and its own sense of settled reality.

The felt crisis of the church is surely because our dominant modes of order, management, and finance are indications of our habits of modernity with settled organizational bureaucratic charts, with clear and unambiguous procedures that determine membership as a practice of welcome and exclusion, with an ordered leadership that depends upon credentials and certification. None of that has been done in bad faith; its enactment, however, has resulted in bad faith practices that at an institutional level circumscribe the message and the messengers. And because our professional identity and livelihood depend on the maintenance of these modernist structures, the survival anxiety of the institutional church is acute, for none of these structures is sustainable in its present form when the stable qualities of modernity are everywhere morphed into the fluidity of a movement. Thus, I imagine that in this very room we can muster as much anxiety about this fissure as may be present anywhere in our society.

4. *It is the pastoral task of the church and its ministers to walk people into the fissure with honesty and to walk people out of the fissure in hope.* The fissure is real. What we sense about free fall of old absolutes and trusted certitudes is a truthful recognition. That reality, however, tempts us to two unhelpful responses.

The first unhelpful response is *denial,* the pretense that it is not so. It is denial to imagine that when we do what we have done better and with more energy, we can curb the loss. In the face of such denial, it is the pastoral task to *traffic in truth telling,* to bear faithful witness that old absolutes are not absolute and old certitudes are far from certain. The church and its ministers are equipped for such truth telling because "the God of all truth," the one who came among us full of grace and truth, is not contained within our old stabilities. It is the truth of the gospel narrative from the exodus forward that the God of all truth is not impressed by or domesticated by Pharaoh or Nebuchadnezzar or Caesar or any of our favorite modes of control. Invariably, the God of all truth operates in, with, under, beyond, and against our structures of pretense, so that the gospel community is a community of truth telling. To be sure, our historic collusion with the pretenses of certitude is long-standing. We are, however, altogether disconnected from such illusion as we have will and trust to live so.

The second unhelpful mode of response to the fissure is *despair,* to imagine that all is lost and nothing can be done, that we must capitulate to the nihilism of brutality. Our tradition knows enough about capitulation to despair. But it knows more than that. It knows about hope. It knows that hope is not a rational argument or an intellectual exercise. Hope is a bodily engagement with the facts on the ground, the astonishing concrete capacity to work newness by a word, a gesture, an act. Despair is the property of those who are passive. The way in which hope counters despair is by concrete action that performs transformational futures where none seemed possible. That is why, in our roll call of hopers, one after another moved on "by faith," in concrete ways, even though they "did not receive what was promised" (Heb 11:39).

Thus, when John asked Jesus if he was the Coming One who was hoped for, Jesus did not provide the Chalcedonian Formula. He answered specifically and concretely without large formulation in a way that all could verify:

The blind see, the lame walk, lepers are cleansed, the dead are raised, and the poor rejoice. (Luke 7:22)

And then Jesus turns back on John defiantly: "What do you think?"

My sense is that the church and its ministers are tossed about by *denial* that refuses the reality of the fissure and by *despair* that succumbs to the fissure. The church with its peculiar narrative, however, counters denial by *unflinching truth telling* and by *relentless hope* that is freighted with new historical possibility. Such truth and hope are, of course, a tall order when we reflect on how dishonest the institutional church has been and how short on hope-filled energy is much of the church. This twofold pastoral task requires that the church recover its peculiar identity of suffering solidarity and the surprise of new life, the marks of Friday and Sunday for which modernity has no receptivity or sensibility. Both liberals and conservatives have muted *the suffering solidarity of Friday* and *the surprise of Sunday new life* to come to terms with modernity. And now, in this hour, we are free to go back to our basics, a going back required by our circumstance.

5. *The church through its ministry is able to perform this defining task of calling people into the fissure in honesty and walking people out of the fissure in hope when it itself is honest about what is lost and when it is actively hopeful for what is new in the goodness of God.* The survival anxiety of the institutional church is a replica of the survival anxiety of old entitled society. It is a survival anxiety that looks backward in the church with its preoccupation with budgets, rules, procedures, programs, buildings, when the truth of our life is elsewhere. This is not for any of us an easy recognition. Nor is it a new situation in the church. Very long ago Jesus responded to the anxiety of his community:

Therefore I tell you, do not worry about your life, what you will eat or what you will drink, or about your body, what you will wear. Is not life more than food, and the body more than clothing? (Matt 6:24–25)

I do not take the challenge this poses lightly, but we may participate in that pageant of honesty and hope. To that honesty and hope, Jesus attests:

Look at the birds of the air; they neither sow nor reap nor gather into barns, and yet your heavenly Father feeds them. Are you not of more value than they? And can any of you by worrying add a single hour to the span of your life? And why do you worry about clothing? Consider the lilies of the field, how they grow; they neither toil nor spin. Yet I tell you, even Solomon in all his glory was not clothed like one of them. But if God so clothes the grass of the field which is alive today and tomorrow is thrown into the oven, will he not much more clothe you—you of little faith? Therefore do not worry, saying, "What will we eat?' Or "What will we drink?" Or "What will we wear?" For it is the gentiles who strive for all these things; and indeed your heavenly Father knows that you need all of these things. But strive first for the kingdom of God and his righteousness, and all these things will be given to you as well. (Matt 6:26–33)

Are you like me, that you find these hard words? Or are you among those who receive these words as emancipatory? This is not a counsel from Jesus to do without. It is rather an awareness that gifts are given in ways we do not expect or understand. This is an attestation that freedom for honesty and hope causes a welling up of abundance . . . risky but generous. It is a daring invitation to join a different economy away from our weary striving.

6. *The Old Testament articulation of this fissure concerns the paradigmatic narrative of the destruction of Jerusalem, the displacement of its leading inhabitants, and restoration of a new community of Torah obedience and well-being.* This sixth thesis is a reflection on how to read the Old Testament in a way that is acutely contemporary for us:

a. We may understand, in the Old Testament, the figurative power of Jerusalem as a theological, political, emotional embodiment of absolute totalism that enjoyed well-being by means of God's full commitment to its well-being:

- Jerusalem was the citadel of power under the dynasty of David.

- Jerusalem was the citadel of certitude with the temple as the media center of monopolized imagination.

- Jerusalem was the citadel of wealth with its power to tax, managed by the scribes who were good at the fine print and who enjoyed an immense surplus wealth.

The capacity of the royal-priestly-scribal leader to meld together hard political-economic power and liturgical fantasy made the city the epicenter of all reality.

b. The underside of this political-liturgical absolute was not pretty; that underside was exposed in the harsh uncompromising poetry of the prophets, who critiqued the city for its exploitation of the neighbor and for its abomination against the holiness of God.[2] Thus, Isaiah can say of Jerusalem:

> How the faithful city has become a whore!
> She that was full of justice, righteousness lodged in her—
> But now murderers! (1:21)

Thus Ezekiel can say of the city:

> This was the guilt of your sister Sodom: she and her daughters had pride, excess of food, and prosperous ease, but did not aid the poor and needy. They were haughty, and did abominable things before me. (16:49–50)

Thus Jesus can say of Jerusalem:

> As he came near and saw the city, he wept over it, saying, "If you, even you, had only recognized on this day the things that make for peace! But now they are hidden from your eyes." (Luke 19:41–42)

The undercurrent of poetic truth telling persisted. For the most part, of course, the managers of the city could drown out that poetry.

They could not, however, drown out loud reality, and so the citadel of entitlement was destroyed. The Patron of the city evoked destruction. That destruction could have been explained in geopolitical terms. But the theological types refused such an obvious analysis. They averred that the end came because the God of all truth could not finally tolerate an idolatrous absolutism. The eternal city proved unsustainable.

And so the liturgy of Israel morphed from the glad Songs of Zion to the book of Lamentations. That book is a full-throated exercise in truth telling that is the work of relinquishment:

> How lonely sits the city that once was full of people!
> How like a widow she has become.
> She that was great among the nations!
> She that was a princess among the provinces has become a vassal. (Lam 1:1)

The city wondered:

> Is it nothing to you, all you who pass by?
> Look and see if there is any sorrow like my sorrow,
> which was brought upon me,
> which the Lord inflicted on the day of his fierce anger. (1:12)

---

2. See Gerhard von Rad, *Old Testament Theology*, vol. 2, *The Theology of Israel's Prophetic Traditions* (Edinburgh: Oliver & Boyd, 1965), 188–277.

There is, to be sure, a trace of hope:

> The steadfast love of the Lord never ceases,
> His mercies never come to an end;
> They are new every morning;
> Great is your faithfulness. (3:22–23)

But finally, after five long poems, the grief ends in petition:

> Restore us to yourself, O LORD . . .
> renew our days as of old. (5:21)

And then, still not knowing:

> Unless you have utterly rejected us,
> and are angry with us beyond measure. (5:22)

Not knowing, because there is no certitude about the future when we are cast off from old realities:

> Utterly rejected?
> Angry beyond measure?

The fissure is real. And then there is a long wait. A long wait is not easy for entitled people who readily and easily count on an all-loving God. But there is a long wait.

c. Only late is the silence of honesty broken. After long enough, there is an eruption of new voices. It is utterly inexplicable that the Hebrew Bible features an explosion of poetry of hope. Who knew that in such a dismal moment there would come the poetry of hope? We know it best from Handel's *Messiah*, but it was on offer before that. Lamentations, the poetry of relinquishment, had offered a sad mantra:

- None to comfort (Lam 1:2)
- None to comfort (1:9)
- None to comfort (1:17)
- None to comfort (1:21)

And then, late in time:

> Comfort, O comfort my people, says your God.
> Speak tenderly to Jerusalem, and cry to her
> That she has served her term,
> that her penalty is paid,

That she has received from the Lord's hand
double for all her sins. (Isa 40:1–2)

The comfort uttered by Isaiah only makes sense when we have been deep into "None to comfort." The geopolitics worked. Cyrus the Persian arrived. But the poetry sees through Cyrus to the Lord of history. The poet takes us into the dialogue that is God:

One voice says, "Prepare the way."
Another says: "Cry out."
But what shall I cry, because it is all grass that withers.
But then another says: of course it is all grass that withers,
But the word stands.
And then this word, called by the poet, "gospel": *"Here is your God"*
(40:3–9).

Here is the Lord of history. Here is the everlasting king. Here is the creator of heaven and earth. Here is the God whom the Babylonians had silenced. Here he is! He is back in play. He comes mighty as a warrior, gentle as a shepherd. He comes and makes all things new. He comes on the trembling lips of a poet who breaks the silence.

Who knew that on the lips of the poet the God of newness would emerge, evoke imagination, energize faith, and empower hope? None of that without poetic lips. None of that without an arena of imagination, a poet who shattered survival anxiety with all things new!

And along with Isaiah we get Jeremiah and his new covenant with God who "will forgive sin and remember iniquity no more" (Jer 31:34). Along with Isaiah we get Ezekiel:

I myself will search for my sheep, and will seek them out. . . . I will seek the lost, and I will bring back the strayed, and I will bind up the injured, and will strengthen the weak. (Ezek 34:11, 16)

This is all poetry, all figure, all imagination, because the poets understood that the memos of Descartes and the syllogisms of Locke would breed no newness.

Thus the memory of Jerusalem is a lens through which to read our fissure:

- *As Jerusalem became an assured absolute,* so our white Western culture has become an assured absolute.

- *As Jerusalem had to be relinquished in grief,* so we are at the brink of honest grief that permits relinquishment.

- *As Jerusalem was restored* on the trembling lips of poets, so our society waits for such lips to tremble with the news of restoration.

7. *The memory of destruction, relinquishment, and restoration is reiterated in the life of Jesus and in the liturgical sensibility of the church.* In the life of Jesus:

- He went about doing good and we hoped he would redeem Israel.

- He was executed by the power of the empire that could not tolerate such a force of newness.

- He was raised to new life.

His story, in Christian rendering, is the reiteration of the story of Israel that moved from domination to relinquishment to restoration. In his life, as in the life of Israel, the restoration is not possible; but it is nonetheless indispensable for the narrative.

We recite that narrative of relinquishment and reception in the Eucharist when we boldly proclaim:

Christ has died, executed by the empire;
Christ is risen, we know not how;
Christ will come again when the future is laden with God's gifts.

The story of ancient Israel consists in walking reluctantly into the fissure, dwelling there in anguish, and walking out of the fissure in buoyant hope. The story of Jesus is the narrative of dying to what is old and receiving what is new. The story of ancient Israel and the church is a narrative of relinquishing what is old and gone and receiving what is new. It is the story of relinquishing and receiving. It is only false ideology that lets us think that *we dare not relinquish* and that *we cannot receive*. It is only the ministry of truth telling and hope telling that will interrupt the deathliness of such ideology.

II

I will now consider two biblical texts that you have as handouts. First, *Isaiah 43:14–21* is a text wherein Israel receives newness. The poem is addressed to displaced Israelites in Babylon who were caught in the web of Babylonian imperialism, who wanted to be back in Jerusalem but who had no way out of their futureless condition in exile. The poem by Isaiah breaks the silence of despair and erupts with new historical possibility. The one who speaks (in the voice of the prophet) is none other than the God of Israel. This silence-breaking speaker is twice introduced by "Thus says the LORD" (vv. 14, 15), indicating that this is more than the speech of the poet. The speaker self-identifies as the redeemer of Israel, the holy one of Israel, YHWH, our holy one, creator of Israel, your king. Three times "your": your redeemer, your holy one, your king; this makes clear that this God is totally committed to the well-being of Israel. This is reinforced by "for your sake" (v.14). The one who has been dormant and is now brought to action in this utterance will defy the power of Babylon and will push proud Babylon to lamentation.

More than that, the one who speaks is the God who enacted the exodus:

who makes a way in the sea,
a path in the mighty waters. (Isa 43:16)

These lines recall the way in which YHWH caused the chaotic waters to drown Pharaoh and his army. The power of Egypt fell exhausted, extinguished, out of business. The deportees could connect to all of that. They relished the old tradition of Exodus. They loved to retell the old, old story. They yearned for the good old days when YHWH had such visible power. They regularly retold the old story in the celebration of the Passover and imagined themselves as players in the drama of emancipation. It was like the Christmas pageant every week!

But then the poet jerks them around in verse 18:

Do not remember the former things,
nor consider the things of old. (v. 18)

Quit talking about the exodus. Quit focusing on past wonders wrought by God. It would be as though a Christian pastor were to say to the baptized, "Quit talking about Jesus and that old memory." Because focus on the past keeps you from attending to now. And then the poet pushes into the present tense and has God self-announce with new first-person verbs:

- I am about to do a new thing.
- I will make a way in the wilderness.
- I will provide rivers in the desert.

- I will give water in the wilderness.

- I will cause rivers in the desert.

And all creatures (of our God and king) will drink: the wild animals, the jackals, the ostriches, and oh yes, my chosen people as well. I will do that!

But then, right in the middle of this bold declaration, the poet puts a taunting question:

Do you not perceive it?

Do you not notice what I am about to do?

Can you not recognize my new initiative on your behalf?

The implied answer is, "No, we do not perceive it, we do not notice, we do not recognize your new maneuver."

We do not because we have settled in despair, and expect nothing. No, we do not notice, because we are looking backward to the good old days of the exodus, the good days of Jerusalem, the good old days of prosperity and security and entitlement and privilege. The question may haunt us: "Do you not perceive?" And if we do not perceive, we will not receive. Thus the exiles, mired in despair and fixed on olden times, almost missed the newness that God is doing.

The poetry of Isaiah, however, is relentless. It will insist that Israel perceive God's newness and receive God's new gifts. The later part of Isaiah is all about identifying the new gifts of God:

- *Receive the new temple* that will be a house of prayer for all peoples (56:7).

- *Receive the new fast* that is to share your bread with the hungry and bring the homeless into your houses (58:6–7).

- *Receive the news* that he is anointed to bring good news to the oppressed and those in prison (61:1–4).

- *Receive the new Jerusalem* that will be quite unlike the old city (65:17–25):

    - The new city where there is no more infant mortality

    - The new city where there is no more confiscation of property

    - The new city where children are not born to calamity

    - The new city where God answers before we call

    - The new city where they will not "hurt or destroy in all my holy mountain."

It is all new . . . beyond old tradition, beyond present despair, beyond Babylonian domination, all new, all given by the poet, all newness to move past what is old and cherished. Do you not perceive it? Or in a replay Jesus, having multiplied the loaves, says to his unnoticing disciples: "Do you not yet understand?" (Mark 8:21).

The second text that you have as a handout is *Psalm 137*. It is likely that it is to be dated a bit before Isaiah 43, but perhaps addressed to the same generation in exile as the poem of Isaiah. The scene is Babylon. The company that speaks is constituted by the leading residents of Jerusalem who had the most to lose, now deported. They are in despair as they remember all they had and have now lost. They are engaged in an act of self-pitying nostalgia. That nostalgia is reinforced, moreover, by the pressure of imperial authorities who mock them; the deportees are so helpless before the powerful authorities who are backed by such powerful imperial gods. As it is reported in their self-pity, their captors required the deportees to sing "the songs of Zion." You know:

- Like Psalm 46: God is our refuge and strength, a very present help in time of trouble.

- Like Psalm 84: How lovely are thy dwelling places, O LORD of Hosts.

The Babylonians mocked them as they sang: How is that working out for you now? They are forced to notice their helplessness and the failure of their God who had not delivered and had not been a present help in time of trouble.

They had this unbearable displacement. On the one hand, it was so hard to sing this stuff that no longer remained persuasive. On the other hand, they would not be talked out of their memory. It became for them a mark of bravery, fidelity, and resolve to stay fixed on the way it used to be in the remembered city. They were determined to remember the good old days in Jerusalem:

If I forget you, O Jerusalem. (v. 9)
If I do not remember you,
If I do not set Jerusalem as my highest joy. (v. 10)

They made the memory a test case for identity. I imagine they outdid each other in their determination to be loyal to the olden days and the olden ways.

They cherished what was gone. And they could readily identify those who had taken it away from them. They could identify the Edomites (the sons of bitches!), their cousins since Esau, who had impinged on them. The Edomites had taken away that to which God had entitled them. And they petitioned YHWH that YHWH should also remember the way in which the Edomites had sacked the city and marred the temple. They could remember the Edomites in their stealth and shameless violence, chanting as they marched, "Tear it down, tear it down." They do not want God to forget that affront to all that is holy.

And they could, by the canals of Babylon, easily identify the Babylonian armies that had assaulted the temple in ruthless irreverent ways. The Babylonians are blasphemous destroyers. In Psalm 74 we get a narrative of their violence against the things of God:

> They set up their emblems there.
> At the upper entrance they hacked the wooden trellis with axes.
> And then, with hatchets and hammers they smashed all its carved work.
> They set your sanctuary on fire;
> They desecrated the dwelling place of your name,
> bringing it to the ground.
> They said to themselves, "We will utterly subdue them";
> they burned all the meeting places of God in the land. (Ps 74:4–8)

The loss must have felt not unlike the destruction, loss, and humiliation at the end of the day on 9/11 when "your enemies" smashed our citadels. Notice: it is "your foes," "your sanctuary," "your name." The destruction is not about us, but it is an assault on you, God. Hard to believe that the terrorists would be so brazen and irreverent as to destroy the citadel of certitude that we have so cherished.

In this shrill Psalm 137 with its embarrassing final verses, we see that Israel is provoked to deep rage concerning those who have taken away what it cherished. That rage could readily turn to massive violence, so massive that it is able and ready to target little bitty babies if they are Babylonian babies. It is the rage against blacks who violate old customs. It is the rage against gays who violate holy rules. It is rage against Muslims, all of them. It is rage against immigrants who bring with them crime and rape. It is blind violence that is beyond control.

And the idea of such violence feels good; makes one "happy":

Happy will we be at the payback.
Happy will we be to kill the children.

Happy will be limitless violence against those who have taken from us what we most treasure. Those who sing this Psalm have relinquished nothing. They are transfixed by what was and remain totally committed to the way it use to be.

I propose that the juxtaposition of these two texts can provide a map for ministry in a society now in a fissure between *what is treasured and lost* and *what is promised but not yet in hand*, the harbingers of which seem frightening. Isaiah 43 is an invitation to receive newness from God, newness that outruns all our old blueprints. The poet of Isaiah 43 knows that in order to receive that newness one must relinquish what is old and treasured. Relinquish it and we are able to receive the newness. But Psalm 137 is a protest voiced by those who have relinquished nothing, who continue to insist with indignation about what is lost, who are resolved to make Jerusalem great again, even if it requires violence toward those who have caused the disruption. Those who speak in this psalm are engaged in nostalgia; they "over remember" old Jerusalem. They do not remember the city as a place of greed and exploitation and violence. They remember an illusionary Jerusalem, and they are ready to kill to have it back. Such a stance of course makes real newness an impossibility. I suggest that these two texts, taken together, are a fair reading of the issues that are alive in most congregations that I know, how to retain what we cherish, how to relinquish what is gone, how to notice new gifts that we do not want to notice. And the pastor who faces into this dangerous, demanding fissure is readily put at risk. That risk is of course acute. But the greater risk is that the people of God will be so preoccupied with what is gone that we miss the new gifts of God by our facing backward.

III

I want now to consider four dimensions of this process of relinquishing what is old and lost and receiving newness that God is giving. I will not pursue a fifth case study concerning congregational life, of relinquishing the modernist church with its programs, budgets, and buildings for the newness of a spirit-led movement of neighborliness.

So here are four zones of fissures that require our engagement:

1. *The crisis of the nation-state and a new internationalism.* I propose that the relinquishment to which we are called is the relinquishment of the absolute nation-state with its never-negotiable boundaries and its senility to pollute the eco-environment without check. Benedict Anderson has shown how nation-states are acts of imagination; he calls them

"imaginaries."[3] That is why we have such endless patriotic rhetoric and repetitions of our national anthem and the bid that our young people should die for an idea. Of course in the United States that mantra of the absolute nation-state has readily morphed into exceptionalism. Already in Cotton Mather the United States imagined itself as the new Israel of God, the new chosen people who have displaced the Canaanites and reduced the Gibeonites to be hewers of wood and drawers of water (see Josh 9:21).[4] That exceptionalism, moreover, has yielded a Manifest Destiny that has authorized a self-righteous imperialism on a global scale.

In the midst of such self-congratulatory exceptionalism, the poet says, "Do you not perceive a new thing?" The new thing that might be identified is a new internationalism in which no nation-state, not the United States, not China, not Russia, will be the essential mechanism for climate control, for arms limitation, for management of limited natural resources, and for protection against crimes against humanity. The failure to relinquish the old doctrine of exceptionalism can only yield a more predatory order and evocation of enemies so that, as James Risen has seen, the protection of the old fossil monopoly will demand a commitment to perpetual war.[5]

The biblical tradition of God's chosen people has been readily appropriated among us. But consider this anticipation of a different future by Isaiah:

> On that day there will be a highway from Egypt to Assyria, and the Assyrians will come into Egypt, and the Egyptians into Assyria, and the Egyptians will worship with the Assyrians. On that day Israel will be the third with Egypt and Assyria, a blessing in the midst of the earth, whom the Lord of hosts has blessed, saying, "Blessed be Egypt my people, and Assyria the work of my hand, and Israel my heritage." (Isa 19:23–25)

The poet anticipates a coming time as a gift of God, when there will be easy transport and communication across all the old boundaries of hostility and self-protection, a highway through chosen Israel between the superpower of the north and the superpower of the south. Beyond that the poet anticipates a time when God will give a new blessing to the nations, designating Egypt as "my people," Assyria as "the work of my hands," and Israel as "my heritage." In coming time Israel will be ranked

3. Benedict Anderson, *Imagined Communities: Reflections on the Origin and Spread of Nationalism*, rev. ed. (London: Verso, 2006).

4. See Sacvan Bercovitch, *The Puritan Origins of the American Self* (New Haven: Yale University Press, 2011).

5. James Risen, *Pay Any Price: Greed, Power, and Endless War* (Boston: Houghton, Mifflin, Harcourt, 2014).

alongside Egypt and Assyria. All will be called by God's pet names, because all of them will be God's chosen peoples. The truth, says the poet, is that God has many chosen peoples, a claim that of course counters exceptionalism. The military culture of the United States makes talk about such relinquishment profoundly hazardous. That, however, does not keep it from being the truth of our faith. As nation-states are "imaginaries," so the newness of God invites to alternative imaginaries.

2. *A second zone of the fissure is racism.* The new surge of white nationalism reinforces advantage, privilege, and entitlement for whites.[6] We are only now becoming aware of how deeply white superiority is written into the fabric of our society, not least into the Constitution, a bargain that has assured that political and economic power would remain in white hands in perpetuity. The coding of this entitlement has been so comprehensive that we whites have scarcely noticed. That coding, moreover, is continuous with the old purity codes of Israel's ancient Torah, which were designed to banish and excommunicate, if necessary by violence, all those who did not qualify tribally. Thus, our society has had its purity codes: "Separate but equal," "We reserve the right to refuse service," "No blacks need apply," no women can be ordained, no gays can be allowed, no immigrants are admitted, no Muslims allowed, a process whereby white privileges are extended and others are disenfranchised because they are not like us. So says Moses:

> No one whose testicles are crushed or whose penis is cut off shall be admitted to the assembly of the Lord. Those born of an illicit union shall not be admitted to the assembly of the Lord. . . . No Ammonite or Moabite shall be admitted to the assembly of the Lord. (Deut 23:1–3)

What a shock it must have been to Ananias when Jesus appeared to him and sent him to Saul:

> Go, for he is an instrument whom I have chosen to bring my name before gentiles and kings and before the people of Israel. (Acts 9:14)

What a shock it was to Peter when the voice in his trance twice said to him:

> Get up, Peter; rise and eat. (Acts 10:13)

Peter refused because he knew the old codes:

6. See Carol Anderson, *White Rage: The Unspoken Truth of Our Racial Divide* (New York: Bloomsbury, 2016); and Edward E. Baptist, *The Half Has Never Been Told: Slavery and the Making of American Capitalism* (New York: Basic Books, 2014).

> By no means, Lord; for I have never eaten anything that is profane or unclean. (v. 14)

But the voice persisted:

> What God has made clean, you must not call profane. This happened three times. (v. 15)

And Peter finally deduced the right conclusion:

> I truly understand that God shows no partiality; but in every nation anyone who fears him and does what is right is acceptable to him. (vv. 34–35)

What a shock it must have been to the earliest Jesus movement to reject purity codes, to refuse tribal identity, and to welcome gentiles into the beloved community.

Failure to relinquish the old tribal codes of entitlement precludes us from seeing the new gifts God is giving, namely, a multiculturalism in which the way of God is ordained in every race, tongue, tribe, and nation. The gospel embrace of gentiles, that is, those outside the tribe, is already underway in the poetry of Isaiah:

> My house shall be a house of prayer for all peoples. (56:7)

And Paul had seen that the promise to the nations via Abraham is already "the gospel beforehand" (Gal 3:8). The fissure between old tribalism and a new multicultural community is a danger zone where the truth of God is at work.

3. *The old memory of unlimited, endless economic growth is a powerful force among us even though it is an impossible, unsustainable fantasy.* That economic growth assumed that the next generation in the United States would be better off than the last, a growth that depended on unlimited natural resources, cheap labor, and on the freedom of the strong to prey upon the vulnerable. That ideology of endless economic growth, fostered by advertising that generated false desires and endless consumerism is taken by the broad middle population as a God-given right.[7]

It matters little in that ideology of deregulation that the public good is

---

7. Ruchir Sharma calls this "nostalgia for a bygone era":

It will be difficult to persuade people to accept the reality of slower growth. . . . The coming era is likely to bring more such experimentation and diversion, but the new math of slower growth will remain. ("Why Trump Can't Make It 1981 Again," *New York Times*, January 15, 2017, SR4.

neglected through a passion for privatization, thus a path toward legitimated inequality and injustice.

That of course is an unsustainable dream. The well-known poetry of
Isaiah anticipates a time to come when all nations will stream to Torah
and disarmament, beating swords into plowshares and spears into pruning hooks. That same oracle, however, is reiterated in the poetry of
Micah, a rural peasant. Micah is grounded in an agricultural economy
unlike the urban Isaiah. To the oracle of Isaiah Micah adds a verse that
might have been written by Wendell Berry:

> They shall all sit under their own vines and under their own fig trees,
> and none shall make them afraid. (Mic 4:4)

Micah understood that disarmament and peace require an important
economic adjustment. It is for sure that our vast military apparatus exists
in order to sustain an unsustainable standard of living that depends upon
the resources of others. But a "vine and fig tree" constitute modest peasant food produced by a modest rural economy. Micah understood that
disarmament and peace will not be possible until the deathly cycle of
consumer self-indulgence is broken. "Vine and fig tree" provide no
meat, no sugar, no self-indulgence, no endless satiation, but the prospect
of an alternative life in which neighbors are not greedy for each other's
produce, goods, or property. As a result, "no one shall make them afraid."
Micah proposes nothing less than the reorientation of the economy away
from consumer desire.

The fissure between *self-indulgent satiation* and *a sustainable modest
standard of living* is an acute issue for all of us. As long as we take endless
growth as a God-given right to consume the world's resources (including fossil fuels), there cannot be and will not be peace or disarmament.
Micah's footnote to Isaiah is a quite remarkable statement of realism that
calls the bluff on life lived as though resources were endless and all that is
required is the possessor to have what we crave.

4. *A further dimension of the fissure concerns exclusionary religious passion
and religious idolatry.* The old world in which many of us still live is
Christendom, the cultural assumption that Christian truth is cosmic, that
Euro-Western geopolitical authority is superior, and that the mission is
to extend the reach of Western Christian domination. The most pernicious expression of this assumption is the "Doctrine of Discovery," the
papal edict of 1493 in which the Vatican gave the European colonial
powers, especially Spain and Portugal, the right to the land, resources,

and populations of the New World.[8] But of course Christendom is more immediate than that, sustained by our triumphal hymns coded as missionary zeal and engaged in entitlements and privilege cast as national or tribal or cultural superiority. The theological hinge of all of that cultural apparatus is the claim, "No one comes to the Father except through me," a terse declaration that has empowered the church and enhanced cultural superiority and political economic aggressiveness (John 14:6).

But of course the exclusionary claims of Christendom are no longer sustainable, because God is birthing *a new ecumenism* in which our most treasured confessional claims have to be reformulated in the presence of others. The obvious test of this emerging reality is that we regularly find more authentic solidarity with confessors of other faiths than we often do among those who confess Christ. That new ecumenism does not call us to abandon our confession; it does, however, require that we state our confession in ways that make room for the credibility of other confessions alongside our own.

I return once more to the poem of Micah 4. The oracle shared with Isaiah 2:2–4 concludes with a summons to the nations that will stream, in a mighty "procession, to Torah and disarmament and peace. But Micah's addition in verse 5 is one of the most stunning verses in all of Scripture:

> For all peoples walk, each in the name of its god,
> but we will walk in the name of the LORD our God forever and ever. (Mic 4:5)

This verse characterizes the procession of the nations on the way to peace, disarmament, and justice. It asserts that these many peoples, on the road together, will walk together, each in the name of its own God. Micah proposes that the procession of peace and justice is so important that it does not linger over confessional differences. On the road together with the Israelites are Canaanites who worship Baal, Babylonians who serve Nebo, Philistines who serve Dagon, and so on. There is no lingering theological argument because the purpose of the parade trumps such distinctions.

The final line of the verse is insistent upon Yahwism:

> We will walk in the name of YHWH our God forever and ever.

---

8. See Steven T. Newcomb, *Pagans in the Promised Land: Decoding the Doctrine of Christian Discovery* (Golden, CO: Fulcrum, 2008); and Lindsay G. Robertson, *Conquest by Law: How the Discovery of America Dispossessed Indigenous Peoples of Their Lands* (Oxford: Oxford University Press, 2005).

We will not abandon YHWH. We will not cease to confess Christ. But we will not be exclusionary. We will find allies among others who worship other gods. The move beyond the exclusionary confessionalism of Christendom allows room for the legitimacy of other confessions. It also begins the slow process of relinquishing the superiority of Christendom that is all wrapped up with racism, precisely because "God shows no partiality."

IV

This strikes me as a huge, dangerous, demanding pastoral agenda of relinquishment and reception:

1. Relinquishment of *exceptionalism* to receive *a new internationalism*

2. Relinquishment of *white domination* to receive *multiculturalism*

3. Relinquishment of *expectations of endless economic growth* to receive *a sustainable standard of living in a context of neighborliness*

4. Relinquishment of *Christendom* to receive a *new ecumenism*

This is not a liberal or progressive agenda. This is, rather, a map of what is happening before our very eyes in the overthrow of an old world premised on privileged violence. The forces that refuse relinquishment (that we ourselves know very well) are very strong and determined, but that is a rear-guard action that will fail. Because God is doing a new thing.

My judgment is that, while we may find allies where we can, the work falls primarily to the pastoral office, because there is no other calling that is situated exactly in this moment of fissure. We have considered that moment in ancient Israel between the determined nostalgia of Psalm 137 and the invitation of Isaiah 43 to a new thing. And now that same conflictual reality is, I propose, operative among us.

I fully understand how very difficult pastoral ministry is now, most particularly in the face of survival anxiety. I do not, moreover, urge kamikaze missions by pastors. I say these things to you because I believe they belong to our pastoral call, because I believe that when we find ways to take up these hard issues in local contexts, we find ourselves emancipated and energized with good courage; we will have come down where we ought to be. I believe, moreover, that we are in a near-Barmen situation and we must be on the alert that we do not become chaplains for the old world. There is no future in such a vocation. It is the truth among us, as it was in Isaiah and as it was Easter day that God is doing a new thing. I have delineated what I think are some marks of that new thing to which attention must be paid:

- a new internationalism
- a new multiculturalism
- a new, lowered standard of living
- a new ecumenism

We are the witnesses. We have perceived it and need use no more energy nursing the comfort of nostalgia.

PART III

Creation and Climate

9.

An Inconvenient "Therefore"

I

The economy of ancient Israel, a small economy, was controlled and administered by the sociopolitical elites in the capital cities of Samaria in the north and Jerusalem in the south. Those elites clustered around the king and included the priests, the scribes, the tax collectors, and no doubt other powerful people. Those urban elites extracted wealth from the small at-risk peasant farmers who at best lived a precarious subsistence life. The process of extraction included taxation and high interest rates on loans. These were financial arrangements that drove many of the peasants into hopeless debt so that they were rendered helpless in the economy. While that arrangement was exploitative, it no doubt appeared, at least from an urban perspective, to be normal, because the surplus wealth and the high standard of living it made possible seemed natural and guaranteed. The powerful people who operated the economy could assume surplus wealth, and the exploited peasants were impotent in the face of that power. The arrangement appeared to be safe in perpetuity.

II

Except that a strange thing happened in ancient Israel in the eighth century BCE (750–700 BCE). There appeared in Israel, inexplicably, a series of unconnected, uncredentialed poets who by their imaginative utterance disrupted that seemingly secure economic arrangement. We characteristically enumerate in that period of Israelite history four prophets—Amos, Hosea, Isaiah, and Micah. They came from various backgrounds, but they shared a common passion and a stylized mode of evocative speech. The "normative" economy of the period had assumed that the economy consisted in only two participants, the *productive peasants* and the *urban elites* who did not work or produce anything but who lived well off of peasant produce. Those uncredentialed poets, however, dared to imagine and to utter that there was, inescapably, a *third participant* in the political economy, namely, *the emancipatory God of the exodus*. In effect, these poets spoke God into the political-economic process, and the presence of that remembered, spoken God of course changed the economic calculus for all parties. These poets invited (required!) the urban elites to reimagine and reconfigure the economy so that they had to answer to the God of covenant, whereas they assumed, prior to the prophets, that they were autonomous economic players who could do what they wanted without restraint.

Specifically, the prophets, with rich variation, spoke "speeches of judgment" whereby YHWH, the God of exodus and covenant, uttered an *indictment* for the ways in which the urban elites had violated God's intention for society. That indictment, moreover, was regularly matched to a *judicial sentence* that anticipated trouble for those who were not restrained by God's commandments. These indictments regularly concerned *injustice* that violated the well-being of vulnerable neighbors or *profanation* that violated God's sovereign intention. The poets, in their daring imagination, were able to assert with rich variation, that violations of human *justice* or violations of divine *holiness* would inescapably be followed by sorry consequences enacted against the offending elites.

III

Here I will consider the imaginative utterance of one of these prophets, Hosea, the only northern prophet of the period, who appeared sometime in the latter part of the eighth century. Hosea is best known for his narrative report that God commanded him to "go love an adulteress" (3:1). This command means that Hosea was compelled by God to step outside the approved conduct of society and to embrace a Torah-violator who could well have been executed for her conduct. That divine command, which Hosea obeyed, caused him to experience, exhibit, and give voice to the pathos (suffering love) in his own life that he then discerned as well in the life of God. He came to understand by his humiliating social experience that life consists not in stern rule keeping but in the exercise of mercy and compassion that move well beyond rules. Among Hosea's utterances of this new awareness that moves beyond quid-pro-quo formal relations are these three poetic utterances:

> For I desire *steadfast love* and not sacrifice,
> the *knowledge of God* rather than burnt offerings. (Hos 6:6)

> Sow for yourselves *righteousness;*
> reap *steadfast love;*
> break up your fallow ground,
> for it is time to seek the Lord,
> that he may come and rain *righteousness* upon you. (10:12)

> But as for you, return to your God,
> hold fast to *love* and *justice,*
> and wait continually for your God. (12:6)

These brief utterances provide a cluster of relational terms that are definitional for Hosea and for covenantal relationships in a society ordered by YHWH. Thus, in 6:6 we have "steadfast love" and "knowledge of God"; in 10:12 it is "righteousness" and "steadfast love"; and in 12:6 "steadfast love and justice." (See also Hos 2:19–20.) This cluster of terms altogether specifies covenantal loyalty that will sustain durable relationships of well-being in every circumstance. The recurring term in all three cases is "steadfast love"; commitment to other covenant partners overrides all other considerations. Hosea understood both that YHWH will practice such durable love and that Israelites are summoned to such durable love of neighbor.

IV

In 4:1-3, Hosea conjured in his poetic imagination, against assumed social reality conducted on a "business model," that YHWH had filed a legal suit against Israel for violating the requirement of steadfast love. Notice that everything depends upon his utterance. Without his poetic courage, the business model of acquisitive economics would seem normal and would not be interrupted or critiqued. But now he has spoken, and the political economy can no longer proceed as before in numbed innocence.

The indictment of this poetic utterance begins with a generic charge:

There is no *faithfulness or loyalty,*
and no *knowledge of God* in the land. (4:1)

Hosea uses the same terms as in 6:6. These terms specify that Israel has
not taken neighborly solidarity seriously but has permitted the exploitative acquisition of wealth to override relational reality. They have treated
the economy as though it were autonomous and without reference to
neighborly reality. The more specific charge against Israel is voiced in
verse 2:

Swearing, lying, and murder,
and stealing and adultery break out;
bloodshed follows bloodshed. (4:2)

This terse catalogue, in very strong verbal form, is clearly an allusion
to the Ten Commandments given at Sinai (Exod 20:1–17). That list of
commands voices in Israel the most elemental nonnegotiable requirements of life with YHWH. The commandments, in Exodus, offer a clear
alternative to the erstwhile exploitative economy of Pharaoh, on which
see Exodus 5:4–19. The commandments insist that God's holiness must
not be reduced to a commodity (Exod 20:1–7) and that neighborly relationships must not be violated in exploitative ways (vv. 8–17). And now,
says Hosea, Israel in its political economy has systematically violated the
commandments. The violation includes exploitation of many kinds:

- *Swearing* (Cursing): invoking divinely caused misfortune on
  others

- *Lying*: false witness in court

- *Murder*: treating human life as expendable

- *Stealing*: sharp economic practice, perhaps wage theft

- *Adultery*: reducing human relations to commodity transactions

This unmistakable reference to Sinai bespeaks an economic practice
whereby human neighbors are regarded as dispensable commodities that
may be readily exploited in the interest of profit and surplus. The intent
of this "speech of judgment" is that such practice is unsustainable and is
sure to evoke a harsh divine response.

V

The next word in the poem, *therefore*, is a rhetorical wonder that recurs often in prophetic utterance. It is a term that connects the *indictment* with the *judicial sentence* to follow. It is as though the poet traces inescapable outcomes and consequences of such violations. Hosea insists that this sorry exploitative urban regime cannot operate with impunity, even if it imagines that it can. There is no such prospect, because in prophetic imagination God presides over the economic enterprise and will not permit such exploitation to go unrequited. This "therefore" is an act of emotive imagination. It does not offer reasons or explanations or trace connections between the indictment and the sentence. Rather, it gives expression to the unrelieved abhorrence of Hosea (and of God) that someone in Israel could treat others in Israel this way.

The judicial sentence that follows the "therefore" is astonishing. The poet names the usual triad of creation: "wild animals, birds, and fish." That is, the creatures *on the earth*, *above the earth,* and the creatures in the waters *around the earth*. Said otherwise, the sentence voices an anticipation for "all who live in it." All creatures of our God and king! All of them are "perishing"; they are disappearing. The reason they are disappearing is because of drought; the phrase "the land mourns" is an idiom for drought. The earth shrivels and dries up and can no longer sustain creaturely life. But "drought" is only a hint of *the total ending of creation:*

> But the description really outruns the limits of a drought or any other empirical situation; it portrays a loss of vitality by land and population that affects every creature, even the fish. The catastrophe is not merely a drought, though partially pictured by drought-vocabulary, but a terrible diminution of life forces which tends to total absence of life.[1]

The poetic, rhetorical sequence of *indictment* and *judicial sentence* linked by "therefore" concerns the socioeconomic violation of neighborliness and the wounding of creation through an acute environmental crisis. The "therefore" is not an exact formulation, for such analysis was not available to the prophet. Nor is it a magical form of supernaturalism, for it is to be noted that no agency of God is mentioned in the sentence of verse 3. It is rather an emotive articulation of abhorrence that assumes and affirms that creation in all it parts is deeply connected to the rule of YHWH, so that the economic violation leads to the environmental dis-

1. James Luther Mays, *Hosea: A Commentary*, Old Testament Library (Philadelphia: Westminster, 1969), 65.

aster. The emotive quality of the words, I judge, aims to appeal to the emotive sensibility of the listening community and so to penetrate the cynical numbness of those who wished the economy were autonomous but who in deep ways know better. Who would have known that violation of the Decalogue would lead to the failure of creation? Well, Hosea would know that! The "therefore" is an ominous recognition that human choices determine future prospects. The human choices, so Hosea attests, have not been good; for that reason the future of creation cannot be good either.

VI

We now hear this poetic utterance at a great chronological, cultural distance. We read it in a public context that evokes a dispute about "protecting the environment" and "maintaining a growth economy." We read it in the context of a scientific dispute about global warming, though the scientific evidence for global warming is not much disputed any more. It is the case that our scientific knowledge fills in the prophetic "therefore" to show that economic exploitation in the interest of growth, surplus, and a higher standard of living by fracking, cutting down rainforests, and increasing fossil fuels for the urban elite and those who replicate the urban elite cannot be separated from the environmental reality.

The final word of the poem, *perishing*, may ring in our ears. We watch the environmental crisis as the Arctic ice melts, as the butterflies disappear due to chemical poisoning of their sources of food, as drought crowds out arable land, as old modes of extravagant living becomes less and less sustainable, as elephant herds are decimated as their tusks become tradable commodities. Not all of this is new; what is new is the scale of exploitation required by a new scale of predatory greed. A high standard of living based on extraction insists that all else (including cheap labor) must be regarded as dispensable commodity. Without such scientific data, Hosea already judged such community-destroying greed to be unsustainable.

We may now ponder the poetic "therefore." We may do so with a grain of salt about "supernatural" agency. We do not believe that God would swoop in and punish. Nor did Hosea! But Hosea did believe that there is a mysterious presence of holiness that sets limits on human choices that violate God's purposes only a great cost. It may be inevitable that we try to adjudicate and negotiate the environmental crisis in a "reasonable fashion" according to our best scientific and economic knowledge. All that may be to the good. But this great issue needs to be framed as a recognition of this *holy mystery* that makes both human freedom and its offspring of acquisitive greed quite penultimate. In light of that inscrutable limit that cannot be disregarded, we are no longer permitted to imagine an acquisitive economy as chooseable, as though there were no long term payback, as though there were no "therefore." Hosea understood that cynical exploitation of the neighborhood cannot finally outflank the divine "therefore."

10.

Accommodation vs. Collusion

An earlier version of this chapter was first presented at the Perkins School of Theology of Southern Methodist University on August 16, 2016.

The urgent necessity for self-care for pastors is well known among us. The matter is urgent because the task entrusted to the pastor now is one of remarkable demand in a society where pastoral authority has greatly eroded, in which expectations of pastors are enormous and complex, and in which the vexing institutional crisis of the church over which the pastor presides is obvious for all to see. The maintenance of pastoral health is urgent as well, in my judgment, because so much of the well-being of our society depends, I have no doubt, on the faithful performance of the pastoral tasks that are possible only when pastors are healthy. I have no special word to speak concerning the usual issues of such self-care. I will therefore consider pastoral health from a somewhat different and perhaps unusual angle.

I

We—pastors but all of us as well—are made in the image of God.[1] We are destined for freedom, responsibility, and truthfulness. We are designated as God's partners in the maintenance and care of creation.[2] That identification "in the image of God" is rooted in the creation narrative.

---

1. See Richard J. Middleton, *The Liberating Image: The Imago Dei in Genesis 1* (Grand Rapids: Brazos Press, 2005).
2. See Terence E. Fretheim, *God and World in the Old Testament: A Relational Theology of Creation* (Nashville: Abingdon, 2005).

But it is given specificity in the church's witness to Jesus as the image of God. Three texts may be cited that invite our attention to the theme of the "image of God." In his thick complex testimony to the resurrection of Jesus, Paul can speak of the "first man" Adam as a living being and "last Adam" as a "life-giving spirit" (1 Cor 15:45).[3] From that he draws the conclusion:

> Just as we have borne the image of the man of dust, we will also bear the image of the man of heaven. (1 Cor 15:49)

The verb rendered in the future, "will bear," can be translated as a jussive, "Let us bear," suggesting that the bearing of the image of Christ is an active decision that we can embrace; we can decide to bear the image of "the man of heaven," that is, the risen Christ. The bearers of that image are invited to a durable resolve:

> Therefore, my beloved, be steadfast, immovable, always excelling in the work of the Lord because you know that in the Lord your labor is not in vain. (1 Cor 15:58)

The defeat of death has created space and opportunity for the exhibit of the image, performed as "the work of the Lord." Easter makes the performance possible and sustainable.

In 2 Corinthians 3:12–18, in his complex argument about the "veil" of our minds being removed so that we can see and know and interpret faithfully, Paul concludes:

> Now the Lord is the Spirit, and where the Spirit of the Lord is, there is freedom. (v. 17)

That freedom leads to the good news that we may be transformed in the same image:

> And all of us, with unveiled faces, seeing the glory of the Lord as though reflected in a mirror, are being transformed into the same image, from one degree of glory to another, for this comes from the Lord, the Spirit. (v. 18)

The new covenant, in the newness of the Spirit, invites us to the exercise of gospel freedom.

---

3. Michael Fishbane offers a Jewish counterpoint to the Pauline contrast in his discussion of the "Adamic self" and the "Mosaic self" (*Sacred Attunement: A Jewish Theology* [Chicago: University of Chicago Press, 2008], 119–24).

In Colossians 3:5–11, which is likely an instruction pertaining to baptism, Paul traces the move from the old self to the new self:[4]

> Seeing that you have stripped off the old self with its practices and have clothed yourselves with the new self, which is being renewed in knowledge according to the image of the creator. (vv. 9–10)

And in that transformative renewal, all old barriers of distinction are overcome:

> In that renewal there is no longer Greek and Jew, circumcised and uncircumcised, barbarian, Scythian, slave, and free; but Christ is all and in all. (v. 11)

In the verses that follow, the new life according to the image of the creator is marked by the signs of holiness:

> As God's chosen ones holy and beloved, clothe yourselves with compassion, kindness, humility, meekness, and patience. Bear with one another and, if anyone has complaint against another, forgive each other, just as the Lord has forgiven you, so you also must forgive. Above all, clothe yourselves with love, which binds everything together in perfect harmony. And let the peace of Christ dwell in your hearts, to which indeed you were called in the one body. And be thankful. (vv. 12–15)

It strikes me that this pastoral guidance is voiced as an imperative: "clothe, forgive!" These are choices that are to be made; that, of course, suggests that one could choose otherwise, not to be clothed in the new self, not to love, not to forgive, not to be thankful. The positive imperatives constitute a tall order. But the writer does not doubt that it is a proper order for the baptized community. Nor does the writer doubt that the community wants to make those choices. The urgency of forgiveness is voiced twice and culminates in love that leads to peace and thanks. The message ends in gratitude expressed in psalms, hymns, and spiritual songs:

> Let the word of Christ dwell in you richly; teach and admonish one another in all wisdom; and with gratitude in your hearts sing psalms, hymns, and spiritual songs to God. And whatever you do, in word or deed, do everything in the name of the Lord Jesus, giving thanks to God the Father through him. (vv. 16–17)

---

4. See Philip Carrington, *The Primitive Christian Catechism: A Study in the Epistles* (Cambridge: Cambridge University Press, 1940).

These three texts, among others, mark those who are "in Christ" who are summoned, empowered, and authorized to a very different life of freedom and energy that is rooted in the gospel and sustained by sacrament and liturgies of thanks, that is to say, by Eucharist. I am aware of course that this characterization of the new self in the wake of Easter pertains to all who embrace Christ. But my interest just now is the way in which this identity of the "image of God" pertains particularly to pastors, both to the lives we live and to our call to act out that image in engagement with other members of the body. Pastors in the image of God are called to freedom, honesty, generosity, forgiveness, love, peace, and thanks. And those with whom we minister fully expect that our lives will overflow with those Easter gestures, either because the act of ordination by way of an inscrutable transubstantiation has made us different (ordination as "order"), or simply because we are paid to be that way (ordination as "office.") And we should earn our keep!

II

I suggest that the health of a pastor—spiritual, emotional, physical—depends on the full glad embrace of an identity in "the image of God," an identity of freedom, grace, generosity, and truthfulness—as in "grace and truth." The embrace and maintenance of that identity of course require attentiveness, intentionality, and discipline. In every way, moreover, the embrace and maintenance of the "image of God" for a pastor, as for everyone else, entail a durable imperative and an endless challenge. For the pastor, the imperative and challenge are acute because the pastor must live her life in public where the imperative and challenge are always on exhibit. It is not in substance a different challenge from that faced by our parishioners, but my subject here is the health of a pastor.

The embrace and maintenance of an identity "in God's image" are a demanding challenge among us because we live in a socioeconomic totalism that is elementally hostile to the "image of God."[5] By "totalism" I mean a system of signs and symbols that make a claim of validity that is all-encompassing, that will allow no challenge or competition, and that will not countenance an act of imagination outside the control of that system of signs and symbols. Such a totalism characteristically has a monopoly on technology and control of the media, so that it sets limits on what can be imagined. It claims to contain all imaginable possibilities

5. For a full characterization of "totalism," see Robert Jay Lifton, *Witness to an Extreme Century: A Memoir* (New York: Free Press, 2011).

and rules all others out of court. Such a totalism, moreover, exercises an invisible authority, so that it is not recognized or acknowledged by those who adhere to it, and in any such case including our own, we are all to some extent subscribers to that totalism that commandeers our imagination and that is inimical to the "image of God" and its practices of holiness, forgiveness, love, peace, and thanks.

1. The totalism in which we live and do ministry, I propose, is the ideology of the market that is in the service of limitless consumerism that receives its religious legitimacy from American exceptionalism. It consists in at least the following five aspects:

- Market ideology is committed to endless growth that requires the endless exploitation of available resources and endless productivity.

- Consumerism consists in the reduction of all of life to commodity with the assurance that the right commodity will keep us safe and happy and prosperous—a claim endlessly attested to by ads for the right drug, the right car, the right sporting equipment, the right computer. The interminable liturgies of television insist that human destiny depends on and is defined by the right objects and products that we do not yet possess—hence, endless striving!

- Our inordinate, unsustainable standard of living is reinforced by the world's strongest military, which is beyond criticism and assures us of ample, limitless natural resources that anywhere in the world rightfully belong to us (our oil!), and so we require "trade agreements" that are aimed at opening new markets for profitable trade and cheap labor.

- All of this is blessed by an uncritical exceptionalism that is permeated with racism, so that such mantras as "Make America Great Again" and "Take Back Our Country" consist in what Ta-Nehisi Coates has termed "The Dream" of white privilege supported by cheap black labor.[6]

- The consumer project depends on endless productivity, which results in the devaluing of members of society who are not "productive," among them the old, the young, the poor, the disabled, the poorly educated and those who do not conform to

---

6. Ta-Nehisi Coates, *Between the World and Me* (New York: Spiegel & Grau, 2015) 102, 110, and passim. What Coates terms "the Dream" is nothing less than white totalism with a vengeance.

consumer norms.[7] The dismissal of the "nonproductive" means that our society lives at the edge of violence toward the non-productive, attested to by the gun lobby, which presents itself as an embodiment of true, virile patriotism.

This is the world that is brought, in very many instances, to the life and worship of the church, without acknowledgment or critical reflection. It is a conservative propensity to align the gospel with this totalism. It is a liberal propensity to imagine that the truth of the gospel can be effectively voiced and performed within the confines of this totalism.

2. This totalism shows up in the church in a passion to maintain a prosperous practice of faith that is in cahoots with the dominant system. And that in turn requires that the church should be the happiest place in town. When the church acts in an accommodating way, it remains focused on privatized individuals and echoes the practices of consumerism that are devoid of any critical perspective on the totalism, or even any awareness or acknowledgment of its existence or force. A gospel of happiness requires that the realities of our common life should remain concealed in a strategy of denial and obfuscation. While advocates of a "prosperity gospel" are the most obvious adherents to such happiness, the same practice can take much more subtle forms.

3. If we consider this totalism theologically, it is clear enough that the totalism I have characterized worships the idol of the golden calf, the one we know from the work of Aaron (Exodus 32). The calf is in fact a young bull, so that we have a "bull of gold." The combination of bull and gold suggests (a) a bull of *fertility and virility* that spills over into control and power; and (b) gold that reduces everything to a *commodity*. That combination, moreover, is the icon of Wall Street, an enterprise that now requires eager applause at its dramatic closing every day even if the market has failed to perform well on that day. It is not for nothing that the golden bull, in Exodus 32, is set for us by Aaron as an alternative to the covenantal God of Mount Sinai, who defined reality in terms of *relationships of fidelity*; it is not for nothing, moreover, that YHWH, the God of covenant, was profoundly pissed off by the emergence of the golden bull, which contradicted the truth of covenant (Exod 32:7–10).

4. This totalism committed to the Bull of Gold yields an anthropology of *happy consumerism* and a theology of *vigorous commoditization*. It is no

---

7. Roland Boer, *The Sacred Economy of Ancient Israel* (Louisville: Westminster John Knox Press, 2015), 203, makes a compelling ironic point when he observes that in ancient Israel the subsistence peasants had to "enable the nonproducing ruling class to maintain the life to which its members had quickly become accustomed." The point is to re-identify who are in fact the "non-producers."

surprise that this totalism, so grounded and expressed, contradicts what we know of a gospel notion of the "image of God."

- The image of God is a vocation of freedom; the totalism does not want freed people but only those who have situated their lives within the totalism.

- The image of God is a vocation of truthfulness; the totalism does not want such honesty but prefers a practice of denial that is often served by a code of euphemisms that mislabel and misconstrue reality.

- The image of God champions mercy that is rooted in forgiveness; the totalism allows for no forgiveness but insists on a tight quid pro quo of accounting for any violation of ideological requirement. Thus, notice that in Exodus 34:9–10, YHWH forgives Israel at the behest of Moses and begins again. The entire future of the covenant is based on that act of forgiveness.

5. I suggest that the deep challenge for all of us, but particularly for pastors, is the embrace and maintenance of the *"image of God"* in a context of this *totalism* that insists otherwise. As a result, we are regularly faced with the danger of being talked out of the image of God so that we define ourselves and our ministry in less demanding, less emancipated ways.

- Thus the pastor may be *talked out of freedom* to say and be one's true self.

- Thus the pastor may *be talked out of honesty*, and so must be endlessly vigilant about what can be said and what must not be said.

- Thus the pastor can *cringe from the public implications of mercy* in the face of a hard quid pro quo system of regulation.

The pastor is charged with exactly the claims that contradict the totalism of our society. The pastor is charged to bear witness to the freedom, honesty, and mercy of the gospel that arise from the wonder of the image of God. When we are talked out of the image of God, our lives and our ministry shrivel in despair, cynicism, or denial. We become incapable of honesty, freedom, or mercy, and we end in fatigue, anger, and isolation. The totalism, present in the congregation, does not mind any of that: despair, cynicism, denial, fatigue, isolation, or anger. All of that is acceptable amid the totalism, and surely preferable to the dangers of freedom, honesty, and mercy.

III

Thus far I have traced out (a) the wonder of being in the image of God, (b) the totalism that opposes the image of God, and (c) the threats posed by that totalism to the image of God. Human health, and in our case clergy health, depends upon the recovery, embrace, and maintenance of our identity as the image of God in an environment that wants to talk us out of that identity. This means:

- a capacity for freedom in a totalism that intends no such freedom of speech or life
- a capacity for honesty in a totalism that wants us to be dishonest about the truth of our common life
- a capacity for mercy that morphs into neighborly justice in a totalism that prefers quid pro quo to rehabilitative mercy

The healthy person—the healthy pastor—must find adequate practices of freedom to say and to be, adequate practices of honesty that refuse the coercion of dishonesty, and adequate practices of mercy that refuse quid pro quo living. That coercion is most often subtle and indirect. But it is very powerful and compelling when one's livelihood is at stake. We are readily aware of the cost of too much freedom and honesty. We can readily assess the cost to one's self. We do not, however, often assess the cost to one's self of a curbed freedom or a curbed honesty that colludes with the totalism at the cost of the image of God.

I have no doubt that attentive self-care is urgent in such an environment. I believe, however, that the disciplines of *evangelical honesty, evangelical freedom*, and *evangelical mercy* are well beyond our conventional notions of self-care.

IV

I am aware of the profound restraints imposed on pastors. For that reason, I want to make a clear distinction between a pastoral strategy of *accommodation* and a pastoral practice of *collusion* in the enterprise of unfreedom and dishonesty. By "accommodation" I mean the knowing practice of unfreedom and dishonesty when it is nonnegotiably required by circumstance. Everything is not ecclesially possible. My own judgment is that in many circumstances less accommodation is required than we assume, when we have sufficient courage to trust the gospel and push the envelope. By "collusion" I mean the uncritical, unrecognized, and unacknowledged readiness to engage in unfreedom and dishonesty as business as usual. Such collusion is a failure to maintain critical self-awareness, so that we can no longer act with intentionality; we simply willingly submit to what is imposed and coerced. I have come to think that the distinction between *knowing accommodation* and *unwitting collusion* is of primary importance for pastoral health.

I want now to explore pastoral health by way of accommodation and collusion by considering the book of Job as a script for clergy health. We may consider that the God of that script is presented, at the outset, as a totalizing force with whom Job must come to terms. Job's coming to terms is risky and demanding; it can be a model for our coming to terms with the totalism that we face. Of course God in the book of Job is not equivalent to our present totalism, which I have identified as market ideology; in the end, under pressure from Job, God turns out to be not a totalizer but an agent for deep engagement.

1. Job is a truth teller who engages in honesty. He pulls no punches in speaking the truth before God. Claus Westermann has shown that Job's speeches repeatedly belong to the genre of lament, complaint, and protest.[8] Thus his initial speech addressed to his friends is shrill:

Let the day perish on which I was born,
and the night that said,
"A man-child is conceived."
Let that day be darkness!
May God above not seek it, or light shine on it.
Let gloom and deep darkness claim it.
Let clouds settle upon it;
let the blackness of the day terrify it.
That night—let thick darkness seize it!
let it not rejoice among the days of the year;
let it not come into the number of the months.
Yes, let that night be barren;
let no joyful cry be heard in it.
Let those curse it who curse the Sea,
those who are skilled to rouse up Leviathan.
Let the stars of its dawn be dark;
let it hope for light, but have none;

8. Claus Westermann, *The Structure of the Book of Job: A Form-Critical Analysis* (Philadelphia: Fortress Press, 1981), 31–66.

may it not see the eyelids of the morning—
because it did not shut the doors of my mother's womb,
and hide the trouble from eyes. (Job 3:3–10)

Job defies the givenness of his life in the world. In 7:11–21, moreover,
Job more directly addresses God (who is not addressed in his opening
speech):

Therefore I will not restrain my mouth;
I will speak in the anguish of my spirit;
I will complain in the bitterness of my soul.
Am I the Sea, or the Dragon,
that you set a guard over me?
When I say, "My bed will comfort me,
my couch will ease my complaint,"
then you scare me with dreams
and terrify me with visions,
so that I would choose strangling
and death rather than this body.
I loathe my life; I would not live forever.
Let me alone, for my days are a breath.
What are human beings, that you make so much of them,
that you set your mind on them,
visit them every morning,
test them every moment?
Will you not look away from me for a while,
let me alone until I swallow my spittle?
If I sin, what do I do to you, you watcher of humanity?
Why have you made me your target?
Why have I become a burden to you?
Why do you not pardon my transgression
and take away my iniquity?
For now I shall lie in the earth;
you will seek me, but I shall not be.

In this series of inquiries, Job calls into question the way in which God
exercises dominion over him.

2. In an almost Promethean way, Job will stand without blinking in
the presence of God. He will not grovel or have his freedom or his honesty curbed by the reality of God. In his last speech before the response
from the whirlwind, Job speaks in confidence and without flinching:

Oh, that I had one to hear me!
(Here is my signature! Let the Almighty answer me!)
Oh, that I had the indictment written by my adversary!

Surely I would carry it on my shoulder;
I would bind it on me like a crown;
I would give him an account of all my steps
like a prince I would approach him. (31:35–37)

This defiant statement follows Job's extended statement of innocence in the same chapter, so that he has full confidence in his legitimacy before God (vv. 1–34, 38–40). There is no groveling or cowering. This is an act of freedom and a readiness for honesty that is filled with chutzpah. Job concedes nothing to the imperious God who at this point still appears to be a formidable totalism.

3. God in the whirlwind answers Job, now for the first time identified as YHWH, the God of covenant (38:1). The divine speeches question the legitimacy of Job's emotive assault on the rule of God. And then, remarkably, the creator God offers a rhetorical turn that we could not have anticipated. The speeches disclose YHWH to be more than and other than an imperious totalizer. For this argument I am deeply indebted to Sam Balentine, who has opened the text in a way I had not seen. Balentine writes:

> I suggest that God's speech may be interpreted not as a rebuke or a denial of Job, but rather as a radical summons to a new understanding of what it means for humankind to be created in the image of God. In this view, it is not silence and submission that God requires. It is steadfast lament and relentless opposition to injustice and innocent suffering, wherever it appears. In this view of the divine speeches, God regards Job not as an aberration within the created order that is to be corrected or eliminated. He is rather a supreme model for humankind that God is committed to nurture and sustain.[9]

More specifically Balentine takes up God's characterization of Behemoth in Job 40:15–24. In the remarkable verse 15 as YHWH begins this part of the speech, YHWH says to Job:

Look at Behemoth, which I made just as I made you.

Study Behemoth that great beast of creation: just like you! Balentine judges that Behemoth is offered to Job as a model for his own life. This impressive, dangerous animal is not simply an exhibit of divine power. It

9. Samuel E. Balentine, "'What Are Human Beings, That You Make So Much of Them?' Divine Disclosure from the Whirlwind: 'Look at Behemoth,'" in *God in the Fray: A Tribute to Walter Brueggemann*, ed. Tod Linafelt and Timothy K. Beal (Minneapolis: Fortress Press, 1998), 260.

is an invitation to Job to reflect on how God has made Job and how God intends Job to be.

a. Job—like Behemoth—is a creature of extraordinary strength and power:

> Its strength is in its loins,
> and its power in the muscles of its belly.
> It makes its tail stiff like a cedar;
> the sinews of its thighs are knit together.
> Its bones are tubes of bronze,
> its limbs like bars of iron. (vv. 16-18)

b. Job—like Behemoth—is summoned to royal splendor:

> It is the first of the great acts of God—
> only its Maker can approach it with the sword. (v. 19)

Balentine anticipates that Job might answer his erstwhile friends:

> Yes, indeed, I *am* like the primal creature who is a near equal to God. I *am* summoned forth and endowed with royal prerogatives and responsibilities.[10]

c. Job—like Behemoth—is worthy of praise (vv. 20–24).

> Here God commends Behemoth to Job as an object lesson in what it means to stand before one's maker with exceptional strength, proud prerogatives, and fierce trust.[11]

The God who has appeared to be a totalizer in fact offers courage and confidence to Job. This is no put-down of Job. This creature of beauty, strength, and royal power is made to be ferocious, fierce, dangerous, threatening, awesome. This is indeed a refusal of the tepid "image of God" out of which Job's friends would have talked him in their attempt to make him docile in a way that would deny his bodily truth and curb his outrageous freedom. This God of the whirlwind countered the silencing attempt of his friends. The friends, it turns out, are the totalizers; they intend Job to be docile and submissive. But not God! This God is no indifferent creator or impervious master.

This God is not so vain as to require glory through the diminishment of Job. This is a God who is full of regal self-confidence and who wants

---

10. Balentine, "'What Are Human Beings,'" 271.
11. Balentine, "'What Are Human Beings,'" 271.

Job in God's own image to have the same fullness of regal self-confidence. This is no put-down of Job, only affirmation, celebration, and extravagant appreciation. Of course there is an edge of risk in this image, as there always is. Because the God who makes this affirmation is no patsy and will not be taken for granted. But Job is called to that risk. Indeed it is only *the daring of Job* that permits us to see that this creator *God is no totalizer*, but is in fact a partner who passes along splendor to the "image." Had Job not made his bold insistence, Job would never have known and would, along with us, have been left in the timidity his friends attempted to impose on him.

4. Job's final utterance in 42:5–6 is notably ambiguous. Our usual translation suggests that Job submits in deep deference to God and in fact retracts his mighty protests. But these verses are in fact deliberately ambiguous and do not intend to flatten Job in that way. They allow room for alternative rendering.[12] For the most part, recent interpreters have refused the notion of docile submissiveness and insist that Job at least holds his own at the end in his response to God. Balentine concludes that, while Job may have a troublesome future, he is not mandated by God to silence and submission:

> They [humans] may not be silent, for silence is unworthy of those who have stood in the divine presence and have learned that creation has been entrusted to them, because they are a "little lower than God."[13]

The recent discussions of these verses by Balentine, Carol Newsom, and Davis Hankins suggests that it is not wise or even possible to settle on a simple translation of these verses, but that it is necessary to leave open possibilities in this life-or-death exchange.[14] In his more recent commentary Balentine concludes:

> This picture of Creator and creature locked in dialogue over matters of mutual concern provides a glimpse of how the creaturely pursuit of justice enacts what it means to be made in the image of God.[15]

Thus, we return to the "image of God." The "image of God" is not a docile submissiveness. It is rather a royal rule of history and freedom

12. Samuel E. Balentine, *Job*, Smyth & Helwys Bible Commentary (Mercer: Smyth & Helwys, 2006) 694, has summarized the current discussion of alternative translations.

13. Balentine, "What are Human Beings," 277.

14. Balentine, *Job*; Carol Newsom, *The Book of Job: A Contest of Moral Imaginations* (Oxford: Oxford University Press, 2003); Davis Hankins, *The Book of Job and the Immanent Genesis of Transcendence* (Evanston: Northwestern University Press, 2015).

15. Balentine, *Job*, 697.

before God. And derivatively, it is a rule and freedom before every total-ism that wants to reduce to silence.

Job refuses to *collude* with the God of the whirlwind. He will not concede sovereignty beyond engagement with YHWH. He does, to be sure, *accommodate* YHWH. What else could he do? YHWH is the cre-ator and will not be disregarded. But that accommodation bears none of the marks of unwitting collusion. Job knows exactly what he is doing. He knows how far he will go, how exposed he is, how careful he must be, how respectful he is required to be. God is veiled in the east wind that is cold. Job must take care to protect himself. As one scholar writes, "There is no arguing with the inevitable. The only argument available with an east wind is to put on an overcoat."[16] That is knowing accom-modation; this, however, is no collusion, no yielding to the wind, only a realistic acknowledgment that it is there and that the wind is cold.

5. The book of Job ends with great affirmation of Job, even if it is a prose ending to which scholars have paid little attention. On the one hand, Job is affirmed as "my servant" who receives reparation at the behest of God (42:7-8). Job's words are accepted as valid: he has spoken "what is right"! One the other hand, Job becomes the occasion for the reconstitution of the community gathered around his vindication:

> The most significant ethical aspect of the prose conclusion is its shift of focus from a subject-centered concern with Job's understanding, activities, and obedience, to Job's role in what constitutes and maintains the cultural, legal, and religious institutions of the community. . . . The prose conclusion, however, shifts the focus toward the community and toward Job's role in what constitutes and maintains the collective.[17]

It is his "right asking" that has salvaged a new community of well-being apart from the illusions of quid pro quo reality advocated by his friends. The world finally cannot be quid pro quo. The restored community lives by the life-giving capacity of the creator who is evoked by Job's honesty:

> The blessing God gives seems to be Job's reward for *not* conforming to his friends' theology.[18]

---

16. James R. Lowell, "Democracy: Inaugural Address on Assuming the Presidency of the Birmingham and Midland Institute, Birmingham, England, 6 October, 1884," *Essays: English and American*, vol. 28, The Harvard Classics (New York: P.F. Collier & Sons, 1909–1914), 7. Cited in Balentine, *Job*, 699.

17. Hankins, *The Book of Job*, 223.

18. Balentine, "What Are Human Beings," 717.

V

The book of Job makes clear that fierce engagement in bold truth telling is the stuff of real life. That *daring engagement* is the substance of the image of God. Job's friends would have talked him out of such fierce engagement, but he refused. He is not talked out of the image of God!

I submit that for the pastor this is a helpful model for life amid totalism. Such a model invites both:

- *engagement before God* without restraint. Job does accommodate YHWH, but Job does not for an instant collude with any notion that lets YHWH be an absolute monarch before whom he must bow.

- *engagement with the congregation* that is modeled here as accommodation but not collusion. Of course there are restraints in a congregation. But they are not absolute and limits must be repeatedly tested. Without such fierce contestation we may find we have been refashioned in the image of the golden calf and the requirements of the totalism. When that happens, our ministry descends into religious kitsch that may please many but that leaves us hollowed out for ministry.[19] Kitsch is decorous object with fake attraction that is in fact without value. In light of the poem of Job, I suggest that when our ministry does not challenge and offend and open news paths, we are likely to be engaged in religious kitsch.

Thus I suggest that the practice of engaged dispute—before God and neighbor—is the only way to avoid kitsch. I arrive at these simple conclusions that I have learned from Job:

- Knowing *accommodation* leaves us free to practice *chutzpah* before God and neighbor.

- Unwitting *collusion* reduces us to a life and ministry of *kitsch* that has no joy or transformative power.

Much is at stake in this either/or of *accommodation* or *collusion, chutzpah* or *kitsch* with which Job struggles. I submit that religious kitsch may readily become a handmaiden of fascism. Those who want to reduce

19. For provocative reflections on kitsch, including "religious kitsch," see Milan Kundera, *The Unbearable Lightness of Being*, trans. Michael Henry Heim (New York: Harper & Row, 1984).

the lively theological engagement of socioeconomic political dimension to an easy alliance prefer kitsch. That easy collusion drifts away from democracy. Job's chutzpah in the image of God precludes the ready fascism of his friends who have signed on with a totalizing God. This is a choice with which we always struggle. Kitsch allows no room for freshness of disclosure of God. Job is a powerful model for us, because he shows us how to withstand seductive kitsch, how to engage in chutzpah and so to be judged by God as having spoken right. The outcome is one of affirmed emancipation that ends in restoration to well-being for him and for his community. The "image of God" is, to be sure, a given; it is, however, a given that summons to engaged intentionality that is a sine qua non of self-care.

11.

Sabbath as Alternative

This chapter was first published in Word & World *36 (2016): 247–56.*

It is a great misfortune that in our United States Puritan legacy, the Sabbath is perceived as a restrictive, killjoy practice to be overcome in emancipated self-actualization. To the contrary, in ancient Israel the Sabbath is a mighty practice that sustains a peculiar faith identity in political economy that seeks eagerly to overcome that peculiar identity that is seen as a hindrance to larger economic effectiveness. That peculiar faith identity, moreover, has immense significance for the healthy ordering of the political economy.

I. Looking Both Ways

It is clear that the Sabbath commandment stands at the center of the Decalogue, the ultimate Torah that characterizes the covenant made at Sinai (Exod 20:1–17).[1] The Sabbath commandment occupies considerable textual space (vv. 8–11). I have learned from Patrick Miller, moreover, that this critical position in the Ten Commandments means that this Sabbath commandment looks both ways.[2] It looks back to commandments 1–3, which concern God; this backward look suggests that the God who gives the commandments practices Sabbath and is a God

1. The themes of this paper are more fully exposited in my book *Sabbath as Resistance: Saying No to the Culture of Now* (Louisville: Westminster John Knox, 2014).
2. Patrick D. Miller, Jr., "The Human Sabbath: A Study in Deuteronomic Theology," *The Princeton Seminary Bulletin* 6.2 (1985): 81–97. In *The Ten Commandments* (Louisville: Westminster John Knox, 2009), 117–66, Miller has provided the finest critical exposition of the Sabbath that we have.

of rest, not a God of endless restless anxious production. But the Sabbath commandment also looks forward to commandments 5–10, which concern neighborly relations. This means that respectful neighborly relations, as detailed in commandments 5–10, are premised on restfulness, so that such relations are not driven by anxious, aggressive, self-protective conduct and policy. The Sabbath commandment looks both ways and provides for a restfulness for both God and neighbor. It is possible to think that such a commandment eventuates in the two great commandments to "love God and neighbor" (Mark 12:28–34), to respect the restfulness of both parties: don't crowd, don't demand, don't coerce.

II. The Gift of Being Re-*nepheshed*

The Sabbath commandment, like all of these commandments, sits in a thick, interpretive tradition. Interpretation is required in order to probe what the commandment might mean in actual practice in particular varied circumstances. Indeed, we are given two quite different normative interpretations of the Sabbath commandment. The one that is familiar to us is in the Sinai event of Exodus 20. In that rendering, the ground for Sabbath rest is creation:

> For in six days the LORD made heaven and earth, the sea, and all that is in them, but rested on the seventh day; therefore the LORD blessed the Sabbath day and consecrated it. (v. 11)

This grounding of Sabbath appeals to the rhythm of creation in a seven-day routine that is performed and acknowledged in the creation narrative (Gen 1:1–2:4a). In that narrative, God rested on the Sabbath day after six days of work (Gen 2:3). God is portrayed as not endlessly at work, not endlessly anxious about the world as creation, not endlessly engaged in its generation or maintenance. God exhibits confidence that the world, infused with God's blessing, has a sustaining capacity of its own.

Perhaps the most interesting and important biblical exposition of this claim is voiced in the more tedious and unfamiliar provision for the tabernacle in Exodus 25–31. In that long detailed instruction by God to Moses, provision is made for an apparatus for divine presence, culminating in the coming of God's glory into the tabernacle (Exod 40:34–38). The instruction is given in seven divine speeches to Moses, each introduced with the recurring formula, "The LORD said to Moses" (Exod 25:1;

30:11, 17, 23, 34; 31:1, 12).[3] It is observed by many interpreters that these seven speeches are designed as a match to the seven days of creation in Genesis 1–2.[4] Moses is instructed to make a liturgical world that articulates creation as it should be, so that Israel, in its worship, may for a time move from the conflicted dangerous world of its circumstance to the rightly ordered world of creation as offered in liturgy. In that sequence of seven divine speeches, the first six concern liturgical furniture and equipment, and provision for proper priestly procedure and decorum. It is something of a surprise that the seventh speech, not unlike the seventh day of creation, is very different and concerns exactly the observance of Sabbath. The rightly ordered world of worship culminates in Sabbath observance (Exod 31:12–17).

In these verses the Sabbath is insisted upon with intense urgency, as a "sign forever" of a perpetual covenant between YHWH and Israel. None of the other provisions in these speeches has that claim attached to it. The rhetoric suggests a binding of the two partners not unlike the commandments in Exodus 20, wherein commandments 1–3 concerning God and commandments 5–10 concerning neighbor are bound together in the fourth commandment.

Notice should especially be taken of the final clause of Exodus 31:17, which concludes the seven speeches of instruction to Moses. It is said that God rested on the seventh day. Our usual translation is that God "was refreshed." Sabbath is for refreshment! Even God requires such refreshment! But the term rendered in this way is a verbal form of the noun *nephesh*, which we usually render as "life, self, soul." The nominal form occurs many times in the biblical text; but the verbal form, as here, occurs only three times in the Hebrew Bible. In Exodus 23:12, it is used in a way parallel to 31:17, which concerns Sabbath rest: "You and your slave and your immigrant shall be refreshed." The other use is in 2 Samuel 16:14. David, fleeing for his life along with his faithful entourage, arrives at the Jordan River and "was refreshed." Each of these uses concerns refreshment, given in the form of rest or enlivening water.

But "refreshed" fails to carry the root word's nominal meanings that we translate as "self, soul, life." A stronger translation of this reflexive verb would be that God, in Exodus 31:17, was re-*nepheshed*, that is, received back "self, life, soul" that had been depleted or diminished by the work of creation. Such a translation indicates the urgency of Sabbath

3. See Joseph Blenkinsopp, "The Structure of P," *Catholic Biblical Quarterly* 38 (1976): 275–92; and P. J. Kearney, "Creation and Liturgy: The P Redaction of EX 25–40," *Zeitschrift für die alttestamentliche Wissenschaft* 89 (1977): 375–87.

4. See Jon D. Levenson, *Sinai & Zion: An Entry into the Jewish Bible*, New Voices in Biblical Studies (New York: Winston, 1985), 111–37.

because the usage recognizes that one' life (*nephesh*) . . . even God's life (God's *nephesh*) . . . can be depleted or diminished, and must be restored by proper Sabbath keeping.

Such as translation makes clear that in Exodus 20:8–11, Genesis 2:3, and Exodus 31:17 Sabbath keeping is no mere incidental practice. It is rather an acknowledgment of the human condition and of God's provision for human frailty and fragility, made clear in the affirmation that even God's own life or self can be depleted and diminished. Thus, Sabbath is a mighty antidote to an economy of depletion and diminishment, because it entails participation in a community that does not believe that human well-being and worth are established by endless productivity. The commandment is thus an act of resistance against such an economy. It is also provision for an alternative way. That alternative in Genesis 1–2 relies on the fruitful blessing of the earth. In Exodus 31 it is reliance on the presence of God as life-giver, assured in the apparatus of the liturgy.

Sabbath, then, is not just a practice. It is a life choice to belong to a different humanity. Michael Fishbane sees that Sabbath is an act of divestment from the productivity of the world, a divestment that knows that life is a gift and not an accomplishment or a possession:

> A sense of inaction takes over, and the day does not merely mark the stoppage of work or celebrate the completion of creation, but enforces the value that the earth is a gift of divine creativity, given to mankind in sacred trust. On the Sabbath, the practical benefits of technology are laid aside, and one tries to stand in the cycle of natural time, without manipulation or interference. To the degree possible, one must also attempt to bring the qualities of inaction and rest into the heart and mind.[5]

The matter of Sabbath keeping as life choice for an alternative existence is echoed in the poetry of Isaiah 56 concerning participation in the postexilic community of Judaism. The prophetic poem makes provision for the inclusion in the community of "foreigners and eunuchs," two groups that some surely wanted to exclude. Most remarkably, their inclusion is premised generally on keeping covenant, but specifically on keeping Sabbath:

> To the eunuchs who keep my sabbaths,
> Who choose the things that please me
> and hold fast to my covenant . . .
> All who keep sabbath,
> and do not profane it,

5. Michael Fishbane, *Sacred Attunement: A Jewish Theology* (Chicago: University of Chicago Press, 2008), 126.

and hold my covenant—
these I will bring to my holy mountain. (Isa 56:4, 6–7)

It is noteworthy that Sabbath keeping is the only specific requirement, which suggests that it is this disciplined act that most distinguishes the community of covenant from the dominant economy of that time. The culminating invitation of inclusiveness is in the wake of Sabbath keeping:

These [foreigners and eunuchs] I will bring to my holy mountain,
and make them joyful in my house of prayer . . .
for my house shall be called a house of prayer
for all peoples. (v. 7)

One might judge that in a Sabbath-less society all would not be welcome at worship because in a production-propelled society, social rank, social power, and social access are sure to be hierarchal, based on worth established by endless productivity. Sabbath is a great equalizer: all are welcome because their worth is not based on productivity, a criterion that foreigners and eunuchs perhaps could not meet.

III. Sabbath as Emancipation

The Sabbath commandment is decisively altered in Deuteronomy; this is the only substantive change in the Decalogue in these verses (Deut 5:12-15). In verse 15 the commandment on Sabbath is no longer grounded in God's rest at creation. Now the grounding is in the exodus event, which was an emancipation from the exploitative labor practices of Pharaoh in Egypt, on which see Exod 5:4-19. The exodus was a decisive disruption of Pharaoh's production schedule that eased the coercive pressure on the bodies of bondaged workers. The exodus is narrated as a one-time event. But the Sabbath is a way of assuring that the memory of the exodus has continuing contemporary force for emancipatory significance. It is to be noted that, in Deuteronomy 5:14, on the Sabbath day, working animals, slaves, and immigrants (those without assured rights) are all "as you," that is, all entitled to rest. The Sabbath is a day of social equalization for those who on all other days are quite unequal.

It is clear that, in the tradition of Deuteronomy, the Sabbath commandment provides the basis for an extended series of economic provisions that are designed to protect the weak from predation.[6] The series includes:

- Restrictions on charging interest on loans (23:19–20)

- Limitation on loan collateral concerning the poor (24:10–13, 17–18)

- Prohibition of "wage theft" by withholding payment to laborers (24:14–15)

- Provision for the widow, orphan, and immigrant (the most economically vulnerable groups in that ancient economy) by leaving agricultural produce after harvest, thus anticipating the pernicious "laws of enclosure" enacted in modern time (24:19–22)

- Limitation of physical punishment in order to maintain human dignity for the guilty (25:1–3)

- Requirement of honest weights and measures in commerce (25:13–16)

All of these provisions are intended to prevent predatory practices against the vulnerable. It is to be noted that twice the motivation for the commandment is remembrance of the exodus (24:18, 22).

It is clear that the tradition of Deuteronomy provides the basis for much of the prophetic critique of a predatory economy. Deuteronomy is the lead tradition that defines social relationships in terms of covenant that regards all the members of the community as neighbors. Thus, the economy is to be a neighborly practice that curbs excessive greed and exploitation in the interest of sustaining social relationships of dignity, respect, and security.

One prophetic articulation concerning Sabbath that lives in the same world as Deuteronomy is the oracle of Amos 8:4–8. The prophet addresses those who exploit the poor by using dishonest weights, who reduce the poor to tradable commodities. In the oracle, God vows disruptive action against the "pride of Jacob," unspecified actions that will cause the land to tremble, that will bring mourning and chaos like an out-of-control Nile River. The image is of an exploitative economy that victimizes those without resources.

What interests us is that such merchants and traders resent Sabbath,

6. See Frank Crüsemann, *The Torah: Theology and Social History of Old Testament Law* (Edinburgh: T&T Clark, 1996), 201–75.

which inconveniently interrupts their sharp commercial dealings. They are eager that Sabbath should end in order to resume their predatory practices. They rightly recognize that the Sabbath is intended precisely to disrupt such practices, to give the vulnerable a respite from exploitation.

It is clear that Sabbath, in the horizon of Deuteronomy, is not only provision for a day of rest. It is in fact a tap root for a political economy that is imagined and practiced differently. In that different economy, economic concerns are subordinated to and governed by neighborly relationships. The economy has no autonomous function, but is designed to serve the common good of the neighborhood.

IV. A Paradigmatic Sabbath

It is indicated in the preamble to the Decalogue that the Ten Commandments are designed as an alternative and counter to the regime of Pharaoh:

> I am the LORD your God, who brought you out of the land of Egypt, out of the house of slavery. (Exod 20:2)

It turns out that the narrative of exodus emancipation is not an isolated event of ancient memory. It is in fact programmatic and paradigmatic for all that follows in Israel. Thus, we may make a case that the entire Decalogue is designed to fend off the pressures and dangers and seductions of all Pharaonic economies.[7] We must be acutely aware of the intensity of Pharaoh's socioeconomic practice. The series of imperatives issued by Pharaoh to his supervisors and taskmasters requires that the Hebrew slaves must be more and more productive of larger brick quotas, even in circumstances that hinder their productivity (Exod 5:4–19). Behind this inflammatory picture of exploitation there is the more sober narrative report of Genesis 47:13–25, which probes how Pharaoh's economic policies worked. It is clear that Pharaoh is an accumulator of land and food, apparently propelled by his double nightmare of scarcity (see Gen 41:1–7). His policy grew out of his fear! Joseph, an erstwhile Hebrew, is presented in the narrative as Pharaoh's willing agent to work against his own Hebrew people. Pharaoh accumulates land and food that eventually amounted to a monopoly. Amid the scarcity resulting from the

---

7. See Walter Brueggemann, "The Countercommands of Sinai," in my *Disruptive Grace: Reflections on God, Scripture, and the Church*, ed. Carolyn J. Sharp (Minneapolis: Fortress Press, 2011), 75–92.

famine, Joseph, on behalf of Pharaoh, systematically takes money from the hapless peasants; then he takes their cattle, their means of production.[8] Finally Joseph takes their land and their bodies into slavery. The narrative can report in summary:

> All the Egyptians sold their fields, because the famine was severe upon them. And the land became Pharaoh's. (Gen 47:20)

Pharaoh's land seizure is reported as a sustained strategy for reducing subsistence farmers to slavery, this assuring that Pharaoh would have an endless, reliable supply of cheap labor among those who had no economic leverage whereby to resist. Pharaoh's strategy is to render people vulnerable to a kind of dependence that is sustained by impossible debt. In his world everything and everyone is reduced to a tradable commodity in which laborers are situated so as to be unable to assert any agency in their own history.

It follows, of course, that in Pharaoh's regime there was no Sabbath rest for anyone. Certainly not for the slaves or for the work animals, and likely not for the taskmasters and supervisors, and surely not for Pharaoh himself. All social relationships in a society without Sabbath rest are reduced to commodity transactions, reinforced by fear, the threat of violence, and, when necessary, real violence (see Exod 1:13–14).

In that world the exodus could be readily remembered through bodily suffering. The Sinai commands are an effort by YHWH, the God of liberation, to counter Pharaoh's policies of coercive commoditization. By keeping Sabbath, Israel practically and bodily imagines a political economy that is not reduced to commodity transactions, an economy wherein even the vulnerable are respected and treated as neighbors who are entitled to security.

The Sabbath tradition in ancient Israel, along with the exodus narrative, was an articulation of reality that could be reenacted and reperformed in many new circumstances. Thus, in usurpatious Jerusalem (and especially in the usurpatious reign of Solomon with his forced labor and tax-collecting prowess), Sabbath issues a mighty protest and alternative. Thus, Sabbath practice is life beyond the reach of the predatory practice of Pharaoh, often belatedly reperformed by those who imitate Pharaoh. We cannot fully understand the Sabbath command, in ancient or contemporary setting, unless we are vigorously alert to the Pharaonic capac-

---

8. Amartya Sen has forcefully contended that famine does not indicate an absence of food but only a scarcity that drives prices of food up (*Poverty and Famines: An Essay on Entitlement and Deprivation* [Oxford: Clarendon, 1981]). The result is that the disadvantaged have no access to food that is indeed available for those with resources; see a case in point in 2 Kings 6:24–7:20.

ity that is endlessly reperformed in economies that are propelled by the logic of scarcity.

V. The Sabbatical Principle

Patrick Miller has shrewdly seen that the Sabbath commandment issues in a "sabbatical principle" whereby the entire practice of political economy is redefined by Sabbath claims.[9] After "the seventh day," the "sabbatical principle" shows up in two major Torah provisions. The provisions evidently derive from Sabbath as they also are according to a regime of "sevens."

First, in Deuteronomy 15:1–18, a pivotal text for the tradition of Deuteronomy, the "year of release" provides that every seven years there is to be a remission of debts. This commandment clearly intends to subordinate the economy to the enhancement of neighborly social relations, so that neighbors count for more than either debts or wealth. Special attention is given to the needy (v. 7). It is evident that the commandment encountered stiff resistance (even as it does now whenever it is taught or advocated). Thus, "Moses" warns against being "hard-hearted" or "tight-fisted" toward the needy. The urgency of the provision is indicated, moreover, by the repeated use of an absolute infinitive, a grammatical device in Hebrew whereby the verb is intensified by repetition that cannot be replicated in translation. This grammatical device is used to intensify no fewer than six verbs in this commandment (more than in any other text), making clear that "Moses" understood that this is the most urgent and most radical of all Torah provisions.

We may pay particular attention to an apparent contradiction if we juxtapose verses 4 and 11. In verse 4, it is assured that if this commandment is performed faithfully, there will "be no one in need among you." ("The poor will cease in the land.") In verse 11, a more familiar statement asserts that "there will never cease to be some in need in the earth." ("The poor you will always have with you.") Thus, verse 4 ("There will be no poor") and verse 11 ("There will always be poor"). But in fact there is no contradiction between the verses. Verse 4 states the *effectiveness* of debt cancellation; verse 11 states the *urgency* of the same policy. The predatory economy of Pharaoh works to have continuing indebtedness in order to assure a supply of cheap labor. Israel's counter-imagination insists that Pharaoh's debt-slave economy need not be practiced and is inimical to YHWH's intent for Israel.

The second provision of the "Sabbath principle" is the "year of Jubilee"

9. Miller, "Human Sabbath," 93–97.

in Leviticus 25; it provides that every forty-nine years (seven times seven), property lost in the rough-and-tumble economy will be returned to its rightful owner, because such landed property is inalienable and is not finally a tradable commodity. Thus, the autonomy of the market is severely limited in the interest of sustaining neighborly relationships.

While it is frequently contested that the proposal for a Jubilee Year has no realistic future, it is important that it is reiterated as the "acceptable year of the LORD's favor" in Isaiah 61:2, a text cited by Jesus in his synagogue appearance, a citation of which he subversively declared:

Today this scripture is fulfilled in your hearing. (Luke 4:21)

It is indeed possible to trace out the Jubilee performance of Jesus in the Gospel of Luke.[10]

It becomes clear that the Sabbath provision in the Torah is not simply a restrictive or coercive requirement. It is rather an act of bodily testimony whereby the faithful insist that economic transactions, in and of themselves, are at best penultimate and are situated in the more ultimate reality of neighborly social relationships. Seen in this way, Sabbath keeping is indeed a subversive act that asserts that Pharaoh's claims of predatory monopoly are to be resisted and are ultimately rejected. *Creation as the basis for Sabbath keeping* (Exod 20:11) insists that the God of covenant, and not Pharaoh, made the world and governs and sustains it. In his hubris, Pharaoh can imagine that the world is his (see Ezek 29:3), but his claim is false. *Emancipation as the basis for Sabbath keeping* (Deut 5:15) is an insistence that the authority of Pharaoh is limited and his claim to cheap bondaged labor is to be rejected. Sabbath is the bodily declaration that persons in the image of YHWH do not belong to Pharaoh; he is not to be obeyed or trusted or feared.

VI. Sabbath as Testimony

Rightly understood, Sabbath is a practice of immense urgency in our contemporary political economy. It is necessary only to recognize that "Pharaoh" in the narrative is a metaphor for all predatory, confiscatory economic practice grounded in and legitimated by idolatry. As a result we are able to see that the tenth commandment, "Thou shalt not be acquisitive" (Exod 20:17), is the climactic point of the Sinai covenant.[11]

10. See Sharon H. Ringe, *Jesus, Liberation, and the Biblical Jubilee: Images for Ethics and Christology*, Overtures to Biblical Theology 19 (Philadelphia: Fortress Press, 1985).

11. See Marvin L. Chaney, "'Coveting Your Neighbor's House' in Social Context," in *The*

The covenant is an act of resistance to and an alternative to the Pharaonic social system. Sabbath is the visible expression of resistance and alternative.

It is evident that our national economy in the United States (writ large as "globalization"), is largely in the hands of Pharaonic interests.[12] The acquisitive oligarchy now largely manages the government and controls the media. It has, moreover, supported a sustained process of deregulation alongside rigged credit laws, inequitable tax arrangements, and low wages that has resulted in a growing gap between a small party of "haves" and a large company of "have-nots" who are economically vulnerable and without leverage. As in ancient Egypt, such inequitable economics skews social relationships. "Pharaoh" is an icon for any political economy that reduces too many to low-wage jobs or no job at all, because there is no protection or safeguard against rapacious practices of the oligarchy for a workforce that is increasingly powerless. (The destruction of labor unions is an element in the strategy of accumulation.) The result is that only the "productive" are seen to have value. The "unproductive" are readily dispensable, most extremely by mass incarceration but more broadly through an arrangement of inadequate housing, unfair schools, and inaccessible health care. The indices of social health all suffer in an economy of restless anxiety in which there is no "rest" for anyone, not among the "producers," who must endlessly produce more, or among the "nonproducers," who are characteristically kept at risk in a Pharaonic system.

The performance of Sabbath is an act of testimony, a powerful antidote to such a dehumanizing system of power. Practically, Sabbath is an insistence on rest for even the most vulnerable among us. Theologically, it is an insistence that the world does not belong to the predators. It belongs to the creator of heaven and earth, who intends that those in God's image cannot be reduced to commodity. This God has never intended that some should be reduced to slavery. This God has never intended that some should be reduced to commodity. This God has never intended that the earth should be plundered for the sake of limitless wealth. Sabbath keeping is a deep affirmation that all of God's creatures, human and nonhuman, should be honored in concrete and practical ways. When Jesus counsels his disciples, "Do not be anxious," he surely intended that the man in the preceding parable with "big-

Ten Commandments: The Reciprocity of Faithfulness, ed. William P. Brown, Library of Theological Ethics (Louisville: Westminster John Knox, 2004), 302–17.

12. Enrique Dussel has most clearly seen the perniciously negative dimensions of globalization (*Ethics of Liberation in the Age of Globalization and Exclusion*, Latin America Otherwise [Durham, NC: Duke University Press, 2013]).

ger barns" should not be the order of the day, the restless man who never observed Sabbath and ended in death (Luke 12:1–31). Jesus surely refused endless accumulation as the purpose of life. He summoned his disciples to stand in solidarity with birds and flowers, trusting creation to know that there is enough for all. Indeed, those trusting creatures are contrasted with Solomon, Pharaoh's son-in-law who continues, within Israel, Pharaoh's restless accumulation. Sabbath is an embrace of *the truth of the abundance* of creation against *the anxious scarcity* that reduces neighbor to threat. Sabbath is a regular, visible enactment of that alternative.

PART IV

Tradition, Memory, and Identity

12.

Memory (I): Amnesia and the
Need to Remember

This chapter was originally given at a colloquium at Columbia Theological Seminary in Decatur, Georgia, on April 20, 2015. The title of the colloquium, organized by Dr. Erskine Clarke, was "The Church Facing the Future: Memory, Hope, and Obedience."

> Another characteristic of this crushing form of economic Darwinism is that it thrives on a kind of social amnesia that erases critical thought, historical analysis, and any understanding of broader systemic relations.[1]

Jesus told a series of kingdom parables. Then he asked his disciples, "Have you understood all of this?" And they answer, "Yes." They answer tersely and unambiguously. And then he took them to the next level:

> Therefore every scribe who has been trained for the kingdom of heaven is like the master of a household who brings out of his treasure what is new and what is old. (Matt 13:52)

He characterizes discipleship as an exercise in agile hermeneutical imagination, a movement of old and new, of tradition and vision. And now for our context I propose it is an agile process of remembering and forgetting for the sake of obedient newness. The aim of such obedient agility is to serve the kingdom of heaven, that is, participate in the coming rule of the God of the gospel in the world. Such participation requires

---

1. Henry A. Giroux, *Neoliberalism's War on Higher Education* (Chicago: Haymarket Books, 2014), 2.

schooling, in the NRSV, being "trained." Or better, being "discipled." The process of old/new, tradition/imagination is not an obvious or natural activity; it requires intentionality and discipline. I take this process of "old/new" as the subject of our reflection in these days. It is clear that some of us would prefer to keep drawing out the old in resistance to the new; some of us would prefer to embrace the new and move away from what is old as quickly as possible. Jesus's terse comment, however, precludes both temptations and summons his followers to the more difficult and challenging enterprise of a both/and rather than an either/or. The practice of old and new as a both/and is not a finger exercise or an experiment in cleverness. It is an urgent preoccupation for participation in the kingdom. When the disciples answered, "Yes," they little understood what was required of them.

I

In ancient Israel, the endless challenge was the articulation and maintenance of a distinct identity in cultural contexts that wanted, whenever possible, to nullify that distinct identity. In the premonarchical period, in the wake of the exodus, the pressure of Pharaoh on the one hand and the seduction of Canaan on the other worked powerfully against a distinct covenantal identity. Israel wanted always to return to the reliable world of Pharaoh and his fleshpots. Israel found it often compelling to go after other gods in the land. It was the tradition, wrought through the steadiness of Moses, Joshua, and Samuel, that preserved distinctiveness.

In the monarchical period, the problem was internal to Israel. The establishment of Jerusalem, with king, temple, and surplus wealth, always wanted to be "like the nations" with a predatory economy sanctioned by the great state myths reflected in the "Songs of Zion." It was the sustained effort of the prophetic tradition that kept summoning Israel back to its odd identity with all of its socioethical implications.

In the vexed exilic/postexilic periods, it was the relentless force of empire that wanted to undo Israelite distinctiveness. In sequence the Babylonian, the Persian, the Greek, and finally the Roman Empire with its overlay of Hellenistic culture found Jewish identity to be a deep inconvenience. As a result, political pressure and cultural expectation wanted to make Jewish oddity at least an embarrassment if not unbearable. We may take the reported temptation of the Maccabean period to "undo circumcision" as a durable epitome of the erosion of distinct identity that was under immense cultural pressure (1 Macc 1:15).

In the face of premonarchical, monarchical, and postmonarchical pressure against peculiar identity, an urgent task in the community was to maintain a distinct identity and vocation that had theological rootage and socioethical implications. It is evident that the primary resource for such maintenance of identity and vocation was narrative saturation, sustained, intentional remembering in which the lines between educational inculcation and liturgical reperformance were completely blurred or disregarded.[2] The leadership responsible for this distinct identity—which we may regard as nearly fanatical—concluded that narrative reiteration was crucial, because such narrative testimony focused on the particular in defiance of imperial universals that dismissed the remembered particularity as impossible. Thus, nurture through educational inculcation and liturgy was taken seriously in order that the people not be embarrassed about the claims of particularity that were in reality embarrassing in a more urbane universalizing venue. So the teachers endlessly attested of Passover:

> When you come into the land that the LORD will give you as he has promised, you shall keep this observance. And when your children ask you, "What do you mean by this observance?" you shall say, "It is the Passover sacrifice to the LORD, for he passed over the houses of the Israelites in Egypt, when he struck down the Egyptians but spared our houses. (Exod 12:25–27)

The point of Passover is to raise the question to which the narrative gives the answer. Parents, moreover, are recruited into saturation education:

> Keep these words that I am commanding you today in your heart. Recite them to your children and talk about them when you are at home and when you are away, when you lie down and when you arise. Bind them as a sign on your hand, fix them, as an emblem on your forehead, and write them on the doorposts of your house and on your gates. (Deut 6:6–9)

The intent is that the recital will provide a narrative horizon and plot for the children. In the narrative at the entry into the land, moreover, one can see a process of typology at work in which "this" is offered as a way to reiterate "that." Thus, in the confusing report on the stones for the crossing of the Jordan River into the land of promise, Joshua can say:

> When your children ask their parents in time to come, "What do these stones mean?" then you shall let your children know, "Israel crossed over the Jordan here on dry ground." For the LORD your God dried up the waters of the Jordan for you to you cross over, as the LORD your God did to the Red

---

2. See Walter Brueggemann, *The Creative Word: Canon as a Model for Biblical Education*, 2nd ed., rev. Amy Erickson (Minneapolis: Fortress Press, 2015), chapter 2.

Sea, which he dried up for us until we crossed over, so that all the peoples of the earth may know that the hand of the LORD is mighty, and so that you may fear the LORD your God forever." (Josh 4:21–24)

The process of question and answer is the same. But the interpretive clue is "as," what Garrett Green has called the "copula of imagination" in which the crossing of the Jordan is an occasion for recalling the crossing of the Red Sea, so that the performed narrative becomes a cluster of narratives, all of which together attest a distinct identity with socioethical implications.[3] The reiteration and reperformance of that cluster were a primary form of resistance against the pressure and seduction of empire that wanted always to refuse the inconvenience of communities of particularity.

II

The remembered, remembering narrative of Israel, however, is not as straightforward as we might wish. The dynamic and complex traditioning process that Gerhard von Rad has articulated so masterfully has, since von Rad, become even more complex and problematic.[4] Not so long ago, thanks to the Albright school, the tradition to be remembered seemed fixed and reliable.[5] Now, however, in a season of skepticism, the matter is acutely complex. Beginning with John Van Seters's proposal that the ancestral narrative of Abraham comes very late, current majority critical opinion has come to judge that the early traditions lack early historical rootage.[6] Specifically, scholars judge that it is in the Persian postexilic period that Israel did much of its creative work in formulating the tradition that it situated and came to think of as old. Whether the material originated then or not, it was a time of immense creative generativity in shaping the tradition as a usable memory. To be sure, such a critical judgment about the memory is unnerving for those who hope for a flat,

---

3. Garrett Green, *Imagining God: Theology and the Religious Imagination* (Grand Rapids: Eerdmans, 1998).

4. Gerhard von Rad, *The Problem of the Hexateuch and Other Essays*, trans. E. W. Treuman Dicken (New York: McGraw-Hill, 1966), 1–78; and more fully in von Rad, *Old Testament Theology*, vol. 1, *The Theology of Israel's Historical Traditions* (New York: Harper & Brothers, 1962).

5. The predominant and summarizing text is John Bright, *A History of Israel*, 4th ed. (Louisville: Westminster John Knox, 2000).

6. John Van Seters, *Abraham in History and Tradition* (New Haven: Yale University Press, 1975). After Van Seters have come much more radical contentions under the flag of "minimalists." Grudgingly scholars have gravitated to much of the argument and conclusion of the "minimalists" concerning the dating and historical reliability of the tradition.

fixed past. But given Jesus's mandate to his disciples concerning interpretive agility, we may be grateful for current critical judgment.

1. The idea of a belated generativity reminds us that the remembered
tradition is dynamic and has vitality.

2. The idea of belated generativity asserts that every "present form" of
the tradition in some part is evoked by context and circumstance, so that
we may every time anticipate some acute contemporaneity in the tradition.

3. The idea of a belated generativity asserts that in any generation
we are not simply passive recipients of the tradition, but, as Ricoeur has
seen, we have a voice in constructing how the past goes.[7] Or, as my
friend Peter Block has said of the Soviet Union, "the past is quite unpre-
dictable." But of course much of the memory of the Old Testament is
open to reformulation in which the new generation always has a voice.
Or, as Moses asserts in Deuteronomy:

> Not with our ancestors did the Lord make this covenant, but with us, who
> are all of us here, alive today. (Deut 5:3)

This sequence of terse words, "us, all of us, here, alive, today," bespeaks
intensity and urgency beyond any settled tradition.

4. The idea of a belated generativity means that the memory is indeed
"thick" in the sense of Clifford Geertz and George Lindbeck, who, following Geertz can say:

> Thick description, it should be noted, is not to be confused with Baconian
> empiricism, with sticking to current facts. It is rather the full range of the
> interpretive medium which needs to be exhibited, and because this range
> in the case of religion is potentially all-encompassing, description has a cre-
> ative aspect. There is, indeed, no more demanding exercise of the inventive
> and imaginative powers than to explore how a language, culture, or religion
> may be employed to give meaning to new domains of thought, reality, and
> action. Theological description can be a highly constructive enterprise.[8]

7. Paul Ricoeur has in many places exposited the continually generative work of the biblical
narrative traditions. See, e.g., *Figuring the Sacred: Religion, Narrative, and Imagination*, trans.
David Pellauer, ed. Mark I. Wallace (Minneapolis: Fortress Press, 1995) 144–66, 236–48. Thus
he can speak of "productive imagination," on which see *A Ricoeur Reader: Reflection and Imagination*, ed. Mario J. Valdés, Theory/Culture Series 2 (Toronto: University of Toronto Press,
1991), 338–54. See also Yosef Hayim Yerushalmi, *Zakhor: Jewish History and Jewish Memory*,
The Samuel and Althea Stroum Lectures in Jewish Studies (Seattle: University of Washington
Press, 1982).

8. George A. Lindbeck, *The Nature of Doctrine: Religion and Theology in a Postliberal Age*
(Philadelphia: Westminster, 1984), 115.

Rather than concern for the historical reliability of the memory, we may follow Erich Voegelin's verdict that the tradition of Israel is "paradigmatic," so that it provides a plot line that is to be reiterated and reperformed in many circumstances.[9] Michael Walzer, to cite a specific example, concludes his study of the exodus tradition in this way:

> First, that wherever you live, it is probably Egypt;
> second, that there is a better place, a world more attractive, a promised land;
> and third, that "the way to the land is through the wilderness."
> There is no way to get from here to there except by joining together and marching.[10]

Thus, we may imagine the agile interpretive community of ancient Israel engaged always in reperformance of the memory, always rooted in the answers that parents give to the children but always recasting the answer as a way that requires both imagination and responsibility. This is an enterprise that has of course continued in rabbinic reflection, not least the rabbi whom we name as Messiah. The agility that requires imagination and responsibility is so urgent among us because of one-dimensional conservatives that want only to reiterate, and because of one-dimensional progressives who entertain such deep doubts about the credibility of the tradition and want to flee to "generic truth."

Agile remembering is in order to sustain oddity in an imperial environment. That oddity must be regularly and imaginatively reperformed. So the oddity is performed, belatedly, in ancient Israel by the Jew Daniel, who was in the civil service of the Babylonian Empire. He refused to eat imperial food lest it "defile" him (Dan 1:8). His notion of "defilement" was undoubtedly based on what were later, perhaps quite late, rules of purity. His performance, moreover, was designed to narrate oddity, and to summon hearers of the tale to an oddity that refused empire.[11] That oddity, so Daniel, characteristically has two markings. On the one hand, the performance of the memory yields *an oddity of holiness* that refuses defilement. Thus, in the great, difficult chapter 7, the poetry concerning the "fourth beast" says:

> He shall speak words against the Most High,
> shall wear out *the holy ones* of the Most High,
> and shall attempt to change the sacred seasons and the law. (Dan 7:25)

9. Erich Voegelin, *Order and History*, vol. 1, *Israel and Revelation* (Baton Rouge: Louisiana State University Press, 1956).

10. Michael Walzer, *Exodus and Revolution* (New York: Basic Books, 1985), 149.

11. See Daniel L. Smith-Christopher, *A Biblical Theology of Exile*, Overtures to Biblical Theology (Minneapolis: Fortress Press, 2002), 137–62, 182–88.

But two verses later, it is affirmed:

> The kingship and dominion and the greatness of the kingdoms under the
> whole heaven
> shall be given to *the people of the holy ones* of the Most High;
> their kingdom shall be an everlasting kingdom,
> and all dominions shall serve and obey them. (v. 27)

The maintenance of holiness matters for the future of the world.

On the other hand, the performance of the memory yields *justice.*
Thus, in unsolicited Jewish advice to the terrified king Nebuchadnezzar,
Daniel advises:

> Atone for your sins with righteousness, and your iniquities with mercy to
> the oppressed, so that your prosperity may be prolonged. (4:27)

Both *holiness and justice* as nonnegotiable elements of Israel's oddity show
up as peculiar testimony amid the empire. That testimony obviously
required immense ability and imagination, so that the memory could
operate with generativity. Everything depended on that memory!

III

We may, however, take the tradition of Hosea as *the great exposition of
forgetting.* Generative remembering is at best inconvenient and can be
costly. The Deuteronomic casting of the tradition in First and Second
Kings, the story of monarchy that provides the time line in which
are situated the several prophets who remember vigorously, exhibits a
Jerusalem establishment that was able to dismiss any claim it wanted to
forget—because remembering was inconvenient and costly. The cost of
remembering is evident in the dramatic encounter of king and prophet
in the narrative of Naboth's vineyard (1 Kings 21). Ahab found the old-
fashioned ideas of community patrimony a great inconvenience to a
commodity-based economy. It was easier to forget the old requirement
of tradition—which Ahab and Jezebel did, to their ultimate shame and
judgment.

The poetry of Hosea, a century after Naboth and Elijah, is a med-
itation about and testimony to the cost of forgetting. It is staged in
northern Israel but was readily reapplied to the destiny of Jerusalem.
Hosea is rooted in the old covenantal traditions that have been mediated
by Deuteronomy. Note well that the phrase "old covenantal traditions"
is itself difficult, because much critical opinion believes that the old

covenantal traditions were formulated in the eighth century, that is, near to the time of Hosea. As usual, we do not know whether "transmitted" or "invented" or "freshly formulated." The users of the tradition did not linger over the question. It is a given, a paradigmatic given in Hosea's poetry, that Israel is bound to YHWH in intimacy, intimacy like that of husband and wife, even if cast in patriarchal terms, or like that of father and son (yet again patriarchal). The tradition will eventually move beyond the patriarchal, but not yet. So here we consider Hosea's texts on forgetting because the "old covenantal memory" was inconvenient and costly, and there were better futures on offer.

1. The defining usage, I suppose, is in *Hosea 2:13:*

> I will punish her for the festivals days of the Baals,
> when she offered incense to them
> and decked herself with her ring and jewelry
> and went after her lovers
> and *forgot me*, says the Lord.

Forgot me! Found better alternatives, "lovers," gods, foreign alliances, sources of security. As you know, this judgment that reeks with futility is the midpoint in the great chapter 2, which moves from divorce (vv. 2–13) to remarriage (vv. 14–23). Here it is the divorce that concerns us. What uncommon poetic imagination to cast social reality bent on self-destruction as a crisis in an intimate relationship! We are so familiar with the imagery that we miss the daring. This God takes as partner not a goddess but a historical people. But that historical people, so their own narrative attests, found it inconvenient:

> For she said, "I will go after my lovers;
> They give me my bread and my water,
> My wool and my flax,
> My oil and my drink. (v. 5).

> She did not know that it was I who gave her
> The grain, the wine, and the oil,
> and who lavished upon her silver and gold that they used for Baal. (v. 8)

It is all about gifts that appear to be commodities. Israel could not connect gift and giver, and so thanked the wrong gods.

> Therefore I will hedge up her way with thorns;
> and I will build a wall against her,
> so that she cannot find her path. (v. 6)

The second "therefore" is long and intense:

> Therefore I will take back my grain in its time,
> and my wine in its season;
> and I will take away my wool and my flax
> which were to cover her nakedness . . .
> I will put an end to all her mirth,
> her festivals, her new moons, her Sabbaths,
> and all her appointed festivals.
> I will lay waste her vines and her fig trees . . .
> I will make them a forest and wild animals shall devour them.
> I will punish her . . . (vv. 9–13)

It is all punishment, except for the last line:

> Because she forgot me!

2. In *chapter 4* Hosea offers a succinct speech of judgment:

> The LORD has an indictment against the inhabitants of the land.
> There is no faithfulness or loyalty,
> and no knowledge of God in the land.
> Swearing, lying, and murder,
> and stealing and adultery break out;
> bloodshed follows bloodshed.
> Therefore the land mourns and all who live in it languish;
> together with the wild animals and birds of the air,
> even the fish of the sea are perishing. (4:1–3)

The poetic connection is amazing. The indictment is an enumeration of the Ten Commandments. The punishment is the dismantling of creation . . . wild animals, birds, fish. The remarkable connection is between violation of commandments and the dismantling of creation, held together by the fragile divine "therefore" that bespeaks cause and effect. The cause is violation of Torah; the effect is loss of creation. The implied positive is that obedience to commandments yields a viable creation. But not here! The connection of a relational kind trades on huge imagination.

The poem continues:

> My people are destroyed for lack of knowledge;
> because you have rejected knowledge,
> I reject you from being a priest to me.
> And since *you have forgotten the Torah of our God,*
> I also will forget your children. (v. 6)

Here it is not "forget me" as in 2:13 but "forget the Torah of the Lord your God." Forget to obey. Forget the oath of obedience. Forget the relationship. Forget and imagine autonomy. Forget and act in self-destructive stupidity. Forget like the archbishop simply forgot his mandate to the poor in his plan for a bigger house. Torah, remembered or forgotten, is not incidental; it is defining and it does not matter much if it is "forget me" or "forget my Torah." Forgetting is an act of one's self outside the narrative memory in pursuit of a better deal.

3. In *Hosea 8:4*, in what seems to be the only wholesale rejection of kingship in prophetic literature, the poet can have God say:

> They made kings, but not through me;
> They set up princes, but without my knowledge.
> With their silver and gold they made idols for their own destruction.

At the end of the chapter, there is this:

> Israel has *forgotten his Maker*,
> and built palaces;
> and Judah has multiplied fortified cities;
> but I will send a fire upon his cities,
> and it shall devour his strongholds. (8:14)

This is a curious juxtaposition of lines. Forgot his Maker. But the act of forgetting is building "big houses." The word could mean "palace" or "temple," that is, engaged in self-aggrandizement. The parallel line is "fortified cities," an arms program of "defense." Money and power, big house and arms, outcomes of amnesia. The implied positive alternative is that remembering one's maker precludes such pursuits of money and power. The impact of forgetting is immediately practical and visible. The divine "but" at the end of the verse concerns fire in the cities, devouring in their fortresses. The outcome of amnesia, says the poet, is destruction.

4. The fourth and final reference in *Hosea 13:4–6*. It begins with a quick retelling of the ancient deliverance:

> Yet I have been the Lord your God
> ever since the land of Egypt;
> you know no God but me,
> and besides me there is no savior.
> It was I who fed you in the wilderness,
> in the land of drought,
> When I fed them they were satisfied.

The generative wilderness left them satisfied outside the zone of Pharaoh's food supply because YHWH feeds. But then the poetry says a second time,

> They were satisfied, and their heart was proud;
> Therefore *they forgot me.*

They got high hearts. They forgot me. They were glad that YHWH had emancipated them. They were glad that YHWH saved them. But then they were no longer enslaved, not hungry, not in need, capable on their own. Now we are back to the rhetoric of 2:23: "forgot me." Thus, the fourfold mantra in these texts is "forgot me, forgot Torah, forgot your maker, forgot me," forgot the tradition, welcomed amnesia, because amnesia permits one to start afresh, encourages autonomy, have control, be self-sufficient.

Hosea sets it up so that Israel forgets and YHWH remembers:

> But they do not consider
> that *I will remember* all their wickedness;
> Now their deeds surround them,
> they are before my face. (7:2)

> Now *he will remember* their iniquity,
> and punish their sins. (8:13)

> *He will remember* their iniquity,
> He will punish their sins. (9:9)

We might wish for more slippage with a God less likely to keep a list of affronts. In this poetry, however, *the remembering God* is as crucial as *the forgetting of Israel.* The clash between divine remembering and Israel's amnesia issues in loss. This is a poetry of loss. This is anticipatory grief, not because the poet is a predictor, but because he knows from the tradition how the world is designed. He is, like every poet, rearticulating in savage ways an inescapable anticipation. The poetry will serve, whether one believes in such a God or not, because it is "inspired," an act of imagination that moves beyond the toxic amnesia of his contemporaries who are so smitten with big houses and good armaments that they have given up the task of imagining.

The outcome of this clash of Israel's amnesia and YHWH remembering is hard to hear:

In 2:13 their forgetting implies complete loss.

In 4:6 their forgetting yields this:

I will forget your children.

In 8:14 their forgetting yields this:

Fire upon his cities,
and it shall devour his strongholds.

In 13:6 forgetting yields this:

So I shall become like a lion to them,
like a leopard I will lurk beside the way.
I will fall on them like a bear robbed of her cubs,
and will tear open the covering of their heart;
there I will devour them like a lion,
as a wild animal would mangle them. (13:7–8)

It is just poetry. It is a thick rendering of the memory. It is memory
become an unbearable performance that resituates, that gives perspective
on the military establishment and the growth economy of affluent arro-
gance. The horror will be relieved by other lines in Hosea. It turns out
that the angry husband will reverse field and love Israel again. It turns out
that the raging father will come to tenderness that interrupts the tirade.
It turns out that "not my people" will again be called "my people." But
the poetry cannot be rushed. It takes lingering as the lover-husband-
father lingers before reversing field. These futures grow from YHWH's
remembering; but they do not in the moment cancel away the high cost
of amnesia.

IV

But if Hosea is the great script of forgetting, Deuteronomy is *the great
script of remembering*.[12] It is likely that Deuteronomy, in some initial form,
was formulated in the eighth century BCE, that is, in the same environ-

12. Paul Connerton (*How Modernity Forgets* [Cambridge: Cambridge University Press,
2009]) proposes that modern societies forget because they destroy or negate the "places" of
memory, and when those places are gone, there can be no remembering. Clearly the forgetting
of place was not a temptation to ancient Israel. Connerton writes of Deuteronomy:

Nowhere is this theology of memory more pronounced than in Deuteronomy. For the
Deuteronomist the test of showing that the new generation of Israel remains linked to the tradition of Moses, that present Israel has not been severed from its redemptive history, is to be met
by a form of life in which to remember is to make the past actual, to form a solidarity with the
fathers. This test is to be met in cultic demonstration; Israel observes festivals in order to remember. What is remembered is the historical narrative of a community. (*How Societies Remember*
[Cambridge: Cambridge University Press, 1989], 46)

ment as Hosea and is addressed to the same crisis. But even if they are contemporary, Deuteronomy is the "senior text," the established script in the Torah attributed to Moses. It establishes the baseline to which Hosea (and after him Jeremiah) can appeal. The remarkable characteristic of Deuteronomy and its articulation of Torah is its determined insistence on the contemporaneity of the tradition. Thus, Deuteronomy, as von Rad has shown, is a mediating step between the remembered engagement of Sinai and the witness of the prophets. Deuteronomy is the rereading of the tradition.

• Thus, already in Deuteronomy 1:5, at the very outset, we are told that Moses "expounded" this Torah. He did not simply reiterate, but he extended and interpreted Sinai in the material to follow. Sinai requires exegesis.

• In Deuteronomy 5:3 as noted, Moses insists upon contemporaneity.

• In the Decalogue itself we are given only one instance of such contemporaneity, but it is an important one. In the fourth commandment on the Sabbath, the grounding of the day of rest is no longer the rest of the creator on the seventh day as at Sinai; now the grounding is that "you were slaves in the land of Egypt" (Deut 5:15). As we will see, this note turns out to be the signature accent of contemporaneity. It is plausible that this accent on the exodus memory was stressed because the eighth century was a time of the growing gap between haves and have-nots that resulted in exploitative policy and practice.[13] Or, as Hosea expressed such an exploitative inclination:

A trader, in whose hands are false balances.
He loves to oppress.
Ephraim has said, "Ah, I am rich,
I have gained wealth for myself;
in all of my gain
no offense has been found in me." (12:7–8)

The tradition of Deuteronomy counters such an illusion by an imaginative act of interpretation.

• In Deuteronomy 17:18, it is urged that the king must keep a "copy" of the Torah primarily to forfend against confiscatory economics. But the term we render "copy" (in Greek *deuteros*), might as well mean a second version, that is, a second version of the memory, a revised version, a revised standard version, or maybe a new revised standard version. In that New Revised Standard Version, appeal to the exodus deliverance

13. On the eighth century, see D. N. Premnath, *Eighth Century Prophets: A Social Analysis* (St. Louis: Chalice, 2003), 1–98.

is primary. So in their singular law concerned with warning the king against usurpatious economic policies, Moses warns not to go to Egypt in order to acquire horses, that is, armaments, since God has said, "You must not return that way again." In 17:16, "Keep away from Egypt!" Keep away from confiscatory economics. Keep away from predatory policy for which the remembered Torah is the primary vehicle of resistance.

The accent on remembering is primary in the sermonic materials of Deuteronomy:

> When the LORD your God has brought you into the land that he swore to your ancestors, to Abraham, to Isaac, and to Jacob, to give you—a land with fine large cities that you did not build, houses filled with all sorts of goods that you did not fill, hewn cisterns that you did not hew, vineyards and olive trees that you did not plant—and when you have eaten your fill, *take care that you do not forget* the LORD, who brought you out of the land of Egypt, out of the house of slavery. (Deut 6:10–12)

Moses knows that self-sufficient affluence will produce amnesia:

> Remember the long way that the LORD your God has led you these forty years in the wilderness, in order to humble you, testing you to know what was in your heart, whether or not you would keep his commandments. . . . Therefore keep the commandments of the LORD your God, walking in his ways and by fearing him. For the LORD your God is bringing you into a good land, a land with flowing streams, with springs and underground waters welling up in valleys and hills, a land of wheat and barley, of vines and fig trees and pomegranates, a land of olive trees and honey, a land where you may eat bread without scarcity, where you will lack nothing, a land whose stones are iron and from whose hills you may mine copper. You shall eat your fill and bless the LORD your God for the good land that he has given you.
>
> *Take care that you do not forget* the LORD your God, by failing to keep his commandments, his ordinances, and statutes, which I am commanding you today. When you have eaten your fill and have built fine houses and live in them, and when your herds and flocks have multiplied and your silver and gold is multiplied, and all that you have is multiplied, then do not exalt yourself, forgetting the LORD your God, who brought you out of the land of Egypt, out of the house of slavery, who led you through the great and terrible wilderness, an arid wasteland with poisonous snakes and scorpions. . . . Do not say to yourself, "My power and the might of my own hand have gotten me this wealth." But remember the LORD your God, for it is he who gives you power to get wealth, so that he may confirm his covenant that he swore to your ancestors, as he is doing today. (Deut 8:2, 6–18)

The sermonic rant summarizes the urgency of Deuteronomy:

- Remembered wilderness sojourn attests dependence on YHWH.

- These gifts of God—land, water, wheat, barley, vines, fig trees, bread—invite self-sufficiency.

- The multiplication of herds and flocks, silver and gold, is a seduction away from memory (see Deut 17:14-20 on the same goods).

- Forgetting invites self-sufficiency just as self-sufficiency invites forgetting.

- Forgetting leads to idolatry and so extinction.

This heavy-handedness causes many Scripture interpreters not to like Deuteronomy (or Moses) very much. Except that it sounds so contemporary!

The sum of these sermons in chapters 6 and 8 is the worry that the new land of affluence into which they had entered was a seduction that would cut them off from their sustaining memory. And if the material is now dated to the exilic period, then perhaps it is a warning to the displaced Jews not to accommodate excessively to Babylonian prosperity. In whatever context the memory is situated, the issue is the same. Memory is a defining resource against every pressure that would talk Israel out of its identity and its destiny as the emancipated people of YHWH. Forgetting constitutes a forfeiture of a destiny grounded in emancipation.

But Deuteronomy is not primarily in a defensive posture concerned to fend off the seduction of Canaanite self-sufficiency or royal self-sufficiency in Jerusalem, or imperial self-sufficiency in Babylon or Persia. The tradition of Deuteronomy is rather concerned with articulating a positive alternative to such self-sufficiency, because self-sufficiency results, Moses understood, in social indifference or, as we now say, "privatization." The positive alternative that Deuteronomy locates in the memory is an economy that serves the common good.

Thus the narrative memory in Deuteronomy is generative of an alternative to self-sufficiency that eventuates in the common good. The positive alternative of memory is cited five times in the Torah provisions of Deuteronomy:

a. The text of overriding importance is the provision for the "Year of Release" in *Deuteronomy 15:1–18*.[14] The text describes (or anticipates) an economy that is subordinated to the common good and that provides a periodic and disciplined cancellation of debts for the poor. The intent is that there should be, in the community of covenant, no permanent underclass. The capstone of the provision is the mantra of Moses:

> Remember that you were slaves in the land of Egypt, and the Lord redeemed you. (15:15)

Moses connects old memory and present obligation.

This teaching about debt cancellation, surely the most radical socioeconomic requirement in the Torah, has remarkable rhetorical features:

It includes six absolute infinitives, that is, the repetition of the verb to underscore its urgency:

- You diligently observe (v. 5).
- Really open your hand (v. 8).
- Willingly lend (v. 8).
- Give liberally (v. 10).
- Really open your hand (V. 11).
- Provide liberally (v. 13).

Moses is greatly insistent on this regulation. Even more so, because he clearly encountered great resistance. Thus he warns against being "hard-hearted or tight-fisted." I have no doubt that Moses would have said about his opponents that they were seduced by an ideology of privatism made possible by their anxiety about their own life. The appeal to the exodus in verse 15 is an indication that Moses intends that the socioeconomic policy practice in Israel should be seen as an imitation of and a continuation of emancipation from Egypt. Observing such a policy is not possible in a society that cannot remember its own deliverance.

b. In *16:3*, at the beginning of the liturgical calendar with it provision for the Passover, direction is given for unleavened bread:

> For seven days you shall eat unleavened bread—the bread of affliction—because you came out of the land of Egypt in great haste, so that all

---

14. See Jeffries M. Hamilton, *Social Justice and Deuteronomy: The Case of Deuteronomy 15*, Society of Biblical Literature Dissertation Series 136 (Atlanta: Scholars Press, 1992).

the days of your life you may *remember* the day of your departure from the land of Egypt.

That is all. Nothing more is said about it. Moses knew that the ritual festival of Passover will keep the memory of emancipation active and perchance lead to an alternative ethic that is not here spelled out. Moses intends that the liturgical imagination of Israel should be so pervaded by the exodus memory that an exodus ethic would inevitably follow. Moses knew what Paul Ricoeur would reiterate, that imagination evokes concepts and concepts produce policy.[15] Imagination is the elemental and indispensable beginning point, imagination that lets ancient memory have contemporary bite.

c. What is implied and inchoate in the festival provision for Passover is made explicit in the Festival of Weeks *(16:11)*. The provision of Moses includes a guest list for the festival:

Rejoice before the Lord—you and your sons and your daughters, your male and female slaves, the Levites resident in your town, as well as the strangers, the orphans, and the widows who are among you. (16:11)

This list is not quite the same as the list for Sabbath rest in the commandment in 5:14. Both lists include "sons, daughters, slaves, and strangers." In the Sabbath list there are included "ox, donkey, livestock." In the festival list we have "Levites, orphans, and widows." Both lists intend inclusiveness. Both lists include vulnerable outsiders who will not be included in the guest lists of a predatory, hierarchical economy. Both lists intend that the people who can pay for the festival will open the festival to the vulnerable without resources. Both lists include "the other."

We can see how Moses works the tradition, because the inclusive list of the "other" is validated by the familiar refrain in verse 12:

Remember that you were a slave in Egypt, and diligently observe these statutes.

Remember slavery. Remember deliverance. Remember food. Remember life as gift. Remember and perform life as gift to those without resources.

d. In *24:10-13, 17-18* we have two regulations from Moses concerning credit, loans, and collateral. In the first of these, Moses provides that, in giving a loan to a neighbor, the creditor cannot enter the house of

---

15. My first reading in this was in *The Philosophy of Paul Ricoeur: An Anthology of His Work* ed. Charles E. Reagan and David Stewart (Boston: Beacon Press, 1978), where Ricoeur adumbrated the way in which imagination generates concepts. He has elaborated on this in many subsequent places.

the debtor to seize collateral. It must be brought out. If the debtor is poor, the coat taken as collateral cannot be kept overnight but must be returned at dusk to the debtor so that the poor person can keep warm at night. The debtor can pick up the coat as collateral the next morning and keep it all day but must return it again at night. Can you imagine doing that for a thirty-year loan! I suggest that Moses intended to make it so inconvenient that the creditor would forgo collateral. In the second provision, Moses commands:

> You shall not deprive a resident alien or an orphan of justice; you shall not take a widow's garment in pledge.

In verse 12 it is the "poor." Here it is "alien, orphan, widow." In both it is the vulnerable without resources, the ones "unlike" the creditors who have lending capacity. Here the holding of collateral is prohibited, whereas earlier it was only made impossibly inconvenient. The end of the second provision has this appeal:

> Remember that you were slaves in Egypt and the Lord your God redeemed you from there; therefore I command you to do this. (v. 18)

Memory has ethical implications; and of course so does amnesia.

Sandwiched between the two regulations on loans in verses 10–13 concerning the poor and in verses 17–18 concerning the widow, orphan, and immigrant is a regulation about wages for workers (Deut 24:14–15). It proposes that one must pay "the poor and needy laborers" and cannot say to them, "the check is in the mail." Payment must be made the day it is earned. Moses already knew about wage theft:

> You shall pay them their wages daily before sunset, because they are poor and their livelihood depends on them. Otherwise they might cry out against you, and you will incur guilt. (v. 15)

The cry of the poor about wage theft is simply an echo, from the memory, of the initial cry of the slaves in Egypt that mobilized YHWH to emancipation. The cry, wherever it is sounded, will evoke healing, emancipatory power.

e. Finally in this inventory of Deuteronomy, I mention *23:19–22*, which has a remarkable symmetry. It is symmetrical because it concerns the three great money crops, grain, wine, and oil. These are the money crops for which Israel, in Hosea, forgot to thank YHWH (Hos 2:8). This commandment is symmetrical because it names the triad of widow, orphan, and stranger, those who characteristically are denied access to the money crops that must be shipped out for profit. The urging of Moses is to forgo some profit and leave some of the three money crops for those without resources:

> When you reap your harvest . . . you shall not go back to get it; it shall be left for the alien, the orphan, and the widow . . . when you beat your olive trees, do not strip what is left; it shall be left for the alien, the orphan, and the widow. When you gather the grapes of your vineyard, do not glean what is left; it shall be for the alien, the orphan, and the widow.

The forgoing of profit means a break in the endless cycle of the predatory economy. The provision is significant enough for Frank Crüsemann that he will say that it is the first governmental social safety net.[16] By this time it will not surprise you that Moses adds:

> Remember that you were slaves in Egypt. (v. 22)

Remembering ancient status as slaves is to remember a time before self-sufficiency; it is to remember a time of wretched needfulness that in this case was answered by the free food of manna. Free food for the resourceless, likely presumed to be the undeserving, the unproductive resourceless, is to break the grip of earned resources and the iron linkage between productivity and sustenance. When the exodus narrative is kept palpably available, Israel can maintain its distinct identity in either a royal or imperial context that wanted to negate that identity in order to reduce everything to a commodity. It turns out that the resourceless triad of widow, orphan, and stranger are not the "undeserving poor" or the forgotten. When the memory has credibility, they are neighbors more like us than different from us.

Thus I propose that the *forgetting in Hosea* and the *remembering in Deuteronomy* taken together provide a matrix in which we may consider the cruciality of memory, the generative energy of memory, and the high cost of amnesia.

- In canonical context, the claims of Deuteronomy are the authoritative backdrop to which Hosea can make appeal in his crisis. Thus, Hosea sounds like an echo of Deuteronomy in his imperative:

---

16. Frank Crüsemann, *The Torah: Theology and Social History of Old Testament Law*, trans. Allan W. Mahnke (Edinburgh: T&T Clark, 1996), 224–34.

> Return to your God,
> Hold fast to love and justice,
> And wait continually for your God. (Hos 12:6)

The "return to your God" is a favorite theme of Deuteronomy, a return to the memory from a land of amnesia. It is remarkable that in Hosea 12:5 we have:

> The LORD of hosts is his name.

But the term rendered "name" is *zēker*, his memorial, his remembrance, his memory. Verses 5 and 6 together are a recall to the claim that the name YHWH itself bespeaks *ḥesed* and *mišpat*, community solidarity in well-being. Hosea's imperative is a summons away from a commodity society freed to a neighborly practice.

• In conventional critical perspective, Deuteronomy and Hosea share an eighth-century context of Israel's predatory economy in which a covenantal, neighborly possibility was deeply at risk, canceled out by the power of commodity.

• In recent critical perspective, the texts are situated in exilic or postexilic context when imperial demand and pressure crowded out distinctive memory. It turns out, in canonical, conventional critical, and newer critical context, the issue is very much the same. If and when Israel can scuttle its distinctive narrative memory with its implied neighborly mandate, Israel can join the dominant practice of anti-neighborliness. Of course in any of these proposed contexts as in our own, the power of amnesia is not to eradicate the memory. It is rather to trim its edges and blunt it sharpness into acceptability. With such trimming and blunting, of course, the identity of the community is compromised, and the demands of vocation are softened to collusion. One always considers in Israel whether Passover and the Festivals of Weeks and Booths and simple narration will suffice against seductive amnesia. But Moses lives in hope:

> Keep these words that I am commanding you today in your heart. Recite them to your children and talk about them when you are at home and when you are away, when you lie down and when you rise. Bind them as a sign on your hand, fix them as an emblem on your forehead, and write them on the doorposts of your house and on your gates. (Deut 6:6–9)

V

Ours is a time of turmoil so that the crisis of remembering and forgetting becomes visible to us. That same issue is present to us all of the time, but in "ordinary" times we do not notice. Here are three texts that occur to me from times of turmoil not unlike our own.

1. *Hosea 2* indicates that YHWH remembers in spite of Israel's recalcitrance. You will recall that YHWH's speech of judgment against Israel ended in verse 13 with the resounding indictment, "You forgot me." The poem, however, does not end there because YHWH continues to remember. As Israel nearly forfeited its destiny in amnesia, YHWH reiterates YHWH's own identity. What follows is a fresh resolve by YHWH to reembrace forgetful Israel. This divine remembrance, so says the poem, will lead to disarmament and to the renewal of creation (2:18). And then, in a most remarkable assertion, YHWH utters a unilateral wedding vow of fidelity toward Israel. YHWH remembers and signs on for the full vocabulary of fidelity that permeates the memory:

> I will take you for my wife forever; I will take you for my wife in righteousness and in justice, in steadfast love and in mercy. And I will take you for my wife in faithfulness, and you shall know the Lord. (2:19–20)

This summary from YHWH's side is not a memory of Israel's recalcitrance. It is rather a divine recall of the depth of faithfulness for which YHWH is both the agent and cipher. The word pair "steadfast love and faithfulness" (later to become "grace and truth") is joined with "mercy" as YHWH's most elemental terms of commitment to Israel. The second word pair, "righteousness and justice," recalls a social vision not unlike that of Deuteronomy and often sounded in the prophets. The fifth term, "compassion," bespeaks YHWH's vulnerable pathos-filled willingness to risk, a term that Hosea will have YHWH speak in a move beyond divine anger:

> My heart recoils within me;
> my *compassion* grows warm and tender. (11:8)

The sum of these five terms is a memory of the entire past of divine fidelity and the resolve of YHWH for the future. It is, moreover, the anticipation of YHWH that such a torrent of divine fidelity will evoke a response from Israel that is better than amnesia, "You shall know the Lord." YHWH's memory is thick and resilient:

The LORD is merciful and gracious,
slow to anger and abounding in steadfast love.
He will not always accuse,
nor will he keep his anger forever.
He does not deal with us according to our sins,
nor repay us according to our iniquities . . .
As a father has compassion for his children,
so the LORD has compassion for those who fear him. (Ps 103:8–10, 13)

2. *Lamentations 3:22–24* shows that Israel is capable of remembering even in the face of terminal destruction. Lamentations is set immediately in the wake of the destruction of Jerusalem when those left behind in Jerusalem faced daily reminders of the loss of temple, city, and political viability. The loss of viable life supports brought with it the loss of hope:

He has made my teeth grind on gravel,
and made me cower in ashes;
my soul is bereft of peace;
I have forgotten what happiness is;
So I say, "Gone is my glory,
and all that I had hoped for from the LORD."
The thought of my affliction and my homelessness
is wormwood and gall!
My soul continually thinks of it
and is bowed down within me. (Lam 3:16–20)

All that Israel's memory had vouched for is now a faded possibility Verse 20 is a remarkable hint of what is to come. The NRSV translates it: "My soul continually thinks of it." But the Hebrew is an infinitive absolute of *zkr*: "My *nephesh* really remembers." My *nephesh* remembers who it was and how it has now been lost. Elsewhere the term *zkr* is almost always rendered "remember," but here in the NRSV it has been reduced to "think," and the emphatic infinitive is reduced to "continually." Notwithstanding such weak translation, the use of the term *zkr* opens a new verse:

This I call to mind.

The term *zkr* is not used here; rather it is, "I return this to my heart." And therefore, as a consequence of such a return, the "this" is a return of sanity in this staggering four liner:

The steadfast love of the Lord never ceases,
His mercies never come to an end;
they are new every morning;
Great is your faithfulness. (Lam 3:22–23)

In the most dire circumstance of despair, the poem can recall the great
terms of fidelity that are filled in the memory with narrative specificity:
"steadfast love, mercy, faithfulness." Here are three of the five that
YHWH reiterates in Hosea 2. As the five words override the disobedience of Israel in Hosea, so here the three words of remembering override
the debacle of Jerusalem. The memory has within it enormous resilience:

The LORD is my portion, says my soul,
therefore I have hope. (Lam 3:24)

We have moved quickly from "all that I had hoped for is gone," to
"therefore I have hope," to "therefore I will hope in him." That passage is
made possible by the substance of the memory. Kathleen O'Conner says
of these verses:

> The taproot of the strongman's hope, the unseen source of his confidence,
> is God's own faithful character, affirmed in many places in the Old Testa-
> ment. In the abundant plural, God never stops showing mercies and loving-
> kindness. Every morning God's newborn mercies surprise and overturn.
> Though the strongman's life is in ruins and trauma encompasses his being,
> in his own deep act of faithfulness, he remembers that YHWH is his "por-
> tion."[17]

But O'Connor will not let us rest easily with that, for she adds:

> The poem could stop here. This passionate outpouring could be the end of
> the strongman's words, his complaint resolved in trust and hope. But the
> strongman's suffering is too deep to be overturned for long by simple theo-
> logical affirmation.[18]

This rememberer has material with which to work; but much work
remains to be done with the memory, to make sure it is not an illusion.
It is that continuing work that the poem continues to address, clear to
the end of the alphabet.

17. Kathleen M. O'Connor, *Lamentations and the Tears of the World* (Maryknoll, NY: Orbis
Books, 2002), 50.
18. O'Connor, *Lamentations*, 50.

3. *Psalm 78* is both an example of remembering and a study in the importance of remembering. The actual remembering on exhibit here is about YHWH's fidelity and Israel's stubborn resistance. Here I call attention to the wise recognition of the process:

> We will not hide them from their children;
> we will tell to the coming generation
> the glorious deeds of the LORD, and his might,
> and the wonders that he has done.
> He established a decree in Jacob,
> and appointed a law in Israel,
> which he commanded our ancestors to teach to the children;
> that the next generation might know them,
> and the children yet unborn,
> and rise up and tell them to their children,
> so that they should set their hope in God,
> and not forget the works of God,
> but keep his commandments;
> and that they should not be like their ancestors,
> a stubborn and rebellious generation,
> a generation whose heart was not steadfast,
> whose spirit was not faithful to God. (Ps 78:4–8)

The memory to be entrusted to the children is about wonders that violate all explanatory categories. The dual purpose of the recall is (a) to keep the commandments in obedience, and (b) to set hope in God. It is grace and law, *Gabe* and *Aufgabe*, but what strikes me is that the proclamation of divine resolve in this psalm is a ground for hope. The hope is in this:

> Yet he, being compassionate,
> Forgave their iniquity,
> And did not destroy them;
> often he restrained his anger,
> and did not stir up all his wrath.
> He remembered that they were but flesh,
> a wind that passes and does not come again. (vv. 38–39)

YHWH is compassionate; YHWH remembered Israelite, human frailty; YHWH forgives. This quality of YHWH permits Israel to imagine a viable future.

The negative counterpart to such remembering in verse 8 concerns the previous generation in its amnesia:

Stubborn and rebellious,
A generation whose heart was not steadfast,
whose spirit was not faithful to God.

The awareness is that remembering leads to a viable life; forgetting leads
to a barbaric society of infidelity and corruption. The teaching task is
urgent.

I add one footnote to the concern of this psalm. The contrast in the
psalm concerning fidelity and infidelity is fairly commonplace. We are
surprised, however, that at the end of the psalm we get a curious turn of
rhetoric that we had not anticipated. Verses 59–62 tell of termination in
divine anger for northern Israel:

> When God heard, he was full of wrath,
> and he utterly rejected Israel.
> He abandoned his dwelling at Shiloh,
> the tent where he dwelt among mortals,
> and delivered his power to captivity,
> his glory to the hand of the foe.
> He gave his people to the sword,
> and vented his wrath on his heritage, (vv. 59–62)

But these verses are simply a setup for what follows. The termination of
the north leads to his choice of Judah:

> He chose the tribe of Judah,
> Mount Zion which he loves,
> He built his sanctuary like the high heavens,
> like the earth, which he has founded forever.
> He chose his servant David,
> and took him from the sheepfolds;
> from tending the nursing ewes he brought him
> to be shepherd of his people Jacob,
> of Israel, his inheritance. (vv. 68–71)

The end of the psalm confirms the divine choosing of Judah, Mount
Zion, and David, the entire Jerusalem establishment. In its final form,
the historical recital is bent to call attention to the divine repudiation of
northern Israel and the elevation of southern Judah. This strikes me as
remote from the tone and texture of the foregoing. Now the psalm and
its memory have been hijacked for ideology; now the children are to be
taught about divine repudiation and divine choosing. The glad psalm has
been captured for the use of Jerusalem. It is a caution to us that history
has its uses, that the past can be used to justify present power arrange-

ments, and the legitimacy of unjust social confiscation. It is likely that this psalm was bent amid the turmoil around the question of northern and southern legitimacy in ancient Israel; it occurs to me that this was not the last time the Bible was used, even in these environs, to settle questions of northern and southern legitimacy, but I will leave that to Professor Clarke.[19]

VI

It remains only for me to say that we live in a time of deep turmoil about the crisis of remembering and forgetting. I suggest that the crisis of scuttling memory is a two-step maneuver among us. First is to recognize that market ideology, which is now totalizing among us, specializes in amnesia and in the ready use of the delete button. Money is readily transportable, places are virtual, community consists in flash mobs, and we live in a fast network of surface relationships. Such a way of life is inimical to memory and wants to empty memory of its staying power.

But the second step in an ideology of commoditization is to fill the space of deleted memory with universal claims and uncontested offers for the maintenance of beauty, youth, wealth, control, security, and limitless well-being. The double process of *emptying memory* and *generating ersatz memory* is vigorous among us.

In the midst of that powerful, seemingly irresistible pressure sits the church and its seminaries. The church and its seminaries are inescapably taken up with the crisis of remembering and forgetting, tempted to amnesia but knowing better. What better finish to this exploration than to recall the wise narrative of William Cavanaugh, who reports on the way in which Chilean bishops found the Eucharist to be the remembering that was a thick counter and antidote to the thin offer of torture in the regime of Pinochet.[20] What the bishops could recall is that "we do this in remembrance." We cannot do that effectively, however, with staying power unless the memory is thick and critical and endlessly on exhibit. Pinochet in Chile much preferred amnesia, a script for death. Our odd evangelical narrative at the table you know very well:

---

19. Editor's note: Erskine Clarke, who organized the colloquium at which Brueggemann presented an earlier version of this chapter, is professor emeritus of American Religious History at Columbia Theological Seminary in Decatur, Georgia. Clarke's work focuses on religion and slavery in the southern United States.

20. William T. Cavanaugh, *Torture and Eucharist: Theology, Politics, and the Body of Christ*, Challenges in Contemporary Theology (Oxford: Blackwell, 1998).

We remember his death;
We proclaim his resurrection;
We await his coming in glory.
It is remembering that makes possible proclaiming and waiting.

13.

Memory (II): Nostalgia and Obligation to Forget

This chapter was originally presented at a colloquium at Columbia Theological Seminary in Decatur, Georgia, on April 20, 2015. The title of the colloquium, organized by Dr. Erskine Clarke, was "The Church Facing the Future: Memory, Hope, and Obedience."

> One of the most persistent ways of reacting to disaster, decline, or powerlessness is nostalgia for an imagined great age in the past, often at the beginnings of the national or ethnic group, and more often than not in the form of the recovery of political and military power and influence.[1]

The generative force of memory was easily compromised in ancient Israel by the temptation to amnesia. On the other hand, it is clear that Israel was tempted in a second way as well by "over-remembering" or by "better remembering," which I will discuss under the rubric of "nostalgia," a deep longing homesickness for the way it used to be. The exile was for Israel a crisis of deep loss—of city, temple, monarchy, of a viable political identity; but it was also a loss of supreme confidence in status as God's guaranteed chosen people.[2] In such a season of loss, it is no wonder that Israel looked back with eager longing for the way it had been, or

---

1. Joseph Blenkinsopp, *David Remembered: Kingship and National Identity in Ancient Israel* (Grand Rapids: Eerdmans, 2013), 126.

2. On the exile, see James M. Scott, ed., *Exile: Old Testament, Jewish, and Christian Conceptions*, Supplements to the Journal for the Study of Judaism 56 (Leiden: Brill, 1997), and derivatively Edward W. Said, *Reflections on Exile and Other Essays*, Convergences (Cambridge: Harvard University Press, 2000). More accessibly, see Daniel L. Smith-Christopher, *The Religion of the Landless: The Social Context of the Babylonian Exile* (Bloomington, IN: Meyer-Stone Books,

the way that they remembered it had been, or the way that they wished it had been. Exile is a troubled time of turmoil with an unsorted mix of remembering and of forgetting, of remembering too little or too much. Here I will consider the latter, the danger of remembering too much. The situation in exile, most scholars think, consisted in an elite community of deported people carried off to Babylon, and a larger population left behind in Jerusalem. The larger community back in Jerusalem is voiced in Lamentations with its nearly unrelieved sadness without consolation.[3] Most of the rest of exilic material comes from the smaller company of elites who had been deported to Babylon.

I

It is the community of elite Jews in Babylon that was much more influential and which engaged in much more nostalgia. Indeed, the people left behind in Jerusalem had little opportunity, I suspect, for nostalgia, confronted as they were with the facts on the ground.

1. The lead text that concerns nostalgia among deported Jews is, I think, obviously *Isaiah 43:14–21*. Second Isaiah is addressed to those exiles concerning the gospel declaration that YHWH will soon permit Jews to go home to Jerusalem. YHWH will do so as the redeemer, creator of Israel:

> Thus says the LORD:
> Who makes a way in the sea,
> a path in the mighty waters,
> who brings out chariot and horse,
> army and warrior;
> they lie down, they cannot rise,
> they are extinguished,
> quenched like a wick. (Isa 43:16–17)

The cadence of "they lie down, they cannot rise, they are extinguished" is an echo of Moses's old song of triumph (Exod 15:1–18). It is clear that the sea imagery is an allusion back to the exodus deliverance; YHWH will perform a new exodus and a new emancipation from imperial bondage!

But the allusion to the exodus turned out, with this audience, not to

1989); and Smith-Christopher, *A Biblical Theology of Exile*, Overtures to Biblical Theology (Minneapolis: Fortress Press, 2002).

3. See Norman K. Gottwald, "Social Class and Ideology in Isaiah 40–55: An Eagletonian Reading," in *The Bible and Liberation: Political and Social Hermeneutics*, ed. Norman K. Gottwald and Richard A. Horsley, rev. ed. (Maryknoll, NY: Orbis Books, 1993), 329–42.

be simply background. It functioned for them to recall the exodus they eagerly remembered. The prophet's listeners were so preoccupied with the old exodus memory that they engaged in nostalgia about that miraculous event that had given them identity as God's chosen people. They were apparently so fixed on the old exodus that they were unmoved by the poetic imaginative testimony about a new contemporary deliverance. Because they did not have the interpretive skills or freedom to turn the memory to the future, they lingered excessively in that past, which now had no emancipatory force. For that reason, the poet chides the exiles for their nostalgic look back:

> Do not remember the former things,
>   or consider the things of old. (43:18)

What a strange thing to say to a displaced people: Do not remember! Do not cling to that past. Because if you cling excessively to the past, you will miss the newness being enacted before your very eyes. The matter is tricky, because without the old memory appeal to it as typology makes no sense.[4] But they apparently held to it one-dimensionally, without the capacity to liberate the memory for future-generating typology. So God, via the poet, insists:

> I am about to do a new thing;
> Now it springs forth, do you not perceive it?
> I make a way in the wilderness
> and rivers in the desert.
> The wild animals will honor me,
> The jackals and the ostriches,
> For I give water in the wilderness,
> rivers in the desert, to give drink to my chosen people,
> the people whom I formed for myself
> so that they might declare my praise. (43:19–21)

The question "Do you not perceive it?" is partly an admonition by the poet, who cannot believe that his people prefer the past to future possibilities. Partly it is reprimand for resistance to the newness that they should welcome.

---

4. On this tricky reuse of the exodus tradition in Second Isaiah, see Bernhard W. Anderson, "Exodus Typology in Second Isaiah," in *Israel's Prophetic Heritage: Essays in Honor of James Muilenburg*, ed. Bernhard W. Anderson and Walter Harrelson (New York: Harper & Brothers, 1962), 177–95; and Anderson, "Exodus and Covenant in Second Isaiah and the Prophetic Tradition," in *Magnalia Dei, The Mighty Acts of God: Essays on the Bible and Archaeology in Memory of G. Ernest Wright*, ed. Frank Moore Cross, Werner E. Lemke, and Patrick D. Miller Jr. (Garden City, NY: Doubleday, 1976), 339–60.

Indeed, there is evidence of such resistance to God's new thing. In Isaiah 45:1, Second Isaiah has declared that Cyrus, the Persian ruler, will be God's new messiah who will permit the Jews to go home. How odd to be delivered by a gentile messiah! Some of his Jewish listeners would have none of it, wanting to be saved by a Jewish messiah. The prophet rebukes those who resist the offer of deliverance:

> Woe to you who strive with your Maker,
> earthen vessels with the potter!
> Does the clay say to the one who fashioned it,
> "What are you making?"
> or "Your work has no handles?"
> Woe to anyone who says to a father,
> "What are you begetting?"
> or to a mother, "With what are you in labor?" (Isa 45:9–10)

"Woe" twice; woe . . . big trouble. These lines trace the way in which clay obeys the potter without question, and the way in which semen keeps moving without objection, and the way in which the fetus moves amid the mother's labor without protest:

> Clay without questioning!
> Semen without objection!
> Fetus without protest!

And says the poet:

> Israel without resistance!

Israel without resistance to God's intended rescue by way of a *goi* messiah! But nostalgia would object; they resisted that deliverance. Because the emancipation must be Jewish, and if not a Jewish messiah, then none at all. Their backward look caused them to resist God's new thing. The new thing, says the poet, is "rivers in the desert," a transformed landscape, a renewed creation, water for wild animals, jackals and ostriches, and for God's own people,

> So that they might declare my praise.

As Moses and Miriam had given praise to YHWH the first time around. But the exiles wanted to drop out of the new movement of God's emancipation, because it did not square with their blessed memory about how it had been and how it must be now. Fossilized memory had made them fundamentalists who refused new possibility.

2. A second text of nostalgia among the deported exiles in Babylon is in the vexed *Psalm 137*. As you know, this psalm is the only one that can be securely dated, "by the waters of Babylon." It is by the canals to which they had been deported. Those alien canals in a strange place evoked sadness and surely self-pity:

> By the waters of Babylon—
> there we sat down and wept
> when we remembered Zion.
> On the willows there we hung up our harps. (Ps 137:1–2)

The phrase "There we sat down and wept" eventually became a stylized phrase, for it is used later by Nehemiah when he heard that Jerusalem remained in a hopeless stage (Neh 1:4).

> For there our captors asked us for songs,
> And our tormentors asked for mirth, saying,
> "Sing us one of the Songs of Zion." (Ps 137:3)

Psalm 137 is a very sad song by people who had lost Jerusalem and yearned for it. More than that, they were required in their new context of hostility to sing the "Songs of Zion" by way of mockery. The "Songs of Zion" are those wonderful psalms that celebrate Jerusalem the best known of which is Psalm 46:

> God is our refuge and strength,
> a very present help in trouble,
> Therefore we will not fear,
> though the earth should change,
> though the mountains shake in the heart of the sea;
> though its waters roar and foam,
> though the mountains tremble with its tumult. (Ps 46:1–3)

The psalm asserts that Jerusalem is safe amid every chaos because the God of Jacob dwells there. But now their captors require them to sing the psalm in order to expose the unbearable contradiction between the old claim and present reality. It turns out that Jerusalem was not safe, and that the God of Jacob could not protect it, or they would not have been deported. The clash between old liturgical claim and present reality created an unbearable dissonance, I think, not unlike the dissonance created on 9/11 between the theological claims of US *exceptionalism* and the extreme *vulnerability* of the day.

The humiliation of such mockery that exposed the contradiction, however, did not lead to remorse or silence. It led to resolve for what was remembered:

> If I forget you, O Jerusalem, let my right hand wither!
> Let my tongue cling to the roof of my mouth,
> if I do not remember you,
> if I do not set Jerusalem above my highest joy. (Ps 137:5–6)

This is a vow among the elites that the old Jerusalem that they passionately remembered would continue to be their hope and their point of reference. All of the mockery and humiliation will not shake loyalty to the old city. It is remembered as their highest joy. Their vows of loyalty are so deep as to wager against a withered hand or a failed tongue, as to say, "We really mean this!"

Now this act of remembering is a positive, a resolve not to be talked out of Jewish identity. But we should consider the Jerusalem they remembered. It is above highest joy. But the Jerusalem they remembered so passionately is not the real Jerusalem. It is a conjured Jerusalem. Or it is a privileged Jerusalem that they had experienced as urban elites that was not experienced by many others. If we take prophetic poetry seriously, Jerusalem was not, for very many people, such a happy place.

- It was a place of economic violence, of cheap labor, loan sharks, and exploitation. It was a place where defense spending to resist imperial threat jeopardized the economy.

- It was a place of political foolishness in which the last king, the one after these first exiles, would renege on the emancipation of slaves.

- It was a place where dangerous poetic types were unwelcome, as Manasseh killed them and Jehoiakim dispatched a posse after one.

- It was a place in which high state liturgies had deeply compromised old covenantal commitments, in which Torah commandments were recited and disregarded, in which self-indulgence by way of surplus wealth was based on peasant productivity.

Of course this is not the Jerusalem remembered in the psalm. Perhaps these elites had lived such a protected life, not impinged upon by such realities, that they did not know. More likely their displacement had earned them a "more perfect" memory, so they screened out the unseemly for the sake of certitude. As in many cases, as people of influence they had not suffered what the poets evidenced. As a result, the Jerusalem they swore to remember was an unreal Jerusalem, an ideological construct of privilege and denial. This they will never forget!

As you know, this deep vow to remember issues in some of the most difficult verses in Scripture. First there is a cry that God should remember the enemies of Jerusalem:

> Remember, O LORD, against the Edomites
> the days of Jerusalem's fall,
> how they said, "Tear it down!
> Down to its foundations!" (Ps 137:7)

It is enough that God remember this threat against the city. This verse does not even suggest that God ought to respond. God will know what to do if God brings it to mind . . . as we bring it to memory. And then from Edom to Babylon:

> O daughter Babylon, you devastator!
> Happy shall be they who pay you back
> what you have done to us.
> Happy shall they be who take your little ones
> and dash them against the rock! (Ps 137:8–9)

Babylon is the devastator of Jerusalem, this same Babylon that now requires of them humiliating songs. Now it is not YHWH who devastated Jerusalem, as the old prophets had insisted. Now it is hated empire. What follows is not an action. And it is not a prayer. It is only a hunger. It is a wish and a hope for revenge, revenge now not to be enacted against the soldiers or the rulers, but against the children!

We cringe at these verses, even though as a child I can remember our church choir vigorously singing these words without awareness of what they said. How could God's people sing such vengeance and imagine such brutality? How could these old deep humiliations and losses be transferred to the fate of Babylonian children? Well, I suggest that nostalgia with attachment to an old imagined city and a deep resolve located in humiliation can readily enough move to unrestrained violence. Such nostalgia is an illusionary world. There never was such a city; the Songs of Zion were never true in the first place, because God does not sign on for real estate. But the drama of ideology by way of liturgy makes many things true that are false. And when made "true," they can be defended and justified by extreme measures. The shift from "We remember Zion" (v. 1) to "remember, O LORD" (v. 7) seeks to recruit YHWH into the memory of Israel, and expects that YHWH will act according to that memory of joy and wonder now lost in humiliation and shame. Nostalgia readily morphs into unmitigated vengeance, and these passions have not yet been exhausted.

3. The "Remember, O LORD" in Psalm 137:7 leads me to a third text concerning the Amalekites. In Exodus 17:8–15 there is a narrative about a remembered combat between Israel in the wilderness and the Amalekites. It is reported that Moses, with his powerful hands held high, led Israel to victory over the Amalekites. But when Moses was weary and lowered his tired powerful hand, he caused Israel to be vulnerable and then defeated by Amalek. But when Aaron and Hur held up Moses's weary hands, Joshua, his aide, defeated Amalek. After the reported victory over Amalek, the Torah narrative adds this note:

> Then the Lord said to Moses, "Write this as reminder in a book and recite it in the hearing of Joshua: "I will utterly blot out the remembrance of Amalek from under heaven." And Moses built an altar and called it, The Lord is my banner. He said, "A hand upon the banner of the Lord! The Lord will have war with Amalek from generation to generation. (Exod 17:14–16)

It is a reminder from God, a "Post-it" note about whom to hate:

> Blot out . . . war to all generations!

This will never end! This must never end! It must never end, because Amalek tried to take advantage of Moses's weariness. Such an attack on vulnerability must be repaid . . . endlessly!

It surprises us, moreover, that in the corpus of commandments in Deuteronomy 12–25, the final commandment, in privileged placement, concerns this same Amalek (Deut 25:17–19). This is the place where Moses wrote it, as instructed. This is the very last commandment in this tradition. It begins with historical review and memory:

> Remember what Amalek did to you on your journey out of Egypt, how he attacked you on the way when you were faint and weary, and struck down all who lagged behind you; he did not fear God. (Deut 25:17–18)

We would not know from this that Joshua had prevailed over the Amalekites. We know only that the Amalekites took advantage of weariness. From that comes the "therefore" of mandate:

> Therefore when the LORD your God has given you rest from all your enemies on every hand, in the land that the LORD your God is giving you as an

inheritance to possess, you shall blot out the remembrance of Amalek from under heaven; do not forget. (Deut 25:19)

Take care of pressing business first. But then blot out the remembrance of the Amalekites from under heaven; do that at your leisure. The phrase is the same as in the exodus narrative: "Blot out" memory. By the time of Deuteronomy, there were no more Amalekites. There was only the memory. But the memory lingers, because the memory of humiliation lingers. It is the memory that is to be blotted out, not the Amalekites, who are long since gone. Israel is to remember to blot out a memory. And the text ends ominously, "Do not forget." Do not forget to blot out memory. It is an odd imperative. But the work of *forgetting* is to *remember* forever.

I judge that this is an act of escalated nostalgia. The root report in Exodus is of a normal battle encounter. Every adversary tries to take an enemy who is weary. What the Amalekites are said to have done is not exceptional. What is exceptional is that the narrative tradition chose to take this routine military encounter and transpose it into a pivotal test of loyal remembering. Israel's humiliation draws Israel to recall past humiliations and keep them available. Israel's memory of humiliation demands eternal negation against a normal enemy, escalated as a product of a continuing imagined enemy. Nostalgia feeds on loss; it also feeds on wounds that are never to be forgotten and therefore can never be resolved. Such a memory, moreover, can be drawn on endlessly in new circumstances, because it is continually a call to arms.

4. The final text I cite is *Psalm 89*. I am not sure it is a text of nostalgia, but I will consider how it might be. Psalm 89:1–37 is a liturgical psalm of the Davidic house. It celebrates God's unconditional commitment to the dynasty enunciated in 2 Samuel 7. It repeatedly asserts, in a favorite word pair, that YHWH will be loyal to the Davidic house:

> I will sing of your *steadfast love,* O LORD, forever,
> with my mouth I will proclaim your *faithfulness* to all generations.
> I declare that your *steadfast love* is established forever;
> your *faithfulness* is as firm as the heavens . . .
> My *faithfulness and steadfast love* shall be with him . . .
> I will not remove from him my *steadfast love,*
> Or be false to my *faithfulness.* (Ps 89:1–2, 24, 33)

In verse 14 the poem utilizes the four great terms for that constancy:

Righteousness and justice are the foundation of your throne;
Steadfast love and faithfulness go before you.

And then the promise to David is explicit:

You said, "I have made a covenant with my chosen one,
I have sworn to my servant David. . . .
Once and for all I have sworn by my holiness;
I will not lie to David. (Ps 89:3, 35)

It ends with a bold rhetorical sweep:

His line shall continue forever,
and his throne endure before me like the sun
It shall be established forever like the moon,
an enduring witness in the skies. (Ps 89:36–37)

This was surely a self-congratulatory liturgical song for the dynasty of
David in the temple of Jerusalem.

In verse 38, however, the psalm shifts abruptly, bringing to voice the
reality of abandonment, likely in exile:

But now you have spurned and rejected him;
you are full of wrath against your anointed.
You have renounced the covenant with your servant;
you have defiled his crown in the dust.
You have broken through all his walls;
you have laid his strongholds in ruins. (Ps 89:38–40)

Toward its end, the psalm asks a pathos-filled question about that same
dominating word pair:

Lord, where is your *steadfast love* of old,
which by your *faithfulness* you swore to David? (v. 49)

And then, finally, a petition:

Remember O Lord, how your servant is taunted;
how I bear in my bosom the insults of the peoples,
with which your enemies taunt, O Lord,
with which they taunted the footsteps of your anointed. (vv. 50–51)

The imperative of remembering is to ask God to remember as we
remember, because circumstance suggests that YHWH has forgotten
YHWH's oath. What YHWH is to remember is the insult, the taunt of

the enemy, perhaps Babylon. Thus, the psalm moves from buoyant affirmation to complaint and lament. It may be that the psalm is a break with nostalgia to consider circumstance; if so, it then does not serve the thesis of nostalgia.

But what if the doxology at the beginning of verses 1–37 drives out the complaint? What if the look back to the glory of Jerusalem leads to a focus on the marvel of David and his dynasty, his royal city, and his permanent assurance from YHWH? It is a huge interpretive question about whether the complaint of verses 38–51 is permitted, in the faith of Israel, to "correct" the buoyant promise, or if the remembered promise will "correct" historical reality. There is evidence to suggest that Israel in exile might have recited the first part of the affirmation without the second part with its insistent candor. Except that we ourselves in the church do just that with this psalm. In the common lectionary, verses from the first part of the psalm are read in ABC lections for the First Sunday after Epiphany, and in year A with Proper 8 in June. In the Episcopal Order of Holy Days, moreover, such verses are read on the Feast of St. Joseph. It will not surprise you that nothing from verses 38–51 is ever heard in the lectionary. We recite the glory of David as it is remembered in the psalm, and do so, taking it with an anticipation of the coming Messiah in the Epiphany season. What we do in that process is imagine that the future will be a recovery and reestablishment of Davidic rule, albeit in the person of Jesus.

Now I should not implicate exilic Israel in the lectionary usage of the later church and maybe they did no such thing. But given the reprimand of Isaiah 43 about remembering too much, one could imagine that in exile there was a lively hope for Davidic restoration and his good old days, as indicated in the prophetic process of Isaiah 55:3; Jeremiah 23:5–6; 33:14–16; and Ezekiel 34:23–24; 37:24–27.

Such hope is evident, moreover, in the political activity of Ishmael, son of Nethaniah, son of Elishama of the royal family in Jeremiah 41:1. There was an active party at work for the restoration of David, and the doxology of divine devotion to David in Psalm 89 would have reinforced that. I dare think, moreover, that the bid to remember taunt and insult in verses 50–51 is a bid for recovery of what has been lost. Thus, even with the complaint, I submit that the psalm functions in hope of restoration, rather than facing forward into the radically changed circumstance of Jewish existence.

Thus, I take the admonition of Isaiah 43, "Do not remember,"

- as an invitation *not to remember old Jerusalem* as passionately as is done in Psalm 137

- as an urging *not to remember Amalek* and all old wounds from generation to generation

- as a resolve *not to remember Davidic promises* so literally

Not to remember is important work among desperate people who remember too much too long too well, so as not to miss the newness God is about to perform among us.

II

As a segue to forgetting in order to make room for newness, I pause briefly for two texts concerning YHWH as the great rememberer. Of course we all want God to remember. We replicate the thief on the cross when we sing, after the manner of Taize:

> Jesus, remember me when you come into your kingdom.[5]

And Paul Tillich has his wondrous sermon on the God who remembers eternally.[6] That, however, is not all. In the great psalm of confession, the psalmist says,

> For I know my transgressions,
> and my sin is ever before me. (Ps 51:3)

Such transgressions we never forget. That confession by the psalmist, however, is sandwiched between two petitions:

> According to your abundant mercy,
> *blot out* my transgression . . .
> Hide your face from my sins,
> and *blot out* my iniquities. (vv. 1, 9)

"Blot out," erase, purge from the record, forget! In his remorse, the psalmist resolves to remember sin forever, as we all inescapably do. But along with that honesty we hope, soon or late, to have transgression forgotten by God. Theologically what counts is that God does "blot out"

---

5. *Glory to God: The Presbyterian Hymnal* (Louisville: Westminster John Knox, 2013), 227.
6. Paul Tillich, "Forgetting and Being Forgotten," in *The Eternal Now* (New York: Charles Scribner's Sons, 1963), 26–35.

and not remember. It is that divine forgetting that makes possible the hope-filled imperatives that follow in the psalm:

> Create in me a clean heart, O God,
> and put a new and right spirit within me.
> Do not cast me away from our presence,
> and do not take your holy spirit from me.
> Restore to me the joy of your salvation,
> and sustain in me a willing spirit. (vv. 10–12)

We may in self-negating nostalgia hold to our guilt. But we are reassured of God's capacity to forgive and forget. That is precisely the promise on which the new covenant is based in Jeremiah:

> I will forgive their iniquity and remember their sin no more. (Jer 31:34)

YHWH "remembers no more" or "remembers not again." This becomes for Jeremiah and for the exilic community exactly the opening for relinquishment of what is old that has failed, and the reception of new possibility beyond the zone of memory. That divine capacity for forgetting is voiced in our best loved psalm:

> He will not always accuse,
> Nor will he keep his anger forever.
> He does not deal with us according to our sins,
> nor repay us according to our iniquities. (Ps 103:9–10)

That statement in the psalm is bracketed in verses 8 and 11 by "steadfast love." The conclusion we may draw is that divine forgetting does not suffer from amnesia but also does not engage in nostalgia. The relinquishment of a failed past is essential to receiving any serious future from God.[7]

III

Given Israel's nostalgia that I have lined out in four texts and given YHWH's capacity to forget, I propose that responsible remembering entails a disciplined refusal of nostalgia, exactly what the great poem of

---

7. Tillich asserts: "Therefore, all life has received the gift of forgetting. A church that does not accept this gift denies its own creatureliness, and falls into the temptation of every church, which is to make itself God . . . if it is unable to leave behind much of what was built on this foundation, it will lose its future ("Forgetting and Being Forgotten," 289).

Isaiah 43 commends. I could think of three relinquishments of nostalgia to which the work of memory now summon us:

1. I believe that in these texts there is a mandate to *forget old wounds* that cannot be healed. That of course is an impossibility, but an impossibility made possible in the gospel. Most of us are masters at nourishing old wounds that we do not want ever to be blotted out. I recall when I led the first Campbell Seminar with distinguished international church scholars, we allotted each member of the seminar ninety minutes to tell his story and to introduce herself. I recall that the well-beloved Janos Pasztor used his ninety minutes to sketch himself in the Hungarian Church. But after ninety minutes he was still only up to 1300, so that he required more time—because nothing has been forgotten in Eastern Europe. A friend of mine told me recently of being on a church venture in Macedonia where a church friend said to him, "I wish all Albanians were dead." Asked why he had such abiding anger, he said, "In 938 they burned our church down." Or a distinguished professor at Emory said not so long ago, "I wish all Palestinians were dead," etc., etc., etc. The harboring of old wounds, including that of the Amalekites and the "Lost Cause" narrative of the Old South is remembering too much too well, which precludes futures. We are all tempted to locate our deep hurts and to dwell there in fateful remembering. So we variously remember:

Remember the Alamo!

Remember the Maine!

Remember Pearl Harbor!

2. I believe that in these texts there is an urging to *forget old monopolies of triumph*. The passionate remembering of Jerusalem in Psalm 137 is a memory of well-being that was based on economic privilege for the urban elites, matched and reinforced by the liturgical monopoly of the Jerusalem temple. *Mutatis mutandis*, nostalgic remembering in our church culture is a memory of religious domination that was fostered by our ideological hegemony and was permitted by what we thought was cultural homogeneity. At the public level, this was the success of Christendom, the establishment, so we then thought, of the United States as a "Christian nation," that is, a Protestant nation in which the articles of faith were treated as nonnegotiable absolutes. At a local level the same assumptions were fed by institutional success measured by goodly numbers, enthusiastic programs, and enough dollars that came with respect and leverage. I experienced the acme of this triumph when, as a student at Union Seminary, I observed President Dwight D. Eisenhower arrive with great pomp and entourage to lay the cornerstone of the new National Council of Churches headquarters opposite Riverside Church.

It seemed "natural" to have the president lay that cornerstone. More recently the political rise of the Religious Right has replicated, for a moment, the success of the progressive mainline.

In displacement, the loss of that triumph has produced a yearning, even a homesickness for remembered well-being that cannot be recovered. That longing is variously expressed as anxiety about "church growth" or, more recently, economic survival. Such remembering produces a desperate wish that if we found the right pastor or the right youth program or the right donor or the right curriculum we can gather all of that remembered glory back. Partly it is a hope, partly it is desperation, partly it is a sense of failure, all of which is a reluctance to recognize that that form of glory is over and gone. Clearly there will be no serious or courageous thinking about the future as long as nostalgia governs our hopes of recovery. And of course romantic political rhetoric reinforces such a longing with a promise of reestablishment of the good old days with a mix of Reagenesque hope stirred in as an unassailable ingredient. So the poet implores, "Do not remember former things!"

3. I believe that in these texts there is an urging to forget some forms of *old national exceptionalism*. Todd Gitlin and Liel Leibovitz have traced the way in which the chosenness of ancient Israel has morphed into the chosenness of the United States in a way that has fed white superiority and legitimated imperial expansionism.[8] There still lives among us a powerful, often tacit form of the memory of US domination in the acquiring of "our oil," in the control of world markets, and in the exploitation of cheap labor around the world. The requirement of such a memory is to walk tall with a big stick, to seek first a military solution to whatever, and to impose our will on others.

Joseph Margulies has chronicled the way in which the crisis of 9/11 and the new awareness of vulnerability have impacted our society.[9] It has led, says he, to a more punitive society that is intolerant of and frightened by any "other," and that in turn has led to tougher laws supported by a new gun culture and the new wave of "Stand Your Ground" laws.

But of course that old proud exceptionalism is gone, even though we eagerly reiterate it. We have no idea yet how to articulate our national identity apart from a triumphal exceptionalism and, as a result, no energy to think afresh. It is at least an embarrassment, perhaps a scandal that it necessitated Vladimir Putin to remind us, albeit mockingly, that every

8. Todd Gitlin and Liel Leibovitz, *Chosen Peoples: America, Israel, and the Ordeals of Divine Election* (New York: Simon & Schuster, 2010).

9. Joseph Margulies, *What Changed When Everything Changed: 9/11 and the Making of National Identity* (New Haven: Yale University Press, 2013).

nation is a chosen nation with claims of exceptionalism.[10] The struggle
for a new national vision apart from the old exceptionalism is wistfully
voiced in the subverting hymn "This Is my Song":

> This is my song, O God of all the nations,
> a song of peace for lands afar and mine.
> This is my home, the country where my heart is;
> here are my hopes, my dreams, my holy shrine;
> but other hearts in other lands are beating
> with hopes and dreams as true and high as mine.
> My country's skies are bluer than the ocean,
> and sunlight beams on cloverleaf and pine.
> But other lands have sunlight too and clover,
> and skies are everywhere as blue as mine.
> So hear my song, O God of all the nations,
> a song of peace for their land and for mine.
> This is my prayer, O Lord of all earth's kingdoms:
> thy kingdom come; on earth thy will be done.
> Let Christ be lifted up till all shall serve him,
> and hearts united learn to live as one.
> So hear my prayer, O God of all the nations;
> myself I give thee; let thy will be done.[11]

The hymn affirms us and our land; but it acknowledges the legitimacy
of other lands and other skies as blue as ours, thus an abandonment of
monopoly. It does still, nevertheless, reiterate the monopoly of Christ's
rule.

I submit that these three refusals of old nostalgia are urgent in our society:

- forgetting old wounds
- forgetting old monopolies of triumph
- forgetting old claims of exceptionalism

10. In a puckish baiting of the United States, Vladimir Putin wrote:

I carefully studied his [Obama's] address to the nation on Tuesday. And I would rather disagree
with a case he made on American exceptionalism, stating that the United States' policy is "what
makes America different. It's what makes us exceptional." It is extremely dangerous to encourage
people to see themselves as exceptional, whatever the motivation. There are big countries and
small countries, rich and poor, those with long democratic traditions and those still finding their
way to democracy. Their policies differ, too. We are all different, but when we ask for the Lord's
blessings, we must not forget that God created us equal. ("A Plea for Caution from Russia," *New
York Times*, September 11, 2012)

11. *Glory to God*, 340.

Each of these has a counterpart in the texts I have cited:

- the wounds of Amalek in Exodus 17 and Deuteronomy 25
- the triumphs of Jerusalem in Psalm 137
- the exceptionalism of David in Psalm 89

Refusal and relinquishment are not easy. A beginning point is to name them and face not only their claim but their capacity to block alternative futures. Perhaps the repeated phrase of Psalm 137:1 and of Nehemiah 1:4 is a clue:

There we sat down and wept.

Weeping might lead to relinquishment, for it is a bodily acknowledgment of loss that is irreversible. That irreversible loss, moreover, must be wept over. Weeping lingers in the night, but joy comes in the morning!

IV

The key text in Isaiah 43 asks in surprise and indignation:

I am about to do a new thing;
Now it springs forth,
Do you not perceive it? (Isa 43:19)

It springs forth but is not ever seen when one is in a posture of nostalgia. It is amazing that the exilic prophets, in the depth of displacement that invited nostalgia and a wish for recovery, had the energy and the courage to identify God's newness that springs forth. The newnesses are given in poetic idiom, because they are at best still inchoate. Here are five such newnesses that contradict old nostalgias.

1. In *Isaiah 2:2–4* there is, as you know, a vision of disarmament (plowshares and pruning hooks) and a refusal to learn war anymore. In ancient Israel, political history had often been cast as a military contest in which Israel tried to compete with its near neighbors militarily, and beyond that dared imagine resistance to the military power of the empire, of course with futility. Thus, the vision of new possibility contradicts the domain assumptions of the Jerusalem establishment.

From that "springing forth" we might notice the nearly complete militarization of our society, in which every pastor knows that one can critique almost anything except the flag and the military. Indeed, in a deadlocked Congress, the only substantive bill that could be passed was for veterans' care, because veterans have become an epitome of national identity. We know, as the prophets knew, that there will be no serious way to security until our common imagination is demilitarized and we forget the glory days of triumph.

2. To the oracle of Isaiah, Micah adds a sober note:

> But they shall all sit under their own vines and under their own fig trees,
> and no one shall make them afraid.
> for the mouth of the LORD of hosts has spoken. (Mic 4:4)

This verse, without parallel in Isaiah, witnesses to a lower standard of living, for Micah imagines a coming future life in terms of modest peasant food of "vine and fig tree" locally produced. The verse attests a quite local economy in which a peasant community eats the home-grown food at hand, thus a challenge to the mega-food corporations and indirectly to the domination of agribusiness that grossly violates the land.

Such an innocent-looking verse comes out of the mouth of the agrarian poet who was in tune with and committed to a peasant economy. He dared to imagine a new world of local, modest well-being. The counterpoint to this vision is the searing anticipation in Micah that Jerusalem, emblem of a mega-economy, could not be sustained in its greedy corruption:

> Hear this . . . you who build Zion with blood
> and Jerusalem with wrong!
> Its rulers give judgment for a bribe,
> its priests teach for a price,
> its prophets give oracles for money;
> Yet they lean on the LORD and say,
> "Surely the LORD is with us!
> No harm shall come upon us."
> Therefore because of you
> Zion shall be plowed as a field;
> Jerusalem shall become a heap of ruins,
> and the mountain of the house a wooded height. (Mic 3:9–12)

It is not often noticed that the dismissal of old, failed Jerusalem (3:9–12) is juxtaposed in Micah to the oracle of disarmament (4:1–4).[12] The juxtaposition of the two poems suggests that the dismissal of the old vision

---

12. But see the important exception of Daniel L. Smith-Christopher, "Are the Refashioned Weapons in Micah 4:1–4 a Sign of Peace or Conquest? Shifting the Contextual Borders of a Utopian Prophetic Motif," in *Utopia and Dystopia in Prophetic Literature*, ed. Ehud Ben Zvi (Helsinki: Finnish Exegetical Society; Göttingen: Vandenhoeck & Ruprecht, 2006), 187–210.

of militarism and its accompanying self-indulgent corruption precluded the new possibility of local peaceableness.

3. Third, Micah adds yet another remarkable verse in 4:5 to the primary poem of disarmament. That oracle envisions a great procession of the nations to Jerusalem, seat of the Torah, which is the script for instruction in peace. But Micah describes that great procession:

> For all the peoples walk,
> each in the name of its god,
> but we will walk in the name of the LORD our God
> forever and ever. (v. 5)

Remarkably, Micah imagines all peoples on the way to peace together. He insists that "we," Israel, will walk in the name of YHWH our God. Of course! But he allows that other peoples will walk in the name of their god. This is astonishing ecumenism that does not insist even on the sovereignty of YHWH. Perhaps Micah had figured out that peace is not possible with an exclusive claim for one's own religion. Perhaps Micah had read Regina Schwartz, who concluded that monotheism is intrinsically violent.[13] In any case, the verse contradicts the exclusionary theological claims of Jerusalem and allows that Jerusalem is an international city of ecumenical possibility on the way to peace.

I hesitate to push further into this newness. But what springs forth, perhaps, is a recognition that even "Christ alone" becomes an anti-peace claim, because other peoples walk in the name of other gods but, the poem imagines, on the road to peace together.

4. That statement in Micah 4:5 prompts me to mention the first poem of Third Isaiah, which advocates for the inclusion of unwelcome foreigners and eunuchs—the unthinkable others—in the temple in Jerusalem. As you know, the poem of welcome concludes:

> These [that is foreigners and eunuchs] I will bring to my holy mountain,
> and make them joyful in my house of prayer;
> their burnt offerings and their sacrifices
> will be accepted on my altar,
> for my house shall be called a house of prayer for all peoples. (Isa 56:7)

The poem intends to contradict all old purity regulations that functioned to exclude.[14] Nostalgia imagines that only "we" who are qualified could

---

13. Regina M. Schwartz, *The Curse of Cain: The Violent Legacy of Monotheism* (Chicago: University of Chicago Press, 1997).

14. See Frederick J. Gaiser, "A New Word on Homosexuality? Isaiah 56:1–8 as Case Study," *Word & World* 14.3 (1994): 289–93.

claim the temple, a nostalgia that would be re-performed later on by Ezra. But here, it is "all peoples," including the disqualified.

It is no wonder that Jesus quotes this text in his drama of "cleansing the temple" (Matt 21:13). The money changers had made economic qualification a condition that would exclude those without resources. Jesus's accent is on prayer, not on "all peoples"; but his stricture is against the reduction of worship to commodity, which is always an exclusionary enterprise. And now the church, along with our national anxiety, struggles with exclusionary assumptions that variously concern race, class, gender, and—beyond that—immigrants and Muslims, and for some of us "conservatives" and for some of us "liberals." Nostalgia for "real Americans" and "Christian America" may be relinquished for the sake of new social possibility that springs forth.

5. The quintessential "springing forth" in the Old Testament is in Isaiah 65:17–25 concerning new heaven, new earth, new Jerusalem. The new Jerusalem is not in heaven. It is the one to which the deportees will be returning, and it will be quite unlike the old city for which they yearned. I mention only two facets of that new city that will spring to reality.

> No more shall there be in it
> an infant that lives but a few days,
> or an old person who does not live out a lifetime;
> for one who dies at a hundred years will be considered a youth,
> and one who falls short of a hundred will be considered accursed. (Isa 65:20)

The verse anticipates long life. It begins with "no more infant who lives but a few days." The cemeteries of old Jerusalem, like the cemeteries of many old cities and like the cemeteries of any violent society in our own time, are strewn with the graves of infants. What an act of imagination that this poet anticipates an end to infant mortality. There will be an end to such deaths because of a peaceable society, because of the valuing of every tiny person, because of good health care. No doubt babies, vulnerable as they are, are the canaries in the coal mines of violent societies. My own town, Cincinnati, ranks fifth among US cities in infant mortality precisely because we lack the health care structure and the health care will that the vulnerable should be protected. A society that "makes it sons (and daughters) pass through fire" in the form of military action is not big on child protection (2 Kgs 16:3; 17:17; 21:6; 23:10). But it may spring forth from the lips of the poet.

And in verse 65:24 we have the articulation of a mother God:

Before they call I will answer,
while they are yet speaking I will hear.

This is a God inordinately attentive and present. That God who attends like a vigilant mother is unlike the state God of retribution, who operates on the basis of merit.[15] This mother God does not sort out which child should be answered, whether a good and deserving child, but answers all before they cry. This cryptic verse reconfigures the communication lines between heaven and earth beyond the control of fear, threat, violence, or merit. It is no wonder that in the new economy,

They shall not hurt or destroy
on all my holy mountain,
says the Lord (Isa 65:25)

Imagine that poetic speaker bearing witness to the new springing forth that would be missed, except for such artistic attentiveness.

V

So what springs forth that we do not yet see? I propose, following Paul Ricoeur, that the parables of Jesus are opportunities for springing forth on the lips of the storyteller, and in the imagination of the faithful that subverts the homesickness of nostalgia.[16] In his study of the parables, John Donahue says that parables are difficult and demanding for us because "we live often in a desert of the imagination."[17] I suggest that it is an inordinate yearning for the past through over-remembering and "improved" remembering that precludes originary imagination. So what springs forth? Well, for starters, the Song of Mary is an act of imagination that sets the key for Luke-Acts. Mary sings of the transformative work her Son will do that eventuates, in the life of the church, in "turning the world upside down" (Acts 17:6). She sings,

He has brought down the rulers from their thrones
and lifted up the lowly;
he has filled the hungry with good things,
and sent the rich away empty. (Luke 1:52–53)

15. Erhard S. Gerstenberger has clearly distinguished the religious articulations of state religion and the religious expressions of clan and family, the latter much more given to intimacy and gentleness (*Theologies in the Old Testament*, trans. John Bowden [Minneapolis: Fortress Press, 2002]).

16. Paul Ricoeur, "Biblical Hermeneutics," *Semeia* 4 (1975): 29–148.

17. John R. Donahue, *The Gospel in Parables* (Philadelphia: Fortress Press, 1988), 212.

Mary anticipates, in the wake of prophetic imagination, that the world will be made new and different in the gospel narrative to follow. And when her son arrived, he was from the outset about turning the world upside down.

- They may have yearned for the good old days when Torah keeping qualified one for "eternal life." But he reminded them that love extended to the neighbor led to the question of neighbor identification. And so he told a story of new springing forth that we call the "Good Samaritan." It turns out that neighborliness does not have to do with acceptable, preferred companions like "us," but simply with "showing mercy" (Luke 10:37).

- They may have imagined that good sons (and daughters) should inherit the land, and rebellious sons (and daughters) should be, as Deuteronomy says:

  > brought out to the elders of his town at the gate of that place.
  > . . . Then all the men of the town shall stone him to death. (Deut 21:19–21)

He, however, interrupted hoped-for well-ordered family values with his narrative of the two sons. The story is in response to the "grumbling" of the Pharisees and scribes: "This fellow welcomes sinners and eats with them" (Luke 15:2). His story contradicts their exclusionary hopes for a return to "normal," the "normal" that Ezra would seek to impose. His story calls his listeners away from such nostalgia to the new order of the kingdom of welcome.

- The laws of purity dictated who could have table fellowship. And when they got back home from exile they would dispute who the real Jews were, the acceptable approved Jews, rather like the real Presbyterians or the real Episcopalians or the real Baptists, those who honored the purity codes. And he told them the story of table fellowship (Luke 14:15–24). It turns out that the future of God is like a banquet which the seats at the table of honor are filled by the disqualified off the street, by those who do not pass litmus tests, who do not own property, and who do not meet production schedules. It is springing forth, he said!

- In their piety they wanted to pray correctly. But he told them a story of alternative prayer that he knew already from the Psalter (Luke 18:1–8). It is the story of a widow, a disenfranchised woman with no resources or advocate. She, however, never doubted, even in court, her entitlement that they had denied. She nagged and nagged the cruel indifferent judge, so much so that she got labeled "importunate." She received justice by refusing to give in. And Jesus adds the zinger:

Pray like that and you will never lose heart. (v. 1)

You may think of and prefer other parables from Jesus. Those are the ones that occurred to me. They are indeed evangelical acts of imagination that permit newness to spring forth in the face of old memories of how the world works.

In my reading about the parables, I was astonished to find this comment by Ulrich Luz, among our best Matthew commentators:

One cannot understand the parables of the kingdom of heaven by exegesis alone. To go to school with the sole teacher Jesus means more than learning to repeat his stories exactly (although it means that also!); it means to invent stories oneself—stories as Jesus told them, but one's own stories, filled with hope and life, covered by one's own life. In my judgment, the inability to do that shows something of the power of tradition in Christian history.[18]

By that last sentence I assume Luz means the over-remembering of tradition that refuses new imagination.

Luz proposes that we flood our imagination with new accounts of kingdom possibility. His negative judgment on "the power of tradition in Christian history" is, I believe, the same as my accent on nostalgia. Tradition has failed when it becomes a barrier to new acts of imagination. And nostalgia wants tradition to do just that. So I imagine that the church, when it engages in faithful forgetting of its over-remembering and witnesses the springing forth from the tradition, will have enough energy and fresh courage for the new territory to which we will return in homecoming.

---

18. Ulrich Luz, *Matthew 8–20: A Commentary*, Hermeneia (Minneapolis: Fortress Press, 2001), 298. My colleague Anna Cater Florence has, in her homiletic pedagogy, invited students to generate new parables. This pedagogy not only generates new material for preaching but inescapably allows students (and preachers) to see the world more thickly.

VI

I have in these two presentations been concerned with the gifts and tasks that relate to the practice of faithful remembering. I have considered the way in which a market ideology invites us to amnesia, to think we live in a timeless, placeless moment without a narrative, for which vacuous praise hymns may be taken as an epitome. I have considered as well the way in which deep anxiety about the present causes us to trust the memory excessively, and to seek escape into an old formulation that seems safe and stable, as though nostalgia would provide an escape from anxiety.

I have the sense that we are tempted to divide ourselves into competing parties:

- *The party of amnesia*, perhaps represented by progressives who are embarrassed about the tradition and its esoteric formulations, who want to scuttle it or explain it away;

- *The party of nostalgia*, which is a backward yearning to recover and reiterate old mantras of certitude.

It is, I propose, the task of faithful traditioning to resist temptations of both amnesia and nostalgia, and to engage the tradition as a normative, elusive, generative enterprise that requires sustained hard work:

- That hard work is the work of agility that is perhaps well expressed by *The Fiddler on the Roof*, who refused to scuttle or to freeze. Such work requires sustained, disciplined self-aware conversation that takes the tradition in its textual specificity seriously and that does not shrink from making daring new moves in present circumstances.

- That hard work of agility is precisely the work of the church and its seminaries, the church as an arena for sustained work that honors the fears, angers, and losses that are so powerful among us, but that does not give in to them. When more and more of our interpretive venues in our society—the courts, the media, the universities—are increasingly domesticated into market ideology that specializes in amnesia but that traffics in nostalgia, the church (along with allies wherever we may find them) as a community of interpretive agility is of singular importance for the well-being of our society.

- The process of agility requires hard work and resists dumbing down to cater to one-dimensional certitudes or to vacuous, rootless fantasies. That agility takes as its working material exactly the complexity of our common life and the holy one who is hidden in that complexity.

After Jesus told that series of parables in Matthew 13, he asked his disciples, "Do you understand all this?" The disciples answered, "Yes." That is all they said, and they likely said that almost immediately, too quickly, while they avoided eye contact. They did not want to admit that they lacked the agility to follow his strange narrative logic. So he parsed it slowly for them:

- Bring out of your treasure, the treasure of the church for Matthew, *what is old;* remember the old, remember the tradition; refuse amnesia!

- Bring out *what is new* from the treasure of the church where the Spirit dwells; it springs forth; resist nostalgia!

Scribes will have failed the kingdom if they bring out only what is old; scribes will have failed if they bring out only what is new. To be faithful, a scribe for the kingdom must be agile with old and new.

A lack of agility works very well in the land of Pharaoh or Caesar. But we are talking about a new regime that he called "kingdom." The kingdom requires, he said, scribes well trained in both old and new. Our training for the assignment continues!

14.

Children (I): Taken as Hostages

A version of this essay was originally delivered to the Children's Defense Fund, 22nd Annual Samuel DeWitt Proctor Institute for Child Advocacy Ministry in Clinton, Tennessee, July 20, 2016.

In the big world of power, children are collateral damage who may happen to be in the way of relentless ambition. They are at best an inconvenient statistic, exceedingly vulnerable to the savage power of predatory confiscation. They are regularly dismissed as nameless and even uncounted in the world of ruthless power. Only in the counter-community that stands over against the big world of power do children register. In that counter-world they have names, identities, and futures. In what follows I will consider three instances of this recurring contest for children between the hard world of indifferent power and the counter-world of sustained fidelity.

I. Pharaoh's Hostages and Knowing Better

The first instance I cite is that of Pharaoh in the exodus story. Pharaoh is, in the Bible, the quintessential representative of savage power. We are given a brief history of Pharaoh whose name we do not know. We are told that, for all of his power, he is devoured by anxiety. As a result, he had two nightmares about scarcity. He dreamed of lean cows eating fat cows, and rotten sheaves of grain eating the good grain (Gen 41:1–7). The most powerful man with the most ample resources is obsessed about running out!

Consequently, Pharaoh initiates a policy of confiscation. He recruits a

Hebrew, Joseph, to activate his policy. And so we are told that the peasants in need of food came to Joseph, Pharaoh's food czar, to get food from Pharaoh's monopoly (Gen 47:13–26). And when the peasants had no money to buy food from the monopoly, and had no cattle to trade for food with the monopoly, Joseph—on behalf of Pharaoh—confiscated their land and reduced the peasants to debt slaves. They were enslaved as cheap labor because they could not pay their food bill!

Pharaoh's monopoly of land and resources was insatiable. Like every aggressive power, Pharaoh wanted more. And in order to have more, he required cheap labor that he had in the form of slaves over which he appointed supervisors and taskmasters. Pharaoh of course is not the last aggressor who accumulated great wealth by way of cheap labor in the form of slavery!

Pharaoh, however, is so anxious that he cuts off his nose to spite his face. In his irrational anxiety, Pharaoh decreed to the Hebrew midwives:

> When you act as midwives to the Hebrew women, and see them on the birthstool, if it is a boy kill him; but if it is as girl, she shall live. (Exod 1:16)

In tradition this decree has been termed "the slaughter of the innocents." Pharaoh's decree gets only one verse in the Bible. But it tells us everything about the crisis of children in the face of state or corporate power. The children are an expendable statistic. Pharaoh does not take the children seriously but acts out of fear to protect his massive monopoly.

So it is with savage power and vulnerable children, seemingly always. But of course even before Pharaoh's decree of death for vulnerable children, we have been given a harbinger of the danger to vulnerable children in the narrative of Genesis. Joseph was the younger brother in the family of Jacob, whom the older brothers despised (Gen 37:4). They wanted to be rid of him. Even Reuben, who did not want to kill him, wanted him gone (37:21–22). So they sold their younger brother to slave traders who took him to Egypt. That is, they sold him into the hand of the ruthless power of insatiable Pharaoh. There is of course an important difference between death and passage into slavery, because he still has a chance for a future. But either way, Joseph was gone, just as the brothers wished him to be. He is for them an expendable inconvenience. They faked his death; they did so decisively and so deceived their father, Jacob. And then, in a brief but moving scene, we are told of Jacob's grief over his lost son. Unlike Pharaoh who did not care and his other sons who did not care, father Jacob is moved to deep grief. He cherishes his young son who is not for him expendable:

Then Jacob tore his garments, and put sackcloth on his loins, and mourned for his son many days. All his sons and all his daughters sought to comfort him; but he refused to be comforted, and said, "No, I shall go down to Sheol to my son, mourning." Thus his father bewailed him. (Gen 37:34–35)

His death is qualified when we are told of his Egyptian placement:

Meanwhile the Midianites had sold him in Egypt to Potiphar, one of Pharaoh's officials, the captain of the guard. (37:36)

Pharaoh, carrier of savage power, predictably appears in the midst of the loss of the child. But Jacob only weeps. He refuses to be comforted for his lost son. Here is the nub of the drama that concerns us. The indifferent brothers can despise Joseph. Pharaoh, the indifferent strong man, can purchase him. But the father weeps. He weeps in perpetuity; he will not be comforted. The loss of his son is incalculable. Joseph is a beloved child, and now he is gone, into the hand of savage power that is always ready to discount the vulnerable.

In the midst of savage power that treats vulnerable children as an inconvenient statistic, entertain the thought that Israel, the company of Moses, is formed as a counter-community of emancipation whose work is to protect the vulnerable, most notably the children! The contest is joined in the exodus narrative between ruthless power that operates with statistics and the community set to protect the vulnerable.

As the issue is joined in the narrative, Pharaoh is seen to be less and less effective, and more and more at risk. As a result, Pharaoh reluctantly engages in compromise and bargaining with Moses. Savage power must come to terms with the force of vulnerable-protecting agency.

In the first instance the Hebrew slaves want to be free to worship YHWH, the legitimator of their freedom. Such worship was an assertion of freedom from Pharaoh and from the Egyptian gods. Thus, the will to worship YHWH was a daring political act; of course it was resisted by Pharaoh. As the narrative advances, however, Pharaoh is increasingly in a weakened position vis-à-vis the slave community. As a result, he must bargain with Moses, even if he bargains grudgingly.

• In Exodus 8:20–29, Moses makes a first request for freedom to worship the emancipatory God. The ground of worship, in the mouth of YHWH, is this:

But on that day I will set apart the land of Goshen, where my people live, so that no swarms of flies shall be there, that you may know that I the LORD am in this land. Thus I will make a distinction between my people and your people. This sign shall appear tomorrow. (Exod 8:22–23)

This is a noticed people upon whom YHWH focuses attention. At first Pharaoh seems to agree with the request, an agreement that would constitute his acknowledgment of YHWH. But Pharaoh's permit to worship comes with a severe limitation:

Go, sacrifice to your God within the land. (8:25)

Moses refuses this unacceptable compromise, for Pharaoh wants to supervise the worship of the God of freedom. Moses gives the reason for his refusal:

It would not be right to do so, for the sacrifices that we offer to the Lord our God are offensive to the Egyptians. If we offer in the sight of the Egyptians sacrifices that are offensive to them, will they not stone us? (8:26)

The double use of the term "offensive" is in fact "abomination." It would fill the Egyptians with disgust and repulsion. We do not know if this is a real objection, or a ploy on Moses's part. He insists that the only viable worship of YHWH must be outside the aegis of Pharaoh, so that YHWH's initial summons to worship and Pharaoh's initial permit come to naught.

• In a second effort, Pharaoh's advisors urge him to cut his losses and to let the slaves go worship YHWH before his regime comes to ruin (10:7). Pharaoh, for a moment, accepts that wise advice and offers to let the Hebrew slaves leave his domain to worship YHWH. But there is a catch:

Go, worship the Lord your God! But which ones are to go? (10:8)

Pharaoh assumes only some will go. Pharaoh sets it up like *Sophie's Choice* in which Moses must decide whom to leave behind. Pharaoh has in mind hostages to be sure that the slaves return to work after worship of the God of freedom. It is this that drew me to the narrative. Pharaoh is unembarrassed about wanting to keep hostages. Indeed, it is the way of anxious regimes, to hold some back for the sake of self-security. The proposal on Pharaoh's part has led me to reflect on the way in which Pharaonic regimes keep hostages, and the way in which the military-industrial-educational monopoly is unembarrassed about keeping our young as hostages, to be sure we all maintain our allegiance to the regime.

Hostage taking among us is in at least three forms. First, it is our military adventurism that requires our young to participate in what has now become perpetual war. As a result, our society is strewn with maimed bodies and crushed psyches, not even to speak of the dead. And for what? For the maintenance of the pyramid of privilege for which these young are sacrificed and to which they will never have access.

Second, we keep many of our young hostages by assuring that they receive inadequate education in disadvantaged schools. It is a policy and a practice that is not very different from "separate but equal," or even more perniciously, to be sure that slaves should not be taught to read well. Because if they read, they grow into freedom. As a result, the endless pool of cheap labor may disappear and the assumed advantage of some is gone. And prison serves to reinforce the coercive maintenance of the labor pool.

Third, so many of our young who get a better education are kept hostage in unpayable debt that marks them for a lifetime. The consequence of such policy is to assure that such indebted ones will and must show up regularly for work . . . forever.

Thus it is not an innocent question when Pharaoh asks, "Which ones are to go . . . not all . . . which ones?"

- Not the cannon fodder that morphs too often into disability

- Not the poorly educated who morph predictably into cheap labor

- Not the well-educated with endless debt

None of these are going free. All of them are predictable hostages.
Moses does not blink or hesitate:

> We will go with our young and our old; we will go with our sons and daughters and with our flocks and herds, because we have the Lord's festival to celebrate. (10:9)

All will go; no hostages! All will go . . . sons and daughters, flocks and herds. All will go, because we are headed to celebrate YHWH, the Lord of freedom, headed to Beulah land. That mantra, "all will go," rings in our ears. It calls to mind Nelson Mandela on Robbins Island. The pernicious apartheid government offered Mandela a freedom deal. He refused, insisting that he would not go until all his companions went with him. All will go! It is the strategy of Pharaoh to separate, to make distinctions, to set some over against others by class distinction, or by race distinction or by ethnic distinction or by gender identity distinction. The freedom of YHWH refuses every such distinction upon which Pharaoh depends, because in the sweep of emancipation, all will go!

Pharaoh cannot compute such a requirement of emancipation, so he must refuse:

> The LORD indeed will be with you if ever I let your little ones go with you! Plainly you have some evil purpose in mind. No, never. (10:10–11)

Pharaoh judges that if they ever get free—all of them—it will be a sign that YHWH, the emancipator, is with them. But not now, not ever . . . "bondage today, bondage tomorrow, bondage forever," in an anticipation of George Wallace. The little ones will never go. They will be hostages to curb emancipation. The little one are the vulnerable:

- the cannon fodder of perpetual war
- the left behind, for separate but equal
- the hopelessly indebted

The little ones, so vulnerable and powerless, are hostages to assure that the bondage system will be perpetual. Pharaoh is decisive: No, Never! . . . end of discussion. Your men may go; the Hebrew is "mighty men," the warrior class. All those who could do the heavy lifting of slavery; they may go; but they will return, because they are bound to their little ones kept as hostages. It works that way:

- When a soldier, the family is supportive of military adventurism.
- When left behind, the family accepts that status for the entire household.
- When left indebted, the family must work hard.

In his cunning calculation, Pharaoh sees that the "mighty men" and the "little ones" are bound together. One need keep only the vulnerable little ones, and all will remain hostages to Pharaoh's system, even the ones who are permitted to go and worship YHWH. So it is "all or nothing." Moses says, "All will go." Pharaoh counters, "All will stay in bondage, including the mighty men, because they love their little ones."

As a reprise Pharaoh makes a third offer to Moses:

> Go worship the Lord. Only your flocks and your herds will remain behind. Even your children may go with you. (10:24)

Even the little children may go; but Pharaoh still has hostages in mind. In the second exchange Moses had asserted, "We will go with our sons and daughters, and with our flocks and herds." Pharaoh goes half way: sons and daughters, but not flocks and herds. Pharaoh calculates that the Hebrew slaves will be drawn back to his commodity system by their possessions. But Pharaoh does not understand the alternative thinking of those who yearn for emancipation. Pharaoh thinks in terms of one commodity at a time. Against that Moses thinks that all these political hostages, sons and daughters, flocks and herds, are all members of the village. And that of course is what YHWH had in mind in the Sinai commandment on Sabbath: all shall rest, including your livestock (Exod 20:10). All shall rest including your ox, your donkey, and your livestock (Deut 5:14). Pharaoh's grudging proposal is a misconstrual because he misunderstands the animals as property rather than as members of the household. But then Pharaoh thinks that way not only about flocks and herds but also about sons and daughters. Everything is a tradable commodity; in a commodity system anyone can be taken hostage; anyone can be left behind; everyone is dispensable.

Moses, not surprisingly, refuses; he knows that a village will prize every member, sons, daughters, sheep, cows, every member. No one is mere commodity:

> Our livestock also must go with us; not a hoof shall be left behind, for we must choose some of them for the worship of the Lord our God, and we will not know what to use to worship the Lord until we arrive there. (Exod 10:26)

Moses offers Pharaoh an excuse; but this is only an excuse. The real reason to take every hoof is that every hoof is precious. All belong to the household of freedom. Not even a hoof is offered to the commodity system.

Thus Pharaoh offers Moses three "compromises":

- Worship but in the land.
- Leave the children as hostages.
- Leave the flocks and herds as hostages.

Moses three times refuses the offer:

- We cannot worship in the land.
- We cannot leave the little one as hostages.

- We cannot leave behind flocks and herds as hostages.

We know the outcome of this story. In the end, on a dark and stormy night freedom prevails.

This task of freedom is endlessly re-performed. It must be endlessly re-performed because Pharaoh's hostage-taking commodity system is endlessly flexing its muscle. The exodus story becomes the curriculum for shaping emancipatory imagination:

> You may tell your children and grandchildren how I made fools of the Egyptians, and what signs I have done among them . . . so that you may know that I am the LORD. (10:2)

Tell the grandchildren! Tell the grandchildren that the contest between hostage taking and the emancipatory alternative is a drama that requires full and continuing participation. If you do not tell the grandchildren this story, they will surely think that Pharaoh's commodity system is the abiding truth of the world. My learning, as I pondered this material for this conference, is a new awareness that we live in a hostage-taking commodity system. And the reason the children need "defense" is that there is a vigorous "offense" against them. The commodity system cannot flourish without hostages. And now we know better than to collude with that commodity system.

II. Unregulated Patriarchy and Knowing Better

According to the singing imagination of Israel, Pharaoh was finished, drowned at sea:

> Pharaoh's chariots and his army he cast into the sea;
> His picked officers were sunk in the Red Sea.
> The floods covered them;
> They went down into the depths like a stone. (Exod 15:4–5)

But of course Pharaoh is always reemerging and recurring as a commodity force, always seeking to take and hold hostages. One form of Pharaoh's reappearance was in the patriarchy of ancient Israel after Israel had settled in the land of promise. The subsistence economy of Israel, organized in village life, was fiercely patriarchal. This meant that all social power resided in male authority that was competent in maintaining social control. Such patriarchal control could be generous and empowering (as with Jacob toward Joseph), or it could be authoritarian in uncaring ways (as with Jephthah with his daughter). No doubt the managers of such a social arrangement had lots of options. At its worst, patriarchy continued Pharaoh's practice of keeping sons and daughters as hostages.

I will begin with one Torah provision that occurs in the midst of a collection of "family laws" in the mouth of Moses. In Deuteronomy 21:18–21 it is provided that if a stubborn and rebellious son does not obey mother and father, he will be taken by his parents to the village elders, who may stone him to death. On any reading this is a harsh and violent treatment of disobedient children that is reflective of the awesome authority of the father in a patriarchal society. Clearly the father has unquestioned authority concerning the son.

But Richard Nelson has helped me to read the commandment in a different way and I am indebted to him. No doubt the readiness to punish disobedient sons (only sons are mentioned in patriarchal horizon) not only reflects the authority of patriarchy; it also reflects the anxiety of patriarchy that faces a "breakdown in traditional family life under the pressures of social change."[1] In village life that lived in a marginal subsistence economy, social change was risky, and the maintenance of social control was important, even if it had to be maintained through harsh measures. The father is all important, and sons (and by inference daughters) are hostages to a social system that put exclusive male authority beyond question. There is no way to make it pretty!

But this commandment in the mouth of Moses suggests two mitigating practices that hint that Israel, early on, knew better than absolute fatherly control. First, the law specifically includes the mother in the treatment of the wayward son, a remarkable fact in a patriarchal society. The father's authority is qualified by the presence of the mother. We may expect that the mother, in practice, might soften the harshness of treatment or at least assure that the father's judgment is under review. Second, the son is to be handed over to the "elders at the gate," to the wise senior leaders of the village. The father, or even both parents together, may not act on their own. The treatment of the wayward son is public business. Thus, one could imagine a circumstance in which the elders might overrule the anger and exasperation of the parents and protect the wayward son. The intervention of the village elders into family discipline suggests that the nurture and discipline of children is a public affair or, said another way, "It takes a village." Because we meet under the aegis of the Children's Defense Fund, our business is to see that the

---

1. Richard D. Nelson, *Deuteronomy: A Commentary*, Old Testament Library (Louisville: Westminster John Knox, 2002), 261.

care, discipline, protection, and well-being of children are a public business that cannot be left to the whim of indifferent fathers or indifferent circumstances that render the child vulnerable. Even in that ancient patriarchal society, children were too important to the community to be at the disposal of unchecked private authority.

Thus, this commandment of Moses articulates a recurring ambiguity in the sensibility of ancient Israel. Its social practice was authoritarian and heavy-handed. It was willing to subordinate the well-being of children to the maintenance of social order and social control. On the other hand, there is indication that they knew better: the presence of "mother" and "elders" constitutes a curb on patriarchy in the interest of the child. It occurs to me that we are now in the midst of that same ambiguity. On the one hand, we are generally willing to subordinate the well-being of the child to social order and social control, as I have indicated, concerning the draft, the left behind, and the hopelessly indebted. Children count for very little in an economy of aggressive commoditization. On the other hand, we know better.

- We know that children are more than cannon fodder.
- We know that the left behind warrant alternative provision.
- We know that hopeless indebtedness is no path to social prosperity.

We know better, but like ancient patriarchy we are slow to move beyond social control for those who do not conform to the rigors of consumer capitalism.

Pharaoh would learn nothing, and so he disappears from the narrative. But knowing better and honoring the worth and dignity of the children are an endless process among us as it was in ancient Israel. These points seem pertinent to me:

1. In the remarkable narrative of King David, the king is not a good father, indifferent at best, harsh at worst. Near the end of his story, however, an astonishing scene occurs. His handsome son, Absalom, had led a coup against his father and tried to seize his throne. Absalom is of necessity killed by David's army. When David learns the news of the death of his son, he does not rejoice that the coup has failed. Instead, for the first time, he shows an emotional response toward his son in a famous scene when he grieves:

The king was deeply moved, and went up to the chamber over the gate, and wept; and as he went, he said, "O my son Absalom, my son, my son Absalom! Would that I had died instead of you, O Absalom, my son, my son!" (2 Sam 18:33)

And then his grief is reiterated:

The king covered his face, and the king cried with a loud voice, "O my son Absalom, O Absalom, my son, my son!" (2 Sam 19:4)

The hard-nosed king calls his dead son by name for the first time in the narrative. At long last he notices him. He notices how deeply linked to him he is, and that his son matters to him. He steps out of his regal role and acts shamelessly like a father. We could have imagined early on that David would be glad to stone his son to death for his insurrection. But now, finally, he knows better. He is a father. And this is his son. In this moment he will forgo all the trappings of royal office, all the performance of monarchy, and move to the unbearable reality of "my son, my son." In death, as not in his son's life, David knows better. It is the process of "knowing better" in which we are engaged,

- knowing better than the brutalizing of children in the hopeless processes of war
- knowing better about relationships in place of commodities
- knowing better about valorization rather than coercion

David learned late; but then he knew better.

2. It is remarkable that in the very book of Deuteronomy with its harsh provision for stoning a disobedient son, the tradition can take special notice of orphans. In a patriarchal society orphans are those without a fatherly advocate or patron. The commandments make provision that when a child lacks a father, the covenant community has a deep obligation to care for the child. Thus:

- You shall share your wealth in a full tithe with orphans who may come and eat their fill (Deut 14:29).[2]
- At the festival of weeks (harvest) you shall provide so that your sons and daughters and orphans may rejoice (16:11). [Orphans are equal to sons and daughters!]

2. These texts characteristically refer to the "triad of vulnerability," widows, orphans, and immigrants. I have omitted reference to widows and immigrants due to my focus, but clearly the case is the same for these vulnerable types as it is for children who are left behind and without viable resources.

- At the festival of booths you will share produce with orphans (16:14).

- You shall leave a residue of grain in the field for orphans (24:19).

- You shall leave a residue of olives in the orchard for orphans (24:20).

- You shall leave a residue of grapes in the vineyard for orphans (24:21).

- Cursed shall be anyone who deprives an orphan of justice (27:19).

Israel knew better! Israel knew it could not abandon its children just because patriarchy failed. Israel knew better and so constituted a community-wide program of care, support, and sustenance. This is indeed a welfare program that runs beyond mere patriarchy. When the father fails, the community covers!

3. Israel comes to see that children are it most precious treasure. When the exile and deportation of Israel happened in the sixth century BCE, the poets found the metaphor of "children-orphans" to be the most poignant image by which to characterize the acute experience of social displacement and abandonment. When their system of social sustenance collapsed, they knew what it was like to be an orphan . . . without an advocate or a patron. So the poet in exilic grief can say:

> We have become orphans, fatherless;
> our mothers are like widows.
> We must pay for the water we drink;
> the wood we get must be bought.
> With a yoke on our necks we are hard driven;
> we are weary, we are given no rest. (Lam 5:3–5)

Gone is the support that makes life possible. To be an orphan is to be a part of unbearable social chaos:

> Women are raped in Zion,
> virgins in the towns of Judah.
> Princes are hung up by their hands;
> no respect is shown to the elders.
> Young men are compelled to grind,
> and boys stagger under loads of wood.
> The old men have left the city gate,
> the young men their music. (Lam 5:11–15)

The poem describes a complete social breakdown. In the poetry, orphans may be reckoned as the canary in the mineshaft of social disorder. When a society cannot or will not care for its abandoned children, only bad things will follow.

So Jeremiah, in a most poignant utterance, can describe social disarray as the loss of children.

> Rachel is weeping for her children;
> she refuses to be comforted for her children,
> because they are no more. (Jer 31:15)

The poetry recalls from Genesis that father Jacob refused to be comforted when his beloved son Joseph was gone and presumed dead. And now, in poetic imagination, it is Rachel, the wife of Jacob and mother of Joseph, who grieves all the lost children of exile, refusing to be comforted. Never mind the loss of king, the loss of temple, the loss of city. Never mind the collapse of the economy. What is felt most deeply that only a poet can probe is the children; they are gone, now hostages of Babylon! The ancient mother of Genesis is recruited as a carrier of grief. She will not be comforted! In mother Rachel Israel knew better. It knew that only the children count; nothing cuts as deep as their loss. There is no substitute for treasured children, all of them. It took the destruction in order that Israel, belatedly, could come to know better.

4. There is a profound reason that Israel knew better. Israel discerned that the usage of "orphan" and the prospect of advocate and patron for "orphan" (crucial in a patriarchal society) was a way of speaking about the God who acted on behalf of Israel. YHWH, the God of Sinai, is the God of orphans. The imagery of "orphan" of course concerns socioeconomic political policy and practice. But it also illuminates the theological tradition that lies behind political economy. The most elemental claim for the defense of children is that God is an advocate for orphans:

> Father of orphans and protector of widows
> is God in his holy habitation.
> God gives the desolate a home to live in;
> he leads out the prisoners to prosperity,
> but the rebellious live in a parched land. (Ps 68:5–6)

In the echoing poetry of Hosea, this God is contrasted with Assyrian military power, for the obligation of military power is never on behalf of orphans or any other who is vulnerable and left behind:

> Assyria will not save us;
> we will not ride upon horses;
> we will say no more "Our God,"
> to the work of our hands.
> In you the orphan finds mercy. (Hos 14:4)

The contrast is sharp and complete. Assyria, as emblem of military might, is the quintessence of commodity, both the possession of commodity and the capacity to secure more of them. None of that will save. The only savior is the God who is in solidarity with the orphans. It is from that theological accent that Israel derived an alternative social policy that refused unregulated patriarchy and that curbed the greedy appetite of military commoditization.

On that basis, Israel, in its prayer, can contrast even "mother and father" who forsake with the Lord who does not forsake:

> Do not turn your servant away in anger,
> You who have been my help.
> Do not cast me off, do not forsake me,
> O God of my salvation!
> If my father and mother forsake me,
> the Lord will take me up. (Ps 27:9–10)

The petition confidently affirms that God is the finally reliable parent.

These three texts from Psalm 68, Hosea 14, and Psalm 27 make clear that Israel knew better because of God. And when Israel cares for orphans, that is, when it defends children, it is acting in a way congruent with the way in which God has acted and continues to act. Because this God occupies the center of Israel's imagination, it follows that no child is left behind, no orphan is left abandoned. The beginning of curbing unregulated patriarchy in the commandment of Deuteronomy 21:19–21 is already grounded in God's own character. Israel knows better, even if it is ever so slow in acting it out.

III. The Jesus Movement and Knowing Better

The Jesus movement is one heir to the tradition of ancient Israel. The early Jesus movement is set in the Roman Empire, which is, in the imagination of the movement, not unlike the old regime of Pharaoh. The early Jesus movement, moreover, picks up the Torah-prophetic legacy of Judaism that refuses the hostage-taking practices of the empire.

We may begin our consideration of the Jesus movement with the account of King Herod in the massacre of innocent children (Matt 2:16). In the Gospel of Matthew that narrative action by Herod is clearly a reiteration and reperformance of the action of Pharaoh in Exodus 1:15–22. As Pharaoh acted violently against the children, so Herod acts violently against the children. Both Pharaoh and belatedly Herod kill the baby boys; they are examples of the violent hostage taking of the empire. The babies are the dispensable collateral damage of predatory military power.

> When Herod saw that he had been tricked by the wise men, he was infuriated, and he sent and killed all the children in and around Bethlehem who were two years old or under, according to the time that he had learned from the wise men. (Matt 2:16)

His reported action evokes in Matthew a citation from Jeremiah:

> Then was fulfilled what had been spoken through the prophet Jeremiah:
>
> > A voice was heard in Ramah, wailing and loud lamentation,
> > Rachel weeping for her children;
> > She refused to be consoled,
> > because they are no more. (Matt 2:17–18)

When the empire works its violent, anxious will, the children always "are not." They are dispensable, to be done in by violence. And the mothers are left to weep in perpetuity, never comforted, because a lost child is a lost child forever beyond comfort. Imagine the costly poetic force:

Refuse to be comforted . . . they are not!

It is in the face of such cynical violence that the Jesus movement makes its counter witness. We may cite three texts from the testimony of Jesus's witness:

1. In Matthew 10:40–42 Jesus dispatches his disciples into risky ministry. He sends them out vulnerable and in this text variously refers to them as "prophet," "righteous person," and "little one." He used the term "little one" to refer not to children but to his vulnerable disciples. We may nonetheless notice the usage, because the disciples in a world of predatory power are not unlike children in an unwelcoming world of hostage taking. The usage bespeaks vulnerable risk and sees that the character of Jesus and his mission are as vulnerable as a child. It is the very vulnerable he sends out who are the harbinger of the alternative world he intends to enact.

2. In Matthew 18:1–7 Jesus voices two teachings concerning a child. In verses 1–5 he invites his disciples to "change" and "become like children," specifically to become humble like a child. This teaching chal-

lenges "cultural assumptions about social status" and sets his kingdom in contrast to the powerful kingdom of Rome, where children are the vulnerable left behind and discounted.[3] The vulnerable children are the example and embodiment of the new rule of Jesus that exposes the falseness of hostage-taking regimes that do not value children:

> The child has no status and no social importance. Jesus challenges his followers not to think in terms of social hierarchies. The "humility" that he recommends involves putting aside such considerations and being willing to become a social "nobody."[4]

In his second terse teaching Jesus issues a protective warning ensuring "these little ones" whom Daniel J. Harrington characterizes as "the marginal ('little ones') and the 'strays.'"[5] Jesus's teaching is a mighty subversion of the usual norms of society. His teaching is an important echo of Moses's insistence to Pharaoh that none of the most vulnerable will be left behind.

3. This accent on the lowliest and the most vulnerable is reinforced in the more familiar teaching of the parable of Matthew 25:31–46, wherein the Son of Man is identified with "the least." In the parable the "least" includes those who are hungry, thirsty, naked, sick, in prison, or a stranger, that is, the ones who do not benefit from the resources of society. The statement does not specifically refer to children. It is, however, no reach to see that the vulnerable disenfranchised children are to be counted among "the least" with whom the Son of Man identifies. Attentive care for children, along with all of the least, is a devotion to the coming Son of Man. More important, neglect of children (among the least) is a failure to receive the coming Son of Man. Characteristically this parable brings the deep, severe expectations of the "end-time" into the immediacy of policy and practice and into the sphere of material resources where the deepest "spiritual" decisions are made.

We may take these three texts from Matthew as a major motif in the teaching of Jesus:

- In Matthew 10:42, it is a cup of cold water for these little ones.

- In Matthew 18:1–7, it is the protection of the little ones and the invitation to become like a child.

- In Matthew 25:31–46, it is ministry to "the least."

3. Daniel J. Harrington, *The Gospel of Matthew*, Sacra Pagina (Collegeville, MN: Liturgical Press, 2007), 266.

4. Harrington, *Gospel of Matthew*, 266.

5. Harrington, *Gospel of Matthew*, 267.

The sum of this teaching, partly shared in the other gospel accounts, provides a summons to refuse the hostage-taking propensity of the empire of Herod and of Rome. The early Jesus movement knows much better than did Rome what could yield a viable social order.

The Jesus movement is in deep continuity with the Torah tradition of the Old Testament. One evidence of that continuity is the way in which the Gospel of Luke appeals to the promise of the final verses of the Christian Old Testament. In Malachi 4:5–6 the Christian Old Testament ends with a final expectation that Elijah the prophet, who had been "taken up into heaven," will return in the end-time. He will have particular work to do when he returns:

> He will turn the hearts of parents to their children and the hearts of children to their parents, so that I will not come and strike the land with a curse. (Mal 4:6)

The risk of Elijah's return is that he will bring a curse on the land. But Elijah, it is anticipated, will act to preclude that curse. What precludes the curse, moreover, is the fresh reconciliation of parents and children who have been estranged, that is, a peaceableness between *the power generation* (parents) and *the vulnerable generation* (children). Thus, this anticipation completes the work begun in Deuteronomy 21:18–21, where patriarchal authority is curbed by mother and by village elders. Now in time to come there is not only unregulated power restrained, but there is complete reconciliation, the "turning of hearts" in care and respect and love.

The final verse in the Old Testament is echoed explicitly in Luke's introduction of the gospel. In Luke's rendering, John the Baptist is a figure like returning Elijah. The angel promises to father Zechariah that his soon-to-be, John,

> Will turn the hearts of parents to their children, and the disobedient to the wisdom of the righteous, to make ready a people prepared for the Lord. (Luke 1:17)

Unlike the anticipation of Elijah in Malachi 4:6, here the turning of hearts concerns only and specifically the hearts of the parents. It is the hearts of the parents—the power generation—that must turn reconciliation to the vulnerable children. The counterpoint is that the disobedient, presumably the children, will turn to "the wisdom of the righteous," presumably to the way of Torah obedience, all of which makes it possible for the Lord to come. Reconciliation with the children is a prerequisite for the new rule of the Messiah to come.

Thus, attentiveness to the children is a hallmark of the Jesus movement, a movement that refuses the hostage taking of the empire in which the hearts of adults are turned against the children. This peculiar accent of the Jesus movement is picked up in the summary statement of the Epistle of James:

> Religion that is pure and undefiled before God, the Father, is this: to care for orphans and widows in their distress, and to keep oneself unstained by the world. (Jas 1:27)

To be "stained by the world" may mean to take advantage of the vulnerable. But that is "bad religion." This statement of James nicely juxtaposes *God as Father* and *orphans* who have no father. The way in which God becomes father to orphans is exactly to care, to see, to look after, and to have regard for. That is true religion! When there is not such positive, active regard for orphans, it means that we have too much imitated the world of power that preys on the vulnerable. True religion transforms orphans into treasured children.

The capstone of such orphan-regarding faith is Jesus's own promise in John 14:18:

> I will not leave you orphaned.

The term in Greek is exactly "orphaned." The paragraph continues to assert that he, Jesus (along with the Father) "will make our home" with them (v. 23). The Jesus movement has the work of transforming abandoned children into safe, well-regarded, at-home sons and daughters, that is, "children of God."

IV. The National Security State and Knowing Better

Thus in three waves we may contrast "hostage taking" and "knowing better."

- In ancient Egypt, Pharaoh always wanted hostages, but Moses knew better.

- In Israel's ancient patriarchy, unregulated fathers treated children as hostages, but the Torah tradition knew better.

- In the New Testament, Herod was at the apex of a hostage-taking regime, but the Jesus movement knew better.

I submit that our own moment of responsible faith is not different from these scenarios. In our case, we live in a National Security State that is committed to perpetual war, in a consumerism that reduces everything and everyone to a commodity. As a consequence, children become statistics for sales reports, military recruitment, prison population, and debt. It is, among us, all about subordinating the future of children to the success of market ideology wherein the money and power flow to the top of the pyramid while increasing numbers of children are left behind. They are left behind in unnoticed and calculated poverty. Or they are left behind through the rat race of privilege that ends too often and too soon for too many in depression that culminates in suicide, so great is the pressure to keep up and compete. But the National Security State, that flies the banner of American exceptionalism, does not compute the cost and lacks the capacity to notice the accumulation of devalued hostages.

But we know better. We know better because we have left no child (not even a hoof!) behind with Pharaoh as a hostage. We know better because the Torah tradition witnesses to the God who is the father of orphans. We know better because the Jesus movement has always understood that "true religion" consists in care for orphans. We know better because we are situated in an alternative narrative. It is this alternative narrative that we act out dramatically in the sacrament of baptism. We use water and words to mark children, as we say, "Sealed as Christ's own forever."

Baptism reiterates the counterstory about children, counter to hostage-taking assumptions and practices of Pharaoh, of unregulated patriarchy and of Herod. Baptism, however, only signifies the counterstory. The performance of the counterstory has to be continued in public practice. It has to be performed by local programs that value and valorize children. It has to be continued by sweeping policies that redeploy societal resources for those whom we dare not leave behind.

With Pharaoh, with unregulated patriarchy, with Herod, and with our own National Security State, both policy and practice are set . . . dead-set! . . . against the children. But we know better! We know that our hearts may be turned toward the children. As they are turned, we may witness the coming of the new regime in which there are no orphans, no left behind, no hostages; none is in hopeless debt, none is a statistic of cannon fodder. We do indeed know better!

15.

Children (II): Given as Sacrifices

A version of this essay was originally delivered to the Children's Defense Fund, 22nd Annual Samuel DeWitt Proctor Institute for Child Advocacy Ministry in Clinton, Tennessee, July 20, 2016.

I have assumed that we are all on the same page about "oppression, justice, children, and our call as people of faith." For that reason I take the liberty of probing with you some curious texts that do not leap immediately to mind.

I

As you may know, the books of First and Second Kings present a four-hundred-year sweep of the monarchy of David in the city of Jerusalem, a four-hundred-year sweep of obscure names that comes to a sorry end. The text, with the urgency of advocacy, sorts out good kings and bad kings and eventually concludes that the bad kings have caused the ultimate destruction of the holy city of Jerusalem. This text, moreover, proposes criteria for what makes a good king or a bad king, that is, what serves the city of Jerusalem well or what places it in jeopardy. The judgments rendered on the several kings are highly stylized and repetitious.

• Near the end of that long historical process, we get a curious phrase four times, that the bad kings have caused their "sons to pass through fire."

Thus concerning King Ahaz (735–715 BCE):

> He did not do what was right in the sight of the Lord his God, as his ancestor David had done, but he walked in the way of the kings of Israel. He even made his son pass through fire, according to the abominable practices of the nations whom the Lord drove out before the people of Israel. (2 Kgs 16:2–3)

Ahaz, moreover, accommodated the great Assyrian Empire of Tiglath-pileser III and imitated his worship.

• In the summary statement of 2 Kings 17:7–18 concerning the failed northern kingdom of Israel, that regime is judged for its theological disobedience. It is said of the northern kings:

> They rejected all the commandments of the LORD their God and made for themselves cast images of the two calves; they made a sacred pole, worshiped all the host of heaven, and served Baal. They made their sons and daughters pass through fire; they used divination and augury, and they sold themselves to do evil in the sight of the Lord, provoking him to anger. (2 Kgs 17:16–17)

• In 2 Kings 21:3–6, Manasseh (687–642 BCE), judged to be the worst of the kings of Judah, is indicted in a similar fashion:

> He erected altars for Baal, made a sacred pole as King Ahab of Israel had done, worshiped all the host of heaven, and served them. He built altars in the house of the Lord, of which the Lord had said, "In Jerusalem I will put my name." He built altars for all the host of heaven in the two courts of the house of the Lord. He made his son pass through fire; he practiced soothsaying and augury, and dealt with mediums and with wizards. (2 Kgs 21:3–6)

• In 2 Kings 23:10 the best king, Josiah (640–609 BCE), purged his realm of pernicious religious practice:

> He defiled Topheth, which is in the valley of Ben-hinnom, so that no one would make a son or a daughter pass through fire as an offering to Molech.

Thus the northern kings are condemned wholesale. Two southern kings, Ahaz and Manasseh, are specifically condemned. And one king, Josiah, is commended for terminating the practice of making children pass through fire. It is easy to notice that in all of these cases, we have the repeated phrase, "pass your son or daughter through fire." That practice is each time cited as a sign of religious misconduct, a brutal practice of violence against children whereby kings sought to secure their own future by making an offering to other gods, notably Baal and Molech.

The phrase itself, "pass through fire," is not explicated in the text, but most interpreters regard it as an act of child sacrifice, as a brutal rendering of sons—even royal sons—to bargain with, persuade, bribe, or appease the gods. Thus, the practice entails sacrifice of royal heirs—the carriers of the future—for present well-being, whether economic prosperity or military success. The barbaric practice was grounded in an assumption that the mysterious powers of holy danger could be tamed and administered by offering our most precious possessions in a patriarchal society, namely, our sons. So the prophet Micah, in a familiar passage, ponders the question concerning sacrifice to God:

> With what shall I come before the LORD,
> and bow myself before God on high?
> Shall I come before him with burnt offerings,
> with calves a year old?
> Will the LORD be pleased with thousands of rams,
> with ten thousand rivers of oil?
> Shall I give my firstborn for my transgression,
> the fruit of my body for the sin of my soul? (Mic 6:6–7)

The question runs from the least precious to the most precious, from calves to a thousand rams to ten thousand rivers of oil, and finally to "my firstborn." Is this what God requires? Micah answers, "No, that is not what God requires." What God requires, as you know from this text is:

> To do justice and to love kindness,
> and to walk humbly with your God. (v. 8)

The kings of Israel and Judah, however, thought otherwise. Bewitched as they were by commodities, they thought a good future depended on the offer of their most treasured commodity, their firstborn son, who was offered to God to purchase well-being.

II

This offensive practice of child sacrifice—passing children through fire—was deeply condemned. But we may pause to consider what in fact was going on. I propose four points of probe.

1. This was a religious rite conducted in anxiety that sought to secure the present at the expense of the future. It was understood in a calculating practice of quid pro quo, of giving this for that, on the assumption that the favor of God could be purchased by the payment of a precious commodity. That is, the world of divine mystery had been reduced to a

commodity transaction, and the sons—even royal sons—were perceived as a *tradable commodity*. The reduction of everything to tradable commodity is an endless temptation, a category mistake that is often made in religion, as, for example, the "sale of indulgences" in the late medieval church. Israel knew of that temptation. In Psalm 50, God is portrayed as mightily resistant to worship as a commodity transaction:

> I will not accept a bull from your house
> or goats from your folds.
> For every wild animal of the forest is mine,
> the cattle on a thousand hills.
> I know all the birds of the air,
> and all that is in the field is mine. (Ps 50:9–11)

God has no need that humans must satisfy. God wants nothing of precious commodities. In the prophetic tradition the continual insistence is that *trusting relationships* and not *tradable commodities* are the proper category for communion with God.

Thus Hosea can declare:

> For I desire steadfast love and not sacrifice,
> The knowledge of God rather than burnt offerings. (Hos 6:6)

This is, moreover, a text quoted later by Jesus, who also resists the commoditization of faith (Matt 9:1–13; 12:7).

2. But from where does this idea of commoditization arise? Do you notice that in all four uses of our phrase, passing sons through fire, other gods are mentioned?

- In 2 Kings 16:3 it is the Assyrian gods who are worshiped on every high hill and under every green tree.
- In 17:7 it is Baal who is worshiped.
- In 21:6 it is "altars erected for Baal."
- In 23:10, it is worship of Molech.

So let us stay with Baal, the most mentioned of these gods. Baal is often said to be a "fertility god," the god who gives rain and makes crops grow, the god who can fructify the earth, that is, make it pregnant (Beulah land). But "Baal" is in fact a code word for the reduction of the mystery of life to manageable commodity manipulation. Baal—along with Molech and a host of other gods—in this polemical rhetoric is understood as an idol, as a manageable object and not subject, as passive object without agency who can do nothing, who has no moral edge, who requires nothing by way of conduct or obedience beyond the regular offer of commodity sacrifices. What happens in a society connected to Baal—as in the Elijah contest at Mount Carmel—is that the social interactive dimensions of humanness disappear and everything becomes a commodity transaction. And when Baal demands commodity, those who take themselves to be made in the image of Baal become managers of commodity transactions. And if things do not work, if Baal does not prosper, if Baal is not satisfied, if Baal is not appeased, then the offer of commodities must be escalated, in terms of quantity, more and more up to ten thousand rivers of oil, or in terms of quality, more precious until the offering includes sons, even royal sons.

3. Do I need to tell you that what happens in such commodity transactions is that religious values and human possibilities are reduced to *economics*? So Baal is a code word for economic reductionism in which everything and everyone is a tradable, usable, commodity. In conventional thinking, moreover, economics is the distribution of scarce goods. There is never enough, never enough to go around, never enough to satiate Baal, never enough to share with neighbors, never enough to have abundance. As a consequence, life consists in the pursuit of more commodities. Everything is priced and no sacrifice of sons or wealth or environment is too great a price to pay for more commodities in a world defined by commodity. Baalism is a tag word for a world in which every human possibility is reduced to commodity.

I may cite two dramatic cases of commoditization in the Bible. In Ezekiel's condemnation of the city-state of Tyre, its commercial enterprise is vigorously condemned:

Tarshish did business with you out of the abundance of your great wealth; silver, iron, tin, and lead they exchanged for your wares. Javan, Tubal and Meshech traded with you; they exchanged human beings and vessels of bronze for your merchandise. Beth-togarmah exchanged for your wares horses, war horses, and mules. The Rhodians traded with you; many coastlands were your own special markets; they brought you in payment ivory tusks and ebony. Edom did business with you because of your abundant goods; they exchanged for your wares turquoise, purple, embroidered work, fine linen, coral, and rubies. Judah and the land of Israel traded with you; they exchanged for your merchandise wheat from Minnith, millet, honey, oil, and balm. Damascus traded with you for your abundant goods because of your great wealth of every kind—wine from Helbon, and white wool. Vedan and Javan from Uzal entered into trade for your wares; wrought iron, cassia, and sweet cane were bartered for your merchandise. Dedan traded with you in saddlecloths for riding. Arabia and all the princes of Kedar were your favorite dealers in lambs, rams, and goats; in these they did business with you. The merchants of Sheba and Raamah traded with you; they exchanged for your wares the best of all kinds of spices, all precious stones, and gold. Haran, Canneh, Eden, the merchants of Sheba, Assyria, and Chilmad traded with you. These traded with you in choice garments, clothes of blue and embroidered work, and in carpets of colored material, bound with cords and made secure; in these they traded with you. The ships of Tarshish traveled for you in your trade. (Ezek 27:12–25).

In the poetry that follows this prose, the targets of prophetic critique are the "merchants" who have reduced social reality to trade, a sentiment most recently voiced by Margaret Thatcher, who famously said, "There is no such thing as society; there is only the market." This indictment of Tyre is echoed in Revelation in its condemnation of Babylon, which is, in context, a stand-in for Rome:

And the merchants of the earth weep and mourn for her [Babylon], since no one buys their cargo any more, cargo of gold, silver, jewels and pearls, fine linen, purple, silk and scarlet, all kinds of scented wood, all articles of ivory, all article of costly wood, bronze, iron, and marble, cinnamon, spice, incense, myrrh, frankincense, wine, olive oil, choice flour and wheat, cattle and sheep, horses and chariots, slaves—and human lives. (Rev 18:11–13)

A quick reading of these two texts might not have permitted you to notice one stunning parallel in them. In Ezekiel 27:13:

They exchanged *human beings* and vessels of bronze for your merchandise.

In Revelation 18:13, at the end of the long list of commodities, as though written with a deep exasperated sigh, "and *human lives*." In both texts, human persons are listed along with all the other commodities. Given these references to slavery in which human persons can be bought, sold, traded, and owned, it follows, surely enough, that when some persons can be readily reduced to commodity, all human persons are placed in jeopardy by such anxious reduction to commodity. The sad result is that there is nothing outside the market that becomes the only norm for value.

4. If you pay attention to the placement of these four texts on "passing through fire," you will notice that they occur in contexts of acute social anxiety as the royal history has run its course. That is, such acts did not occur in the narrative of David or Solomon, when all appeared to be

well. They occur when the leadership is at its wits end and these practices are undertaken to stave off big trouble.

In the case of Ahaz, his action was to stave off the threat of Syria and then the greater threat of Assyria, that is, Iraq. In the summary statement of 2 Kings 17, the action was taken to protect the capital city of Samaria. In the case of Manasseh, the king was tempted in his long reign to self-sufficiency, a policy that brought him great prophetic judgment in 2 Kings 21:12–15.

It is no wonder that the prophets polemize against all such practices. Jeremiah can say:

> And they go on building the high place of Topheth, which is in the valley of the son of Hinnom, to burn their sons and their daughters in the fire—which I did not command, nor did it come into my mind. Therefore, the days are surely coming, says the LORD, when it will no more be called Topheth, or the valley of the son of Hinnom, but the valley of Slaughter: for they will bury in Topheth until there is no more room. (Jer 7:31–32; see Jer 19:4–5; 32:25)

And Ezekiel can say:

> I defiled them through their very gifts, in their offering up all their firstborn, in order that I might horrify them, so that they might know that I am the LORD. (Ezek 20:26)[1]

In the end the prophetic critique concerns not just particular acts but the entire frame of reference that has distorted social policy and social practice. The process of commoditization has violated the character of YHWH and the covenant Israel has with YHWH. That relationship depends upon interpersonal trust and obedience that pivots on regard for the neighbor. In a commodity practice, the neighbor simply disappears. The ultimate absence of neighborliness is having your sons and daughters pass through fire as a way to secure one's well-being.

III

Now at midpoint in my presentation, I want to pause to comment on a novel by Ian McEwan, *The Children Act*.[2] It is the story of a boy, Adam Henry, the son of Jehovah's Witness parents, who has leukemia. The

---

1. See Jon D. Levenson, *The Death and Resurrection of the Beloved Son: The Transformation of Child Sacrifice in Judaism and Christianity* (New Haven: Yale University Press, 1993), 43–45.
2. Ian McEwan, *The Children Act: A Novel* (New York: Doubleday, 2014).

parents, because of their faith, refuse medical treatment for Adam. But a suit is brought to override the will of the parents, a suit to be heard by Judge Fiona Maye. Fiona, the judge, has in her awareness a previous case in Britain wherein the authorities took children away from their parents because of an accusation of devil worship. But she reports to her husband on the outcome of that case:

> It turns out there was nothing. No secret rituals, no Satan, no abuse. Nothing happened. It was a fantasy. All the experts and important people were sharing a delusion, a dream. Eventually, they all came to their senses and were very ashamed, or they should have been. And very slowly, the children were returned to their homes.[3]

This memory evokes in Fiona sympathy for the will of the parents, a sympathy reinforced for her by Adam himself. Adam is a true believer in the faith of his parents and gladly cites biblical texts to show why blood transfusion is evil and must be rejected:

> He presented himself as a spokesman for his sect when he said that he and his congregation wanted to be left alone to live by what they knew to be self-evident truths.[4]

The novel focuses on the trial and the decision that the judge must make. In the end, Fiona rules against the parents for the sake of Adam's welfare:

> In short, I find that A., his parents and the elders of the church have made a decision which is hostile to A.'s welfare, which is this court's paramount consideration. He must be protected from such a decision. He must be protected from his religion and from himself.[5]

Thus the trial ends. But the novel is extended because Adam shows up at the door of Fiona's house. There develops between the judge and the boy a deep engagement wherein Fiona clearly steps outside her professional capacity. Adam is now grateful for her ruling, glad it has been made. He reports to her that his parents are joyous as well. It has been a transgression of their faith, but they are not guilty of it, and their son has been saved.

But Fiona reflects. She reflects on the children that have come before her in many contested family cases:

3. McEwan, *Children Act*, 105.
4. McEwan, *Children Act*, 117.
5. McEwan, *Children Act*, 127.

And the children? Counters in a game, bargaining chips for use by mothers, objects of financial or emotional neglect by fathers; the pretext for real or fantasized or cynically invented charges of abuse, usually by mothers, sometimes by fathers; dazed children shuttling weekly between households in coparenting arrangements, mislaid coats or pencil cases shrilly broadcast by one solicitor to another; children doomed to see their fathers once or twice a month, or never, as the most purposeful men vanished into the smithy of a hot new marriage to forge new offspring.[6]

She reflects further that in such conflicted cases there is always money:

And the money? The new coinage was half-truth and special pleading. Greedy husbands versus greedy wives, maneuvering like nations at the end of a war, grabbing from the ruins what spoils they could before the final withdrawal. Men concealing their funds in foreign accounts, women demanding a life of ease, forever. . . . And beyond Fiona's reach . . . children tortured, starved or beaten to death, evil spirits threshed out of them in animalistic rites, gruesome young stepfathers breaking toddler's bones while dim compliant mothers looked on . . . indifferent neighbors selectively deaf to the screaming and careless or hard-pressed social workers failing to intervene.[7]

Finally she sends Adam away. Before she does, she kisses him on the mouth. And she is left, as the novel ends, having to explain all of this, honestly as she can, to her husband who has been estranged in an affair and who is now coming to reconciliation.

It is a novel about complexity and conflict, about a judge who is deeply conflicted, and who cannot fence out her own internal reality that leads her to have passion for the child she has saved. Like a good novel, this one ends with no easy resolution. We are left with deep wonderments; Fiona is left with her own emotional churning in the midst of her marital conflict. It all sounds to me like making a son pass through fire. It is, moreover, not just any son; this is "Adam" who is in God's likeness, who is every son, any son or any daughter who is in the image of God.

Adam is made to pass through the fire of his parents' legalistic faith. They are ready to sacrifice him for the sake of their faith. He is a pawn of their law. It is the work of the court to protect the child. Fiona discerns that legal action to protect is more difficult than a court ruling. Because in the end, Adam is still left, cut off from his parents, not quite cut off but not wanting to be with them. He yearns to be with Fiona, but he cannot

6. McEwan, *Children Act*, 137.
7. McEwan, *Children Act*, 138.

be. He is left, at the end, as a displaced child, not finally passing through fire but not exempt from it. And what the judge deals with along with her estranged husband is left unresolved.

I am left with the two questions that Fiona poses: "And the children?"[8] "And the money?"[9] Children . . . money. What an interface! The children have to do with fragile but essential relatedness that neither the parents nor the judge manages well. The money has to do with control, mastery, security. They go together. But they cannot both be ultimate. If children are of ultimate importance, then the anxious pursuit of money cannot be right. If money is the real thing, then children are at best incidental to our life. We are always choosing. Fiona, as a judge, saw the choosing that people do, sometimes choosing for children, sometimes choosing for money, sometimes being ambiguous, living in denial and finally in violent despair. She asks and we must ask, "And the children? . . . And the money?"

IV

You may think I have taken much too long to get to my argument. I have done so because I want to consider the ways in which we make our children "pass through fire" as a present practice among us.

1. Our present practice of that ancient ritual is because we, as a society, are completely committed to a *commoditization of reality*. Everything and everyone is reducible to a commodity that can be bought and sold and owned and traded and used. I suppose that the taproot and high mark of such reduction was slavery, which was practiced from the beginning of our Euro-American society, in both the north and the south. The capacity of one person to "own" another person was the taproot of huge wealth in our society. Thus, the deep reality of what is "owed" to the erstwhile slave community is an anticipation of commoditization that needed to demean and dehumanize some to legitimate their social usefulness. The sequence from slavery to Jim Crow to the New Jim Crow makes clear that there is a strong racist element to commoditization.

It is then an easy step from racism to extend commoditization to all parts of our political economy to see that social life is a zero-sum game of winners and losers, and that winning is paramount, no matter what the cost is to anyone else. Everything of worth has a market value and needs to be priced, so that only those with resources have access. Commoditization inevitably brings with it a relentless competition to determine

8. McEwan, *Children Act*, 137.
9. McEwan, *Children Act*, 138.

winners and losers. Policies are designed to reward winners and punish losers.

And perhaps the last step of commoditization is that we ourselves, our very persons are reduced to technical apparatuses that can be fixed like a machine. So we have come to regard ourselves as candidates for technical repair, made clear in TV advertising that is saturated with drugs that can fix anything including failing virility. Thus, we have technical fixes for any human ailment, all set in survival games, or better, hunger games, or thirst games in which we are admonished to "stay thirsty" for the next product, never yet satisfied, never yet adequate, never yet at peace or at rest, because we must always pursue one more commodity that finally will make us safe and happy.

What disappears in such commoditization are the depths and heights of human loyalty or the wonder of truth, beauty, and goodness, or the kind of human connection that requires no commodity engagement to flourish and so offers nothing that can be marketed on TV. The dominant value system of our commodity society is to marginalize that human dimension, a marginalization that is epitomized in the loss of the arts from school budgets and the making of money as the definition of a "career" and therefore the measure of education.

2. As the ancients engaged in *idolatry*, so does our society. In that ancient world it was tagged in biblical polemic as "Baal." Baal was a demanding object to be worshiped, never subject, never agent, never a lively character who could act. Baalism is a code word for reducing everything to objective relationship without the ingredients of justice, righteousness, steadfast love, mercy, or faithfulness. The dominant narrative of idolatry is the golden calf of Aaron (Exodus 32). The calf—better, the young bull—is symbol of virility; one can imagine that young bull having a four-hour erection. And it is made of gold. It is a commodity, a precious commodity. Thus, the combination of *calf* and *gold* yields a precious commodity of virility that is offered as a substitute for a free relational God who comes and goes in freedom. It is that freedom of God (including the forty days of absence by Moses) that requires an alternative god who has no freedom and is never absent. It is the trade-off of a free, faithful God for an icon of precious metal that is the deep crisis of ancient Israel.

In our society, it is exactly a calf of god, a bull of gold, who sits in front of our national temple, the Stock Market on Wall Street. That golden bull of Wall Street promises well-being and make endless demands. The great icon of commodity has arranged social power in a pyramid in which "value" perforce gravitates to the top.

If we think about that icon that combines gold and virility and ask about its dramatic performance, it is clear, is it not, that the televised sports of football—college and professional—is the great liturgy of commoditization whereby virility is on exhibit. And the entire enterprise is about gold, about fabulous concentrations of wealth all surrounded by celebrity that celebrates success in the world of gold plus virility, all given tone by poorly paid "cheerleaders" who in fact never lead any cheers but who add sex to money and virility.

3. It turns out that the precious icon of a golden bull is not about religion, except as religion is the legitimator for *economy*. It turns out that the gold bull is about the value of those who have reached the top of the pyramid. It turns out that "approved religion" in our society is a set of symbols that endorses individualism, that keeps systemic power hidden, that legitimates power to sustain an unsustainable standard of living for the entitled.

The economic assumption of a Baal-propelled commoditization, given legitimacy by the bull of gold, is that there are scarce goods. There is not enough of oil or water or land for everyone. Such items cannot be free, because they are not available in abundance. For that reason, one must endlessly qualify, endlessly produce in order to endlessly merit a payout. And because the process is "endless," it is infused with profound anxiety of not having done enough, not having earned enough, not having become enough, not having been enough yet . . . thus no free lunch!

There are, from time to time, efforts to "regulate" the predatory economy to assure that the left behind or the left out have a small portion of the wealth. But the long effort is to deregulate, because regulation gets in the way of pure market ideology that governs our social relationships.

Of course, that anti-neighborly stance is made complex and problematic in "Christian America" because that faith tradition endlessly features "the neighbor" who is entitled to a viable portion of the common good. As a result, the interface of religion and economics is an endless process of remembering the God of Abraham. So we sing without any irony:

America, America! God shed his grace on thee,
And crown thy good with brotherhood from sea to shining sea![10]

But the God of bounty and brotherhood must be morphed into the domain of capitalist individualism that compromises "brotherhood" for the sake of some at the expense of others. The Bible to which we make appeal concerns the God of emancipation and abundance, bread from

---

10. "O Beautiful for Spacious Skies," in *Glory to God: Hymns, Psalms, & Spiritual Songs* (Louisville: Westminster John Knox Press, 2013), 338.

heaven and from amber waves of grain; but this God is pushed back into the fear and scarcity and monopoly of Pharaoh, in the interest of unstable wealth and security that reduce all others to unnoticed forms or bondage. Thus, our economy has an uneasy interface with the faith we claim to profess, because that covenantal faith in fact contradicts the economy we take as definitional for "the American dream."[11]

4. The drama of *commoditization, idolatry,* and *predatory economics* ends in the process of making *our children pass through fire.* The ideology of the Jehovah's Witnesses in the novel urges that adherence to the ideology is more important than Adam's health and welfare. And so the ideology of *commodity,* legitimated by *idolatry* and acted out as *economics,* insists that the market ideology counts for more than the children. I have already said that "passing through fire" is a willingness to sacrifice the future, that is, our children, for the sake of present well-being. So count the ways in which our children pass through fire, that is, are sacrificed in order to sustain our commoditization via idolatry. I can think of three dimensions of compromising our children.

a. Most obvious is *the military arrangement* of an all-volunteer army. Our all-volunteer army takes matters of war and peace away from the citizens and entrusts them to the managers of the pyramid. The managers of the pyramid, in the interest of resource control (oil) and market control, do not mind the expenditure of young lives for the sake of ideological advances. The all-volunteer army depends—to some large extent—on those who have no alternative way to enter the capitalist economy but find value, order, and viable money in the service of the military. The managers of the pyramid do not mind that we are committed to perpetual war with no exit strategy, because the costs of the war are paid by sons and daughters other than their own sons and daughters. The high cost of such adventurism is evident not only in the devouring debt but in the maimed bodies and crushed psyches that contribute to an endangered society. Of course it is noble and patriotic to assure good care for vets; but that is no good trade-off for the endless military adventurism and a war-based economy. These maimed bodies and crushed psyches are indeed our sons and daughters who have passed through fire. And they have passed through the fire in order to satisfy the insatiable requirements of the golden bull of wealth and virility, a contemporary Baalism.

b. An endless commitment to fossil fuels is before our very eyes, making our existence vulnerable. The extreme cost of that commitment is

---

11. See Ta-Nehisi Coates, *Between the World and Me* (New York: Spiegel & Grau, 2015), for a critical assessment of the white dream of America that Coates calls "The Dream."

in the interest of a growth economy in order to sustain our accustomed standard of living. The commitment is propelled by the insatiable hunger and thirst for more. As a result we are coming to the end of water resources and fossil resources. And that is seconded by *the ravages of the earth* that makes our context unlivable. In the ancient world they soured the land of their enemies with salt so that it would not produce. And now we sour the land of our enemies with chemicals. And we extend the souring to "disadvantaged neighborhoods" that become dumping grounds for unwelcome waste. We make creation into an unlivable chaos. And we imagine—as we always do at the top of the pyramid—that privatized privileged zones of well-being can be set apart from such ruin. But of course they cannot be. And so we bequeath an unlivable world to our grandchildren, who will pass through fire in their effort to sustain human community in an unlivable environment.

It is ironic that voices of fear constantly protest against the national debt because they do not want to leave such a debt to our grandchildren. The same voices, however, have no critical thought about leaving an unlivable environment to our grandchildren. And so we may imagine that in two or three generations, our sons and daughters will pass through the fire of unsustainable creation, all because of endless commoditization offered to the idols of commodity in the form of unregulated economics.

c. The commodity system leaves too many of our sons and daughters to pass through the fire of hopeless *poverty*. In an article on November 18, 2015, Eduardo Porter reports that "16 million Americans live on $8.60 or less a day." He continues:

> The American antipoverty strategy, so focused on choosing between good and bad guys, those worthy or unworthy of public assistance, is shaped by this ignorance. It exposes the inadequacy of viewing poverty as personal failure and the limitations of relying so heavily on providing low-income working Americans with a tax break to encourage better behavior, get a job and just stop being poor. Deep poverty . . . is an ecosystem where bad individual decisions occur within broken environments, where the social glue has come unstuck. Cognitive abilities and character are important at the individual level, but they can't be clearly separated from their environment.[12]

He concludes:

---

12. Eduardo Porter, "Electing to Ignore the Poorest of the Poor," *New York Times*, November 18, 2015, B4.

There's a reason. Even as the Black Lives Matter campaign and the movement to raise the minimum wage gains steam, the deeply poor remain politically unorganized. They may not even rate a tax cut.[13]

The hopeless situation of the poor is not an aberration or an accident. It is an inevitable outcome of an economy of greed that is propelled by the reduction of all to commodity, and the consequent disappearance of human empathy and effective human caring.

It was high irony that on the same day in the *New York Times* (November 18, 2015) on the page opposite the Porter article was a piece by Matthew Goldstein on the apparent overreach of Cyrus Vance Jr., district attorney for Manhattan.[14] The article reported on a dozen young people who worked for a bank who were charged by Vance with a "systemic scheme" to sell fraudulent mortgages to Fannie Mae. They did so by inflating the qualifications of the mortgage applicants. That sounds like routine fraud. But the striking photograph shows the young people all in procession, chained together and stooping down to hide their faces from the photographer. It looked like they were passing through fire. They were acquitted, but not before they performed the drama of shame.

The photograph lingers. It lingers because, whether guilty or not, these sons and daughters had found a way to get ahead in the commodity system. They were willing and able to do what was required to join the pyramid club. I suppose the only saving grace is that they were ashamed enough to want to hide their faces. They knew better; they had not yet forgotten that they knew better.

The juxtaposition of these two articles on the same day, one on $8.60 day and one on dishonest inflation of qualifications for loans, suggests that the passing through fire of commodity is a seduction for the haves who serve Baal even as it is a death sentence for the have-nots. The result for haves and have-nots is an economy that is skewed away from viable humanness and is a high cost for all parties.

Alice Skirtz has written a study entitled *Econocide: The Elimination of the Urban Poor* that traces the action of the City Council, the Chamber of Commerce, and the financial leadership of Cincinnati that has for twenty years been systematically eliminating the poor from the city.[15] The visible part is gentrification; the hidden part is that it is intentional policy. The elimination of the poor is based on the conviction that some are

13. Porter, "Electing to Ignore," B4.
14. Matthew Goldstein, "Harsh Light on Vance," *New York Times*, November 18, 2015, B5.
15. Alice Skirtz, *Econocide: The Elimination of the Urban Poor* (Washington, DC: NASW Press, 2013).

dispensable, because they do not produce; they do not have resources to purchase, and so they are without value in an ecosystem of commodity. The dispensability of the poor sounds to me not unlike the ancient dispensability of sons and daughters, if that is what is required to satisfy the gods of commoditization.

5. There are no doubt other dimensions of this process of passing through fire. But these three facets together, *military maiming and despair, environmental dislocation*, and the *dispensability of the poor* together yield *a culture of violence* that is an intrinsic element in the commodity system. That violence was already undertaken by Pharaoh against the Hebrew slaves as he treated them "ruthlessly" (Exod 1:13–14). It is a violence perpetuated in the old slave system of the United States. It is a violence, moreover, continued by our current public practice, overtly through police brutality in which police are cast in the role of the old plantation "drivers," but covertly in a system of pay-day loans, low wages, inequitable taxation, and stratified housing, education, and health care that serves the pyramid scheme. It is the same uncaring that blithely raises the Social Security age to sixty-seven or sixty-eight or seventy, a decision made by wealthy members of congress who have never done a day of manual labor. They do so in order to extend the working life of the voiceless in the service of a skewed system. Commoditization breeds violence, and the gods who legitimate such a system regard violence as the cost of doing business and maintaining a system in which cheap labor enhances the life of the nonlaborers.

6. I noted in my textual analysis that all of these references to passing sons and daughters through fire occur *near the end* of the historical recital as Jerusalem—home of the urban elites—moved to an inexorable termination.[16] The sacrifice of sons and daughters reflected urgent anxiety about the coming end.

The cluster of such texts near the end leads me to suggest that our passing of sons and daughters through fire via *militarism, environmental violence*, and *poverty* shows how anxious we are about *the termination of an unsustainable system*. We may make palliative gestures to resist that end for a long while. We may face, eventually, internal revolution. Or we may fade in a whisper, no longer to believe our own mantras of exceptionalism. Surely passing sons and daughters through fire, a nar-

16. Paul Krugman, in speaking of the climate crisis, has asked if the Republicans would destroy civilization in their refusal to face the reality of the crisis ("Republicans' Climate Change Denial Denial," *New York Times*, December 4, 2015, A35). The climate crisis evokes for Krugman, as for many others, rhetoric of "the end." *Mutatis Mutandis*, one can propose that such an anticipated "end of civilization" is indeed a result of passing sons and daughters through fire.

cotic refusal to notice what we are doing, is an act of futility, because the sacrifices are offered to a god who cannot save.

V

Or dare we imagine that fresh obedience to the God of emancipation might matter. We do not know. But in the hope that it might matter, I line out, as my last move, two texts that imagine a life-generating alternative.

1. My first text is *Hosea 2*, the fullest, most complete dramatic prophetic text we have. It is the drama of divorce and remarriage, and it is cast in deeply patriarchal terms. That is, Israel is a whoring wife and YHWH is an indignant husband. The roles could have been reversed, given our gender equity, so that Israel could be cast as the whoring husband and YHWH could be the indignant wife.

Either way, Israel is accused of misconstruing its life. She imagined that her lovers (gods of commodity) gave her life resources: bread, water, wool, flax, olive oil (v. 5). She refused to recognize that it was YHWH, the creator and Lord of the covenant, who sustained her in need:

> She did not know that it was I who gave her
> the grain, the wine, and the oil,
> and who lavished upon her silver and gold that they used for Baal. (v. 8)

Israel used the gifts of YHWH for Baal. Israel used the free gifts of covenant for the perversion of covenant. YHWH, in response, is no easy mark and could not be taken for granted. YHWH has no patience with the worship of commodity or for the gods of commodity.

And so the poem arrives at the big prophetic "therefore" (v. 9). YHWH is no patsy, and so speaks of the termination of Israel. Then comes a series of forceful divine resolves that bespeak deprivation and termination, the kind of deprivation that will cause some to live on $8.60 a day and some to cower in chains and in shame before the photographers:

> Therefore I will take back my grain in its time,
> and my wine in its season;
> and I will take away my wool and my flax,
> which were to cover her nakedness. (v. 9)

And then loss of consumer goods, by war or by famine:

- I will uncover.
- I will put an end.
- I will lay waste.
- I will make a forest.
- I will punish. (vv. 9–13)

This is a God—unlike Baal—who has agency, who can act, who will not be mocked! And it is all because Israel forgot: forgot covenant; forgot that creation belongs to the creator; forgot Torah obedience. Forgot fidelity. Forgot neighbor, forgot, because commoditization produces amnesia. Forgot everything about being human, and so reduced all transactions to commodity.

But here is the news! The poem does not end at verse 13 with its sad conclusion, "Israel forgot me." YHWH, the Lord of fidelity, will not stop at termination. Thus in verses 14–23 there are anticipations of restoration by the great God of fidelity. YHWH, unlike Baal, will give an open "door of hope" beyond military arms, beyond a ruined environment for those who have been left behind (v. 15). Imagine that! The news is that Israel (along with the creation) does not need to be left wretched!

Notice in these verses:

- Baal will have his name washed out of their mouths (v. 17). *Baal-talk will cease* and Baal worship will end. Removing Baal—the god of commodity—is like taking down the wrong flag.

- There will be a *restoration of creation*, the end of the environmental crisis caused by Baalism and the mad worship of commodity:

  I will make a covenant on that day with the wild animals, the birds of the air, and the creeping things of the ground. (v. 18)

- There will be *disarmament*, the end of reliance on the military and its weapons:

  I will abolish the bow, the sword, and war from the land. (v. 18)

- There will be a will be *a renewal of both creation and of covenant:*

  The earth will answer the grain, the wine, and the oil,
  and they shall answer Jezreel;

and I will sow him for myself in the land.
And I will have pity on Lo-ruhamah,
and I will say to Lo-ammi,
"You are my people";
and he shall say, "You are my God." (vv. 22–23)

This poem anticipates full recovery of Israel and all creation by disarmament, by renewed environment, by the end of the worship of commodity.

And it all pivots on new vows of fidelity that God makes to God's people, the very people who had forgotten all their vows of fidelity:

And I will take you for my wife forever. I will take you for my wife in righteousness and in justice, in steadfast love, and in mercy. I will take you for my wife in faithfulness, and you shall know the LORD. (vv. 19–20)

Notice these five big words, because they are the truth of our life: *Righteousness, justice, steadfast love, mercy, faithfulness*!!! They are the words that belong to and come from the Lord of the covenant. They are the words that never are on the lips of Baal; they are words that never come up in the world of commodity. But they are true words that open to new futures, to doors of hope.

So notice the poem in its two parts:

- Verses 2–12 consist in *truth telling* about the unbearable costs of commoditization and loyalty to Baal.

- Verses 13–23 consist in *hope telling* about covenantal possibility through fidelity.

In these latter verses there are no impossible demands from Baal, no insatiable appetite, no sons or daughters passed through fire. There is only the generative recovery of good life in good creation. It is required that we move our imagination to the second part of the poem, but only after we have lingered in honesty concerning the first part. That move of imagination toward *righteousness, justice, steadfast love, mercy, and faithfulness* is a move that can be made, in rhetoric, in economics, and in practice. The outcome of that move is to be named again as the beloved of God. It is possible!

2. The second poem, *Jeremiah 22:13–19*, comes later. It concerns one of the last kings in Jerusalem, Jehoiakim, who helped preside over the disastrous termination of the city. Woe to him! Woe to the king of termination! Big trouble to the king of termination! And here is why:

[He] builds his house by unrighteousness,
and his upper rooms by injustice;
who makes his neighbor work for nothing,
and does not give them their wages . . .
But your eyes and heart are only on your dishonest gain,
for shedding innocent blood,
and for practicing oppression and violence. (vv. 13, 17)

The king, at the top of the pyramid club in Jerusalem, is the greedy user of others. He operates in unrighteousness and injustice. He pays low wages and engages in wage theft. He sheds innocent blood, which means he treats some as dispensable. He is a practitioner of oppression and violence. He does all of that because he thinks that a splendid house (McMansion) and big upper rooms and a cedar-paneled office will enhance him. He is willing to trade off his neighbors for the sake of commodity gains. He is cast as a pure type of commodity worshiper, even if the name of Baal does not occur in the poem. He is the chairman of termination who will come to a sorry end (vv. 18–19). He will not be grieved or remembered in his death; he will end in shame and abandonment. The portrayal of this king, Jehoiakim, is a model for the practice of commoditization that is grounded in injustice and leads to violence.

Remarkably, the poet breaks his poem open to imagine otherwise (vv. 15–16). He features the father of this ignoble king. The father is Josiah, a good king who had not forgotten his covenantal grounding. We are told that Josiah, the father, unlike the son, specialized in justice and righteousness. The father prospered, says the poem, because he intervened for the poor and the needy. He is a total contrast to his son. Father and son contrast *covenant* and *commodity*. They also contrast outcomes. The father: it was well with him; he prospered. The son: forgotten in shame, because commoditization has no good outcomes.

And then the poet gives us one of the most stunning lines in the Bible. YHWH says, "This is to know me!" Knowledge of God is intervention for the poor and the needy. Josiah knew that. He knew that solidarity of haves and have-nots is the way to well-being. It is not a surprise that in 2 Kings 23:10 he is the king, the only king, who prohibited the practice of passing sons and daughters through fire. He knew a more excellent way that values sons and daughters.

VI

Conclusion: *The gods of commoditization are operative and powerful.* They cannot, however, keep their promises. The Bible and the living tradition of the church attest to an alternative. It is a covenantal tradition that refuses to pass sons and daughters through fire. It is a neighborly tradition that revolves around the five terms that are never on the lips of Baal. It is a generative tradition that connects the poor and needy to the future of God. When there is convergence of the poor and the needy with YHWH, there (and only there) is livable future, a future that refuses the deathly demands of Baal.

16.

Mentoring across Generations

This chapter (here with minor changes) was first published in Mentoring:
Biblical, Theological, and Practical Perspectives, *Cam Murchison and
Dean Thompson, eds. (Grand Rapids: Eerdmans, 2018). Reprinted by permission of the publisher.*

Mentoring as an *idea* is a quite modern notion. The *practice* of mentoring,
however, is very old. It is as old as social relationships in which one person knows things that would help another person flourish with wellbeing and success. Characteristically (but not always), mentoring is a
relationship between someone of an older generation with more experience providing guidance and counsel for someone in a younger generation.

The practice of mentoring, moreover, is an acknowledgment that this
social relationship works amid the ambiguity of continuity and discontinuity. On the one hand, there is continuity, as the older person or
both persons assume that wisdom and know-how from an earlier experience still pertain and are relevantly operative for the younger person.
On the other hand, the relationship assumes, when honest, an awareness of discontinuity, for circumstances and possibilities for the younger
person are different; one cannot simply replicate or reiterate old wisdom without recognizing that a leap of imagination is required in order
that the wisdom of older experience can be recalibrated for new circumstance. Thus, the mentoring relationship depends for its effectiveness on
both honoring what has been learned from the past and recognizing that
"new occasions teach new duties." In what follows I will consider several
examples in the Old Testament of that venturesome process and the way

in which remembered experience is mobilized as guidance for new circumstance.

I

It is appropriate to begin our investigation of mentoring in the Old Testament with reference to the wisdom tradition and most particularly Proverbs. The very term *wisdom* by which we designate the books of Proverbs, Job, and Ecclesiastes refers to the accumulated learning of the community over time that is passed from generation to generation. This accumulated learning has arisen from actual experience, observation, and discernment about how the world works, and even though the wisdom literature variously stylizes and reduces those empirical data to standard (normative) articulations, their rootage remains quite practical.

The practicality of this accumulated tradition over time has two dimensions to it. On the one hand, it is quite pragmatic. The wise know what works and what fails to work toward success, security, wealth, or a good reputation. That is why there is advocacy concerning hard work, the avoidance of debt, the shunning of bad companions, and the danger of wanton speech. On the other hand, the legacy of the proverbs is devoted to identifying modes of life and conduct that are in sync with the will of the creator. As a result, wisdom teaching is labeled "creation theology" because it is a reflection on how the world works as it has been ordered by the creator God. While some interpreters have attempted to distinguish between *pragmatic, secular learning* and *theological wisdom*, it is not possible in the ancient world to make such a distinction. What "works" is what is in sync with God's will for creation. That legacy of wisdom, based on experience and observation, is an offer to the younger generation. James Crenshaw has observed that this treasury of experience was passed on with great authority to the next generation so that it remained important even when problematized:

> This treasury from the past came with certain claims of authority and therefore placed new generations in a context of decision. . . . In a sense, the legacy from the past comprised faith reports, and devotion toward parents complicated matters enormously. The tendency was to accept these faith reports at face value, even when they contradicted the personal experience of later generations.[1]

---

1. James L. Crenshaw, *Education in Ancient Israel: Across the Deadening Silence,* Anchor Bible Reference Library (New York: Doubleday, 1998), 125.

Crenshaw further observes that the receiving voice of the younger generation is "the missing voice" in the tradition:[2]

> The usual speakers in the Book of Proverbs are parents, both father and mother. They teach their children in the privacy of the home. . . . To shape character in the youth, parents rely on insights accumulated over years of experience by the community at large. These fresh discoveries, stated in succinct form are presented as statements demanding assent because they represent a consensus. Such sayings need not be argued or defended; they just are.[3]

Thus it is plausible to think that the mentoring of the wisdom tradition was one-directional; except that the poem of Job bears witness to critical restlessness with such an authoritative tradition so that, as the book of Job has it, a radically different articulation was required in order to resonate with lived experience.

The stylized mentoring in the wisdom tradition is from father to son, so that we get a chorus of "Listen, my son."

> In Proverbs, the father-to-son setting continues through chapters 1–9 and is assumed occasionally elsewhere in the book. . . . Twice, the father associates his teaching with that of the youth's mother (1:8 and 6:20), but she never speaks directly to the son.[4]

There is no doubt that this teaching is highly stylized, but surely it reflects the patriarchal setting of the tradition.

An important exception to masculine figures of speech in Proverbs is the words of "King Lemuel," who repeats "an oracle that his mother taught him" (31:1) This mentoring took place in the royal household, but it might be the admonition that any mother would give to a son, a warning about dangerous sex and the risks of alcohol. Beyond that, the mother summons her royal son to exercise royal authority in a particular direction:

> Speak out for those who cannot speak,
> for the rights of all the destitute.
> Speak out, judge righteously,
> defend the rights of the poor and needy. (Prov 31:8–9)

Yoder comments on this counsel:

2. Crenshaw, *Education in Ancient Israel*, 187.
3. Crenshaw, *Education in Ancient Israel*, 133.
4. Christine Roy Yoder, *Proverbs*, Abingdon Old Testament Commentaries (Nashville: Abingdon, 2009), 13.

The mother implores Lemuel to do his job, to enact and protect just laws and judgments and to advocate for the poor, whose lack of voice and powerlessness she captures with the expressions "mute" and "those passing away." When people cannot speak—*especially* when they cannot—the king must speak for them.[5]

In this wisdom tradition, for the most part there is no "comeback" from those who are addressed, an indication that the tradition of accumulated wisdom has great authority. It is evident, moreover, that it is all about sons, without reference to "daughters," what one would expect in patriarchal setting. Indeed, the reorientation from patriarchy to an inclusive "sons and daughters" is itself an example, in our own time, of the way in which mentoring requires discontinuity and a leap of imagination to new social reality.

II

From the *early narrative materials* of the Old Testament, I will review three instances of mentoring, recognizing that the textual evidence is terse; it requires and permits extensive "unpacking" according to our theme.[6]

1. *Jethro and Moses* (Exodus 18:1–27). In the wake of the exodus and the crisis of food and water in the wilderness, Moses was left with the task of consolidating the erstwhile slave community into a sustainable institutional form. Fortunately, his father-in-law, Jethro, came to his rescue and mentored Moses on the management of that onerous process. The meeting between Jethro and Moses is highly stylized and couched in phrasings of theological awareness. Moses greets Jethro in solemn deference, and they exchange greetings of mutual concern (v. 7). Moses bears witness to Jethro concerning the exodus deliverance, and Jethro responds in kind (vv. 8–12).

Then the narrative moves beyond conventional formula to practical matters. Jethro observes Moses functioning as judge and administrator of the people. Before he mentors Moses, he must be sure he has rightly sized up the situation. The exchange between them radically alters Moses's assumptions and actions:

---

5. Yoder, *Proverbs*, 292.

6. By "early narrative materials" I refer to the time that the text purports to narrate. I raise no critical question here concerning the historical origin of the text.

- Jethro questions Moses in a way that has a note of reprimand:

  > What is this that you are doing for the people? Why do you sit alone, while all the people stand around you from morning until evening? (v. 14)

- Moses explains that he is acting responsibly (vv. 15–16a).

- Jethro, in a more extended speech offers Moses specific advice: "I will give you counsel" (v. 19).

Moses had not asked for such counsel and likely would have continued his burdensome task without critical reflection. Jethro intrudes into Moses's busyness with a series of imperative recommendations:

> v. 19: You should represent the people before God.
>
> You should bring their cases before God.
>
> v. 20: Teach them the statutes and instructions;
>
> make known to them the way they are to go.
>
> v. 21: You should look for able men;
>
> set such men over them.

Conclusion:

> Let them sit as judges for the people at all times; let them bring every important case to you, but decide every minor case themselves. So it will be easier for you, and they will bear the burden with you. If you do this, and God so commands, then you will be able to endure, and all these people will go to their home in peace. (vv. 22–23)

Jethro proposes a new judicial structure that will ease Moses's work, and he urges Moses to focus on his most important tasks. Moses heeds Jethro's counsel and undertakes new practices whereby he shares responsibility (vv. 24–25). Jethro's uninvited wisdom rescued Moses from his overcommitment to his work and reminded Moses that he needed help and that alternatives were available. Jethro is a model mentor, who identifies the crisis, suggests a solution, and permits greater effectiveness by Moses with less personal cost. Well done!

2. *Moses and Joshua* (Numbers 27:18–23). There is no doubt that the tradition intends to exhibit Joshua as the successor to Moses and is at some pains to establish his authority in that role. Joshua functions in the narrative as an aide to Moses, assisting Moses in his various tasks, notably as military leader (see Exod 17:9–14, 24:13, 33:11, and Num 11:28). It is clear that Joshua, in his role as aide to Moses, is being instructed and groomed to assume leadership.

The most interesting part of their relationship, I judge, is the way in which Moses takes care to fully authorize Joshua to carry on his work:

- He changes Joshua's name, thus giving him a new identity in the tradition (Num 13:16).

- He authorizes him to be shepherd of the sheep by laying hands on him (Num 27:18–22; see Deut 34:9). The latter text notes that Joshua is "full of the spirit of wisdom," surely a result of having been with Moses for so long.

The specificity of mentoring is evident in two accent points. On the one hand, Moses "charges" Joshua with a mission to complete the transition into the new land:

> Be strong and bold, for you are the one who will go with this people into the land that the LORD has sworn to their ancestors to give them; and you will put them in possession of it. It is the LORD who goes before you. He will be with you; he will not fail you or forsake you. Do not fear or be dismayed. (Deut 31:7–8)

On the other hand, in Numbers 11:29, when Joshua tries to stop the prophesying in the camp, Moses reprimands him:

> Are you jealous for my sake? Would that all the LORD's people were prophets, and that the LORD would put his spirit on them! (Num 11:29)

Then entire narrative process shows the way in which Joshua is prepared for leadership. By their companionship in which he is the compliant junior partner, Joshua is inculcated into Moses's vision of what can be done and must be done. Moses is effectively shaping him for the hard work that is to come.

3. *Eli and Samuel* (1 Samuel 3:1–18). This narrative is well known. The young Samuel is "under care" to the decrepit priest, Eli. Sleeping in the temple, Samuel is three times addressed by YHWH, but, young as he is, he does not know it. It remained for the aged Eli to recognize what was going on, so that he instructed Samuel on how to receive the address from God. In our church reading, we regularly read only through verse 10, the result being a lovely little romantic tale. The sharp edge of the text, however, is after verse 10. Faithful to the advice of Eli, Samuel listens for the divine word that is given as prophetic oracle (vv. 11–14). It is astonishing that in the very temple over which Eli presides God declares that God will terminate the priestly house of Eli:

For I have told him that I am about to punish his house forever, for the iniquity that he knew, because his sons were blaspheming God, and he did not restrain them. Therefore I swear to the house of Eli that the iniquity of Eli's house shall not be expiated by sacrifice or offering forever. (vv. 13–14)

It is no wonder that the young Samuel was "afraid to tell the vision to Eli" (v. 15). Eli, however, is not corrupt as were his sons. He is a faithful priest who does not flinch from the divine declaration. When Samuel reports the divine verdict against his house, Eli responds:

It is the LORD; let him do what seems good to him. (v. 18)

This narrative has important aspects of mentoring. Samuel would not have received the divine word except for Eli's guidance. Beyond that, Eli and Samuel enjoy full confidence and trust in each other, so that Samuel can overcome his fear and tells Eli all. Eli, I suggest, is a model mentor. He understands that the child whom he mentors must grow decisively beyond him. He does not try to control or restrain Samuel but fully accepts that Samuel must move into an arena that not only outruns Eli but in fact turns in negativity against Eli. Good mentoring requires release of the one mentored to go beyond the horizon and interests of the mentor.

III

From *the prophetic tradition*, I will comment on two instances of mentoring.

1. *Elijah and Elisha* (1 Kings 19:19–21). The narrative encounter between the two is terse. It is dominated by the threefold use of the term *follow*. In the first usage, Elisha proposes to follow Elijah. In the second use (in English translation of a different term) Elisha turns back from Elijah, and in the third usage he follows Elijah. He becomes Elijah's "aide," the same word that was used for Joshua. That is all. Elijah gives him no instruction or command. Except that "follow" surely means to be in the company and under the instruction of Elijah. The casting of his mantle over him, moreover, is an act of designation.

Their relationship, brief as it is, continues in the final scene of Elijah's life (2 Kgs 2:1–12). In this narrative, Elisha promises three times:

- I will not leave you (v. 2).
- I will not leave you (v. 4).

- I will not leave you (v. 6).

He is totally committed to Elijah. He then asks from Elijah "a double share of your spirit" (v. 9). We are not told that he received it until the next paragraph when his companions observed his mighty act and drew the conclusion:

The spirit of Elijah rests on Elisha. (v. 15)

This is all accomplished in the narrative without any utterance by Elijah except for his quite enigmatic statement about bequeathing his spirit to Elisha. Clearly Elijah has mentored Elisha by his presence, his courage, and his performance. By being so closely committed to him, Elisha "inherits" his transformative capacity. The mentor has given his disciple a capacity to continue his subversive work, which is detailed in the narratives that follow.

2. *Hulda and Josiah* (2 Kings 22:14–20). I am not sure this counts as mentoring, because the prophet Hulda never meets with Josiah. But she does address him. In the wake of finding the scroll in the temple, the closest advisors of King Josiah approach Hulda to consult with her. Verse 18 makes clear that they come to Hulda at the behest of the king. They wondered what to make of the onerous words of the scroll, presumably the disastrous curses for covenant disobedience in Deuteronomy 28, the book that is commonly identified as the scroll that had been found. Hulda's response to their inquiry is in two parts. First, in verses 15–17, she issues a characteristic prophetic speech of judgment. In verse 16 she confirms the threat of the scroll that there will be a coming disaster on Jerusalem and its inhabitants. In verse 17, introduced by "because," the death sentence of verse 16 is justified by an indictment for covenantal disobedience and the worship of other gods in defiance of the first command of Sinai. This oracle is surely a cliché of familiar prophetic rhetoric.

What surprises us and what I think may qualify as mentoring is the fact that in verses 18–20 Hulda makes an exception to the speech of judgment and directly addresses the king himself, even though he has not come to see Hulda. This second part of her oracle has the same structure in reverse as the preceding, marked by "because . . . therefore." The "because" of Josiah is that he has taken the scroll seriously and has effectively engaged in penitence and humbleness before its great threat (vv. 18–19). He has acted out his humbleness by tearing his clothes (see v. 11) and by weeping in sad repentance. That is, he did not respond to the scroll with royal imperviousness but knew himself to be addressed. He is a true child of the Torah.

As a result, Hulda can promise the king, with a "therefore," a peaceable death in which he will not have to witness the savage undoing of Jerusalem. The king will be immune to the threat of covenant curses evoked by disobedience to the Torah. That Josiah in fact died a violent death at the hand of his enemy does not discredit the assurance offered at the time (see 2 Kgs 23:29–30). Mentoring is not omniscient but makes the best judgment available at the time. It cannot control or predict the outcome of any choice but invites the one mentored to take chances on the future on the basis of best choice.

In the case of Hulda and Josiah, there is no doubt that in framing the literature as it is, Hulda is a "plant" designed to voice the Deuteronomic urgency that Josiah is made to perform. That larger concern, however, does not detract from the narrated specificity of Hulda-to-Josiah. Her mentoring of the king is a reinforcement of Josiah's life choices. In 2 Kings 23:25 Josiah's life choice is given in a quite stylized generic way. In Jeremiah 22:15–16, by contrast, it is expressed with more specificity concerning "justice and righteousness" for the "poor and needy."

IV

The Hulda–Josiah narrative provides a fine segue to consider *mentoring among royal figures.* Here I will cite three instances of such mentoring.

1. *Hushai, Ahithophel, and Absalom* (2 Samuel 15–17). In his rebellion against his father, David, Absalom has available two mentors, and he must choose between them. On the one hand, he has available the sobering mentoring of Ahithophel, whose "wise" counsel was like the "oracle of God" (16:23). He advised Absalom to commit an overt act of defiance by publicly usurping the authority of his father by dramatically seizing his father's concubines. The alternative mentor is Hushai, who had been recruited by David to infiltrate Absalom's coup and subvert the more practical advice of Ahithophel (15:32–37). In contrast to the simple but strong stratagem of Ahithophel, Hushai, in a quite bombastic speech, counsels Absalom to huge military gestures that were quite impractical (17:7–13).

The narrative is arranged so that Absalom had to choose between the two counselors. In the end,

> Absalom and all the men of Israel said, "The counsel of Hushai the Archite is better than the counsel of Ahithophel." For the LORD had ordained to defeat the good counsel of Ahithophel, so that the LORD might bring ruin on Absalom. (17:14)

Hushai had been mandated by David to "defeat for me the counsel of Ahithophel" (15:34). And so it happened. It is as though Absalom's judgment was impaired so that he could not see how foolish was the advice of Hushai. Hushai counsels Absalom to make the wrong choice, which led to his wholesale defeat. Mentoring does not occur in contexts of simple innocence. Mentoring is most important in the midst of complexity when difficult choices have to be made. In this case, Absalom chose, but chose wrongly, perhaps because of being seduced by the sweeping rhetoric of Hushai.

In the end, however, the narrator lets us know what Absalom could not have known, that "the LORD had ordained" that Absalom would follow the wrong mentor. The term that the NRSV renders "ordained," *ṣwh*, means "to command." The narrator does not comment on this astonishing disclosure. The acknowledgment made in this verse is a recognition that historical choices are not clear and rational. They are rather complex, and the route to decision making is so hidden that room is allowed for the surreptitious working of God, even in ways that we do not recognize. This narrative voices an awareness that a choice of mentors and a decision about strategy is finally in the hands of God. The narrative, aware of the limits of human wisdom and human imagination, resituates all mentoring in a cloud of unknowing. The end of the narrative is an echo of the conviction that wisdom finally is not control; it is yielding to a cunning reality beyond our best wisdom:

> No wisdom, no understanding, no counsel,
> can avail against the LORD.
> The horse is made ready for the day of battle,
> but the victory belongs to the LORD. (Prov 21:30–31)

Gerhard von Rad comments on these verses:

> Its aim is, rather, to put a stop to the erroneous concept that a guarantee of success was to be found simply in practicing human wisdom and in making preparations. Man must always keep himself open to the activity of God, an activity that completely escapes all calculation, for between the putting into practice of the most reliable wisdom and that which then actually takes place, there always lies a great unknown.[7]

Thus, all mentoring is sharply relativized.

2. *David and Solomon* (1 Kings 2:1–9). There is no reason to suppose, in the scope of the royal narrative, that father David had any ongoing

---

7. Gerhard von Rad, *Wisdom in Israel*, trans. James D. Martin (Nashville: Abingdon, 1972), 101.

connection of intimacy with his son and heir, Solomon. It is only on his deathbed that David offers counsel to his son. Indeed, it is his last act and last utterance in the narrative, after which his death is reported (2:10–12). The verses of deathbed counsel of king to prince are like a last will and testament.

In 2:1–4 David gives counsel to Solomon that fully expresses Deuteronomic conviction:

> Be strong, be courageous, and keep the charge of the LORD your God, walking in his ways and keeping his statutes, his commandments, his ordinances, and his testimonies, as it is written in the law of Moses, so that you may prosper in all that you do and wherever you turn. (vv. 2–3)

Everything depends on Torah obedience. The father counsels his son to "do the right thing." David himself has not been a spectacular Torah keeper. In this scene, it as though David undertakes deathbed repentance or reparation and gives covenantal advice to his son, even if that advice contradicts the ruthless way of his own life. Indeed, Nathan had accused David directly of violating Torah (2 Sam 12:9). That violation, however, does not tell against mentoring. Many mentors have learned the hard way and give counsel to "do better than I have done."

That Torah-oriented Deuteronomic counsel, however, is juxtaposed directly in verses 5–9 with a very different counsel that sounds more authentically like what David might say. Now David expresses no piety, but offers the crassest kind of pragmatism in which he urges his son to protect himself and his coming rule by hard-nosed realism against those who had opposed the father and who constitute an ongoing threat to the son:

- Concerning Joab, his ruthless general who had done his dirty work: he is to be eliminated:

  > Act therefore according to your wisdom, but do not let his gray head go down to Sheol in peace. (v. 6)

David's horizon is here limited to "your wisdom," the same limited orientation with which David earlier assured Joab concerning the murder of Uriah:

> Do not let this matter be evil in your eyes. (2 Sam 11:25)

An unfortunate translation has eliminated the intentional parallel between "your eyes" in 11:25 and "YHWH's eyes" 11:27. This is wisdom with a very "low ceiling," limited to quite visible self-interest.

- Concerning Barzillai: David counsels generosity as payback for Barzillai's previous hospitality and support (v. 7). Perhaps this counsel is designed to soften the brutality of his extended advice to his son, or to exhibit royal generosity in the midst of royal violence.

- Concerning Shimei, a continuing advocate of the rival rule of Saul's family: David urges brutal retaliation (vv. 8–9). As with Joab, David urges Solomon to act because you are a "wise man." Clearly David's notion of "wisdom" amounts to calculating self-protection and self-advancement, a kind of political shrewdness that contradicts the long-term intent of Torah wisdom. This recommendation to kill Shimei is David's final utterance.

In the narrative that follows, Solomon readily follows through on David's mentoring and proceeds to eliminate his enemies. In a sequence not unlike the violent sequence in *The Godfather*, Solomon, via Benaiah his general, eliminates all of his rivals and would-be challengers: Adonijah (v. 25), Joab (v. 34), and Shimei (v. 46). In the narrative report of implementation, the advice to "deal loyally" with Barzillai is not mentioned. Moreover, Abiathar, who did not make David's hit list, now appears in Solomon's narrative of execution. Solomon does not kill the priest "at this time," but clearly the royal threat lingers over Abiathar (vv. 26–27).

The juxtaposition of verses 1–4 and verses 5–9 is stunning; the editor, moreover, takes no trouble at all to comment on or to justify the contradiction. But mentoring can be like that, filled with contradictions as the mentor may send mixed messages reflective of both *noble ideals* and *ignoble self-interest*. In this case as in so many cases, the counsel of emotive self-interest prevails. Solomon became a Torah keeper (1 Kgs 3:12–13). That commitment, however, fades as Solomon goes farther down the road of self-aggrandizement with predatory tax policies, forced labor, economic greed, and compromising religious commitments. Perhaps he takes his father's ambiguous counsel as warrant for his own deeply compromised reign. The Deuteronomist belatedly hopes for better concerning Torah obedience (see 1 Kgs 6:11–13, 9:4–5), but it is a disappointed hope.[8]

3. *Mordecai and Esther* (Esther 4:10–17). The Persian imperial household of Ahasuerus was an arena, like many such arenas, for hardball in which contending parties played for keeps. Early on, the queen, Vashti, is banished because she refuses the summons of the king. Her successor, Esther, is fully aware of the risks of disobedience to the royal whim. With word of Haman's vendetta against the Jews, Mordecai, a big player in royal affairs, urges Esther, the queen, to make supplication to the king on behalf of the Jews. Tim Beal describes Esther's speech of refusal as a "long way of saying no" (vv. 10–11).[9] It is in this ominous circumstance that Mordecai mentors Esther to think beyond conventional royal protocol and to run risks commensurate with the danger to the Jews. She, however, will not be commanded by Mordecai, who seeks to mentor her to risky conduct.

In response to Esther's refusal, the counsel of Mordecai becomes more urgent and more demanding. He warns Esther that she will not in any case be safe because she refuses to act. Then he summons her afresh to risk:

> For if you keep silence at such a time as this, relief and deliverance will rise for the Jews from another quarter, but you and your father's family will perish. Who knows? Perhaps you have come to royal dignity for such a time as this. (v. 14)

Esther's response is an acceptance of the challenge of Mordecai (v. 16). After an extended pause for fasting, she is prepared to run the risk of confronting the king. By this remarkable exchange, Esther is transformed into an active agent. In verse 8, Mordecai seeks to command Esther. By verse 17, she will now command Mordecai. His role as her mentor is crucial to the narrative. His role shows the way in which mentoring may amount to a call beyond conventional prudence to take a leap of faith and to run great risks. Mentoring may be wise, but it is not always prudent. Sometimes it is a way to summon one to become a bold history maker. In what follows in the narrative, Esther does, in response to the challenge of Mordecai, play a decisive role in the history of her people and in the history of the empire. Mentoring in this case is the trigger

---

8. See Walter Brueggemann, *Solomon: Israel's Ironic Icon of Human Achievement*, Studies on Personalities of the Old Testament (Columbia: University of South Carolina Press, 2005), 139–59.

9. Timothy K. Beal, *The Book of Hiding: Gender, Ethnicity, Annihilation, and Esther*, Biblical Limits (New York: Routledge, 1997), 71.

that turns the course of history. Mordecai does not flinch from putting his prodigy at risk in the service of an urgent cause.

V

It is clear from the examples I have cited that mentoring allows for a great variety of styles and strategies. In each case, the mentor seeks to guide the advisee in a particular direction; in these cases, the mentoring advice is characteristically accepted.

It does not surprise that, in this *Torah-dominated*, YHWH-focused tradition, much of the mentoring is an urging to stay faithful to YHWH and to YHWH's Torah. Such an urging, however, often has in purview a particular outcome. Thus:

- Moses charges Joshua that the land promised by YHWH may be received; he has YHWH declare:

    Be strong and bold, for you shall bring the Israelites into the land that I promised them; I will be with you. (Deut 31:23)

- Eli counsels Samuel to listen for YHWH's will, even if that divine word subsequently tells against Eli and his house:

    Go, lie down, and if he calls you, you shall say, "Speak, LORD, for your servant is listening." . . . "It is the LORD; let him do what seems good to him." (1 Sam 3:9, 18)

- Elijah summons Elisha to "follow" and gives him, at the end, the power of his spirit:

    You have asked a hard thing; yet, if you see me as I am being taken from you, it will be granted to you; if not, it will not. (2 Kgs 2:10)

- Hulda commends Josiah because he had been humble and penitent, Hulda has YHWH say:

    Because your heart was penitent and you humbled yourself before the LORD, when you heard how I spoke against this place, and against its inhabitants, that they should become a desolation and a curse, and because you have torn your clothes and wept before me, I also have heard you, says the LORD. (2 Kgs 22:18–19)

There is a commonality in these instances, for each mentor is singularly committed to the rule of YHWH, and urges in each case trusting obedience to YHWH.

There are, however, important variations on our defining theme, so that mentoring may go in many specific directions:

- The advice of Jethro to Moses (that he heeded) is quite practical concerning the organizational development of his administration.

- The mentoring that David provides for Solomon is profoundly ambiguous. One has the impression that the real force of the words of the father to the son is a call to purge one's adversaries and so to eliminate their potential threat, all the Torah talk notwithstanding.

- Hushai's advice to Absalom is cynical and calculating. In fact Hushai has intentions that are wholly contrary to the good outcomes he ostensibly offers to Absalom.

- Mordecai's urging to Esther is a summons beyond conventional self-interest to risky action for a larger good.

In these latter four cases, appeal to YHWH is less than central:

- Jethro alludes to God (not YHWH!) in his rhetorical flourish, but that is clearly not essential to his guidance.

- David begins with an appeal to YHWH and to YHWH's Torah; such reference appears to be only pro forma in light of what follows.

- Hushai's imaginative counsel makes no reference to God, though we are able to know what Hushai does not know, that YHWH is deeply implicated in his manipulative mentoring words.

- As close as Mordecai comes to such divine reference is an allusion to "another quarter" that suggests more is under way here than that which Esther perceives (4:14).

Clearly mentoring moves readily back and forth between an acute theological sensibility and quite practical awareness of specific tasks that need to be accomplished.

Our beginning point in "wisdom" has an appropriate concluding counterpoint with reference to Deuteronomy, as Deuteronomy is likely much shaped by sapiential interpretive tradition.[10] *The commanding voice of Deuteronomy* clearly intends to recruit the next generation into the salvific memory and its durable requirements. Thus, the mentoring advice of Deuteronomy is consistently to adhere to the Torah tradition as the singular path to life and well-being. Thus, in Deuteronomy 6:7, following the *shema'*, Moses urges Israel:

> Recite them to your children and talk about them when you are at home and when you are away, when you lie down and when you arise. Bind them as sign on your hand, fix them as an emblem on your forehead, and write them on the doorposts of your house and on your gates. (Deut 6:7–9)

Moses proposes saturation socialization.[11] In Deuteronomy 6:20–25, moreover, the normative memory is to be told to the children in order that they should not fall into indifferent amnesia. The counsel of Deuteronomy is to heed the Torah, which is Israel's true wisdom:

> See, just as the LORD my God has charged me, I now teach you statutes and ordinances for you to obey in the land that you are about to enter and occupy. You must observe them diligently, for this will show your wisdom and discernment to the peoples, who, when they hear all these statutes, will say, "Surely this great nation is a wise and discerning people!" For what other great nation has a God so near it as the LORD our God is whenever we call to him? And what other great nation has statutes and ordinance as just as this entire law that I am setting before you today? (Deut 4:5–8)

Michael Fishbane has noticed the intense urgency in the counsel of Deuteronomy. He concludes, albeit in a patriarchal mode:

> The teaching of the fathers in Deuteronomy 6:20–25 is an attempt to involve their sons in the covenant community of the future, and undoubtedly reflects the sociological reality of the settlement in Canaan. The attempt by fathers to transform their uninvolved sons from "*dis*temporaries" to *con*temporaries, i.e. time-life sharers, is an issue of supreme and recurrent significance in the Bible.[12]

---

10. See Moshe Weinfeld, *Deuteronomy and the Deuteronomic School* (Oxford: Clarendon Press, 1972).

11. See Walter Brueggemann, *Biblical Perspectives on Evangelism: Living in a Three-Storied Universe* (Nashville: Abingdon, 1993), 94–128.

12. Michael Fishbane, *Text and Texture: Close Readings of Selected Biblical Texts* (New York: Shocken Books, 1979), 81–82.

Thus, the mentoring process hopes for continuity in the practice of Torah wisdom. As every wise mentor knows, however, the ones advised have freedom and may make leaps into newness that are remote and discontinuous from what the mentor has in mind, sometimes for evil, sometimes for good (see Gen 50:20).

PART V

Best Practices for Tenacious Solidarity

17.

The Psalms: Tenacious Solidarity

An earlier version of this chapter was delivered at Xavier University on September 20, 2016, on the occasion of Xavier's acquisition and exhibition of a copy of the Saint John's Bible.

I am so pleased that Dr. Melcher has invited me to this happy occasion, more so because we have known each other since her ancient days of graduate study, even more so because she has done this on our way out of the door into retirement.[1] That the university is acquiring the St. John's Bible is an occasion of great moment, and I am glad to be included in that wondrous happening. The Saint John's Bible is a most remarkable gift to us that reminds us of the depth, antiquity, and beauty that belong to the legacy of Holy Scripture as we stand amid the cadences of many fathers and mothers. Psalms, moreover, is an offer of the text that is most important to us for its pastoral power, wisdom, and honesty. It is, in addition, a script that overrides our sectarian differences as we voice our common faith, and that brings Jews and Christians together in the worship of the Holy One of Israel. On all these counts, the publication and the reception of this particular book of Psalms are due cause for joy, praise, and thanksgiving.

I

It is impossible to make any generalization about Psalms because it speaks in many voices from and into many circumstances. Nevertheless, I will

---

1. Editor's note: Sarah Melcher is professor emeritus of Hebrew Scriptures at Xavier University in Cincinnati, Ohio.

risk a generalization without needing to force everything into it. I have asked, Why is it that the Psalter has such durable power among us?

The durable power and authority of the Psalter are that it concerns covenantal fidelity, surely the deepest urge and hunger that are elemental to our humanness. The critical term in Hebrew for that covenantal fidelity is *hesed*, variously translated as "loving kindness" or "steadfast love." I prefer to translate it as *"tenacious solidarity."* It is the witness of the scriptural tradition and of the Psalms in particular that God is an agent and character of tenacious solidarity who has pledged abiding fidelity to Israel and then, through Jesus, to the church, and ultimately to creation. This means that the Bible is cast in relational categories that finally resist our efforts to reduce its claim to logical, syllogistic, or "reasonable" articulation, even though we continue to try to make such reductions. God is witnessed through this script, in the life of Israel and the church, as one who is ready and able to be in solidarity with, one who makes promises, issues directives, and keeps faith. Humanity, by way of Israel, is identified as and summoned to be creatures of solidarity, both in solidarity with God through love as obedience and solidarity with our neighbor through mercy, compassion, and justice. That solidarity, as partner to God and to neighbor is one of deep tenacity. It is for that reason that the Bible, in poetic idiom, often drifts toward marital imagery, because it is in those marital relationships or with that imagery that we speak most urgently about solidarity "for better, for worse, in sickness and in health."

But like all honest relational solidarity, the tenacity witnessed in Psalms is acutely dialogical, that is, an open, dynamic, ongoing, risky interaction that refuses settlement or closure, that is always moving into new circumstances to new crises and new possibilities. The dynamic quality of this interaction of tenacious fidelity indicates the following:

1. In Israel's prayers and songs there really is someone on the other end; this is real talk addressed to someone who we claim is listening attentively. It is our modern embarrassed propensity to want to reduce this theological interaction to psychological practice, so that the Psalms become a script for catharsis or wholeness. And surely the Psalms serve that purpose. But they cannot, in covenantal reckoning, be reduced to such a dimension. The marvel of this poetry is that we, after Israel, dare to affirm that this is real interaction with a seriously engaged partner.

2. But, second, because this interaction is genuinely dialogical, our frequent theological assumption of the priority of God is called into question. This is a theological transaction in which either party can take the lead. Thus, in the great familiar hymns of the Psalter, God is high, lifted up, awesome, and powerful. In much of the Psalter, however, Israel

in its laments assumes priority in the relationship, takes the initiative, and addresses God in imperatives, as though to command God; and God very often accepts that calculus. This is an interaction of playfulness, risk, and openness that violates our usual theological expectations.

3. And, third, the doxological quality of this tradition concerning tenacious solidarity is not always affirmative. In the poems that we know and love best, such as Psalm 23, such solidarity is deeply confirmed. Thus "surely goodness and *hesed* will follow me all the days of my life" (23:6). But of course it is not always so in our experience or in the Psalter. Because the drama is relational and both parties exercise freedom, life is often experienced and voiced as *hesed* violated. We are familiar with the prophetic statements that critique and condemn Israel for covenantal fickleness. We are less willingly attentive to Israel's vigorous accusation against God for God's failed fidelity. Israel discerns that God is free and is not an automaton of reliability. Thus, in the dread Psalm 88 Israel can say:

> O Lord, God of my salvation,
> when at night, I cry out in your presence,
> let my prayer come before you;
> incline your ear to my cry . . .
> Every day I call on you, O Lord;
> I spread out my hands to you . . .
> But I, O Lord, cry out to you;
> in the morning my prayer comes before you. (88:1–2, 9, 13)

And no answer! In the end Israel can threaten God:

> Do the shades rise up to praise you?
> Is your *hesed* declared in the grave,
> or your faithfulness in Abaddon? (88:10–11)

That is, dead people do not celebrate God, and if you let me die, there will be one less singer of your praise. In Psalm 89 the Psalmist in deep pathos can say:

> Lord, where is your *hesed* of old,
> which by your faithfulness you swore to David? (89:49)

Israel knows, as God's *hesed* fails, that solidarity from God is much less than tenacious. Since this is dialogic, even that can be brought to speech.

II

Thus, I am able to note four features of this dialogue of fidelity that gives staying power:

1. The Psalter is *an exercise in emotional extremity* that defies ordering through restraint. This is talk in which no secret is hidden; nothing is held back. Those who speak are permitted to give voice to the full range of unrestrained emotion. Thus, the great hymns of the Psalter soar in praise and thanks and ecstasy. The extreme example, I suppose, is Psalm 150, which dissolves in self-abandonment before God; the speaker summons the temple orchestra, instrument by instrument, to do the glad work of praise. Or, alternatively, in Psalm 148 the singer summons angels and sun and moon and sea monsters and snow and wind and creeping things and kings and young women to join the praise, because our tongues are not adequate to what must be sung. Can you imagine all of creation dissolving into glad doxology before the Holy One with nothing of the restraint of ecclesial propriety?

But the Psalter knows the counterpoint of negativity in which *ḥesed* is violated by God or by neighbor. And all of that violation by God and by neighbor, all of that guilt and shame, all of that anger and rage and vengeance, all of that alienation and abandonment are brought to speech. Because the Psalter understood, even before Freud, that we are speech creatures, and our full humanity, all of it, must be brought to speech.

2. While we know about such emotional freedom in a therapeutic culture, what strikes us in this emotive exercise of extremity is that it is all *uttered in the presence of God*. Interaction with the God of covenant is not reduced to the strictures of obedience and deferential praise as some authoritarian forms of faith would have it. It is, rather assured and affirmed that this dialogic practice with God concerns the full scale of our life, positive as praise and negative as complaint. The result is that life, before the lectionary committee exercised its censure, is all before God, the one who not only speaks to command but who listens even when put at risk by our utterance.

3. But more than that, this emotive exercise that has transformative impact is done *in the midst of the congregation*. Thus, Israel is pledged to praise God "in the great congregation." It is contested and less clear that the negative voicings were so public. I judge that the articulations of lament, complaint, and protest were not done in private. In the book of Job, Job utters his laments in the presence of his friends. Erhard Gerstenberger has proposed that there were "rituals of rehabilitation"—what

we might call "therapeutic interventions"—by trusted members of the community who gathered to aid in the speech before God that would call God to account and summon God to engagement in circumstances of need.[2] Fredrik Lindström, moreover, has shown that in the psalms of lament there are no confessions of guilt, because the one in need, in the presence of neighbors, did not grovel or even repent but spoke as one who had been victimized and was in need of succor.[3] The point was to insist that fidelity from elsewhere had failed and so there was need for restoration. Thus the famous accusation of Psalm 22, "My God, my God, why have you forsaken me," was enough in public that it could be remembered and quoted and used again when divine fidelity had failed. The neighborhood calls God back to fidelity.

4. Fourth and finally, this dialogue of fidelity in which Israel speaks before God and neighbor in emotional extremity, is *highly artistic in its casting.* We do not know the origin of the psalms. But we know that they arose in the practice of the community and were used and reused, treasured, refined and transmitted, so that over time they became the reliable codes of articulation for the community of covenant. They became the readily recognized forms through which Israel spoke and sang its most urgent truth. We may identify two elements in such artistry that are worthy of the artistry of the Saint John's Bible. The first is termed by scholars "genre."[4] That is, these recurring utterances and modes of expression were found to be reliable over time in the most urgent dimensions of life. In such awesome and demanding moments, we did not have to start fresh and reinvent the wheel, because we already knew what to say and how to say it in this community of self-aware voicing. In any community that survives through time, reliable, trusted utterance is required, so that we rehearse old patterns of speech at birth, at weddings, at death, at departure, and at arrival. We still say, "I love you" . . . as time goes by. Indeed, such occasions do not require clever or innovative speech, but reliable speech, knowing ahead of time what to say and how to say it. Belonging to the community means to know and trust the codes. That is why in any "mixed marriage" it can be difficult because

2. Erhard S. Gerstenberger, *Der bittende Mensch: Bittritual und Klageleid des Einzelnen im Alten Testament*, Wissenschaftliche Monographien zum Alten und Neuen Testament 51 (Neukirchen-Vluyn: Neukirchener Verlag, 1980).

3. Fredrik Lindström, *Suffering and Sin: Interpretations of Illness in the Individual Complaint Psalms*, Coniectanea Biblica: Old Testament Series 37 (Stockholm: Almqvist & Wiksell International, 1994).

4. See Erhard S. Gerstenberger, "Psalms," in *Old Testament Form Criticism*, ed. John H. Hayes (San Antonio, TX: Trinity University Press, 1974), 179–223; and Barbara Green, *How Are the Mighty Fallen? A Dialogical Study of King Saul in 1 Samuel*, Journal for the Study of the Old Testament: Supplement Series 365 (Sheffield: Sheffield Academic Press, 2003), 55–115.

one does not know the codes of the in-laws. When we do not know the "how" of speech, we are likely to misconstrue the "what" of speech. Thus, we can identify the patterns of speech that recur from psalm to psalm in the same genre; we can guess at the circumstance out of which they came and to which they bear witness. And we can readily transfer that pattern of speech to our own life circumstance. We do it all the time and do not notice that we do it. Modernity places the accent on innovation. But our deepest moments require not new speech but old trusted speech that sounds the cadences of the community in its incessant practice of risk and assurance.

The second artistic point is that Hebrew poetry is characteristically expressed in poetic parallelism so that the same statement is offered twice or thrice, each time in different terms. Robert Alter, moreover, has shown that the second line of poetry often intensifies and deepens the claim of the first line.[5]

These two artistic features—highly stylized patterns and double or triple parallel lines—abetted by a rich field of venturesome images and metaphors permit the articulation of profound emotional extremity. This means that the poetry not only lets human reality come to speech; it brings it to speech in a way that is formed according to the long-term wisdom of the community. "Formed" expression means that each time we utilize a psalm we participate in a long recurring artistic gesture whereby our particular speech is joined with and reiterates the cadences of the community that has long been speaking its most intense emotional extremity before God in the midst of the congregation. In this way Israel not only knows *what* to say in every circumstance. It knows *how* to say it in a way that joins the ongoing dialogue over the generations. The use of the complete repertoire of the Psalter schools us in dialogic practice and permits us to join the conversation about fidelity, which is the most important conversation in town. The artistic forms are known and treasured by many mothers and fathers before us who share with us the recurring crises in the practice of fidelity. These forms, moreover, draw God into the ongoing crisis as well, so that the very recital of a psalm is something of a sacramental act, an act whereby the presence of God as listener and respondent is mediated to us.

In what follows I have selected three Psalms that I take to be fairly representative of that covenant interaction in which we may participate. I have selected them because they give evidence of that fidelity (*ḥesed*) as tenacious solidarity as the subject of our deepest interaction with God and neighbor.

---

5. Robert Alter, *The Art of Biblical Poetry* (New York: Basic Books, 1985).

III

Psalm 103 is a familiar and greatly beloved psalm because it offers to us wondrous assurance. It is unfortunate, in my judgment, that in liturgical use we line out a psalm, line after line, as though it were a continuous, repetitious, monotonous one note. In fact, this psalm—or any psalm—cannot be well read in such a way because it flattens the rhetoric. It is much preferable, I suggest, to recognize that a psalm is a series of rhetorical riffs or poetic clusters that are not well served by our usual liturgical renditions. In this Psalm 103, I propose that there are four such rhetorical riffs, each of which requires attention, over each of which liturgical attention might be given by repetition of its cadence or by expansive imagination that extrapolates.

The psalm is framed by a double (triple?) imperative at the beginning, "bless, bless" (vv. 1–2) and by a fourfold imperative, "bless, bless, bless, bless" at the conclusion (vv. 20–22). The imperative verbs suggest that the singing community can, in a rhetorical gesture, "bless" (that is, enhance) the character of God. The object of the verbs, in all cases, is "the Lord," the creator and the one who covenants with Israel. Those summoned by the imperatives includes not only the "self" at the beginning and the end but angels, mighty ones, God's troops (hosts), ministers (ambassadors), all creatures, and then finally "me." The speaker has so much eagerness to enhance YHWH that she is unable to do it all; she needs the community to join the praise. She needs not only all earthly creatures but all the inhabitants of the heavenly court and company of God. The psalm mobilizes all reality in the magnification of God.

The body of the psalm provides four reasons why heaven and earth are summoned to praise YHWH. Such extravagance is clearly a performance of emotional extremity, an exuberance and passion that go beyond reason. This is a response to the tenacious solidarity of YHWH.

1. The first rhetorical riff in the psalm in verses 3–5 features five participles that assert YHWH's characteristic and recurring activity. It is YHWH, none other, who "forgives, heals, redeems, crowns, and satisfies." In this remarkable recital, Israel summarizes its entire awareness of YHWH, the one who does the pastoral work of forgiveness and healing, the one who does the emancipatory work of delivery, the one who does the creation work of satiation, and at the center of the recital is our term *hesed*, the one who crowns with steadfast love and mercy. The conclusion is that "being young" is not chronological; it is covenantal. The "young," the ones with vigor and energy and daring, are those who are

on the receiving end of God's participles. What better than to soar as an eagle!

> Even youths will faint and be weary,
> and the young will fall exhausted;
> but those who wait for the LORD shall renew their strength,
> they shall mount up with wings like eagles,
> they shall run and not be weary,
> they shall walk and not faint. (Isa 40:30–31)

They shall run to bless the Lord!

2. The second riff, verses 6–8, alludes back to the exodus, already signaled in the third participle, "redeem." The reference is explicitly to Moses; with another participle verse 6 voices an awareness that the exodus work of the emancipation of the oppressed is work that YHWH does all of the time. Thus, this sixth participle could have been attached to the first five, but it is placed as the beginning of a new riff.

Beyond the Mosaic deliverance in verse 6 is the Mosaic instruction of verse 7. This is a reference to the negotiation that YHWH and Moses conducted after the violation with the golden calf. Finally, exasperated by recalcitrant Israel, YHWH in Exodus 34:6–7 can just blurt out YHWH's own true identity:[6]

> The LORD, the LORD,
> a God merciful and gracious,
> slow to anger,
> and abounding in *steadfast love* and faithfulness,
> keeping *steadfast love* for the thousandth generation,
> forgiving iniquity and transgression and sin. (Exod 34:6–7)

The center of that ancient declaration is the double use of *ḥesed*: "abounding in *ḥesed*, keeping ḥesed for the thousandth generation." The psalmist knows the exodus narrative and this self-assertion by YHWH. The psalmist need not reiterate the entire statement from that tradition, only the usable part of it. As a result, in our psalm verse 8 is a reiteration of ancient disclosure; YHWH is marked, as Israel does not doubt, by mercy, graciousness, patience, and *ḥesed*. Thus, this second riff, again with *ḥesed*, gives ample reason to bless YHWH.

3. In the third riff, verses 9–14, the psalmist takes up one of the two deepest human issues, namely, guilt and alienation. The reality of sin and alienation is recognized but not dwelt on. Indeed, the church has used

---

6. See Nathan C. Lane, *The Compassionate but Punishing God: A Canonical Analysis of Exodus 34:6–7* (Eugene, OR: Wipf & Stock, 2010).

much more energy on sin than does the psalmist. Instead, what we have is a glad assurance of God's generous response to human sin. It is no wonder that it was in the study of the Psalms that Luther received his great insight about the grace of God.

The news is that God does not stay angry, because of God's tenacious solidarity stated in verse 8. Thus, verses 9–10 break out of any quid-pro-quo calculus; God who will not be captive to anger and retaliation. Two images are mobilized to declare divine generosity. First, an appeal to the spaciousness of creation. The heavens are high above the earth. The east is far distant from the west. The spaciousness is almost unimaginable, certainly to the ancients, but even to us as we know more about space even beyond Pluto. The speaker is dazzled by this distance beyond measure that becomes a way to express the distance between human sin and God's inclination. Too bad that moralism has imagined that God is preoccupied with our guilt and failure, such a small God who is not inured to *hesed*.

The second image concerns a father–son relationship expressed in patriarchal fashion, an anticipation of Jesus's parable of a lost son and a lost father. The father-God is marked by a womb of compassion, so that this father acts like a tender mother. We get a double use of "compassion," thus "womb, womb," an echo of the poetry of Isaiah:

> Can a mother forget her nursing child,
>   or show no compassion for the child of her womb?
> Even these may forget,
>   yet I will not forget you.
> See, I have inscribed you on the palms of my hands. (Isa 49:15–16)

This father-God is like a mother-God who will nurse the baby, who has written the baby's name on her sleeve, who will not be separated from her baby.

But then, in verse 14, it is as though the familial imagery is too small. Now the poet returns to creation with an allusion to Genesis 2, humankind from dust. The creator remembers that we are dust and need not expect so much of us. The father-mother remembers the fragile baby, the feeble irresolute teenager. Lower expectation from the parent is the order of the day because the parent God shows *hesed*, not because of us but because of God, who is the final bearer of *hesed*. This is the God who forgives all our iniquities and who heals all of our diseases. Our chosen alienation is overcome by the wide embrace of the God of all *hesed*. We are embraced dust!

4. The fourth rhetorical riff, verses 15–18, takes up the second great human crisis, mortality. Indeed, Ernest Becker has seen that our denial of death is the central preoccupation of our human life.[7] It is because of our fear of death that we want more military strength and more guns. It is because of our fear of death that we want to keep others from having access to our store of material blessings from God. It is because of our fear of death that we act in abusive ways toward each other and toward ourselves. It is because of that same fear that we have an inordinate need to be right in ways that excommunicate the other.

The psalmist is honest about his life and ours. Yes, we are mortal. Yes, we will die. Yes, we are like a flower that fades. Yes, we are like grass that turns brown. Yes, we are blown away; for the most part we are not remembered or bothered with, leaving no trace in the sand. No denial here. No pretense. No strategy for survival. No mad science to preserve our bodies or our sperm or our special brain. If we look back to verse 14, we are all about dust. It turns out that our passion for longevity is a hoax. We will not stay young by the right drug or the right exercise or the right cosmetic surgery. Which of you by being anxious can add a millisecond to your life? Thus, the faithful acknowledge:

> For all our days pass away under your wrath;
> our years come to an end like a sigh.
> The days of our life are seventy years,
> Or perhaps eighty, if we are strong. (Ps 90:9–10)

The acknowledgment is followed by a prayer:

> So teach us to count our days
> that we may gain a wise heart . . .
> Let the favor of the Lord our God be upon us,
> and prosper for us the work of our hands—
> O prosper the work of our hands! (Ps 90:12, 17)

It is a prayer and a ready recognition, not a denial.

But then our psalm turns in verse 17 with a disjunctive preposition: "But!" To counter the reality of mortality we get, "The *hesed* of YHWH is for always." The *hesed* from YHWH does not cancel death. It persists in and through and beyond death. And that is enough for the psalmist.

So notice about this psalm. If I have rightly discerned four rhetorical riffs along with the introduction and the conclusion, each of the four clusters pivots on the *hesed* of YHWH:

7. Ernest Becker, *The Denial of Death* (New York: Free Press, 1973).

- YHWH crowns you with *hesed* and mercy (v. 4).
- The LORD is slow to anger and abounding in *hesed* (v. 8).
- So great is his *hesed* toward those who fear him (v. 11).
- But the *hesed* of YHWH is forever (v. 17).

It is no accident that this term keeps turning up in this rhetoric. It is Israel's best word concerning the ongoing dialogue with YHWH. Over time Israel has learned that this is the defining mark of YHWH. Over time Israel has learned that this is how we talk, this is how we know what to say, this is how we live.

One can imagine, in ancient Israel or in a contemporary congregation, a four-year-old standing alongside parents, reciting this psalm. The four-year-old does not know Hebrew, does not know the word *hesed*, but says it anyway. Because that is what Mom and Dad say. That is how we speak. That is how we talk. That is what we say. When we talk this way, we advance the dialogue with God and neighbor. When we talk this way, we mark a territory of fidelity. The four-year-old does not ask if this is true. It is a drama of the way Mom and Dad treat me, in my unexpressed guilt and in the fearfulness of danger I keep unspoken. I know about guilt and fear. But we talk this way and then we act this way and *hesed* becomes the world we inhabit.

Or one can imagine a teenager, sullen in church, if in church at all, head down, not reciting the psalm but vigorously and ostentatiously resisting the word of Mom and Dad, not for a minute believing this babble about *hesed*—except after church, counting heavily on this *hesed* for the grace of the day. Or maybe dismayed because the *hesed* of Mom and Dad is not really reliable. But having in reserve the cadences of *hesed* that remain behind the fragile *hesed* of Mom and Dad. Maybe signing on for it; maybe refusing it and seeing that it is a fraud but being haunted by the cadence, partly yearning, partly knowing better, but in any case haunted. The psalm plants *hesed* at the center of our guilt and our mortality. No wonder the voices of heaven and earth must be mobilized in gladness.

IV

The dialogue concerning tenacious solidarity continues in *Psalm 86* in a very different way. In contrast to the hymn of Psalm 103, Psalm 86 is a fairly conventional lament psalm in which the subject is not the wonder of YHWH, Lord of *ḥesed*, but the urgent situation of the speaker. Like other psalms that utilize the code of lament, the speaker addresses YHWH in an attempt to receive the attention of YHWH and from that the positive intervention of YHWH in the vexed life of the speaker. We may see that this psalm is segmented into three rhetorical clusters, though the delineation of these subclusters is not completely clear.

In the first rhetorical cluster, verses 1–7, we see the primary features of this code. The pattern consists in a series of imperatives followed and reinforced by a series of "motivations." The imperatives include,

- incline
- preserve
- save
- gladden
- give ear

The speaker does not hesitate to address YHWH with imperatives on the assumption that the covenantal dialogue works in both directions, and the speaker has a right to make these askings.

It is as though in some bewilderment or indifference YHWH hears the imperatives but is not moved by them. We can imagine that YHWH, high and holy, asks, "Now why would I obey your imperatives?" The question is not asked but implied, and the speaker responds with a series of motivations, reasons why God should act in response. The motivations are often introduced by the small particle, "for":

> For I am poor and needy. (v. 1)
> For I am devoted to you. (v. 2)
> For to you do I cry all day long. (v. 3)
> For to you, O Lord, I lift up my soul. (v. 4)
> For you O Lord, are good and forgiving,
> abounding in *ḥesed* to all who call upon you. (v. 5)

The reasons characteristically concern both the speaker's desperation and the identity of YHWH. This last motivation in verse 5 is of special interest. It is as though YHWH had forgotten that YHWH is pledged to *ḥesed,* goodness, and forgiveness, pledged since the declaration of Exodus 34. Now YHWH is forcibly reminded of YHWH's true covenantal identity with the expectation that, once that covenantal identity is remembered, YHWH will act accordingly. In this rhetorical cluster, that reminder to YHWH in the final petition likely turns out to be more powerful than the earlier motivations that focus on the speaker's need.

In the second rhetorical cluster, verses 8–13, there is a departure from the normal code of lament. These verses begin with a doxology in verses 8–10 asserting that YHWH is incomparable; no other god does what YHWH does; for good reason all nations will worship and glorify only YHWH. The purpose of the doxology is to call YHWH out, to remind YHWH of YHWH's singular identity and vocation. There is no other god bound in covenant like this one. There is no other god who acts covenantally like this one. Indeed, there is no other god like this one bound to *hesed*, committed to tenacious solidarity. The doxology in verse 10 refers to YHWH's "wondrous things," a term that concerns the miracles that YHWH has performed on behalf of Israel. Thus, for all the claim of universalism in verse 9, the particularity of covenant is accented in verse 10.

In verse 11, the speaker voices two imperatives, "teach, give." These imperatives, however, are not like those in verses 1–6. Here they are an application to be properly instructed as a witness to the wonder of YHWH. Give me a heart to conform to your character, to walk in your way, and to honor your reputation (name). The imperatives of verse 11 are followed in verse 12 by a pledge to be wholly committed to YHWH. The verb looks ahead: "I will give you thanks . . . after you teach and lead me." The rhetorical unit concludes with a motivational doxology that matches the opening doxology of verses 8–10. The basis of the entire interaction is: "Great is your *hesed*." Thus, we can see that in this unit from verse 8 forward, the poetry is moving toward the statement about YHWH's *hesed*, which is evidenced in the "wondrous things" and which is to be acknowledged in glad praise by the speaker. It is as though the speaker has been brought out of the needfulness of verses 1–6 and now relishes the goodness of life amid that *hesed*.

In the third cluster, verses 14–17, we are introduced to a different motif of lament, namely, the description offered to God of the trouble out of which the lament arises. The speaker has previously said that he is "poor and needy" (v. 1) and is in "a day of trouble" (v. 7). But now we get more specificity in verse 14. Notice the abrupt address: "God!" That is, "Listen up!" Listen up to my trouble:

The insolent rise up against me;
a band of ruffians seek my life,
and they do not set you before them. (Ps 86:14)

I am surrounded by thugs. This most likely does not mean street violence. Most often it seems to refer to careless, slanderous people in the
village who abuse one's reputation. In a shame culture such speech is
immensely damaging and one is helpless before it. My reputation and
therefore my future are being put at risk. It is especially interesting that
in the third line of the verse, it is asserted that the ruffians not only
damage me, but they do not treat you, YHWH, very well either. The
laments characteristically seek a way to show God that there is something at stake in all of the trouble for God as well as for the speaker. The
trouble not only jeopardizes me; it puts you, YHWH, at risk as well, and
therefore you should act. Act for your name's sake!

There is an abrupt move from "insolent ruffians" in verse 14 to "you"
in verse 15. The two verses provide a sharp contrast to show how
YHWH is quite unlike the insolent ruffians. Unlike them, YHWH is
merciful, gracious, abounding in *hesed* and faithfulness. The insolent ruffians know nothing of mercy, grace, *hesed*, or faithfulness. The psalmist
repeats the classic mantra from Exodus 34 that we have seen already
in Psalm 103:8. This sequence of terms asserts YHWH's character and
YHWH's covenantal responsibility.

It is on the basis of this doxology (which contrasts YHWH with the
troublemakers) that the psalm ends in a new series of imperatives in
verses 16–17:

- turn
- be gracious
- give
- save
- show

These requested actions will demonstrate YHWH's true character, will
honor covenant, and will expose the insolent ruffians as nobodies. The
psalm concludes with two verbs of completed action:

- You have helped.
- You have comforted me.

It is as good as done. It is done! The speaker has complete confidence
that YHWH can be relied on to honor covenant and to restore what
has been lost to insolent ruffians. The restoration concerns a good name
(reputation) and a good future.

When we put the three rhetorical clusters together, we can see that the dramatic movement of the entire psalm is from the initial "poor and needy" (v. 1) to "helped and comforted" (v. 17). This dramatic movement is accomplished according to the reliable *hesed* of YHWH mobilized through this psalm. But the trigger for that dramatic movement is the daring, demanding self-announcement of the speaker who is willing to risk insistent imperatives in the presence of the God before whom all the nations bow down. The sweeping doxologies to YHWH are only a supporting role for the real action that concerns the desperate and helpless speaker. We should notice two important points that contradict conventional assumptions. First is the assumption here that God can be indifferent and unengaged and has to be persuaded to act. Such persuasion, moreover, takes the form of a doxological reminder that seeks to flatter YHWH into action. Second is the recognition that the speaker need not be excessively deferential before YHWH, but has some right to assert and a legitimate insistence to make. YHWH is pledged to tenacious solidarity. The speaker is entitled to tenacious solidarity. But it requires some liturgical *chutzpah* to move the drama of YHWH's pledge and Israel's entitlement.

Perhaps you will have noticed that in each of these three subclusters of the psalm *hesed* is pivotal. In the first subcluster, verses 1–7, the speaker in verse 5 repeats the old formula of *hesed* that asserts who God is and how God should act. In the second subcluster, verses 8–13. which has a more didactic tone, the opening doxology of verses 8–10 is matched by the concluding assertion of *hesed* in verse 13. In that verse, as in verse 17, the speaker uses a verb of completed action: "You have delivered." In the third subcluster, verses 14–17, YHWH, unlike the insolent ruffians, is a *God of* hesed. Thus, in verse 5 in the first cluster, in verse 13 in the second cluster, and in verse 15 in the third cluster, it is all about *God's* hesed. This repeated accent on *hesed*, however, is not a witness to others. It is addressed to YHWH, as though to insist upon God's *hesed* about which YHWH has, until now, been negligent.

This dialogical poetry addresses YHWH, covenantal partner, with great insistence. This is especially clear in a rhetorical element in the Hebrew that is not recognizable in our translations. In Hebrew, the second-person singular pronoun "you" is most often attached as part of the verb. But Hebrew also has an independent second-person singular pronoun that stands apart from the verb. It is often used for special emphasis. It does not occur often, but when it is used it often comes along with the pronoun attached to the verb so that we get a double "you, you." In this psalm, unlike any other that I know, we get six uses of the independent pronoun for purposes of accent that suggests the great intensity of this articulation. The six are:

- You are my God (v. 2).
- You are good and forgiving (v. 5).
- You are great (v. 10).
- You are our God (v. 10).
- You are a God merciful and gracious (v. 15).
- Because you, YHWH, have helped (v 17).

The independent pronoun is used in some of these cases because there is no finite verb to which to attach the pronoun. Nonetheless, the sum of these uses is a voicing of great intensity. The repeated uses call attention to the bold, direct address to YHWH that is in part an affirmation of YHWH but in part a summons to YHWH, that is, a calling out of YHWH.

We can imagine this psalm in liturgy, even though we do not often use it so. It is all imperative and motivation—in conventional context reason enough to avoid it. But when we are bold enough to use such a prayer in our assemblage, the routine is interrupted by urgent contemporaneity. This poetic imagery, if we pay attention, invites us to connect our utterance to our life experience. Mostly we live in a world that is without God. In that world, it is all rough and tumble, thrust and rush that run toward violence. The inventory of insolent ruffians can reach all the way from an unkind coworker or colleague to an unbearable older sibling, to street assault to rumors and realities of terrorism before which we are left helpless and desperate.

In the face of such ruffians we know about being helpless. We are, however, not helpless when we are adequately schooled in this strident rhetoric of insistence. This lament psalm, along with many others, does not suggest that we engage in doxological denial to pretend there is no danger. Nor do such psalms suggest that we shrink away in cowardice. Rather the lament psalms suggest that, as tenured members of covenant, we take the initiative on the basis of our entitlement. We have been invited into tenacious solidarity, and now we insist upon it. A by-product of such speech is the recovery of nerve, courage, and freedom enough to announce ourselves. The central point, however, is that God can be summoned back to God's true self and to God's proper covenantal work. We have here, in this psalm, a script for such daring summons whereby we also become our true selves and may return to our proper work.

V

Psalm 109 is a poignant poetic piece that should be held in reserve for very special circumstances. In it the unidentified speaker makes two extended statements, one that concerns the failure of a neighbor and one that looks to God as an alternative.

The psalm is divided into three unequal parts. In the first part, verses 1–5, the poem is introduced as an address to God and a petition that God should intervene in his vexed life. Verses 2–3 describe for God the jeopardized circumstance of his life with an accusation against those who are his adversaries. They are labeled as "wicked" and sound like the "insolent ruffians" of Psalm 86. They have broken faith by speaking destructive slander that will destroy even a good person in a social circumstance where a good reputation counts for all. Even more, the speaker describes himself as one who has "loved" his adversaries, that is, acted as a good neighbor (as in "Love thy neighbor"). For his good actions toward them, however, they have returned evil. Their evil destructiveness is gratuitous. Nothing the speaker has done merits such a negative response. As a result of their action, his life is at risk; for that reason he speaks to God with intensity and urgency.

In the extended second part of the Psalm, verses 6–20, we have a long address to God in which the speaker proposes to God the kind of punishment that should be meted out to his adversaries. Note at the outset that our translations regularly introduce this part of the psalm with "they say," putting the violent rhetoric that follows into the mouth of the adversaries, as though the speaker were quoting them. (Or alternatively, these verses are put in quotation marks, a move that accomplishes the same thing, as though it is all a quotation from his enemies.) But in fact there is nothing in the Hebrew that justifies "they say" or quotation marks. This is not a quotation whereby the violent rhetoric can be transferred to another. This speech is the speech of the initial speaker. And while we, in our modern nicety, might be offended by such rhetoric and wish it had not been said, it is probable that the speaker intended every syllable of it and is not embarrassed at all by voicing such deep emotion.

These verses propose (a) that God should appoint a "wicked man," that is, a "hanging judge" to try those whom he accuses, (b) that a guilty verdict be brought against them, and (c) that a detailed punishment should be inflicted on them. Like many victims of violence, this speaker knows ahead of time how the trial should come out.

What follows is a series of jussive verbs that are commendations to the "hanging judge" in the hope that the judge will be as severe as possible with the accused, so grave is the affront of the offender. We are offered the most vigorous extended wish for vengeance in all of Scripture, a thirst for vengeance that fills out the wish of Lamech in Genesis 4:24:

> If Cain is avenged sevenfold,
> Truly Lamech seventy-sevenfold.

Seventy-sevenfold will be sufficient, but not less than that; the rhetoric sounds familiar to us from contemporary witnesses who often say after an execution, "At least justice was done." This is a cry for justice in confidence that God and the judge appointed by God are committed to such justice.

It is all a death sentence:

- few days
- wife a widow, children orphans
- property forfeited
- family line cut off (vv. 8–13)

In verses 18–19 the speaker imagines that curse, the imposition of death upon another, is like oil that soaks in or like clothing that envelops him. The offender is inside and outside a carrier of curse.

We may notice in particular the wish of verse 12:

> May there be no one to do him *kindness*,
> nor anyone to pity his orphaned children.

This term "kindness" is a weak translation of our word *ḥesed*. May no neighbor show him *ḥesed*, none to do tenacious solidarity toward him. And the reason for this wish is that he himself "did not remember to do *ḥesed* (kindness)" (v. 16). That is the sum of this affront. He was no good neighbor. He was incapable of neighborly solidarity; for that reason all of these wishes constitute hope that he in turn will be denied such neighborly solidarity. Indeed his lack of *ḥesed* led him to "pursue the poor and needy and the brokenhearted to their death" (v. 16).

In verse 20 this plea for retaliation has been exhausted. It ends in this verse with a reference back to the initial charge of verse 5:

They reward me evil for good. (v. 5)
... who speak evil against me. (v. 20)

The speaker has exhausted human possibility and knows there is no hope for *hesed* from such human neighbors.

But then, in the third part of the poem, verses 21–31, the mood and the address shift abruptly: But you, Lord YHWH! The turn is from human failure to divine possibility. Now the speaker, so filled with vengeance, dares to address God with an imperative petition: Act for me! Act for me because no neighbor will. The petition bids God to act for the sake of God's reputation ("name's sake"). God wants to be known for solidarity, so show me solidarity. And the second line of the parallelism is:

... because of your *hesed* (kindness), deliver me.

On the basis of your tenacious solidarity (*hesed*), deliver me! Deliver me from a hopeless social circumstance of slander. This second imperative, "deliver me," is followed by an extended motivation:

For am I poor and needy [see v. 16],
and my heart is pierced within me.
I am gone like a shadow at evening;
I am shaken off like a locust.
My knees are weak through fasting;
my body has become gaunt.
I am an object of scorn to my accusers;
when they see me, they shake their heads. (Ps 109:22–25)

The speaker has no resources or possibility. It is all up to God.

In verse 26 we get more imperative petitions: "help, save ... according to your *hesed*." In verses 27–29 we return to jussive wishes that bid God reverse the threat and transpose it into a blessing for the speaker. The outcome that assumes the good response of the *hesed*-performing God is well-being. God will save the needy whose lives are at risk (v. 31). And the speaker will give thanks and praise in the throng of those who trust YHWH and count on *hesed* (v. 30).

This third section begins in petition and ends in thanks, trusting that all will be restored because God is an agent of tenacious solidarity. Thus we get a complete contrast between the failed neighbor (vv. 5–20) and the blessing God (vv. 21–31). In the first sequence everything is deathly; but the turn to God who will hear, who will act, and will deliver leads to new life.

It occurs to me that this psalm pivots on the *four uses of* ḥesed, two in each of the two speeches. In the first, the wish is for no ḥesed for the adversary (v. 16) because he had shown no ḥesed (v. 12). This is a world so filled with enmity that it is without ḥesed. The alternative world occupied by YHWH is one saturated with ḥesed. For that reason, the petition appeals to God's ḥesed:

- because of your ḥesed deliver me (v. 21)

- Save me according to your ḥesed (v. 26)

It matters decisively in the world of the psalms that the ḥesed-doing God is a character in the drama of creation. The conviction of the Psalter is that this God of ḥesed can indeed be summoned into the world by urgent petition. This psalm does not say so, but I imagine that, because the psalms are praxis and not only mere rhetoric, the performance of ḥesed is present in the life of the community that names the God of ḥesed.

I said at the outset that this psalm should be reserved for special circumstances. This is no ordinary prayer, and for most of us it violates our sense of propriety. My standard pedagogical ploy in taking up a psalm is to ask, Who is speaking here? Who would use this psalm and find it helpful? Certainly it is not my psalm and I would not say this, because my life has sufficient ḥesed in it that I can manage. I asked this question of this psalm once in class. And my student, Linda, answered promptly. She said, "This is the statement voiced by a woman who has been raped." (I learned later that Linda herself had been violated in that way). Her response would not have occurred to me. But she knew beyond a shadow of a doubt. She knew about a world of violence void of ḥesed. She knew about being abandoned without any advocate. This was her special circumstance, and she found this prayer to be compellingly appropriate. She knew about the authenticity of rage before God. And she knew about the turn to the God of ḥesed, but only after the vengeance had been given full voice.

So I thought about such a special circumstance:

- I could imagine a mother in Iraq just as her son had his head blown off by a bomb.

- I could imagine a poor black person in our economy amid the enduring legacy of slavery that has dropped him into despairing poverty and incarceration.

- I could imagine Jeremiah Wright, on behalf of many African Americans, saying "God damn America."

- I could imagine a cry of the vulnerable against exploitative institutions of all kinds that render helpless without an advocate.

This is emotional extremity addressed to God. This is emotional extremity voiced in the congregation of those who are engaged in the work of *hesed*. This is such extremity artistically expressed by a series of jussives that pivots abruptly to "But you, Lord YHWH." This is not everyday talk. But we keep it in reserve for the times when we are left exposed without *hesed*. We may be glad that the psalm does not end with verse 19. It ends with thanks (v. 30), that *hesed* YHWH stands at the right hand of the needy (v. 31).

VI

I have traced these three long psalms, perhaps trying your patience:

- In *Psalm 103* we have seen *hesed* at every turn, repeating the old mantra from Sinai operative in the midst of our guilt and our mortality.

- In *Psalm 86* we have seen a bid for *hesed* in the midst of tribulation when God must be called out, again with the old formula.

- In *Psalm 109* we have seen a turn from failed human *hesed* in the neighborhood to the ultimate source of reliable *hesed* in YHWH.

Everywhere in these extended psalms we have found the rhetoric of *hesed*, its reliability, its absence, its failure, and it capacity to summon. Such overt preoccupation with *hesed* is not everywhere evident in the Psalter. I dare suggest, nevertheless, that *hesed* is everywhere the subtext of the Psalter, because it is the deepest need of the human heart, the deepest desire of the human community, and the deepest mark of the God who occupies this poetry. Psalms is our most elemental script for the ongoing work of *hesed* that is both our proper rhetorical practice and our proper bodily investment. We, in the image of this God, are intended for tenacious solidarity.

VII

I perhaps do not need to say, in conclusion, that the continuation of this dialogue about fidelity is an urgent task for the sake of the well-being and future of our society. It is urgent because the dominant claims (and therefore the dominant rhetoric) of our society are skewed away from matters of fidelity. Indeed, dominant modes of discourse and practice aggressively contradict such a way of speaking and of living.

Among the markings of a way of speech and life that contradict the way of *ḥesed* are the following:

- We are witnessing a *monetization of social relationships* and thereby a *reduction of relationships to commodity transactions.* The outcome is that human persons become tradable commodities. And in the midst of acute economic inequality, many vulnerable persons thereby become disposable and dispensable commodities.

- We are witnessing a reduction of bodily human reality to a series of *technological fixes.* Thus, staying manly simply requires a drug for virility. Staying young simply requires cosmetic surgery. Managing high-energy children simply requires more screens to entertain them. The attractiveness of technological fixes for dense human reality is a denial of the organic truth of the human body and the body politic.

- We are witnessing a passion for individualism that sustains market ideology that reduces our imagination and policy formation to *instrumental reasoning* in which the thick and inscrutable human questions—questions of fidelity—are bracketed out as nonexistent. We settle for policy formation that is contained within the myopic world of monetization, commoditization, and technical reason. The erasure of liberal arts in our society is a sign and a measure of the way in which instrumental reason has displaced the complexity of the human body and the body politic.

In the face of these onslaughts of dehumanization, the continuation and maintenance of a dialogue about fidelity are an urgent task. It is that dialogue that generates futures, that sustains neighborhoods, and that holds prospect for peace with justice. By way of reflection on these three psalms—a hymn, a lament, and a profound cry for vengeance—I mean to suggest that Psalms is a primary script for that conversation that exposes the dominant claims of our society to be inadequate and finally false. The performance of this counterscript requires, to be sure, immense imagination. But it also evokes that imagination that is evident in the long history of performance. The liturgical performance of the psalms is not simply an incident in liturgical sequence. It is a frontal act of resistance to dehumanization and the modeling of an alternative of interactive fidelity as a way in the world.

The decision of Xavier University to acquire the Saint John's Bible is an immense moment in the life of the university and for our city. The beauty and majesty of this articulation of Scripture are testimony to the deep truth of our faith. Happily, an early fascicle of that wondrous rendering is of Psalms, or we would not be here tonight.

18.

The Prophets: Holy Intrusions of
Truth and Hope

An earlier version of this chapter was delivered at a preaching symposium at the George W. Truett Seminary of Baylor University, on September 11, 2017. The title of the symposium was "The Significance of Preaching from the Prophets to the Present."

The work of the prophets in ancient Israel was to deliver a truth-telling, hope-evoking word in a society that wanted neither the truth that was too hard to bear nor hope that was impossible to entertain.

I

The world in which these ancient prophets did their work was a world of concentrated power and wealth that sought a monopoly of technology and imagination. The purpose of that wealth and power, on the one hand, was to *control all technology* in a way that assured military domination and economic mastery. An early instance of this is reported in 1 Samuel 13:19–22 concerning Philistine control of technology:

> Now there was no smith to be found throughout all the land of Israel; for the Philistines said, "The Hebrews must not make swords or spears for themselves"; so all the Israelites went down to the Philistines to sharpen their plowshare, mattocks, axe, or sickle. . . . So on the day of battle neither sword nor spear was to be found in the possession of any of the people with Saul and Jonathan.

But then the text adds the surreptitious, unexplained note:

But Saul and his son Jonathan had them. (v. 22)

On the other hand, the purpose of wealth and power is to *control all imagination*, a control that was accomplished by liturgical hegemony in the performance of the temple. The royal hegemony intended to create a comprehensive world in which nothing was thinkable, imaginable, sayable, or doable outside the confines of that control. The best word that I know for such an all-encompassing system *totalism*. I appropriate the term from Robert Lifton, who over time has studied some of the great totalisms of the modern world, including the cult of National Socialism in Germany and the war machine in Japan.[1]

The totalism of the royal period of the Old Testament is embodied in the Jerusalem establishment of king, temple, and the scribal culture founded by Solomon that lasted for four hundred years. (Its complement for a time was the totalism of the capital city of Samaria in northern Israel). That socioeconomic, political, liturgical regime was all-encompassing, establishing itself through a combination of taxes (see 1 Kgs 4:7–19), tribute from commercial domination (see 1 Kgs 10:14–25), and forced labor (see 1 Kgs 5:13–16, 9:20–22), all of which permitted the urban regime to enjoy surplus wealth. That surplus wealth, moreover, was grandly exhibited in the Solomonic temple, which tied the economic excess of Solomon to the will of the creator God. It is clear that this urban regime had a monopoly on all important technology that was, not surprisingly, devoted to military dominance; and surely no force of media could compete with the grand imagination of the liturgical performance of the temple. Thus, all of life came to be contained within and defined by the categories of the regime. Consequently, the regime could readily come to think of itself as an absolute match for the will of God, with the priests on the royal payroll having ready access between the earthly domain of Solomon and the heavenly domain of YHWH.

The extended historical episode of the Davidic dynasty is the defining example of totalism in ancient Israel. It is, however, only one of a series of totalisms in the memory of Israel, each of which could pretend to absolutism. Pharaoh could claim, according to the imagination of Ezekiel:

The Nile is my own; I made it for myself. (Ezek 29:3)

---

1. Robert Jay Lifton, *Witness to an Extreme Century: A Memoir* (New York: Free Press, 2011). See especially 67–68, 381. See also chapter 1 for a fuller discussion of this concept.

Thus in the memory of Israel, Pharaoh's Egypt was, well before Solomon, a totalism that was ruthlessly exploitative. (It does not hurt to notice that Solomon was the son-in-law of Pharaoh. He married the boss's daughter and joined the family business of totalism; 1 Kgs 3:1, 7:8, 9:24, 11:1.)

And of course the later Jewish community in the Old Testament faced a succession of totalisms, each of which imagined itself as absolute, each of which practiced aggressive policies in the service of absolutism, and each of which relied on a grand liturgy to justify its claim. Thus, Babylon under Nebuchadnezzar could imagine its absoluteness. In the poetic imagination of Isaiah, we get this from Babylon:

> I shall be mistress forever . . .
> I am and there is none beside me . . .
> No one sees me. (Isa 47:7, 8, 10)

Persia, the successor empire to Babylon, is treated somewhat more generously in the Old Testament. But Bruce Lincoln has chronicled the way in which the Persian regime was ruthless and engaged in the crudest forms of torture to silence alternative imagination. Lincoln concludes, concerning the Achaemenids in Persia, that such aggression required three convictions:

> 1) a starkly dualistic ethics in which the opposition of good/evil is aligned with that of self/other and correlated discriminatory binaries; 2) a theology of election that secures the ruler's legitimacy by constituting him as God's chosen agent; and 3) a sense of soteriological mission that represents imperial aggression as salvific action taken on behalf of divine principles, thereby recoding the empire's victims as it beneficiaries.[2]

The ultimate successor to Persia as totalism, via Alexander and the Hellenistic kingdoms, was the Roman Empire, the totalism in the midst of which the Jesus movement had its inception. We are aware, from our Christian texts, of the way in which Roman military, judicial, and tax-collecting power permeated even the remote territory of Galilee.

Each of these totalisms in sequence operated in roughly the same way. When necessary, the regime used raw power; but it preferred softer persuasion to establish the legitimacy and the necessity of the regime. In order to maintain this claim and practice, it was necessary to refuse and resist any thought, imagination, utterance, or action to the contrary. Of course there were those who did not subscribe to the dominant ideology

---

2. Bruce Lincoln, *Religion, Empire, and Torture: The Case of Achaemenian Persia, with a Postscript on Abu Ghraib* (Chicago: University of Chicago Press, 2007), 95.

and who did not benefit from the concentration of wealth; they engaged in alternative thought and action of a subversive nature. Already under Pharaoh, Moses embodies such a force that Pharaoh must first restrain and then finally, in desperation, expel:

> Rise up, go away from my people, both you and the Israelites! Go, worship the Lord, as you said. Take your flocks and your herds, as you said, and be gone. (Exod 12:31–32)

The memory concerning the regime of Solomon is not different. The regime had from the outset constantly to be on guard against those who dared to imagine that there were life possibilities beyond the sphere of the regime. Solomon's violent seizure of the throne, according to the narrative, required him to forcibly eliminate opponents:

> So King Solomon sent Benaiah, son of Jehoiada; he struck him [Adonijah] down, and he died. (1 Kgs 2:25)

> Then Benaiah son of Jehoiada went up and struck him [Joab] down and killed him. (1 Kgs 2:34)

> Then the king commanded Benaiah son of Jehoiada; and he went out and struck him [Shemei] down, and he died. (1 Kgs 2:46)

But then, in 1 Kings 11:29 the prophet Ahijah, the Shilonite, evoked in Jeroboam a thought about leading a revolution against the house of Solomon, a revolution that came to fruition in the next chapter (1 Kgs 12:1–19). In the subsequent royal narrative, we know that Ahab and Jezebel, in the north, regarded Elijah and Elisha as enemies of their regime and killed many prophets (1 Kgs 18:4, 13). Amaziah, the priest in the royal sanctuary of Bethel, moreover, banished the prophet Amos (Amos 7:10–17). Manasseh contradicted the commands of Moses and "shed much innocent blood" (1 Kgs 21:16), and King Jehoiakim sent a posse to kill Jeremiah (Jer 36:26).

A totalizing regime cannot tolerate dissent or subversion. Thus, as is necessary, totalizing regimes must silence dissent, must prohibit subversion, must control artists, must banish poets, and when necessary must kill prophets. Such brutality is required because dissenters, subversives, artists, poets, and prophets invite thought that the regime is not absolute, that its claims to legitimacy are not ultimate, that its policies are not beyond criticism nor its practices beyond destabilization.

Do I need to alert you, before I move on, that it is increasingly in such a totalism of military consumerism, endorsed by uncritical exceptionalism, that we live? As a successor to Rome, the US Empire prefers the soft legitimacy of liturgical imagination (NFL) but, when necessary, will resort to coercive practices. Witness our public ambiguity concerning torture! Closer to home, witness the silencing vigilance of adherents to the totalism in our own communities and congregations!

II

It is important that the regal time line of the Davidic house in the books of Kings is not given to us in a royal chronicle. It is rather given to us in a theological commentary that footnotes the royal sources (see 1 Kgs 11:14, 14:19). That theological commentary is commonly termed "Deuteronomic" because it had behind it the book of and tradition of Deuteronomy. It is clear that in the final form of the text, the prophetic sequence over the centuries of the royal house in Jerusalem cannot be understood apart from the book and tradition of Deuteronomy, which provide interpretive categories and evoke the imagination of the interpretive community.

Deuteronomy is the normative and model interpretation of the Sinai covenant. It casts all of Israel's life in terms of the Sinai covenant with YHWH, so that Israel may rely on YHWH's promises and respond positively to YHWH's commands. Gerhard von Rad has seen that the book features the dynamics of "law preached," so that the utterance in the mouth of Moses is presented as "expounding" the Sinai Torah (Deut 1:5), and so that it is a matter of intense immediacy to Israel:[3]

> Not with our ancestors did the Lord make this covenant, but with us, who are all of us here alive today. (Deut 5:3)

The outcome of that dynamism is that the Torah commandments here take up matters in the daily life of Israel that were not at all on the horizon of Sinai.

In his classic article "The Problem of the Hexateuch," von Rad saw that the structure of Deuteronomy consists in four elements:

1. Historical presentation and hortatory material

2. The reading of the Torah (Decalogue)

3. The covenant is sealed

---

3. Gerhard von Rad, *Studies in Deuteronomy*, Studies in Biblical Theology 9 (Chicago: Henry Regnery, 1953), 16.

4. Blessings and curses[4]

This becomes the classic structure of covenant through which the prophets can be understood.

The defining point is that here "Moses" traffics in the defining "if" of Sinai:

> Now therefore, if you obey my voice and keep my covenant, you shall be my treasured possession out of all the peoples. (Exod 19:5)

The "if" is a statement of conditionality that substantively amends (corrects?) the unconditional promise of YHWH to Abraham that became the grounding of the Davidic covenant. The "if" that permeates Deuteronomy binds future blessings and curses to the obedience or disobedience of the commandments (see Deut 30:15–20). Obedience to Torah determines whether Israel will live long in the land; disobedience to the Torah will lead to land loss, the abrogation of the promises, and the disappearance of Israel, which will become absorbed into Canaanite culture.

The expansive interpretive reach of Deuteronomy brings every sphere of life under the rule of YHWH. On the one hand, the tradition accents that Israel is YHWH's holy people, so that the life of Israel should resonate with the holiness of YHWH. The tradition indicates practices (disciplines) of holiness that are essential for the life and well-being of Israel. On the other hand, this expansive interpretive tradition pays acute attention to matters of economic justice, insisting that the conduct of the economy must be subordinate to the practice of neighborliness with which YHWH is peculiarly concerned. That is, unlike the "Canaanite economy," which reduced everything to commodity, Deuteronomy insists that commodities must be assessed and handled with reference to social outcomes. The recurring litmus test for a proper economy is that the public accepts responsibility for the security and well-being of the "widow, the orphan, and the immigrant," three populations that are acutely vulnerable in a patriarchal society. It is the well-being of the neighbor that imposes a restraint (regulation) on the unfettered practice of acquisitiveness.

Two commandments in particular may be noted in this regard. First, in Deuteronomy 17:14–20, the only commandment in the Torah concerning monarchy, the acquisitive capacity of the king is curbed so that the king is not free to pursue the accumulation of horses, chariots, gold,

4. Gerhard von Rad, *The Problem of the Hexateuch and Other Essays* (New York: McGraw-Hill, 1966), 27.

silver, or wives—five commodities that occupied the acquisitiveness of the urban establishment of Jerusalem. Second, in Deuteronomy 15:1–18 Moses preaches "a year of release" during which debts are to be canceled, most particularly debts held against poor people. The tradition is determined to prevent in Israel any permanent economic underclass.

With this general imperative for holiness and justice, the tradition of Deuteronomy asserts that the future well-being of Israel depends not on wealth (gold and silver) or upon power (horses and chariots) but on a viable neighborhood, which requires inconvenient attentiveness on the part of the powerful, that is, the ones who occupy and benefit from the urban establishment of Jerusalem. Thus, the covenant articulated in Deuteronomy is demandingly counterintuitive for those who know how to take advantage of commercial dealings. The "if" of Moses is uncompromising.

From that tradition, we have a theological presentation of the royal history of Jerusalem in First and Second Kings from Solomon to the destruction of the city. In his classic study von Rad has seen that this narrative recital of kings is an ongoing contestation between the claims of the royal covenant, which was taken to be an unconditional blank check to David, and the Torah "if" of Deuteronomy.[5] The narrative is constructed according to the royal time line, but with particular interruptions of prophetic assertion. These interruptions are, on the one hand, editorial commentary by the "historian." On the other hand, there are two extended "prophetic pauses" that interrupt the royal narrative. First there is the extended narrative concerning Elijah and Elisha (1 Kings 17–2 Kings 10), which occupies about one-third of the entire narrative. On the other hand, there is the narrative of Isaiah in 2 Kings 18–20 (see Isaiah 36–39). These two major interruptions suggest that the royal time line is vulnerable to prophetic intrusion. More than that, already in the Solomon narrative, the Deuteronomic "if" looms large as a way to correct any royal illusion about unconditionality:

If you walk in my ways, keeping my statutes and my commandments, as your father David walked, then I will lengthen your life. (1 Kgs 3:14)

If you will walk in my statutes, obey my ordinances, and keep all my commandment by walking in them, then I will establish my promise with you, which I made to your father David. (1 Kgs 6:11)

5. Von Rad, *Studies in Deuteronomy*, 74–91.

If you walk before me . . . then I will establish your royal throne over Israel forever. . . . If you turn aside from following me . . . then I will cut off Israel from the land. (1 Kgs 9:4–7)

In this horizon, the future of Jerusalem depends on Torah obedience. The narrative is put together, moreover, to end with the destruction of the city, taken as a vindication of the Deuteronomic claim. It is telling that in this review of royal history—a history of wealth and power—only two kings, Hezekiah and Josiah, are given unqualified approval as Torah keepers. Near the end of the narrative, Josiah is cited as the model royal Torah keeper even though he came too late to save the city:

Before him there was no king like him, who turned to the Lord with all his heart, with all his soul, and with all his might, according to all the law of Moses, nor did any like him arise after him. (2 Kgs 23:25)

I have taken so long with the tradition of Deuteronomy as Torah and as royal history in First and Second Kings because together the Torah and the history constitute the ground through which the role of prophetic preaching can be understood. The royal history is presented as a totalism of power, wealth, technology, and imagination. But the narrative allows for episodic intrusions that disrupt the totalism. I shall suggest in what follows that it is the burden of prophetic preaching in ancient Israel to make intrusions into the royal totalism in order to interrupt and subvert the illusion of ultimacy in Jerusalem. I intend to imply that that intrusion continues to be the test of prophetic preaching. The marks of holiness and justice expose the illusion of absolutism in a self-satisfied system of easy self-sufficiency. That is what Jesus, as a child of Deuteronomy, did amid the Roman Empire, which was sustained by Jewish collusion. And it continues to be the test amid every contemporary totalism.

III

Because the totalism wants to silence, banish, or eliminate every such unwelcome intrusion, the tricky work is to find standing ground outside the totalism from which to think the unthinkable, to imagine the unimaginable, and to utter the unutterable. The totalism would have us think that there is no such possible ground outside the totalism, so that the claim of these ancient prophets is to speak a word that comes from elsewhere without the approval or consent of totalizing authority. Thus, it is to make a claim of authority that will not be contained within the totalism, an authority that dissents from and contradicts the absolutism of the totalism.

Many attempts have been made to understand the claimed authority of prophetic utterance in ancient Israel. Robert Wilson, among others, has offered a sociological analysis, situating authority in the social passion of a group or subgroup for which the prophet speaks.[6] Wilson has seen that some prophets represent peripheral groups (special interest groups!) and some are central prophets (voices of the authorized establishment). This approach suggests that the prophets are not loners but are representatives of distinct advocacy groups.

Much more attention has been paid to psychological analysis of the prophets, best represented by the older study of Johannes Lindblom, *Prophecy in Ancient Israel*.[7] Lindblom reviews all sorts of modern analogues to peculiar psychological phenomena, but of course such analogues do not in fact give us access to the claims made by and for these ancient prophets.[8]

If we focus on the claims made in the prophetic tradition itself, we may consider two quite familiar formulae that assert authority that did not seek to receive any endorsement from the totalism. First is the formula, "The word of the Lord came to me." This formula in fact explains nothing. Norman Habel has studied the highly stylized reports of "prophetic calls."[9] The clear stylization of "prophetic calls" suggests that these are not actual individual reports of actual personal experience but are more or less like the standard applications sent to seminary admissions committees. Scholarship, however, suggests that behind the formulae is the imaginative, poetic, mythic claim of having been in the very presence of God. The mythic device for this claim is a "divine council," a meeting of the gods over which YHWH, the high God, presides.[10] When the council of gods makes a decision, messengers are dispatched to announce the divine decision on earth, variously angel messengers but also human agents who have been in the council and who bring the divine decision to earth. Thus, Amos can say:

---

6. Robert R. Wilson, *Prophecy and Society in Ancient Israel* (Philadelphia: Fortress Press, 1980).

7. Johannes Lindblom, *Prophecy in Ancient Israel* (Philadelphia: Fortress Press, 1976).

8. See Thomas W. Overholt, *Channels of Prophecy: The Social Dynamics of Prophetic Activity* (Minneapolis: Fortress Press, 1989).

9. Norman Habel, "The Form and Significance of the Call Narratives," *Zeitschrift für die alttestamentliche Wissenschaft* 77 (1965): 297–323.

10. See Patrick D. Miller Jr., *Genesis 1–11: Studies in Structure & Theme*, Journal for the Study of the Old Testament: Supplement Series 8 (Sheffield: JSOT Press, 1978), 9–26.

> Surely the LORD does nothing
> without revealing his secret
> to his servants the prophets. (3:7)

More directly, Jeremiah will dispute with his adversaries that he has been to the divine council and so has an authentic divine message, whereas his opponents have no such legitimacy and are making up their word:

> For who has stood in the council of the LORD
> so as to see and to hear his word?
> Who has given heed to his word
> so as to proclaim it? (Jer 23:18)

Jeremiah has God dismiss his adversaries as phonies:

> I did not send the prophets, yet they ran;
> I did not speak to them, yet they prophesied.
> But if they had stood in my council,
> then they would have proclaimed my words to my people. (23:21–22)

More familiarly, the same imagery operates in Isaiah 6:

> Then I heard the voice of the LORD saying, "Whom shall I send and who will go for us?" And I said, "Here am I; send me!" (Isa 6:8).

The report of Isaiah appears to be echoed in the call of Second Isaiah, which reports a conversation in the divine council that culminates in this mandate to the prophet:

> Get you up on a high mountain,
> O Zion, herald of good tidings;
> Lift up your voice with strength,
> O Jerusalem, herald of good tidings.
> Lift it up, do not fear:
> Say to the cities of Judah:
> Here is your God! (Isa 40:9)

Most notorious is the narrative of Micaiah ben Imlah, who reports that he witnessed the divine council when YHWH approved a plan to lie to King Ahab and so to seduce him into self-destruction:

> Then one said one thing, and another said another, until a spirit came forward and stood before the LORD, saying, "I will entice him." "How?" the LORD asked him. He replied, "I will go out and be a lying spirit in the mouth

of all his prophets." Then the LORD said, "You are to entice him, and you shall succeed; go out and do it. (1 Kgs 22:21–22)

The tradition thus insists that the word spoken by the prophets is not the prophet's own word but is a word given by God outside the totalism. It cannot therefore be dismissed but must be heeded.

The second formula operates to the same effect: "Hear the word of the Lord." This standard introduction to a prophetic oracle is an assertion that the word to be spoken is not "my word" but is a word given by God that is not from within the totalism and so is not subject to the consent of the totalism. The two formulae make an authorizing claim that cannot be "objectively" established.[11] My judgment is that the two formulae, "The word of the LORD came to me," and "Hear the word of the LORD" are elusive assertions that attest to a deep inexplicable compulsion, albeit a divine compulsion, in which the prophet is called beyond the human self to run great risks, to exercise daring boldness, and to engage in imagination that finally transcends the person of the prophet. For any particular prophet it is likely that many factors—family, education, socialization, vested interest—all taken together shape the word uttered. But the word uttered cannot be explained by the sum of such factors. It is indeed from beyond; the prophet runs such great risks because it is not possible to do otherwise. Thus, Luther, "I cannot do otherwise." Or Martin Luther King, in his "kitchen experience" reports that God spoke to him, "Martin, do not be afraid." What else would propel Desmond Tutu to defy the apartheid government with such joy? What else would evoke a readiness in Dan Berrigan to suffer long-term imprisonment? What else would cause any contemporary local preacher to tell the truth about racism or economic inequality? Such utterance is not cost effective, even if it is as cunning and careful as possible. Thus, "I could not help myself. I could not do otherwise." That word, moreover, is always spoken into a vigilant, resistant totalism that wants to silence. It was a profound question then as now: Is it possible that there is a word, an utterance that is not contained within the totalism of power, wealth, imagination, and technology? From this perspective, preaching that is not from elsewhere in fact is religious kitsch that functions, just as Karl Marx said, as an "opiate of the people," a religious exercise that is safely contained within the comfort zone of the totalism. One can see why the tradition struggles about how to report this, because it is finally elusive. But then, holy intrusiveness is inescapably elusive, thus beyond the reach of every totalism.

11. See Sheldon H. Blank, *"Of a Truth the Lord Hath Sent Me": An Inquiry into the Source of the Prophet's Authority* (Cincinnati, OH: The Hebrew Union College Press, 1955).

IV

I will focus on the prophet Jeremiah because I believe his book gives us best access to the issues that concern us in prophetic preaching. Jeremiah appeared as an outsider in Jerusalem at a moment of acute crisis, a crisis not unlike our own in which public leadership and public assumptions of chosenness brought on huge trouble. I will comment on four matters.

1. The editorial introduction to the book of Jeremiah is quite remarkable. It locates the words of Jeremiah according to the royal time line:

> It [the word] came in the days of King Josiah son of Amon of Judah, in the thirteenth year of his reign. It came also in the days of King Jehoiakim son of Josiah of Judah, and until the end of the eleventh year of King Zedekiah son of Josiah of Judah. (1:2–3)

The report alludes to three kings, father Josiah the good king, son Jehoiakim the evil king, and his brother Zedekiah, a pitiful cowardly figure. That is, the book of Jeremiah is aimed at concrete political, historical reality that evokes words, not unlike the way the Gospel of Luke situates the narrative by naming the public leadership (Luke 3:1–2). This specificity anticipates that the people will go into exile:

> . . . until the captivity of Jerusalem in the fifth month. (Jer 1:3)

The juxtaposition of these three kings, good, evil, and cowardly, indicates a social situation of great instability and risk. The editor, moreover, knows where this history is headed.

The culmination of the royal time line will be in destruction, dislocation, and displacement that expose the illusion of particular chosenness. Notice there is nothing here about generic matters, and there is no harping on specific issues. Prophetic imagination here is aimed at underneath issues of the way in which in God's world, chickens come home to roost.

The prophet Jeremiah, moreover, is identified as belonging to "the priests who were in Anathoth." The reference serves to remind every knowing reader of the episode in 1 Kings 2:26–27, wherein King Solomon banished Abiathar, a priest from Anathoth back to his hometown because he had backed the wrong royal candidate. That means that Jeremiah belongs to a four-hundred-year brooding resentment for the way in which his priestly family had been maltreated by the crown. That means in turn, does it not, that Jeremiah is not an innocent man; he brings resentment to his words.

Beyond that the editor identifies the words that follow in the book in this way:

> The words of Jeremiah, son of Hilkiah of the priests who were in Anathoth in the land of Benjamin to whom the word of the LORD came. (Jer 1:1)

The specificity is careful. In the tribe of Benjamin, not royal Judah; Anathoth, locus of banishment; son of Hilkiah, perhaps the same Hilkiah who found the scroll of Deuteronomy for King Josiah (2 Kgs 22:8). But notice when we bracket these details this cunning formulation:

> The words of Jeremiah . . . to whom the word of the LORD came.

The phrasing makes an intimate connection between the prophetic word and God's word possibly given in the divine council. In the face of that intimacy, however, the phrasing also makes a distinction. The two are not the same. The editor does not puzzle out how the connection and distinction are to be understood with reference to any prophetic text. But the phrase puts us on notice that we are dealing with divine word factored out as human word. The word is given with all the specificity of locale, grudging, and resentment, but linked in an intimate way to a word beyond human words.

Benjamin Sommer, a distinguished Jewish theologian, has recently written about the matter in a book entitled *Revelation and Authority*, in which he wants to combat any simple literalism concerning the Bible as God's word.[12] He resists a "steno theory" as though Jeremiah were a stenographer. Instead, Sommer proposes a "dialogical aspect of the Bible" that "rests in its oral character." The dialogical part, following Martin Buber and Franz Rosenzweig, allows for this holy God and this human receiving agent to be engaged together in pursuing authoritative articulation that comes from elsewhere. Such a formulation precludes any simple literalism. Jeremiah is not speaking God's word. It also precludes any Enlightenment assumption that the preacher is just making up and offering opinions that pretend to be God's word. This really is from God and it really is from Jeremiah. I would think this suggests that the word comes in anguished, daring brooding through which we are led beyond what we thought.[13] Such brooding, I suspect, requires a holy life that is not rushed and weary with a thousand chores but that brings best effort

---

12. Benjamin D. Sommer, *Revelation and Authority: Sinai in Jewish Scripture and Tradition*, Anchor Yale Bible Reference Library (New Haven: Yale University Press, 2015).

13. This depth has been compellingly probed by Abraham J. Heschel, *The Prophets* (New York: Harper & Row, 1962).

and best energy to the deep awesome confrontation with the living God, who has a decisive say in the life of the world that is not an echo of any of our favorite ideologies. It is such brooding that evoked the well-known laments of Jeremiah that bespeak his deep and inescapable engagement with this God. Thus, as we read Jeremiah, we must attend to this tricky dialogic reality. And as we ponder our own preaching, we must attend to this tricky reality of having a word other than our own word that must become, before we speak it, our own word.

Quoting Heschel, Sommer goes on to say:

> Judaism is based upon a minimum of revelation and a maximum of inter-pretation. . . . There is a partnership of God and Israel in regard to both the world and the Torah.[14]

"Minimum revelation" means we get this terse utterance. "Maximum interpretation" means we have much work to do. And, not unlike Karl Barth, Sommer insists that we must

> put aside that fearful distinction separating what is in the Bible, what our Sages said, and what modern biblical criticism says.[15]

It is all of a piece, revelation and interpretation!

2. The situation of Jeremiah is given in his stylized call narrative. After Jeremiah is summoned by God and after Jeremiah resists YHWH as much as he is able, YHWH responds with this mandate:

> See, today I appoint you over nations and over kingdoms,
> to pluck up and to pull down,
> to destroy and to overthrow,
> to build and to plant. (1:10)

This assignment permeates the final form of the text of Jeremiah. It charges the prophet to perform acts, not mere utterances, in the conviction that words matter, because words generate reality, which is why words are so dangerous. The mandate consists in two parts, *destruction*, which is given in four words ("pluck up, tear down, destroy, overthrow"), and *construction*, which is given in two words ("plant and build"). Of the four negative verbs, two match the two positive ones, so that "pluck up" goes with "plant" in an agricultural image, and "pull down" goes with "build" as an architectural image.[16] The two negatives

---

14. Sommer, *Revelation and Authority*, 29.
15. Sommer, *Revelation and Authority*, 232.
16. It is worth noting that Paul, in his affirmation of his ministry, utilizes exactly these two

are reinforced by two more verbs ("destroy, overthrow") that have no positive counterpart here.

This sequence of two matching sets of verbs is a focus of the entire thematic of the book of Jeremiah, reappearing in its key parts:

> At one moment I may declare concerning a nation or a kingdom, that I will pluck up and break down and destroy it . . . and yet at another moment I may declare concerning a nation or a kingdom that I will build and plant it. (18:7–9)

> I will build them up, and not tear them down; I will plant them, and not pluck them up. (24:6)

> And just as I have watched over them to pluck up and tear down, to overthrow, destroy, and bring evil, so I will watch over them, to built and plant. (31:28)

> I am going to break down what I have built, and pluck up what I have planted, that is, the whole land. (45:4)

The different uses evidence the enormous plasticity of the tradition as these uses serve very different intentions. But they are, taken together, the sum of prophetic preaching. It is the work of honest truth telling to utter and expose the termination of all reality that is not in sync with God's purpose. It is the work of buoyant hope telling to utter and anticipate and imagine the emergence of a new historical reality that is being birthed by God. So that you can easily connect this to our preaching task, I provide this clue:

a. The negative verbs in the New Testament have morphed into *the crucifixion of Jesus*, which exposed the world of Caesar, Herod, and Pilate as a non-world that could not be sustained. The crisis is God's great plucking up of an illusionary world of fear, scarcity, greed, and violence. We have no better articulation of this ongoing work of plucking up and tearing down than the summons of Paul to the divided congregation at Corinth:

> God chose what is low and despised in the world, things that are not, to bring to nothing the things that are. (1 Cor 1:28)

Does it take your breath away? This little community, not rich, not

---

images of restoration: "I planted . . . like a skilled master builder I laid a foundation" (1 Cor 3:6, 10). He asserts to the Christian congregation: "You are God's field [planted], God's building [built]" (1 Cor 3:9). This coheres with Paul's readiness to allude to Jeremiah.

powerful, not of noble birth, had as its vocation the nullification of the illusionary world of power, wealth, and nobility.

b. The positive verbs in the mandate to Jeremiah in the New Testament have morphed into *the Easter of Jesus*, which becomes the inexplicable starting point for a new world of peace and justice in which the blind see, the lame walk, the dead are raised, and the poor rejoice. We have no better articulation of that ongoing work of anticipating and welcoming a new life than in the doxological articulation of Paul in his assurance to the congregation in Rome:

> . . . in the presence of the God in whom we he believed, who gives life to the dead and calls into existence the things that do not exist. (Rom 4:17)

That is what it means to "plant and build." It is done, moreover, by utterance of hope and possibility that are grounded in God. Notice that both the news of plucking up and tearing down and the news of planting and building fall outside the totalism. The totalism does not believe it will be plucked up and torn down; and the totalism does not believe that there can be real newness. Thus, I propose that in the phrasing of 1:10 (with its reiterations), Jeremiah is a *harbinger of the crucifixion, which brings to naught the things that are,* and a *harbinger of Easter, which calls into existence things that do not exist.* Both acts—"plucking up and tearing down" and "planting and building"—are not simply moments in the church year. They are the ongoing work of the people of God, and they are the ongoing theme of prophetic preaching. I imagine that prophetic preaching, a human agent to whom the word of the Lord has come, is a continuing enterprise of bringing to naught the things that are and calling into existence things that do not exist. Prophetic preaching depends on the assurance that there is a living God who terminates what fails and who births what gives life. To trust that assurance, moreover, means to be rooted outside the totalism that accepts neither claim. The hard part is that such preaching is located outside the totalism while our institutional home base of members, budgets, programs, and pensions is thoroughly located in the totalism. It is no wonder that we are all tempted to kitsch.

It is for good reason that Ronald Clements can write of the prophetic canon:

> We can at least understand the value and meaning of the way in which distinctive patterns have been imposed on the prophetic collections of the canon so that warnings of doom and disaster are always followed by promises of hope and restoration. . . . So also the Former and Latter Prophets, comprising the various preserved prophecies of a whole series of

inspired individuals, acquired an overarching thematic unity. This centered on the death and rebirth of Israel, interpreted theologically as acts of divine judgment and salvation.[17]

The whole of the prophetic canon is shaped according to this double theme. But Jeremiah makes it specific. In his resentment, he can speak of a failed city that cannot be sustained. In his deep faith he can speak of restorations that are beyond explanation. He does not explain, because he is a poet.

But his poetry has intense specificity. We have only a bit of text. But we preachers engage in maximum interpretation. We interpret maximally so that our own exceptionalism of military consumerism that is powered by scarcity, fear, and greed is seen as failing and unsustainable, not by arms, not by racism, not by rage, not by anything, because God is not mocked. We interpret maximally in order to welcome new planting and building, as God authorizes a new multiculturalism, a new ecumenism, and a new international network of peace and justice; it is all at hand! That newness threatens the totalism that has deployed privilege differently. So it was in ancient Jerusalem. And this Jeremiah, an outsider from Anathoth dared to say, "The word of the LORD came to me," "Hear the word of the LORD."

3. What began in the instantaneous words of the prophet became the durable words of the book of Jeremiah. Oracle from the prophet becomes the prophetic scroll through a process of editing. The transposition from oracle to scroll assures that utterance of the hard word of the one to whom the word of the Lord came can be transmitted and reheard. So Sommer can write:

> The living voice of God . . . has been preserved in a seemingly "frozen" written medium. The biblical narrative has been formed in such a way that, paradoxically, its siren forms call forth its original "spokenness."[18]

The word does not remain frozen word in the text. It is the voice of the living God accomplished by imaginative interpretation.

This move from word to script is reflected in the remarkable text of Jeremiah 36. We are told that Baruch the scribe:

> wrote on a scroll at Jeremiah's dictation all the words of the LORD that he had spoken to him. (36:4)

---

17. Ronald E. Clements, "Patterns in the Prophetic Canon," in *Canon and Authority: Essays in Old Testament Religion and Theology*, ed. George W. Coats and Burke O. Long (Philadelphia: Fortress Press, 1977), 49, 53.

18. Sommer, *Revelation and Authority*, 181.

Baruch wrote it all down. The authorities of the Jerusalem totalism were astonished by the scroll and were highly suspicious, so that they vetted Baruch carefully. Finally, after much care, suspicion, and investigation, they were persuaded of the authenticity of the scroll and its authority and took it to the king, Jehoiakim. The king, head of the Jerusalem totalism, did not welcome the scroll. He immediately recognized the scroll to be a threat. In response, Jehoiakim did two things. First he ostentatiously shredded the document:

> As Jehudi read three or four columns, the king would cut them off with a penknife and throw them into the fire in the brazier, until the entire scroll was consumed in the fire that was in the brazier. (36:23)

Second, he sent the secret police to apprehend both the prophet and the scribe. He thought to silence the voice from elsewhere that threatened the totalism with its truth-telling, hope-telling alternative. The text laconically reports:

> And the king commanded Jerahmeel the king's son and Seraiah son of Azriel and Shelemiah son of Abdeel to arrest the secretary Baruch and the prophet Jeremiah. (36:26)

The verse adds tersely, "But the Lord hid them." The LORD protected the carriers of his word from elsewhere. We may believe, following Wilson, that high officials in the king's own government were sympathetic to the prophet, were alarmed by the king, and wanted him curbed. Thus, they would have protected prophet and scribe. Either way, we are told that Jeremiah and Baruch would not quit in fear or be deterred by the power of the totalism:

> Then Jeremiah took another scroll and gave it to the secretary Baruch son of Neriah, who wrote on it at Jeremiah's dictation all the words of the scroll that King Jehoiakim of Judah had burned in the fire; and many similar words were added to them. (36:32)

This is an amazing account of how prophets yielded to scribes.[19] The scribes are not prophets. They are the ones who wrote and kept and interpreted the prophetic text. They are the learned in Jerusalem who became "a culture of interpretation."

I tell you this because I think it is an assurance to us. I assume that many of you are like me: you do not want or intend to be so daringly

---

19. See Philip R. Davies, *Scribes and Schools: The Canonization of the Hebrew Scriptures*, Library of Ancient Israel (Louisville: Westminster John Knox, 1998).

prophetic. But the scribal scroll gives us an alternative possibility for faithfulness. We do not need to generate dangerous oracles. It is sufficient, in my judgment, to be interpreters of the scroll we already have in hand, to let the people of God have informed access to the scroll that is the carrier of the spoken word, so that by way of serious interpretation the written form calls forth its original "spokenness."

I cannot tell you how important this is. Because, given institutional reality, not many of us will be ready or able to be prophetic as was Jeremiah. I am struck, moreover, by how little people in many congregations know the prophetic text and how little they care about the text. It is as though congregations listen to the scroll, if at all, with ears shaped by ideologies of denial and despair that produce numbness. I have observed that very few people even listen to the text read in church. As a result, church people have little sense of the large picture of Scripture and little attention for tracing out the detail of a text. But it is our task nonetheless. So if you are like me and do not want to be excessively prophetic, then consider scribal work, which, by bold imaginative interpretation, exhibits an alternative. It is an alternative that lies outside the totalism. It is an alternative to illusionary Jerusalem. It is an alternative to military consumerism. But it requires different preaching. Have done, then, with clever introduction. Have done with illustrations that seldom illustrate; let the text be the illustration. Help the community of the baptized see, against our totalizing culture, that our tradition concerns "bringing to naught the things that are" and about "calling into existence things that do not exist." Prophetic preaching is the news that there is a public zone of well-being that is not sponsored, managed, or controlled by or limited to the claims of the totalism.

V

The reality of the prophetic text preserved in the biblical canon is that it has futures. Scholars term this the *Nachleben* of the text, its afterlife, or its continuing influence. There are later texts that quote and allude to these texts, resituating old remembered texts in quite new circumstances where they may speak afresh. No prophet, certainly not Jeremiah, anticipates or aims at such an afterlife for prophetic words. Passionate prophets are intensely fixed on the historical crisis in which they find themselves. Paul, in his letters, did not know he was writing durable Scripture. Luther knew nothing about bold futures for his "Here I stand." Martin Niemöller knew nothing about futures for his riff "Then they came for me—and there was no one left to speak for me." Martin Luther King did not know what futures would follow from "I Have a Dream." But the word is remembered and taken with continuing pertinence and vitality. Such texts have an afterlife because such truthful words continue to ring true in new contexts.

The text of Jeremiah, oracle become scroll, has a powerful afterlife that is quite explicit five times in the Old Testament. His words were found to be continuingly compelling:

- Grief over the violent, untimely death of the good king Josiah continues in ancient Israel:

   Jeremiah also uttered a lament for Josiah, and all the singing men and singing women have spoken of Josiah in their lament to this day. (2 Chr 35:25)

We have no such lament from Jeremiah; but perhaps Lamentations, credited to Jeremiah, serves as such a lament for Josiah and for all that he embodied.

- The tradition remembers the tricky, ambiguous interaction between Jeremiah and King Zedekiah:

   He [Zedekiah] did what was evil in the sight the LORD his God. He did not humble himself before the prophet Jeremiah who spoke from the mouth of the LORD. (2 Chr 36:12)

The tradition assumes that kings are accountable to prophets, thus contradicting the old royal totalism. Indeed, disrespect to the prophet is rated among the king's most grievous affronts against God.

- Jeremiah's anticipation of the length of exile is taken as a fixed point of the time for restoration to the land (29:10):

   To fulfill the word of the LORD by the mouth of Jeremiah, until the land had made up for its sabbaths. All the days that it lay desolate it kept sabbath, to fulfill seventy years. In the first year of Cyrus of Persia, in fulfillment of the word of the LORD spoken by Jeremiah, the LORD stirred up the spirit of King Cyrus of Persia so that he sent a herald throughout all his kingdom and declared in a written edict: "Thus says . . . ." (2 Chr 36:21–22; see Ezra 1:1)

Thus, Jeremiah's oracle against Babylon that anticipated the fall of Babylon to Persia is taken as a harbinger and cause of the restoration of deported Israel back to the land, an anticipation that is now enacted by

Cyrus. Jeremiah not only supplies the time line but also the prophetic assurance that it will happen.

In Daniel 9:2, Jeremiah's anticipation of "seventy years" of punishment is again taken as foreknowledge of the length of the exile and the time of restoration:

> In the first year of his [Darius's] reign, I, Daniel perceived in the books the number of years that, according to the word of the LORD What interests us is the quotation attributed to Jeremiah to the prophet Jeremiah, must be fulfilled for the devastation of Jerusalem, namely, seventy years.

In the New Testament, Jeremiah continues to be alive and well. In the Gospel of Matthew, Jeremiah is cited by name three times:

- Most important, in Matthew 2:17 Jeremiah's allusion to Rachel weeping over destroyed Jerusalem (30:15) is reiterated with Rachel weeping over the slaughter of the innocents. In this way Jeremiah is made to anticipate the contradiction that the baby Jesus is to the kingdom of Herod.

- In Matthew 16:14 Jeremiah's presence is so palpable in the imagination of this society (or of this evangelist) that Jesus is taken to be, among others, a returned Jeremiah. The tradition judges that it was not yet finished with the powerful voice of Jeremiah.

- In Matthew 27:9–10, Jeremiah is credited with a quotation concerning the blood money paid to Judas:

> Then was fulfilled with had been spoken through the prophet Jeremiah, "And they took the thirty pieces of silver, the price of one on whom a price had been set, on whom some of the people of Israel had set a price, and they gave them for the potter's field, as the LORD had commanded them."

What interests us is the quotation attributed to Jeremiah does not come from Jeremiah, though it may allude to Jeremiah 32:6–15. Some manuscripts have the words credited to Isaiah or Zechariah, and Richard Hays judges that at best "it is only very roughly approximates Zechariah 11:13."[20] Jeremiah, however, is so compelling that he draws the attribution to him. In all, Hays cites thirty-nine allusions to Jeremiah in the Gospel of Matthew. Among these citations a great many concern Jere-

---

20. Richard B. Hays, *Echoes of Scripture in the Gospels* (Waco, TX: Baylor University Press, 2016), 159–60.

miah's "temple sermon" (Jeremiah 7) through which Jesus critiques the Jerusalem temple as "a den of robbers." A great deal is made, moreover, of the promises of Jeremiah 31 concerning the end of exile. Hays allows that Jeremiah's imagery of "Torah written on the heart" (31:34) in important ways anticipates Matthew's treatment of the demands of Torah with special attention to the Beatitudes.[21]

Beyond the gospel uses, I cite two other elements of the *Nachleben* of Jeremiah in the New Testament. First, in Paul's lyrical rendering of a "theology of the cross" he culminates with this counsel to the Corinthian congregation:

As it is written, "Let the one who boasts, boast in the Lord." (1 Cor 1:31)

The words are "written" in Jeremiah 9:23–24, wherein the prophet castigates reliance on wealth, might, and wisdom and commends instead steadfast love, justice, and righteousness. It turns out, in Paul's articulation, that Jeremiah is a voice of the "theology of the cross."[22]

Finally, in Hebrews 8:8–12 the writer quotes Jeremiah's "new covenant" from 31:31–34. The writer does so in order to assert the "new covenant" in Christ that abrogates the old covenant, but the writer could not do so without appeal to Jeremiah, which raises questions about what, exactly, is new about the "new covenant." Even if the text borders on supersessionism, it could do so only by going through this citation that re-presents the prophet's past promises.

Now I have taken this long on the *Nachleben* of the prophet's oracles-become-scroll for two reasons. First, when we do prophetic preaching, our words have an afterlife. They linger in the ears of the congregation of listeners. That may be to our detriment, because we would rather such words might be forgotten. But they also linger to fuel the imagination of the community so that prophetic possibility continues in force. Thus, such preaching generates a world of imagination that is stitched together by word, gesture, and image that may resurface in other contexts we little suspect. One never knows, as Jeremiah did not know.

The other reason I comment on *Nachleben* is that such afterlife from a text requires an imaginative alternative interpreter who has the capacity to carry remembered prophetic utterance into new circumstances beyond the horizon of the prophetic speaker. Imagine that! We may be a part of the afterlife of a prophetic text! We may carry remembered cadences of a prophet into new circumstances to permit the prophet to

21. Hays, *Echoes of Scripture*, 120.
22. For a very different accent on "crucifixion" in Jeremiah, see H. Wheeler Robinson, *The Cross in the Old Testament* (Philadelphia: Westminster, 1955).

respeak the original "spokenness." That process is called "textual preaching." It is textual preaching that deliberately intends to make the force and passion of the old prophet freshly operative and available in new circumstances.

What I have said about Jeremiah may be generally said of the entire prophetic corpus:

1. It is human speech of one to whom the word of the Lord has come by way of participation in the oral character of the tradition.

2. The themes of prophetic preaching are "pluck up and tear down, plant and build":

> For God chose what is low and despised in the world, things that are not, to bring to nothing things that are. (1 Cor 1:28)
> . . . in the presence of the God in whom he believed, who gives life to the dead and calls into existence the things that do not exist. (Rom 4:17)

"Plucking up and tearing down, planting and building" are acts rejected and resisted by the totalism. Both Friday and Sunday are resisted by the totalism.

3. The oracle of utterance becomes written scroll; we may be cast as scribes who are "trained for the kingdom":

> Therefore every scribe who has been trained for the kingdom of heaven is like the master of a household who brings out of his treasure what is new and what is old. (Matt 13:52)

4. We may be both participants in the afterlife of prophetic texts and generators of new prophetic texts that themselves may have a vigorous afterlife.

VI

All of this is very, very difficult, as it was then. I am under no illusion about prophetic preaching in local congregations that are most often themselves proponents of the totalism. Such prophetic preaching requires deep communion and sly imagination, but finally there is no escape from the vocation of truth telling and hope telling. I would not be honest if I did not report that I believe our moment calls for such truth and hope. Cathleen Kaveny, in her book *Prophecy without Contempt* says this about prophetic preaching:

> Chemotherapy can be dangerous. It kills healthy cells as well as diseased ones. To improve the overall health of the patient, therefore, it must be used both accurately and sparingly. The same can be said of the moral chemotherapy of prophetic discourse. More specifically, as I argued earlier, the use of prophetic language in a particular context disrupts the normal functioning of a deliberate community. It renders the normal interactions of mutual reason giving impossible because the audience's only avenues of response to a prophetic statement are either to acquiesce to the prophet's demands or to engage in what amounts to an ad hominem attack. Prophets, therefore, need to acknowledge and take responsibility for the troublesome side effects of their moral chemotherapy.[23]

Kaveny goes on to say that "ordinary moral language" that is generally acceptable must sometimes be disrupted by "extraordinary forms of moral discourse." It puts the expositor at risk but is indispensable for the saving of life. So imagine the danger to all parties in such prophetic discourse, a danger to be run only if to counter sickness unto death. Prophets characteristically appear in such a time as our own when sickness to death is seen to be at hand.

I finish with a word from Ezekiel, who had from God a very difficult vocation as God's sentinel. In the tight logic of the God of Ezekiel, it is this way to the sentinel:

> Whenever you hear a word from my mouth, you shall give them warning from me. If I say to the wicked, "You shall surely die," and you give them no warning, and do not speak to warn the wicked from their wicked way, in order to save their life, those wicked persons shall die for their iniquity, but their blood I will require at your hand. But if you warn the wicked, and they do not turn from their wickedness, or from their wicked way, they shall die for their iniquity; but you will have saved your life. (Ezek 3:17–19)

The lives of those in God's company are at risk. It ill serves to withhold from them the word of truth and the word of hope that is the word of life.

---

23. Cathleen Kaveny, *Prophecy without Contempt: Religious Discourse in the Public Square* (Cambridge: Harvard University Press, 2016), 315.

19.

The Torah: Back to Basics,
from Jesus to Moses

This chapter was first published in Journal for Preachers *41, no. 1 (Advent 2017): 11–20.*

The abrupt turn of our national political economy toward uncritical populism (with a tilt toward fascism) has bewildered many preachers including this one. That turn has made preaching for many of us even more difficult and demanding, because ideological sensibilities are so acute, and every utterance seems freighted with risk. That turn, however, has also made preaching more urgent, because it signifies that we are in a time of forgetfulness, or what Michael Fishbane has called "mindlessness."[1] It is as though in raw and ready ideological dispute we have forgotten the glue of the national good. And a spin-off of that forgetfulness means that we have to some extent in the church forgotten the ties that bind us in the gospel to the living God and to each other.

I

In such a season of forgetfulness (mindlessness), I suggest that we preachers must go back to the basics of what we must remember that we have forgotten. Or in Fishbane's parlance, we must be intentionally "mindful" in a context of pathological mindlessness. When we go back to basics, I propose that we may (without being excessively didactic) bear witness

1. Michael Fishbane, *Sacred Attunement: A Jewish Theology* (Chicago: University of Chicago Press, 2008).

to the ethical completion of the good news or in Dietrich Bonhoeffer's language, that we may exposit the "cost of discipleship." My impression is that with a generous accent on God's good grace, we are very close to "cheap grace" in order to reassure and comfort in a way that requires no costly or even inconvenient decision. The ethical completion of the gospel tradition is everywhere evident. It is voiced at Sinai in response to the Decalogue:

> All that the LORD has spoken we will do and we will be obedient. (Exod 24:7)

In Jesus's ministry it is "follow me," which means to cease to follow the path of Rome:

> Jesus calls us o'er the tumult of life's restless sea;
> day by day his sweet voice soundeth saying, "Christian follow me."[2]

In Paul's language, it is to be "of the same mind," which means to "look to the interest of others" (Phil 2:4–5) that our minds may be renewed and transformed with what is good and acceptable and perfect (Rom 12:2). Cultural Christianity among us comes packaged as a reassurance that there is no compelling "ask" in the gospel, or the "ask" among right-wing Christians is simply an echo of dominant cultural values. In truth, however, the gospel is a summons to be different, think differently, imagine differently, save, spend, and invest differently, and act differently. I recognize that in exploring the "cost" of discipleship it is futile in most venues to focus on current hot-button issues; better in my judgment go back to basics that lie behind such issues.

The "basics" concerning "cost" are most succinctly put in the two "great commandments" (Matt 22:34–40, Mark 12:28–34, Luke 10:25–28). In Mark they asked Jesus for the first commandment; he answered, "You cannot have one; you get two." You cannot separate God and human reality. In response to Jesus, the scribe conceded that all the punctilious requirements of piety count for nothing in the face of the two commandments. In Luke the lawyer knows the answer, and Jesus promises him that the two commandments will bring life; the negative implication, I take it, is that neglect of these two commandments will inescapably bring death. In Matthew, Jesus concludes his response by affirming:

---

2. "Jesus Call Us," lyrics by Cecil Frances Alexander, in *Glory to God: The Presbyterian Hymnal* (Louisville: Westminster John Knox, 2013), #720.

On these two commandments hang all the law and the prophets. (Matt 22:40)

The "law and prophets" refers to the Torah of Moses (law) and the prophetic corpus, that is, in sum the "canonical" tradition of Judaism. To say it all "hangs" on these two commandments evokes the interpretive verdict of Paul, who, it turns out, is not so fixed on grace that he cannot notice the commandments:

For the whole law [Torah] is summed up in a single commandment, "You shall love your neighbor as yourself". . . . Bear one another's burdens, and in this way you will fulfill the law of Christ." (Gal 5:14, 6:2)

Paul seems indeed to reduce the two great commandments to one, but for Paul the first is surely implied and assumed in the second. Thus, I propose that a preacher who seeks to be a pedagogue about the "cost" might spend energy expositing the two great commandments that together constitute the mark of difference for those who have been called to discipleship. Such an exposition can avoid simplistic reductions and over time can fully articulate the riskiness of an alternative life in gospel faith. Over time this would also entail a recovery of baptism as a serious world-changing sacrament.[3]

II

The first great commandment, love of God, is quoted in the gospel from Deuteronomy 6:5. This gives the preacher an opportunity to help the congregation rediscover (or discover for the first time) Deuteronomy. It may also be that the preacher will discover Deuteronomy for the first time. Clearly, for almost all church people Deuteronomy is part of an undifferentiated mass of old stuff easily dismissed. But "back to basics" surely requires that the preacher must spend time in Deuteronomy, because that book is the dynamic center of covenantal theology that was actively on the horizon of Jesus and the early church.

A beginning point is to discern the dynamic tradition that Deuteronomy practices and embodies. The book is clearly rooted in the old Mosaic memory and so is presented as the teaching of Moses. The work of Moses in this belated text is to rearticulate the covenant for a new time, place, and circumstance, namely, life in the land of promise. Thus,

---

3. See R. Alan Streett, *Caesar and the Sacrament: Baptism, a Rite of Resistance* (Eugene, OR: Wipf & Stock, 2018). Streett proposes that in quite explicit ways baptism in the early church imitated imperial practice and served as an alternative to the imperial rite that it imitated.

at the outset Moses is said to "expound" this Torah (1:5). That is, Moses exposited the old memory of Sinai and by expounding he gave fresh articulation and extended the rule of God into spheres of life that were not in purview at Sinai.

In 5:3, moreover, Moses declares:

> Not with our ancestors did the LORD make this covenant, but with us, who are all of us here alive today.

Moses indicates that the dynamism of the covenant requires ongoing imaginative interpretation that precludes any package of fundamentalism or the certitudes of "originalism." Deuteronomy is exactly such imaginative interpretation that transposes the covenant for a context of royal power and a predatory political economy, perhaps in the eighth century BCE.

The core mandate of the covenant is exactly "love of God":

> You shall love the LORD your God with all your heart, and with all your soul, and with all your might. (6:5)

But then Moses, in Deuteronomy, proceeds to show at great length that "love" means obedience to the commandments (chapters 12–25). This extended corpus of commands discloses the character and will of the God whom we are to love fully, without reservation, by our intentional, disciplined acts. That is, love is a *praxis*, action informed by the normative narrative of covenant to which we have sworn allegiance.

Our "love of God" reflects, is responsive to, and corresponds to the character of this God who is disclosed here, and Christians say more fully in Jesus of Nazareth. For starters we may identify three marks of this covenantal God that are to inform our obedience:

1. The God of covenant is a *forgiving* God who "restores the fortunes" after God's people have been wayward and recalcitrant (Deut 30:3; for use of the same phrase, see Jer 29:14; 30:3; 33:7, 11, 26). In response, God's people are to be a forgiving people. This is evident in what is the core command of Deuteronomy, "the year of release" in Deuteronomy 15:1–18. It is provided that debts should be canceled, most particularly the debts of poor people, every seven years. This commandment shows that "forgiveness" is elementally an economic process that concerns the forgiveness of debts. Thus, in one version of the Lord's Prayer we pray that our debts may be forgiven. God does not want anyone to be permanently in hock. God does not want there to be a permanent underclass

in hopeless debt; God intends that our economy should be subordinated to and in the service of covenantal neighborliness.

This mandate of forgiveness is voiced (then and now) in a debt-propelled economy in which the "haves" depend upon the cheap labor of the "have-nots" and keep the "have-nots" permanently in debt so that they can be devoured by interest rates (see Deut 23:19–20). It is clear that Moses encountered resistance to this radical act of forgiveness, for he declares that God's people should not be "hard-hearted or tight-fisted" when it comes to forgiveness of debts (15:7). The antithesis of forgiveness is *bookkeeping* or scorekeeping in which careful records are kept (at least in memory) so that we know who owes whom, who has offended whom, and who must "make payment," whether monetary or relational.[4] This bookkeeping mentality allows no slippage for human need or vulnerability but requires full, unadjusted paying up. Thus, the poor must "earn food stamps," immigrants must "qualify," and those who default end with eviction, deportation, or imprisonment.[5] Covenant people are to act differently as an act of love of God, not only in face-to-face dealings but in policy formation, so that a forgiving community and a debt-canceling economy are acts of "love of God."

2. The God of covenant is *a God of hospitality* who welcomes into the community and into the political economy those who are inconvenient. This is the God who

> executes justice for the orphan and the widow, and who loves the strangers, providing them food and clothing. (Deut 10:18)

Imagine God making provision for food and clothing for those outside "the tribe"! That provision, moreover, is said to be an "execution of justice," so that the needs of orphan, widow, and immigrant are not charity but a just right. From this it promptly follows that the covenant people are to act as YHWH acts:

> You shall love the stranger, for you were strangers in the land of Egypt. (Deut 10:19)

The faithful are to replicate the hospitable action of God. As a result, the commandments of Deuteronomy are preoccupied with practical hospitality toward the vulnerable (the poor, widows, orphans, immigrants), who by their presence are "entitled" to economic viability (Deut

---

4. I am grateful to Peter Block, who suggested to me the term "bookkeeping" as an antithesis to forgiveness.

5. See Matthew Desmond, *Evicted: Poverty and Profit in the American City* (New York: Crown, 2016).

24:10–15, 17–22). The resources of the community are to be distributed not on the basis of power but on the basis of presence and need.

This act of mandated hospitality toward the vulnerable is contrasted with the condescension of "charity."[6] Charity, which so many people and so many congregations embrace, is not a serious recognition of the legitimate claims of the needy but only a gesture of patronage by the "haves" out of their surplus that can be done without cost or much inconvenience. Moses clearly has in mind covenantal hospitality that is committed to justice and not to condescending patronage. Thus, the commandments make provision for the protection and performance of the "right" of the vulnerable, which goes well beyond charity.

3. The God of covenant is a *God of generosity:*

> The LORD your God will make you abundantly prosperous in all your undertakings, in the fruit of your body, in the fruit of your livestock, and in the fruit of your soil. For the LORD will again take delight in prospering you. (Deut 30:9)

The sermonic rhetoric of Moses functions to remind the covenant people that all that they have is a gift of God's goodness:

> When the LORD your God has brought you into the land that he swore to your ancestors, to Abraham, to Isaac, and to Jacob, to give you—a land with fine, large cities that you did not build, houses filled with all sorts of goods that you did not fill, hewn cisterns that you did not hew, vineyards and olive groves that you did not plant. (6:10–11)

> When you have eaten your fill and have built fine houses and live in them, and when your herds and flocks have multiplied, and your silver and gold is multiplied, and all that you have is multiplied. . . . Do not say to yourself, "My power and the might of my own hand have gotten me this wealth." But remember the LORD your God, for it is he who gives you power to get wealth. (8:12–13, 17–18)

Imagining that one is self-made and self-sufficient can lead to cynical parsimony: The money is mine; I don't owe anything to anyone." The propensity in our predatory economy to deny generosity toward the vulnerable is a function of the illusion of self-sufficiency, in which the awareness of the "neighbor" disappears from consciousness. We then enjoy a torrent of self-congratulatory, self-preoccupied greed that regards the needy neighbor as a threat, not entitled to any generosity.

---

6. I am grateful to John McKnight, who suggested to me the term "charity" as an antithesis to hospitality.

The impetus for generosity, in the rhetoric of Moses, is found in the awareness that God is the creator who gives all good gifts. ("We give thee but thine own.") These gifts are to be shared generously as the creator has been generous.

The tradition of Deuteronomy incessantly warns about "other gods" who are precluded by the first commandment of Sinai, "No other gods" (Exod 20:3–6, Deut 5:6–10). In Deuteronomy the "other gods" are ciphers for all who oppose the covenant God of forgiveness, hospitality, and generosity. The cipher "Canaanite" signifies a social practice that reduces all relations to monetary transactions and reduces all neighbors to commodities. Thus, the "religion of Baal" comes with the socioeconomic practices of *bookkeeping* (not forgiveness), *charity* (not hospitality), and *parsimony* (not generosity). The religious symbols of Baal are to be destroyed because they are icons of the commoditization of human relationships and thus the denial of neighborly attentiveness (Deut 7:5).

It requires no imagination at all to see that our own contemporary monetization of social relationships (concerning health care, tax policy, bank deregulation) serves to enhance the powerful with endless expansion of economic resources at the expense of the vulnerable who are without resources. Such monetization of social reality permits and authorizes the endless predatory exploitation of the vulnerable other. In the midst of that economy where we now live, to "love God" is a mighty alternative to the idols, an act that intends to interrupt such practice and policy.

> Jesus calls us from the worship of the vain world's golden store,
> from each idol that would keep us, saying, *Christian, love me more.*"
> In our joys and in our sorrows, days of toil and hours of ease,
> still he calls, in cares and pleasures, *"Christian, love me more than these."*[7]

Thus, the Torah of Deuteronomy, a first guideline on how to "love God," is a "glimpse of a new order that is the kingdom of God."[8] The "kingdom of God" is not a never-never land of "life after death" as we so easily conclude when we reduce faith to "spiritual" matters to the neglect of the material. It is rather an alternative practice of social relationships that correspond to the social practices of the covenantal God. I propose that a "back to the basics" approach invites the preacher to exposit "love of God." It is unnecessary and unhelpful for the preacher to take sides or speak about the great theoretical codes of capitalism, socialism,

7. "Jesus Call Us," in *Glory to God*, #720.
8. Patrick D. Miller, *Israelite Religion and Biblical Theology: Collected Essays*, Journal for the Study of the Old Testament: Supplement Series 267 (Sheffield: Sheffield Academic, 2000), 502.

and so on, for those dogmas constitute a distraction from the first great commandment to love God without reservation. There is more to be said about the first great commandment than is offered in Deuteronomy. That book, nevertheless, is a poignant place from which to begin. Since the scroll remains unopened in much of the church, this may be a fresh pedagogical moment in which the preacher can replicate Ezra:

> So they read from the book, from the Torah of God, with interpretation. They gave sense, so that the people understood the reading. (Neh 8:8)

III

The second great commandment, love of neighbor, is quoted in the gospels from Leviticus 19:18.[9] As was the case with Deuteronomy, this gives the preacher a chance to help the congregation rediscover (or discover for the first time) Leviticus. It may also be, again, that the preacher will discover it for the first time. Clearly, for almost all church people Leviticus is part of an undifferentiated and disregarded mass of old stuff readily dismissed. The only exception is that we may pick out a few preferred verses from the book, for example, Leviticus 18 with which to flail gays. But "back to basics" surely means that the preacher must spend time in Leviticus because it is a launching pad for an ongoing disputatious reflection on the holiness of God's people, a question that was actively on the horizon of Jesus. Thus, his dispute in Mark 7:1–23 on "what goes in" and "what comes out" as defiling is all about holiness. When we recite the creed, moreover, we affirm the "one, *holy*, catholic, and apostolic church," surely without excessive reflection on holiness.

The teaching point for the preacher is that God's people (all of the baptized community) are called to holiness that corresponds to the holiness of God:

> You shall be holy for I the LORD your God am holy. (Lev 19:2)

The verses that immediately follow allude to the commandments on honoring mother and father, keeping Sabbath, and refusing idols and images (vv. 3–4). We may assume that the remainder of the Decalogue is also implied in the statement, so that "holiness" comes to mean keeping Torah.

Leviticus constitutes a long reflection on the form that holiness may take for the people of God; clearly the book reflects an ongoing dispute

---

9. See Lenn Evan Goodman, *Love Thy Neighbor as Thyself* (Oxford: Oxford University Press, 2008).

among the priests about the nature of holiness, a discussion and dispute that continue among us. I suggest that one important question about holiness concerns one's posture toward "the other." There is ample evidence in Leviticus that holiness requires careful avoidance of the *other* because the other will defile and contaminate. Thus, holiness runs in the direction of cleanness and purity.[10] As is readily recognized, Leviticus 19 is peculiarly and strategically positioned between chapters 18 and 20, which are preoccupied with prohibited "distorted" sexual relationships. And even in chapter 19 we encounter worry about possible dangerous "mixing":

> You shall not let your animals breed with a different kind; you shall not sow your field with two kinds of seed; nor shall you put on a garment made of two different materials. (Lev 19:19)[11]

From this fear of "mixing" it is an easy step to fear of human "mixing." Thus, later on, in the interest of maintaining a "holy tribe," Ezra is warned about the danger that "the holy seed (semen) has been mixed" (Ezra 9:2). Such a concern is surely an anticipation of modern fears about "mixed races." And, while all of that seems old fashioned in an embarrassing way, Bill Bishop, in his book *The Big Sort* has chronicled the way in which "red" and "blue" people are self-selecting to like-minded communities of work, housing, and worship; conservatives and liberals currently want to live in communities of pure ideology . . . echoes of the holiness agenda of Ezra![12]

It is clear in Leviticus 19, however, that there is a counterpoint of holiness that purposes a very different way with "the other." I suggest that we might perceive in the holiness tradition a continuing escalation and expansion of positive engagement with the other, an engagement that anticipates the judgment of Emmanuel Levinas that the "face of the other" is where we meet the truth of our lives.[13]

1. The commandment of 19:18, quoted in the gospels, alludes to *love of self* along with love of neighbor. There is no doubt that the covenantal

---

10. See Richard Beck, *Unclean: Meditations on Purity, Hospitality, and Mortality* (Eugene, OR: Cascade Books, 2011).

11. Mary Douglas has established a major thesis that impurity and profanation in the old holiness codes was constituted by having things out of place, in the wrong place, or mixed with other things inappropriately (*Purity and Danger: An Analysis of Concept of Pollution and Taboo* [1966; repr., New York: Routledge, 2005]).

12. Bill Bishop, *The Big Sort: Why the Clustering of Like-Minded America Is Tearing Us Apart* (Boston: Mariner Books, 2009).

13. Emmanuel Levinas, *Totality and Infinity: An Essay on Exteriority* (Pittsburgh: Duquesne University Press, 1969).

tradition advocates a healthy self-respect, a self-respect that is reflected and voiced in the lament psalms, which freely state before God the legitimate claims of the self.[14] Such a healthy sense of self, which is indispensable for generative love of neighbor, is very different from the narcissistic self-indulgence of so much of our selfie culture. Healthy self-regard as a component of holiness does not need always to advertise and exhibit the self. Such exhibits are not necessary when the self is healthy.

2. But of course the commandment of 19:18 is occupied with the neighbor: *Love neighbor* as much as self! "Neighbor," in the tradition, means fellow members of the covenant community, all its members who are distinguished from "foreigners who are not neighbors." But of course the tradition and most especially Jesus keeps the question open: "Who is my neighbor?" and continues to expand the zone of neighborliness. But even before that zone is greatly expanded, this trajectory of interpretation envisions a neighborhood for the common good in which the self is not free to keep from the neighborhood what is required for viability. Thus:

> With justice you shall judge your neighbor. (Lev 19:15)

Holiness is characterized as justice for the neighbor, a practice that assures viable sustenance for all the neighbors! The same accent, moreover, is clear in the tenth commandment, which sounds the word *neighbor* three times in its prohibition of acquisitiveness:

> You shall not covet your *neighbor*'s house; you shall not covet your *neighbor*'s wife, or male or female slave or ox or donkey, or anything that belongs to your *neighbor*. (Exod 20:17)

And in our much-cited verse 18, love of neighbor is a counter to vengeance or grudge, thus affirming the legitimacy of the neighbor. It is, moreover, remarkable that this accent on neighbor is situated exactly in the holiness tradition. Thus, engagement with the neighbor is a way to "take time to be holy." This teaching surely witnesses against the holiness trajectory of purity and cleanness that accents disengagement from the neighbor who may contaminate.

3. This vision of love of neighbor is pushed further in our chapter with attentiveness to the *poor neighbor:*

---

14. See Nicholas Wolterstorff, *Justice in Love*, Emory University Studies in Law and Religion (Grand Rapids: Eerdmans, 2011), 94–97, on "Is Self-love Legitimate?"

> You shall not strip your vineyard bare, or gather the fallen grapes of your
> vineyard; you shall leave them for the poor and the alien: I am the Lord your
> God. (19:10)

The poor have a special claim on the community, which has obligation
to provide an adequate safety net that precludes all "laws of enclosure."
Indeed, care for the poor is seen in the tradition to be an equivalent to
knowledge of God:

> He [the king] judged the cause of the poor and needy;
> Then it was well.
> Is this not to know me, says the LORD. (Jer 22:16)

The wisdom tradition, moreover, sees the special linkage of the poor to
God:

> Those who oppress the poor insult their Maker;
> But those who are kind to the needy honor him. (Prov 14:31)

It is an easy step from here to the instruction of Jesus:

> Just as you did it to one of the least of these who are members of my family,
> you did it to me. (Matt 25:40)

4. While the "poor" are noticed and supported by the community, the
text reaches further toward "the other" with reference to *the immigrant
(alien).*[15] The immigrant is named along with the poor in verse 10. But
more important is this:

> The alien who resides with you shall be to you as a citizen among you; you
> shall love the alien as yourself, for you were aliens in the land of Egypt: I am
> the LORD your God. (Lev 19:34)

The phrasing is exactly the same as in verse 18: "neighbor as yourself,"
"immigrant as yourself"!

Verse 34 is quite remarkable. Holiness means embrace of the other
who is not a member of "our tribe." Though the holiness tradition of
Leviticus does not go further, we notice in Deuteronomy that along
with the immigrant come *the widow and the orphan,* so that we may take

---

15. On the "stranger," see Frank Spina, "Israelites as *gērîm,* 'Sojourners,' in Social and Historical Context," in *The Word of the Lord Shall Go Forth: Essays in Honor of David Noel Freedman
in Celebration of His Sixtieth Birthday,* ed. Carol L. Meyers and M. O'Connor, Special Volume Series, American Schools of Oriental Research 1 (Winona Lake, IN: Eisenbrauns, 1983),
321–35.

this triad of the vulnerable as the ultimate agenda of holiness. Holiness has to do, in this trajectory, with restorative practices toward the vulnerable who have been diminished by the hard-hearted, tight-fisted practices of predation.

5. To be sure, this tradition in the Hebrew Bible does not go as far as "love your *enemy*," an extension of Torah that was voiced by Jesus.

> But I say to you, Love your enemies and pray for those who persecute you, so that you may be children of your Father in heaven. (Matt 5:44)

It is worth noting that this paragraph of instruction by Jesus ends in this way:

> Be perfect, therefore, as your heavenly Father is perfect. (v. 48)

This is a recasting of Leviticus 19:2. Jesus links *love of enemy* to *the imperative to be holy!* Thus, we may see that this mapping of the other imagines an always extended, always expanding zone of neighborliness that constitutes holiness: *self . . . neighbor . . . poor . . . immigrant (widow and orphan) . . . enemy!* In his assault on the punctilious piety of the "scribes and Pharisees," moreover, Jesus attests that the weightier matters of the Torah (that is, the practice of holiness) consist not in scrupulous tithing but in "justice, mercy, and faith" (Matt 23:23). Jesus continues to up-end the holiness tradition, an impulse already activated in Leviticus 19.

The preacher may reflect on the "task of othering" that belongs to holiness and may acknowledge the vigorous contestation in which folks (all of us!) are engaged: the other as neighbor or the other as threat. I commend *The Clash Within*, in which Martha Nussbaum considers the way in which each of us hosts a "clash within" concerning the *welcome* of the other and *fear* of the other.[16] That "clash," suggests Nussbaum, is inescapable. What matters is how we manage it; it will be managed in more healthy ways when it is named and processed in honest ways. The matter of the *other* remains unsettled for each of us; for that reason the issue compels attention from the preacher. The covenantal tradition, even in Leviticus, has a dynamic notion of "othering," and there is no more urgent issue now before our society with its propensity to exclusionary fear and tribal anxiety. There is more to be said about "love of neighbor" than Leviticus 19. But this is a teachable place in which to begin.

---

16. Martha Nussbaum, *The Clash Within: Democracy, Religious Violence, and India's Future* (Cambridge: Belknap Press of Harvard University, 2008).

IV

"Back to basics" means, I suggest, articulating and processing the profound either/or of our baptisms, an either/or as old as Moses, as urgent as Jesus, and as contemporary among us as the recognition of our monetized political economy. I have found most helpful the either/or of Paul's articulation of "the desires of the flesh" and "the fruit of the spirit." I am deeply informed by the discussion of Brigitte Kahl, who understands Paul's discussion of "the law" in Galatians as a challenge to the Roman Empire (and even, I extrapolate, as a challenge to the US "law of money and sex").[17] That is, the "law" that preoccupies Paul is not the Torah of Judaism but the rule and expectation of the empire. The empire of Rome had its requirements and expectations for making it big in the empire; the requirement was readiness to participate in a predatory political economy. That dominant value system, everywhere imposed, specialized in "the desires of the flesh," which consisted in mean-spirited self-promotion and uncaring self-indulgence. The empire functioned to generate appetites that could be satisfied only by antineighborly action. Paul offers an inventory of behaviors that arise from the embrace of such appetites:

> Now the works of the flesh are obvious: fornication, impurity, licentiousness, idolatry, sorcery, enmities, strife, jealousy, anger, quarrels, dissensions, factions, envy, drunkenness, and carousing, and things like these. (Gal 5:19–21)

It will require some careful pedagogy to let people see that "the desires of the flesh" are not simply drugs, alcohol, and sex but are practices of antineighborliness that put the satiation of the self at the center of reality. Paul's awareness is that one cannot subscribe to the values of the predatory economy of sex and money and not have these social outcomes.

The baptismal alternative is to refuse participation in that dominant value system (a refusal enacted by Daniel in Daniel 1) in order to practice an alternative of covenantal neighborliness toward the neighbor, the poor, the immigrant, and the enemy. Neighborliness requires a refusal of the militarized consumerism that is justified by US exceptionalism,

---

17. Brigitte Kahl, *Galatians Re-Imagined: Reading with the Eyes of the Vanquished*, Paul in Critical Contexts (Minneapolis: Fortress Press, 2010).

even as Rome knew itself to be "exceptional."[18] Opting for neighborliness (love of neighbor) yields the fruit of the spirit:

> The fruit of the Spirit is love, joy, peace, patience, kindness, generosity, faithfulness, gentleness, and self-control. There is no law against such things. (Gal 5:22–23)

As Paul knew, one cannot have that "fruit" while participating in the dominant "law" of the empire.

It is the work of the preacher to connect the dots. Our participation in the dominant system is so "normal" that we do not notice. As a result our life is caught up in endless TV ads, mostly concerning new cars and more drugs that will kill us. It is assumed among us that more consumer goods will make us happy. It is assumed that more aggressive militarism will make us safe. It is assumed that more soccer practices will make us more ready for college applications. It is assumed that more spectator sports will give us companionship. It is assumed that anger toward Muslims is appropriate and can be unrestrained. All of these assumptions are sponsored by the empire and are regarded as "normal." It is assumed that it is okay to treat "the other" as a commodity or as an object without merit who qualifies for no respect, compassion, or justice. It is remarkable that Paul frames his catalogues of "desires of the flesh" and "fruit of the spirit" by these two remarkable neighbor assertions that I have cited above:

> For the whole Torah is summed up in a single commandment: "You shall love your neighbor as yourself. . . . Bear one another's burdens, and in this way you will fulfill the law of Christ. (Gal 5:14, 6:2)

Kahl concludes:

> Apart from the works of imperial law, these faith works of love for Paul are indispensable, an insight that has been obscured by the abstract Protestant antithesis of faith versus works. Love of neighbor as yourself as the complete fulfillment of Torah (5:14) and the "new" law of Christ (5:6; 6:2) does not abandon Jewish law as such but rather the competitive and combative hierarchy of self and other that is at the core of Roman imperial *nomos*.[19]

---

18. Robert Paarlberg has shown the way in which US exceptionalism lies behind the national epidemic of obesity (*The United States of Excess: Gluttony and the Dark Side of American Exceptionalism* [Oxford: Oxford University Press, 2015]).

19. Kahl, *Galatians Re-Imagined*, 271–72.

It is the *nomos* of the US empire that is on offer as the alternative to the two great commandments. That alternative, as we are now seeing so unmistakably, is lethal and makes a functioning humane community impossible.

This is a "back to basics" and on three counts. First, these slices of tradition and these elemental texts (Deuteronomy, Leviticus) are not known or available in the church, surely not in the lectionary. Second, the dots are not connected in the dominant narrative of the empire, and the empire has a great stake in making sure that they remain unconnected. Third, the two great commandments, with their enormous public implications, are themselves pre-political. They are in themselves accessible and without immense grand theory or ideology. They are "on the ground" elemental spin-offs of affirming that we are "sealed as Christ's own forever."

The task of the preacher, I propose, is to connect us to these old mandates of the tradition and to connect the dots from there to contemporary social reality and to the contemporary attitudes, actions, and policies that arise from these connections. To do this urgent pedagogy, I think, will require preachers to do textual study in more attentive ways and to read more widely concerning "the empire of force" that so compels us.[20] I am aware that preachers do not have time for all of this. I wonder if the urgency of our context where God has put us requires an intentional shifting of priorities for the preacher to consider what the people of God now most require for living out our baptisms in faithful ways. "Back to basics" arises as an urgent task from the awareness that the truth entrusted to us contradicts the dominant narrative of imperial exceptionalism.

20. See James Boyd White, *Living Speech: Resisting the Empire of Force* (Princeton: Princeton University Press, 2006).

Appendixes: Futures in Biblical Studies

Appendix A: Prophetic Studies

This chapter was originally published as "Futures in Prophetic Studies," in The Oxford Handbook of the Prophets, *ed. Carolyn J. Sharp (New York: Oxford University Press, 2016), 655–65.*

Of course no one knows about the future of study of the prophets, but two things seem clear. First, we are likely to be surprised by new emerging methods and perspectives, new critical judgments, and new interpretive extrapolations. Second, we are sure to continue rich diversity in method, perspective, critical judgment, and interpretive extrapolation. More than surprise and diversity we cannot know.

I

No doubt scholars will continue the well-worn paths of study. On the one hand, critical work will continue, both to ponder (and construct) historical settings of "original" utterance/writing, and to consider the processes for arrival at the "final form of the text." We will continue to observe close source analysis and dissection, largely a German enterprise, and we will likely see "final form" drawn later and later.

On the other hand, interpretive focus on the "canonical" "final form" of the text will continue to trace the large thematic coherences of prophetic literature, thematic coherence deftly articulated by Ronald Clements:

> This message concerned the destruction and restoration of Israel, but special emphasis was attached to the latter. This was because this restoration was still looked for in the future, while the destruction was believed to have already taken place. The prophets therefore were felt to have foretold the future, but in certain very broad categories. . . . [D]istinctive patterns have

been imposed on the prophetic collections of the canon so that warnings of doom and disaster are always followed by promises of hope and restoration. . . . The various preserved prophecies of a whole series of inspired individuals acquired an overarching thematic unity. This centered on the death and rebirth of Israel, interpreted theologically as acts of divine judgment and salvation.[1]

I find this approach most helpful but am also aware that this approach is at times tempted to be reductionist in the interest of more dogmatic commitments. Both of these approaches—critical and canonical—will continue to energize our common work.

Beyond these staples of the discipline, newer ways of reading—feminist, postcolonial, reception history—will claim more and more of our attention. As more interpretive voices from outside the old hegemonic establishment gain a hearing, we will increasingly notice that the prophetic texts are not objects to be analyzed but lively voices that continue to engage in compelling contemporary ways.

II

I take this opportunity, however, to focus on my own interests in research, for likely most of us anticipate such futures in scholarship in terms of what we ourselves might hope to do. Since I have been at this task so long, I think it is not necessary that I should do so covertly. My interest and expectation for future study of the prophets are much more in an interpretive or hermeneutical direction, although I am attentive to and informed by more critical work. I will identify four facets of such interpretive work that are attempts to take seriously methods and perspectives that move in an interpretive direction beyond critical preoccupations. Texts that are as durable and generative (and "classic") as these continue to evoke interpretation that will run risks for the sake of a faithful contemporary reading.[2]

1. *Rhetorical criticism*, the signature term of my teacher, James Muilenburg, is an attempt to take seriously the actual articulation of the text with all of its subtlety, ambiguity, and cunning.[3] One of the problems

---

1. Ronald E. Clements, "Patterns in the Prophetic Canon," in *Canon and Authority: Essays in Old Testament Religion and Theology*, ed. George W. Coats and Burke O. Long (Philadelphia: Fortress Press, 1977), 42–55 (45, 49, 53).

2. On the "classic" in Christian horizon, see David Tracy, *The Analogical Imagination: Christian Theology and the Culture of Pluralism* (New York: Crossroad, 1981).

3. See Phyllis Trible, *Rhetorical Criticism: Context, Method, and the Book of Jonah* (Minneapolis: Fortress Press, 1994).

with much critical and canonical work is that in the end there is not much attention to or interest in what the text actually voices. I anticipate that attention to rhetorical specificity of the prophetic texts will continue to be generative for us. It is crucial that most of the prophetic corpus is expressed in poetry that posits an open-ended imagination not governed by any settled epistemology. Poetic idiom insists on elusiveness that matches both the surprise of quotidian reality and the inscrutability of "surplus" in the midst of that lived reality. Thus Seamus Heaney could say:

> The poet is on the side of undeceiving the world. It means being vigilant in the public realm. But you can go further still and say that poetry tries to help you be a truer, purer, wholer being.[4]

Mutatis mutandis, prophetic poetry is a summons to ancient Israel to be a "wholer" people in the context of the reality of YHWH's purpose and will. It was said of Heaney at his death about his own poetry that he was "anxious that his lyrical gift not cushion hard truth."[5] So it is with these ancient prophets who speak in such a lyric of hard truth that served to undeceive, both about denial and about despair. Such an accent on rhetoric requires great attentiveness to image and metaphor, on which see, for example, the now dated but still exemplary essay of Muilenburg on the images of "adversity."[6] Attentiveness to such playful, elusive matters pushes us to go beneath the flat work of historical criticism and the larger thematizing of canonical approaches.

More than that, the rhetoric serves the anticipatory capacity to envision a world other than the taken-for-granted world that is in front of us. If we take the destruction of Jerusalem in 587 BCE as a pivot point in prophetic literature, then we may say that pre-587, the taken-for-granted world was that of the royal-priestly establishment of the city with its mantras of chosenness, and post-587, the taken-for-granted world was variously an imperial power that imagined itself to be ultimate and beyond answering to anyone for anything (see Isa 47:7–10). The "undeceiving" of prophetic discourse insisted on a world that these hegemonic centers of power, both pre-587 and post-587, had erased from awareness. The poetry, through all kinds of astonishing and affron-

---

4. Quoted in Margalit Fox, "He Wove Irish Strife and Soil into Silken Verse," *New York Times,* August 31, 2013, B12.

5. Francis X. Clines, "Seamus Heaney, Poet of 'the Silent Things,'" *New York Times,* August 31, 2013, A14.

6. James Muilenburg, "The Terminology of Adversity in Jeremiah," in *Translating and Understanding the Old Testament,* ed. Harry Thomas Frank and William L. Reed (Nashville: Abingdon, 1970), 42–63.

tive imagery, refuses such erasure and insists on this other world that is before, behind, and beneath the conjured world of hegemonic power. Such a mode of discourse is inherently subversive, as it voices a sub-version of reality that refuses the dominant version. So much is inchoate in the "rhetorical criticism" of Muilenburg, a continuing project of subversion in our interpretive work.

2. The capacity to take seriously such a subversive alternative to settled taken-for-granted public reality requires a move beyond a critical mode to what Paul Ricoeur has termed a *"post-critical" perspective*.[7] By and large, critical scholarship, generated in the eighteenth to nineteenth centuries as a rejoinder to rigid orthodoxy, is contained within the permits of Enlightenment rationality wherein the character of YHWH who dominates prophetic poetry is viewed variously as a "paper God" or as simply a new inclination in "religious history." Enlightenment rationality could not seriously entertain such a God as attested by the prophets, a real character or a lively agent.

Of course not! But it is Ricoeur's "second naiveté" that knows that and yet can in good faith consider the voicing of such a character and such a world that comes with YHWH as a lively option to be considered.[8] Thus, I anticipate that postcritical work, outside the regime of conventional criticism, might entertain this lively character without whom the prophetic literature loses most of its seriousness.

The form critics of course have taught us that prophetic discourse, before and after 587, is largely constituted by speeches of judgment and promissory possibilities, both genres of which bear the voice and come with the authority of YHWH.[9] The utterance of such speeches of judgment amounts to an insistence that there are *nontransgressable limits* to human conduct and to public policy. The utterance of *promissory possibility* attests that there are, in the human process, ongoing *originary stirrings of fidelity* against circumstance, no matter what. Both such *nontransgressable limits* and such ongoing *originary stirrings of fidelity* against circumstance no matter what depend upon the utterance and sanctions of YHWH as given in prophetic discourse. Our common critical bent is to ask if such claims concerning the shape of lived history might be said

7. Paul Ricoeur, *The Symbolism of Evil* (Boston: Beacon Press, 1967), 352, and many other places in his writings.

8. Ricoeur, *Symbolism of Evil*, 352; and see Mark I. Wallace, *The Second Naiveté: Barth, Ricoeur, and the New Yale Theology*, Studies in American Biblical Hermeneutics 6 (Macon, GA: Mercer University Press, 1990).

9. See Claus Westermann, *Basic Forms of Prophetic Speech* (Philadelphia: Westminster, 1967; repr., Louisville: Westminster John Knox, 1991); and Westermann, *Prophetic Oracles of Salvation in the Old Testament* (Louisville: Westminster John Knox, 1991).

otherwise without the "supernatural" claim of a character and agent. To the question, we may honestly answer that of course it could be said differently, as, for example, in much sapiential articulation. But the fact is that the prophets characteristically do not say it otherwise; they say it this way with appeal precisely to such a character and agent. As a result, we must ask, what is lost if the agent who utters is explained away, or what is gained if the character who speaks is taken seriously? Like every good poet, these poets had no accidental words. They no doubt utilized the rhetoric of character and agent with great intentionality. The effect of such intentionality—in considering these two prophetic dominant genres—is that both nontransgressable limit and originary stirrings of fidelity are grounded in a personal, passionate resolve that causes our conversation about the world to be one of unnerving contestations of fidelity and infidelity. Such a remarkable claim—to which we have grown much too accustomed—is an astonishing claim. Thus, I judge that the casting of lived reality in terms of contestation about fidelity depends upon such rhetoric that is a counter to the common reductionisms of technical reason and commodity transactions. Such postcritical insistence is acutely upstream in our critical world, which wants to honor the norms of rationality all around us, norms that preclude such agency. But then, I have no doubt that the ancient processes of utterance, transmission, and canonization required the same acute upstream quality. I suggest that our capacity for such upstream interpretation is a faithful counterpoint to that ancient work, as hazardous today as it was then (on which, see Amos 7:10–17, Jer 36:26, and Isa 50:6).

3. Appreciation of such rhetoric in a postcritical frame of reference moves in the direction of *postcolonial study*. The categories of "empire-colony" imply that interpretation in the colony continues to be done on the terms imposed by the empire. No doubt in that ancient world of Babylonian and/or Persian hegemony, moreover, that temptation was acute and often observed in order to accommodate the requirements of empire. At the same time, however, poetic idiom linked to the agency of YHWH permitted utterance and expectation that refused to be contained in imperial categories. *Mutatis mutandis*, if the interpretive community of church, synagogue, or guild is a colony with a distinctive perspective, we are able to see about ourselves that as a colony we tend to operate with the assumptions of empire. In our case, that means within the rationality of the Enlightenment that has morphed into market ideology that requires and limits certain modes of expression that serve certain horizons of public possibility. Postcolonial interpretation, against such an imposed or assumed inclination, at least may entertain the chance

that reality can be voiced and lived outside of or over against dominant expectations. Thus, it is not an accident that playful attempts at the contemporaneity of prophetic utterance do not normally arise in the tenured guild but arise among the socioeconomic-political outliers who are not inured to guild rationality or to imperial requirement. It is exactly such an outlier perspective that permits and evokes fresh readings that let us see and hear afresh what is at stake in prophetic utterance.

But, of course, such risky alternative to imperial requirement evokes all kinds of necessary accommodations that may arise from actual threat or intimidation. Thus, we are to see the prophets engaged in endless contestation in which there are various voicings of alternative and voicings of accommodation. The reason for that, obviously, is that a stance of emancipated possibility is not a settled state; it is rather a restive impulse that waxes and wanes. Such ebb and flow, moreover, is discernible not only in ancient texts but in our own interpretive work as well. The articulation of a counterworld that refuses the requirements of empire is endlessly contested and results in an uneasy ambiguity.

Thus, I imagine that the ancient voices—and perhaps our own contemporary interpretation—may be not unlike the risks of peasant work that James C. Scott has discerned in his several studies.[10] Resistance to dominant power by relatively powerless people with few "weapons" is a delicate process of caution, vigilance, and risk-taking, but not risks that are too hazardous. I can imagine that in the face of the Jerusalem establishment, or later in the face of imperial power, prophetic figures variously ran risks, sometimes more boldly than at other times. And I can imagine that we, situated as we are in "colonies" with distinct identities, variously may run interpretive risks, sometimes more boldly than at other times. The nature of these poetic voicings and the nature of dominant context require that our reading be in some way engaged in the contestation that is mapped out in these texts.

4. It is clear that *reception history* will gain increasing traction in our work in time to come. Reception history is the awareness that meanings in texts are not all given by the text but arise "on the other end" in the act of reading or hearing the text. Against an assumption that a text has one "original" meaning in one "original" context, reception history is the recognition that we "receive texts" with great imagination, propelled by the insistences of our own context in which we receive. The emergence of reception history as a method (if it is a method) is a resolve to accept

10. James C. Scott, *Weapons of the Weak: Everyday Forms of Peasant Resistance* (New Haven: Yale University Press, 1985); and Scott, *Domination and the Arts of Resistance: Hidden Transcripts* (New Haven: Yale University Press, 1990).

such imaginative reception not as a mistake but as a serious, legitimate enterprise to be appreciated as a pivot point of the process of engaging an ancient text that claims authorization beyond our reason.[11]

From the perspective of historical criticism, reception history is in principle out of bounds. To be sure, much reception history is quite quixotic; some of it is grotesque, especially interpretation that makes easy and direct connections between the ancient utterance and contemporary events. But the practice should not be judged by its most objectionable examples. Clearly, much of what we now call "reception history" was often a serious attempt at theological exposition and interpretation done in good faith. The old mantra that "God has yet more light to break forth from his word" and the contemporary mantra of my church, The United Church of Christ, that "God is still speaking" indicate a readiness to move beyond what might be identified as "original" meaning.[12] The possible legitimacy of such reception, moreover, is made even more compelling when we recognize that a good deal of so-called objective interpretation has been in fact a disguised form of reception history. Beyond that, I cannot think of a study of the prophetic literature that does not contain within it some tacit act of "reception," that is, meaning found "on the other end." For all of these reasons, I believe that urgent interpretive questions are the following: How shall we practice reception history ourselves in our own emerging social context? How shall we be trustworthy receivers? I pose the questions with four reference points:

a. How shall we receive prophetic texts in a closed world of scientism that is exemplified by the most notorious of the so-called "new atheists"? The potent combination of technical reason and the reduction of all of life to commodity that can be measured and managed makes the question of "reception" an urgent one. Our conventional criticism has been ready to accommodate prophetic literature to that dominant ideology, or at best to take snippets of "justice" (as in Amos 5:24) without considering the systemic issues of a dominant narrative that is increasingly a narra-

---

11. Since first writing this essay, a welcome and important book on the theory of reception history has been published by Brennan W. Breed, *Nomadic Text: A Theory of Biblical Reception History*, Indiana Series in Biblical Literature (Bloomington: Indiana University Press, 2014).

12. The formula comes from a sermon of John Robinson in 1620 when the Puritans set out to the New World. He affirmed that more of light and truth yet could be given in and through Scripture. See Edward Winslow's account of the sermon in *Hypocrisie Unmasked: A True Relation of the Proceedings of the Governor and Company of the Massachusetts against Samuel Gorton of Rhode Island*, a 1916 reprint of the 1646 original in the Library of Congress.

tive of death.[13] I suggest that Robert Jenson has it about right when he concludes:

> We must summon the audacity to say that modernity's scientific/metaphysical metanarrative . . . is not the encompassing story within which all other accounts of reality must establish their places, or be discredited by failing to find one.[14]

His reference point is Darwin, but from Darwin it is an easy move to connect his critique more generally to the social context of dominant culture. The dominant narrative of Western capitalism, expressed as scientism and commoditization, is not an adequate narrative for the long-term sustenance of a viable public life. The prophetic literature, like much else in the Bible, counters that dominant narrative with a narrative of neighborly justice and a theocentric focus that centers on the holiness of God. Thus, justice against injustice and holiness against profanation become life-or-death issues. Our "reception" of this literature puts a very different agenda before us about public policy and social relationships.

b. How shall we receive prophetic texts in a world of military globalism wherein the combination of military and economic power carries all before it? That combination of power, moreover, is increasingly in the hands of a privileged, protected oligarchy that cares hardly at all about the common good or about the crisis of the environment. Its hubris has been eloquently expressed by Francis Fukuyama, even though Fukuyama himself has happily forsworn the arguments of his well-known book *The End of History and the Last Man*.[15] In that context, we are met in prophetic literature with narrative, song, and oracle, peculiar utterances that have behind them no coercive power, either military or economic. The capacity of this collage of utterances, moreover, is the enactment of "sign," a primitive performance of elusive reality that impinges upon the settled arrangements of power. We may ponder how it is that the performance of sign in that ancient world was taken seriously, either in the entitled world of Jerusalem or later in the midst of arrogant imperial power. But that is what we have been given . . . signs in the context of originary utterance:

---

13. The verse from Amos is engraved at the Martin Luther King Memorial in Montgomery, Alabama. It is likely that most who visit the memorial have little understanding of the narrative world of Amos or the socioeconomic crisis to which his words refer.

14. Robert W. Jenson, *Canon and Creed*, Interpretation (Louisville: Westminster John Knox, 2010), 120.

15. Francis Fukuyama, *The End of History and the Last Man* (New York: Free Press, 1992).

- So Amos can report visions of curses and finally an end (Amos 8:1–3)

- So Isaiah can refuse Ahaz's defiance and issue a sign, a time-clock carried by a "virgin" (Isa 7:10–17)

- So Jeremiah can command a rock into the river to anticipate the fall of mighty Babylon (Jer 51:63–64)

The signs are not in a vacuum. They live and bear meaning only in a world of holy resolve that is not at the behest of violent power. The sign, issued in a variety of contexts, runs toward "the sacramental," always constituted by concrete contextual performance that defies settled regimes and refuses settled power arrangements. Historical criticism has been ready to explain or explain away such signs; but we have evidence in our own time of the helplessness of worldly power in the face of such signs. That wonder runs all the way from the Eucharist in Pinochet's Chile to Nelson Mandéla at a rugby match.[16] Each time we read such texts and imagine their performance, we are invited to a critique of sign-vacant power and to an alternative that allows for transformation that is not available in conventional settlements.

c. How shall we receive prophetic literature in a society of denial? The old dominant ideology of chosenness in Jerusalem insisted upon proclaiming false peace:

From the least to the greatest of them,
everyone is greedy for unjust gain;
and from prophet to priest,
everyone deals falsely.
They have treated the wound of my people carelessly,
saying, "Peace, peace,"
when there is no peace. (Jer 6:13–14; see 8:10–11)

Hananiah is a parade example of how old conviction had morphed into an ideology that permitted denial (Jeremiah 28). The denial is, first of all, a denial concerning social reality; but that denial is matched by a dismissal of YHWH as agent and character:

---

16. On the Eucharist as transformative act and sign in Chile under Augusto Pinochet, see William T. Cavanaugh, *Torture and Eucharist: Theology, Politics, and the Body of Christ* (Oxford: Blackwell, 1998). As the first black president of South Africa, Nelson Mandela went to a 1995 rugby match between the South Africa Springboks and the New Zealand All Blacks for the Rugby World Cup. Mandela wore a Springboks team shirt and cap, performing presidential identification with what was, in that context, primarily a White Afrikaner team. It was a majestic gesture and a magical, transformative moment for South Africa.

> . . . those who say in their hearts,
> "The Lord will not do good,
> nor will he do harm." (Zeph 1:12; see Jer 5:12)

And now we live in a US society of denial in which "pretend" is the hallmark of dominant ideology. Thus, it is readily claimed that more weaponry makes safe. We eagerly trust that the economy will recover and all will soon be well. We think short-term about "natural resources" and refuse to consider the long-term savaging of creation. In the face of such pretend, comes this ancient poetic truth telling:

- Against military security:

> But you refused and said,
> "No! We will flee upon horses"—
> Therefore you shall flee!
> And, "We will ride upon swift steeds"—
> Therefore your pursuers shall be swift!
> A thousand shall flee at the threat of one,
> at the threat of five you shall flee
> until you are left like a flagstaff upon the top of a mountain,
> like a signal on a hill. (Isa 30:15–17)

- Against easy economic recovery:

> Like a cage full of birds,
> their houses are full of treachery;
> therefore they have become great and rich,
> they have grown fat and sleek.
> They know no limits in deeds of wickedness;
> they do not judge with justice
> the cause of the orphan, to make it prosper,
> and they do not defend the rights of the needy.
> Shall I not punish them for these things? says the Lord,
> and shall I not bring retribution on such a nation such as this? (Jer 5:27–29)

The poem ends with a double question. No reader can doubt the intended answer.

- Against environmental indifference:

> I looked on the earth, and lo, it was waste and void;
> and to the heavens, and they had no light.
> I looked on the mountains, and lo, they were quaking,

and all the hills moved to and fro.
I looked, and lo, there was no one at all,
and all the birds of the air had fled.
I looked, and lo, the fruitful land was a desert,
and all its cities were laid in ruins.
before the Lord, before his fierce anger. (Jer 4:23–26)

In the face of such mendacity, the poetry erupts. It erupts because of deep impassioned conviction. It erupts, so the prophets say with their formula, "Thus saith the Lord," because there is a holy resolve that is dissatisfied. It may even erupt among us, because we receive it, whatever our notion of "revelation" might be, as a word that will not be disregarded. We say "not disregarded" because it is heard as compellingly offensive in contemporary vacuums of entitlement. It is offensive because it will not make peace with "pretend."

d. How shall we receive prophetic literature in a hand-wringing society of despair that reaches the conclusion that nothing can be done? We are, in our society, very close to such a conclusion when we are honest. The problems are too big and complex, the political will is too weak, ergo the future is lean indeed. Our mood will shortly be not unlike the near despair of exiled Israel:

My way is hidden from the Lord,
And my right is disregarded by my God. (Isa 40:27)

The Lord has forsaken me,
my Lord has forgotten me. (Isa 49:14)

Our bones are dried up, and our hope is lost;
we are cut off completely. (Ezek 37:11)

And then, in a burst of poetry, there is a counter:

The days are coming . . .
In that day . . .

In that day . . . restoration! In that day, shalom! The days of disarmament (Isa 2:2–4)! The days of renewed social relationships (Jer 33:10–11)! We have among us no more thick utterance of hopeful possibility in the face of despair than that of Martin Luther King Jr., "I have a dream." In his utterance, King reiterated the prophetic refusal to accept despair, precisely because of originary stirrings of fidelity about which he had no doubt.

Now, of course, this reading of reception history comes close to "preaching." It is not, however, preaching in any way that we usually understand preaching, nothing here of coercion, authoritarianism, closure, moral scolding, or dogmatism. This reception is rather a note of elusive expectation that lets ancient words touch present social reality. And when that word touches a new context, there is transformative potential.

III

I suggest that all of these methodological options that move beyond historical criticism will be major accents in the future study of the prophetic corpus. It is a happy prospect, in my judgment, that many younger scholars no longer assent to "the wall of separation" between critical study and theological exposition with an edge of contemporaneity, a wall that is the legacy of Enlightenment rationality. That "wall of separation" was an acutely "modern" notion, reflective of the valuing of "objective" possibility. Whatever else one may make of the term *postmodern*, this is certainly "post" to the old assumptions of objectivity that are no longer on the horizon. All of these practices that I have enumerated—rhetorical, postcritical, postcolonial, reception history—require the interpreter to be dialogically engaged diligently with a text that is "still speaking." It is in the nature of the canonical process that the ancient texts have been produced, shaped, and transmitted for subsequent use. These several methods are, in my judgment, faithfully in sync with canonical intentionality.[17] The prophetic corpus is shaped for reperformance and interpretation, so that future study, to some extent moving beyond the recovery of "original meaning," will perforce include some decisive measure of contemporaneity in the task of exposition. I believe, beyond that, that our social, cultural context of crisis evokes and requires, as an ethical matter, such engagement as an available elusive antidote to our current lethal preoccupation. Testimony in the prophetic corpus is shaped canonically for long-term retelling. It is testimony that always and everywhere disrupts what had been thought to be settled.

17. See J. A. Sanders, "Adaptable for Life: The Nature and Function of Canon," in *Magnalia Dei, The Mighty Acts of God: Essays on the Bible and Archaeology in Memory of G. Ernest Wright*, ed. Frank Moore Cross, Werner E. Lemke, and Patrick D. Miller Jr. (Garden City, NY: Doubleday, 1976), 531–60.

Appendix B: Biblical Theology: Testimony vs. Totalism

This chapter was originally published as "Testimony that Breaks the Silence of Totalism," Interpretation: A Journal of Bible and Theology 70 (2016): 275–87.

In my book *Theology of the Old Testament*, I organized my study around the rubric of "testimony."[1] I appealed to the rubric of testimony and the metaphor of litigation to suggest two matters: first, such testimony is originary; it evokes reality that is not available unless uttered. This is my attempt to make a case for a nonfoundational approach to biblical theology that need not adhere to the dominant forms of rationality in society. Second, such testimony is endlessly contested, so that our own practice of interpretation is participation in that ongoing contestation.

Implied in my appeal to such a practice of testimony and such an image of litigation is the claim that YHWH, the subject of Israel's testimony, is presented (a) as an originary character who cannot be "explained," no matter how much we work at a "history of religion," and (b) as both agent and subject of contestation as the testimony of Israel attempts to articulate this character who defies every easy articulation. Thus, I proposed that the work of testimony is originary as a compelling match to the subject of the testimony, YHWH. It is, it follows, an ongoing challenge in biblical theology to articulate this originary character, so that the character of YHWH and our utterance of that character are not domesticated by a rationality that in fact contradicts the character attested in the text.

---

1. Walter Brueggemann, *Theology of the Old Testament: Testimony, Dispute, Advocacy* (Minneapolis: Fortress Press, 1997).

I

I had not seen so clearly, when I pursued the rubric of testimony as a use for biblical theology, that "testimony" is a match for "totalism." By "totalism" I mean a social-political, economic, cultural, theological enterprise that is all-encompassing, that monopolizes both technology and imagination, and that will allow no voice that contradicts the claims and power of the totalism. The best rendition of such totalism known to me is that of Robert Lifton, who has studied recent forms of totalism and who enumerates the "deadly sins" of such enterprises that concern "milieu control" and "mystical imagination."[2] A more philosophical approach to the same issue is offered in the defining study of Emmanuel Levinas, *Totality and Infinity*.[3] By "totality" Levinas means a completely self-contained arrangement of reality that resists the open-endedness of "infinity."

In the ancient world of the Bible, totalism took the form of empire that occupied territory, taxed its subjects, relied on great liturgically enacted myths, and insisted on compliance in a way that precluded local tradition and local freedom. Thus, in the Old Testament we get a series of empires—the paradigmatic account of Pharaoh and the historical sequence of Assyrian, Babylonian, and Persian rule, culminating in Hellenistic imperial culture and finally the severe power of Rome.[4]

Mutatis Mutandis, contemporary interpretation of the Bible lives and works amid a totalism that controls both the technologies of power and the limits of imagination, so that nothing is imaginable outside the control and administration of the political economic oligarchy that goes under the banner of "market ideology," which in the United States is linked to the broad claims of patriotic exceptionalism accompanied by immense military force. The visible expression of this totalism is the huge concentration of wealth in the hands of a few; the measure of the effectiveness of that totalism is that it is nearly impossible, even for communities of religious passion and resolve, to imagine anything outside the control of the totalism. Such market ideology is not to be confused with the actual market, but now has become a "principle for regulating

2. Robert Jay Lifton, *Witness to an Extreme Century: A Memoir* (New York: Free Press, 2011), 67–68, 381.
3. Emmanuel Levinas, *Totality and Infinity: An Essay on Exteriority* (Pittsburgh: Duquesne University Press, 1969).
4. See Richard A. Horsley, ed., *In the Shadow of Empire: Reclaiming the Bible as a History of Faithful Resistance* (Louisville: Westminster John Knox, 2008).

social relations."[5] A triumphant market ideology schematizes all social relationships:

> Schematically three categories of people result from such forced development. First, a small class of ultra-rich who can accumulate much wealth while spending ostentatiously. Second, a varying number of people in an intermediate position. They represent the middle classes, those who balance production and consumption. Finally, there are the poor, excluded from the sharing of wealth, and preoccupied by problems of mere survival.[6]

The economic outcome of such social relationships is this:

> Development tends to produce shortages for a great number of people as the condition of excess for a small minority.[7]

This political-economic monopoly is ordered by Enlightenment rationality. The consequence of such an arrangement is described by Enrique Dussel in this way:

> Modernity must be understood to include its peripheral alterity. Modernity would then encompass all of the following: (1) Its hegemonic core; (2) the *dominated* peripheral colonial world, as part of the "world system"; and (3) the sectors of the world that have been *excluded* from this system, as its exteriority.[8]

Such totalism, ancient or contemporary, has such force that its impact is characteristically to silence views to the contrary.[9] In the Old Testament I suggest that the paradigmatic narrative of such silencing is the confrontation of the prophet Amos with the priest at Bethel. The political regime of Israel (the Northern Kingdom) finds the voice of Amos unbearable and so issues a verdict of silence:

> O seer, go, flee away to the land of Judah, earn your bread there, and prophesy there; but never again prophesy at Bethel, for it is the king's sanctuary, and it is a temple of the kingdom. (Amos 7:12–13)

5. Gerald Berthoud, "Market," in *The Development Dictionary: A Guide to Knowledge as Power*, ed. Wolfgang Sachs, 2nd ed. (New York: Zed Books, 2010), 79.

6. Berthoud, "Market," 87.

7. Berthoud, "Market, 87. See also the concept of "market fundamentalism" in Naomi Oreskes and Erik M. Conway, *The Collapse of Western Civilization: A View from the Future* (New York: Columbia University Press, 2014), 37.

8. Enrique Dussel, *Ethics of Liberation in the Age of Globalization and Exclusion*, Latin America Otherwise: Languages, Empires, Nations (Durham, NC: Duke University Press, 2013), 46.

9. For a compelling exposé of silence imposed from above, see Sue Curry Jansen, *Censorship: The Knot That Binds Power and Knowledge* (Oxford: Oxford University Press, 1991).

The priest who represents the regime understood quite well that control of religious discourse and the central sanctuary is intimately linked to the control of political-economic possibilities. For that reason, silencing the prophet left the religious symbols beyond critique in the hands of the regime.

When we consider the interface of *interpretation* and *silence*, we may entertain an awareness that the rise of "historical criticism" in the eighteenth and nineteenth centuries, perhaps designed to thwart religious scholasticism and fundamentalism, served to conform interpretation to the requirements of dominant rationality. That is, historical criticism, with its effective capacity to "explain away" so much in the text, left the text more-or-less amenable to dominant rationality, thus a form of silencing. One may notice, moreover, that much so-called "progressive Christianity" lives comfortably with the canons of Enlightenment rationality and is ready to explain away or disregard what does not fit. Such an interpretive strategy in the end constitutes a willingness to be silenced by the force of the rationality of the dominant regime. It is characteristically evident that such conformity assures that the radical imperatives of the textual tradition are safely toned down.

II

It is my thought, then, that "testimony" has a capacity to break the silence that is imposed by the totalizing regime. Thus, I propose that the paradigm of "totalism-testimony" is a useful way to think about the future of biblical theology, because it is likely that the silencing capacity of our current totalism will become only more aggressive and comprehensive. The silence cannot be broken by staying safely within the confines of the totalism but requires speech "from elsewhere" that in the textual tradition is grounded in the character and purpose of YHWH, thus, "Thus saith the LORD."[10] It is useful to mention what Dussel makes of the notion of "counterdiscourse." While there may be counterdiscourse right within European modernity (so Bartolomé de Las Casas), Dussel is right to insist that such counterdiscourse is dependent upon voices of the other from outside the European system:

> Bartolomé de Las Casas would not have been able to formulate and articulate his critique of the Spanish conquest of the Americas if he had not himself lived in the periphery and heard the cries and witnessed the tortures to

10. See Walter Brueggemann, "Silence Broken from 'Elsewhere'" (paper presented at the Annual Meeting of the Society of Biblical Literature, San Diego, California, November 22, 2014).

which indigenous people were being submitted. It is that Other who is the actual origin of this counterdiscourse that took root in Europe.[11]

Dussel insists, then, that a study of thought,

> in Latin America, Asia, and Africa is not a task that is anecdotal or parallel to the study of philosophy *as such* (which would be that which is European in character) but instead involves the *recovery* of a history that incorporates the counterdiscourse that is nonhegemonic and that has been dominated, silenced, forgotten, and virtually excluded—that which constitutes the alterity of Modernity.[12]

It is my thought that testimony, in ancient Israel and in the early church, constituted such counterdiscourse that spoke out against the several totalisms that dominated the ancient map.[13] It is my conviction that the comprehensive power of market totalism calls for an either/or, even if it may be strategically in the form of dialogue. That either/or is put most boldly by Robert Jenson:

> We must summon the audacity to say that modernity's scientific/metaphysical metanarrative . . . is not the encompassing story within which all other accounts of reality must establish their places, or be discredited by failing to find one. . . . As pop scientists urge over and over, the tale told by Scripture and creed finds no comfortable place within modernity's metanarrative. It is time for the church simply to reply: this is certainly the case, and the reason it is the case is that the tale told by Scripture is too comprehensive to find a place within so drastically curtailed a version of the facts. Indeed, the gospel story cannot fit within *any* other would-be metanarrative because it itself is the only true metanarrative—or it is altogether false.[14]

Thus, the testimony of Scripture—and the derivative testimony of theological interpretation—cannot be confined in the critical categories of modern Enlightenment rationality, because such containment silences the One to whom testimony is made. Such testimony thus must refuse to dwell in the narrative of the market, and must see that the counterdiscourse in fact attests a counternarrative that is unacceptable to the dominant rationality and to dominant forms of political-economic power that

---

11. Dussel, *Ethics of Liberation*, 45.

12. Dussel, *Ethics of Liberation*, 46.

13. Dussel proposes that such counterdiscourse from the periphery is an "essential co-constitutive dialogue" (*Ethics of Liberation*, 45).

14. Robert W. Jenson, *Canon and Creed*, Interpretation (Louisville: Westminster John Knox, 2010), 120.

depend upon that rationality. It is an appeal to an alternative metanarrative that it takes—with Jenson—as "the only true metanarrative."

Current attention to "trauma theory" may be important for the grounding of testimony outside totalism. Trauma theory makes clear that acute pain and loss evoke truth-telling in the face of silencing. Most helpful in this regard is the rereading of the book of Jeremiah by Kathleen O'Connor according to trauma theory. O'Connor sees the cluster of realities that lie behind the testimony of the book of Jeremiah:

> Haunting memories, broken language, benumbed souls, and impenetrable grief compounded by the collapse of faith—these common effects of disaster and trauma coalesce into heavy burdens that victims can carry for decades and even for generations.[15]

The most remarkable reality in O'Connor's acute study is that in this environment of unbearable wound, with the destruction of language, language was rediscovered. It was given: "Thus saith the Lord." It is speech given beyond the aegis of the regime, beyond the cadences of the liturgy, and beyond the permit of the Torah. In oracle and in narrative, YHWH, said to be the source of the disaster, is called back into play, is called to account, but is also counted on for healing, restoration, and possibility. O'Connor has shown how the testimony of the book of Jeremiah refuses all of the old certitudes and, by image, metaphor, narrative, and daring poetic expression, brings YHWH back to speech and back into play in the lost world of Jerusalem.

The acute insight of O'Connor concerning this uncompromising text has been given programmatic articulation by David Carr, who proposes that the biblical literature has emerged within and in response to a series of traumatic events.[16] If Carr is correct that testimony arises in trauma, then it should not surprise that the speech of trauma comes from outside the totalism and bears witness to a Reality that the totalism is unable to contain, even as it is unable to silence the witnesses to that Reality.

III

One possible future for biblical theology is to take seriously, contend with, and extend the speech of testimony that is propelled by pain to tell the truth that contests the totalizing regimes that generate the pain.

15. Kathleen M. O'Connor, *Jeremiah: Pain and Promise* (Minneapolis: Fortress Press, 2011), 26–27.

16. David M. Carr, *Holy Resilience: The Bible's Traumatic Origins* (New Haven: Yale University Press, 2014).

1. The changed map of guild membership and guild methods gives reason to expect that this work of testimony vis-à-vis totalism is likely to be a durable and generative enterprise. Thus, many interpretive voices sound outside the old Western hegemony that agreed, either knowingly or unwittingly, to conform to totalizing rationality. On the one hand, the various liberation trajectories of interpretation—feminist, queer, and postcolonial among them—no longer accept the canons of the old hegemony and its old methods. On the other hand, the influence of Mikhail Bakhtin's philosophy of language and literary theory represents new possibilities.[17] Bakhtin's attentiveness to multivoiced possibility and dialogic interaction within the text gives the lie to any single, settled meaning. The ideology of the market, like any totalizing regime, cannot tolerate such dynamic pluralism because it specializes in certitude and control. The restless openness of newer methods by interpreters grounded in less-regulated interpretive methods means a refusal to let the text settle in one meaning.

2. There is no doubt that the Western church has been largely co-opted by Enlightenment rationality and the demands of market ideology. The theological result of such co-optation has been either fundamentalism that reduces God to formula or progressivism that yields such an anemic God that there can be no lively witness to bear. In the hands of such churches, the God of the gospel has withdrawn to safe familial life and has retreated from the public domain, that is, has been rendered innocuous.

But of course the church in its fidelity is otherwise. For that reason, biblical theology that is done in the service of the church is attentive to testimony that takes issue with totalism. There is a reason that much of the great growth of the church in venues outside Western hegemony is marked as "Pentecostal." Faithful Pentecostalism is led by the Spirit, who refuses to be contained in any form of totalism, thus with a capacity to bring otherwise to speech and action and to generate zones of freedom that make human life possible. It is my hunch that, as the totalism of market ideology grows more ominous, it will fall to the church, even in the modern West, to find voice to bear witness to the opposition.

3. The church may bear witness, as did ancient Israel and the early church, to the character of the God who in sovereign freedom accepts no accommodation to totalism, who is an embarrassment to Enlightenment rationality. This is a God who breaks the silence of the regime. Thus, at

17. On the importance of Bakhtin, see Barbara Green, *Mikhail Bakhtin and Biblical Scholarship: An Introduction*, Semeia Studies 38 (Atlanta: Society of Biblical Literature, 2000).

the outset of Israel's testimony, in its paradigmatic narrative, the God of Israel speaks:

Let my people go. (Exod 9:1)

The phrase is an imperative addressed to Pharaoh. Pharaoh is not accustomed to being addressed at all, and certainly not in an imperative. That imperative, to be sure, is finally performed by human agents. Moses and Aaron do the heavy lifting. They do so, however, only after and because of the holy authorization from elsewhere, to break open the totalism.

At the end of Israel's canonical testimony, the God of Israel confronts the law of the Medes and the Persians. The great mark of that law is that it cannot be changed, violated, or circumvented (Dan 6:8). It is an absolute as that regime attests. Every totalizing regime claims that it is an absolute beyond change!

The issue is joined, however, between Daniel, a quintessential Jew, who is committed to another law, the Torah of Moses. The contest is law versus law. The Torah of God, however, is vouched for by a God who is an agent of change. Thus:

Blessed be the name of God from age to age,
for wisdom and power are his.
He changes times and seasons,
deposes kings and sets up kings;
he gives wisdom to the wise
and knowledge to those who have understanding. (Dan 2:20–21)

This capacity for change guarantees that the absolutism of Nebuchadnezzar cannot be sustained. The advocates of the law of the Medes and the Persians continue to insist:

Now, O king, establish the interdict and sign the document, so that it cannot be changed, according to the law of the Medes and the Persians, which cannot be revoked. (Dan 6:8; see vv. 12, 15, 17)

The narrative, however, testifies to otherwise. In the end, even Nebuchadnezzar is glad for the change wrought by YHWH. Even this master of the totalism glimpses, on occasion, a better reality. And so he sings, in defiance of his own absolute interest:

For he is the living God, enduring forever.
His kingdom shall never be destroyed,
And his dominion has no end. (Dan 6:26–27)

Between the paradigmatic narrative of the exodus at the outset of testimony and the narrative testimony to the God who can change in Daniel, there was a long contestation about the relevance of YHWH to actual life in the world. There were detractors:

> They have spoken falsely of the LORD,
> and have said, "He will do nothing.
> No evil will come on us,
> and we shall not see sword or famine." (Jer 5:12; cf. Zeph 1:12)

This verdict might be the mantra of human hubris or the sorry chant of human despair. Either way, the alleged speakers do not deny the existence of YHWH; they deny only the capacity of YHWH to make a difference. They imagine a God who has finally conformed to the totalism, for good or for evil. That tradition knows well about the gods of the regime who are without active potential (Ps 115:4–7). The gods are as passive and irrelevant as the regime could require them to be. The truth-telling voice of the text knows even more, that the gods of irrelevance are a narcotic: those who worship them become passive conformists like them (115:8)!

But of course Israel refuses the totalism of a managed earth and a silenced heaven. In contrast to the idols who are given full mocking characterization, the God of Israel receives only one verse:

> Our God is in the heavens;
> He does whatever he pleases. (115:3)

But that one verse is enough; God is elsewhere (in heaven), not on earth to be administered by the dominant regime. This God, moreover, acts in complete freedom, doing what is pleasing to God. No need to conform, no rule to obey, no limit to honor, no overlords to appease! The lyric doxological affirmation of verse 3 concerns a God who can say, "Let my people go," and deliver, and who can change the unchangeable laws of the Medes and the Persians, a living God capable of wonders. This God, via the poet, will break the imposed silence:

> For a long time I have held my peace,
> I have kept still and restrained myself;
> Now I will cry out like a woman in labor.
> I will gasp and pant. (Isa 42:14)

The poetic witness has YHWH admit that the imperial silencing by Babylon has been accepted too long. Now that silence is dramatically broken. It is broken by fresh imagery. It is broken by the God attested in imagery that nullifies the virile control of Babylon. It is broken by the gentle God who will gather the lambs (40:11). It is broken like a mother with generative freedom to birth newness in the face of a regime that wanted no newness. The silence is broken by the gasping panting God filled with resolve and passion and originary possibility. This new divine initiative escapes the administration of the totalizing regime. Now this birthing-mothering God acts in defiance.[18] The series of first-person verbs that follow makes clear that the totalizing regime has been unable to rob this God of power and agency. Before this birthing God finishes, in verse 17 the gods of the empire, the gods of absolute and perpetual control, are shamed in their impotence. They cannot stop new life from emerging in their very midst.

IV

Two concessions concerning that argument are to be faced. First, I am aware that Jack Miles and Richard Friedman have made a compelling argument that in the later parts of the Old Testament the agency of God fades away, and we are left with human agency. Friedman begins his book in this way:

> God disappears in the Bible. . . . The Bible begins, as nearly everybody knows, with a world in which God is actively and visibly involved, but it does not end that way. Gradually through the course of the Hebrew Bible . . . the deity appears less and less to humans, speaks less and less. Miracles, angels, and all other signs of divine presence become rare and finally cease.[19]

He concludes:

> With over two hundred years still left to the story, there are no more fires from the sky, no more miracles, public or personal, no more angels, seen or unseen, no more cloud and glory, no more "and Yahweh said to X." The only remaining visible channel to God is the Temple, housing the ark in Jerusalem, and it is destroyed by the Babylonians in fire.[20]

His conclusions lead him into a reflection on the modern formulation of the death of God, à la Friedrich Nietzsche and Fyodor Dostoevsky.

18. The God who speaks defiantly in these verses is surely a companion in the company of Shiphrah and Puah (Exod 1:15–22).

19. Richard Elliott Friedman, The Hidden Face of God (San Francisco: HarperSanFrancisco, 1995), 7.

20. Friedman, Hidden Face of God, 25.

Jack Miles, in a thicker presentation, reaches a similar conclusion:

> At length, the Israelites took charge of their own lives. Eloh and Yah were still honored, but their home was understood to be in heaven now; little was expected of them on earth. . . . Annually, a religious drama was celebrated recalling the epic of Israel and the gods.[21]

God has withdrawn as a visible, palpable agent in the world. This conclusion does not lead Miles, like Friedman, to the modern question of "Death of God." It leads him, rather, back to the ancient Greek tragedies, to a God who is

> trapped within its contradictions. . . . He cannot escape. He is trapped as Hamlet is trapped—in himself.[22]

In his final assertion, Miles offers a trace beyond tragedy:

> That God is the divided original whose divided image we remain. His is the restless breathing we still hear in our sleep.[23]

Both of these acute readings of the text mount an immense challenge to any straightforward notion of testimony amid totalism, for there would seem in such a conclusion not much left to say by way of testimony. With a God dead (Friedman) or trapped (Miles), totalism would seem to prevail.

The text itself, however, does not readily give in to such a modernist surrender to totalism of a tragic kind. The reality is that the *immediacy* of God has been lost, and we are left with *mediation*. Miles himself acknowledges this:

> If the Tanakh were tragedy, God having learned the truth about himself through his relationship with mankind, above all his relationship with Job, would end in despair. But the Tanakh is not tragedy, and the Lord God does not end in despair. . . . The Tanakh refuses tragedy and ends, as a result, in its own kind of muddle, but its protagonist ends alive not dead.[24]

The mediation is officially left to Torah and to temple.[25] But in fact the most compelling mediation is in narrative that refuses the imperial

---

21. Jack Miles, *God: A Biography* (New York: Knopf, 1995), 401.
22. Miles, *God: A Biography*, 408.
23. Miles, *God: A Biography*, 408.
24. Miles, *God: A Biography*, 404.
25. See Brueggemann, *Theology of the Old Testament*, 567–704.

reduction of memo.[26] Narrative, such as the stories of Ruth or Esther, leaves open the possibility of inexplicable newness that is performed by human agents but that hints regularly of another agency that is beyond the administration of any human agent, whether Ahasuerus or Nebuchadnezzar or Cyrus or even Boaz. There is a defiant emergence in such narratives that is not directly credited to YHWH but that would be trivialized without some such assignation. The theological word for that undercurrent of defiant emergence and inexplicable newness is "providence," the ability of the creator God to see-ahead (*pro-video*) and so to *pro-vide* what is needed for the Jews around Esther or Ruth the Moabite, mother-to-be of a leading Israelite.

Biblical interpretation is not surprised by the "disappearance" or hiddenness of God:

> What calls for chief mention here is that fact that the experience of God's hiddenness, just as the experience of his presence, is an integral part of Israelite faith. Both experiences derive from the nature of God himself. He is both hidden and present, both near and far away. This is precisely the dilemma which faith in God presents. It is not, however, a dilemma that undermines Israel's faith, though it does stretch it to its farthest dimensions.[27]

In Balentine's knowing hands, it is clear that the "disappearance" of God is not a belated "running out of steam" or "God losing interest" in the human and/or Israelite project. It rather belongs recurringly to the reality of life in the world. It is only our trepid tradition of interpretation that is surprised or troubled by that hiddenness.

It is clear that amid seasons of divine "disappearance" or hiddenness, Israel kept to its testimony. In oracle, song, and narrative it intends to mediate defiant emergence and inexplicable possibility. The old narratives could be indeed taken as a "hidden transcripts" that sustain peculiar identity in the face of totalism.[28] Such narratives attest defiant emergence and inexplicable possibility that continue to draw upon the old, more explicit claims for YHWH. They are, however, claims that cannot be said loudly in seasons of acute totalism. They are, however, kept at the ready for the time when the moment is right, when courage is mustered and freedom is performed. Thus it is, in my judgment, a mistake

---

26. See Walter Brueggemann, "Poems vs. Memos," in *Ice Axes for Frozen Seas: A Biblical Theology of Provocation*, ed. Davis Hankins (Waco, TX: Baylor University Press, 2014), 87–113.

27. Samuel E., Balentine, *The Hidden God: The Hiding of the Face of God in the Old Testament* (Oxford: Oxford University Press, 1983), 172.

28. See James C. Scott, *Domination and the Arts of Resistance: Hidden Transcripts* (New Haven: Yale University Press, 1990).

to imagine that we have a linear unilateral movement from the big public God to the hidden, disappearing God as Miles and Friedman propose. We have rather an ongoing two-track testimony, covert and overt, that surfaces or not, depending on the prospect for such testimony amid totalism. That prospect for testimony depends not only upon the opinions and permits of the empire but upon the nerve and courage of the testifying community. The witnessing community is not defeated by absence. The divine character is not nullified by disappearance. Miles's "restless breathing" is the same restless breathing that dismisses the adherents of totalism who are "no help" because they have no "restless breath" (Ps 146:3–4).

Second, it is clear that the testimony of Israel is not a consistent unilateral attestation to the emancipatory character of YHWH. We of course have ample evidence of testimony in the Old Testament that wants to resist and nullify such emancipatory efforts in an attempt to conform to and embrace the totalism that Israel knew so well. Time would fail to attend to all of the studies concerning patriarchal sexism, the propensity to violence, and exploitation in the name of YHWH, among many other concerns. Those careful studies in the church and in the stubborn insistence of the guild require us to see more honestly the totalizing propensity in the biblical texts, to see how YHWH is implicated in that textual propensity, and to see the inescapable contemporary spin-offs of that propensity. Given such analyses, the emancipatory trajectory of the testimony of Israel is often lost or submerged in such a critical awareness.

But then, such acknowledgment of totalism within the text and such readiness to conform to totalizing practices are simply evidence that the testimony of Israel (and of the interpretive trajectories) is inescapably contested and in dispute. We may notice one example of such contestation. In the narrative of the dedication of the temple, the totalizing quality of Solomon's pageant is on full display in the anthem of 1 Kings 8:12–13. That totalizing affirmation makes YHWH resident in and patron of the temple. That claim, however, is promptly challenged by alternative testimony. In 1 Kings 8:9 it is attested that the ark contained no such palpable deity but only the tablets of the Torah. More frontally, the pageantry of Solomon is immediately and deftly challenged in a doxological mode:

> But will God indeed dwell on the earth? Even heaven and highest heaven cannot contain you, much less this house that I have built? (1 Kgs 8:27)

This is not, as Friedman might suggest, witness to the disappearance of God into the heavens; it is rather a refusal of the king's totalism.

This example could be readily multiplied; however, it is enough to suggest that the testimony of Israel is endlessly contested, and interpreters of that testimony participate in that ongoing contestation. If this reading of "testimony amid totalism" is useful, then our interpretive work is to see when, how, and in what ways the textual tradition conforms to a totalizing propensity and when it concerns emergent defiance and inexplicable possibility that refuse totalism. Focus on this question means that biblical theology is indeed practical theology. I have no doubt that the overriding human question for us is how viable life (human life and the life of all creatures) is sustainable in the death-dealing totalism that we face. This is the recurring question in this textual tradition. One can see over time how the emancipatory text and its contestation can be preempted (often by Christians and now by some Jews) to serve legitimated brutalizing totalism. The text, however, is not defeated and totalism has not won, even in our own time, because the text is occupied by this emancipatory character who is the subject of both the testimony and our interpretation of the testimony.

V

It is not very difficult to carry this framing of "testimony amid totalism" into the New Testament. I can suggest three obvious cases for such a framing of New Testament interpretation.

1. The gospel texts are alert to the prospect of "persecution" and being called before "the authorities." The officials of the Roman Empire continue to perform the burdens of totalism.[29] In the "testimony" of Luke, the disciples may anticipate that their own faithful future will be a replication of the destiny of Jesus, who was called before the authorities, the masters of Roman totalism, who finally executed him:

> The arrests and persecution of the disciples will become occasions for them to give testimony. . . . The persecution of the disciples, however, does not exceed what Jesus himself experiences. He, too, is about to be arrested and brought before Pilate and Herod.[30]

---

29. See *Empire in the New Testament*, ed. Stanley E. Porter and Cynthia Long Westfall (Eugene, OR: Pickwick, 2011); and Douglas E. Oakman, *Jesus, Debt, and the Lord's Prayer: First Century Debt and Jesus' Intention* (Eugene, OR: Cascade Books, 2014).

30. R. Alan Culpepper, "The Gospel of Luke: Introduction, Commentary, and Reflections," in *The New Interpreter's Bible*, ed. Leander E. Keck (Nashville: Abingdon, 1995), 9:401.

The disciples will be called to account precisely because their testimony contradicts and becomes unbearable to the totalism of Rome (Luke 21:12–15).

2. In Acts, the apostles are regularly called into imperial courts to further explain and justify their testimony. Their preaching has been insistently about the resurrection of Jesus, the impact of which is to "turn the world upside down" (Acts 17:6). That is, testimony to Easter unsettles and challenges the settled hegemony of Rome:

> They are all acting contrary to the decrees of the emperor, saying that "there is another king named Jesus." (Acts 17:7)

The programmatic effect of the early church in Acts is to articulate and perform a way of life that subverts the life authorized by the totalism.

3. Brigitte Kahl's recent reinterpretation of Paul's Letter to the Galatians understands Paul's critique of "the law" as a reference to Roman law and thus a reference not to the Torah of Judaism but to the sum of Roman totalism.[31] In light of Kahl's argument, we can see that the gospel is an emancipation from "the yoke of slavery," a declaration that is hauntingly reminiscent of the emancipatory work of YHWH in the exodus. The apostle articulates a gospel yielding a life not defined by the empire. Second, Paul is fully aware that the force of totalism leads to destructive conduct that he labels "the desires of the flesh" (5:16; see vv. 19–21). Alternative to that is "the fruit of the Spirit" made possible for those who no longer participate in the fearful life of the empire (5:22–23). The deep either/or in Galatians, as Kahl demonstrates, is between coercive Roman law and the gospel of freedom, or between the "desires of the flesh" and the "fruit of the spirit." This either/or pertains to the life of the church and to the greater well-being of the common good (6:10).

It is entirely possible that I have overstated the case and have been too reductionist about the framing of "testimony amid totalism." I have no doubt that readers will sort that out and make their own judgments. I offer this framing of our interpretive work because I believe that the current claims of market ideology, managed by a greedy, indifferent oligarchy, are the defining social reality of our time. If subversion of and alternative to that totalism are at all possible, I have no doubt that it will be seeded by texts that feature an emancipatory character who authorizes an emancipated existence. My insistence is that biblical theology is not a fringe exercise in the work of the institutional church. It is, rather, an

31. Brigitte Kahl, *Galatians Re-Imagined: Reading with the Eyes of the Vanquished*, Paul in Critical Contexts (Minneapolis: Fortress Press, 2010).

exercise that concerns life or death. Those who engage in such biblical theology have an opportunity to participate in this great contestation. I am filled with hope that new methods and new voices that elude the Western hegemony will lead us in fresh directions that call into question every easy coming to terms with the present totalism.

Appendix C: Biblical Interpretation

An edited version of this chapter was published as "Multitudes of Moseses," The Christian Century 133, no. 21 (October 12, 2016).

We have ample evidence that interpretation of biblical texts is a tricky, problematic business. Here are three assumptions I make for what follows:

1. Every serious biblical reader participates willy-nilly, wittingly or unwittingly, in interpretation wherein new meanings are found in or imposed on the text. A biblical text is an open field of imagination that requires interpretation.

2. No serious reader of a biblical text does objective reading, because interpretation is a tilting, imposing process. The interpretation we perform on the text may be evoked by our context of reading, or it may be to support vested interest or ideological conviction that often remains unacknowledged.

3. Because the text is an open field of imagination, the text gives enormous permission for imaginative imposition. But because the text is a concrete bodily system of signs and images, the text also imposes limits on our tilt of interpretation. Not every reading of a text is permitted; some are refused by the text itself.

I

The trigger for my discussion that follows is a quite remarkable book by Theodore Ziolkowski, *Uses and Abuses of Moses: Literary Representations since the Enlightenment.*[1] Ziolkowski takes up the rich varied interpre-

---

1. Theodore Ziolkowski, *Uses and Abuses of Moses: Literary Representations since the Enlightenment* (Notre Dame, IN: University of Notre Dame Press, 2016).

tive legacy of the Moses tradition of the Old Testament in the modern period. He is primarily interested in renderings of Moses in art, music, and literature and finds evidence everywhere. He cites Heinrich Heine and George Eliot in the nineteenth century and observes that in the twentieth century writers such as Günter Grass, Graham Greene, William Faulkner, and Ignazio Silone returned "to the biblical pattern as the basis for fictional plots." Along the way Ziolkowski pauses for Nietzsche, Schoenberg, Herzl, and Rilke. He sees that in Jewish rendering Moses can be variously pro-Zionist or anti-Semitic. He connects to the muckraker Lincoln Steffens as well as Bruce Barton and the inevitable Cecil B. DeMille. Drawing close to our own time we get to Zora Neale Hurston. One is nearly overwhelmed by the mass of detail in this remarkable study. Ziolkowski has no great critical theory about this panoply of uses, and he does not reflect critically on when it is that use turn into abuse. He does, however, clearly recognize that some of these interpretations constitute abuses of the tradition. His detailed exposition of the many uses and abuses amounts to a "reader response" report.

In the end Ziolkowski observes that, even given "this biblical indeterminacy," there are three nonnegotiable "special traits" concerning Moses that have intrigued writers, namely, Moses as *leader and liberator* of his people, as *lawgiver*, and as *prophet*. These "traits," which dominate the narrative, exercise some restraint on interpretation. It is a restraint that is intrinsic to the text itself. In that regard Ziolkowski moves beyond a collection of reader responses to what is now termed "reception history," that is, the long-term account of various readings that in sum indicate what the text both means and does. The most important study of this method and perspective is by Brennan Breed, *Nomadic Text: A Theory of Biblical Reception History*.[2] Subsequent readers are called by this sum of interpretations to operate within such emerging parameters of meaning. While Ziolkowski's book is one-sided in its accent on reader response without proportionate attention to critical assessment, his account implies a great deal about the restraint present in the text itself.

Because Ziolkowski is primarily interested in interpretation through the arts, he does not give as much attention to the political uses of the Moses tradition. For this accent reference may be made to Bruce Feiler, *America's Prophet: Moses and the American Story*.[3] Feiler explores the con-

---

2. Brennan W. Breed, *Nomadic Text: A Theory of Biblical Reception History*, Indiana Series in Biblical Literature (Bloomington: Indiana University Press, 2014).

3. Bruce Feiler, *America's Prophet: Moses and the American Story* (New York: William Morrow, 2009).

tinuous appeal to the Moses tradition in the political discourse of the United States. He shows that since the beginning of European settlement in North America and the subsequent founding of the republic until now, attention to Moses has dominated political rhetoric. He concludes that Moses is a much more central figure in such discourse than is Jesus.

II

Ziolkowski presents texts *ad seriatim* without worry about either continuity or any attention to reading communities that support such "strong readings." That, however, is not the way in which most of us read Scripture. For the most part Scripture is read through membership in a reading community that accepts its own trajectory of reading as normative, even if not "objective." Membership in such a reading community depends upon and is nurtured by acceptance of certain habits, assumptions, methods, and outcomes. Such membership permits a reading community to accept these habits as normative and rightfully faithful to the text itself, even permitting the bootlegging of vested interest and ideology that mostly remains tacit.

In Christian tradition we can identify three such reading communities with different reading habits. (There are more than that. I do not doubt, moreover, that one could, *mutatis mutandis*, find the same varied habits in Jewish reading of the text.)

1. There is what I would term "creedal" reading, which assumes that the biblical text fits readily and easily with the normative confessions of the church. For example, the new series Brazos Theological Commentary on the Bible is written by theological scholars who do not linger over historical-critical matters.[4] In Old Testament study the most important advocate of such "canonical reading" has been Brevard Childs, though he himself did not go very far in that direction, checked as he was by his great critical learning.[5] Such a creedal reading, for example, places great accent on "the fall" in the Genesis narrative, a claim that historical-critical reading now regards with some question. Appeal to this reading is reinforced by the liturgies and lectionaries of the church, most especially in their ready "unproblematic" linkage of Jesus as Messiah to Old

4. See, for example, R. R. Reno, *Genesis*, Brazos Theological Commentary on the Bible (Grand Rapids: Brazos Press, 2010); and, Jason Byassee, *Psalms 101–150*, Brazos Theological Commentary on the Bible (Grand Rapids: Brazos Press, 2018).

5. On Childs's influential work, see *The Bible as Christian Scripture: The Work of Brevard S. Childs*, ed. Christopher R. Seitz and Kent Harold Richards, Biblical Scholarship in North America 25 (Atlanta: Society of Biblical Literature, 2013).

Testament texts. Childs's insistence on reading Isaiah 53 directly with reference to Jesus as the Suffering Servant exemplifies how such readings take Christian confessions as normative constraints beyond which they do not permit the text to go.[6]

2. We can identify a reading community and trajectory that were formulated amid the seventeenth-century scholasticism in Calvinism and Lutheranism that reduced theological claims in the Bible to formulaic certitude. In Lutheranism Martin Chemnitz and in Calvinism Francis Turretin moved in scholastic directions by employing methods of syllogistic reasoning that reduced to testable propositions Scripture's witness to gospel truth. This was and is an interpretive approach that contradicted the evangelical freedom that Luther and Calvin had enunciated and led to the conclusion that the Bible was without error, that is, infallible.

Faced with "modernism," this reading community at the turn of the twentieth century morphed, with a major assist from Princeton Seminary, into fundamentalism that reduced the meaning and intent of the text to a precise package of legitimated claims. In *The Authority and Interpretation of the Bible*, Jack Rogers and Donald McKim have shown how the major theological teachers at Princeton Seminary for a very long time distorted the evangelical witness of Calvin by rendering Calvin through the scholastic prism of Francis Turretin.[7] Because Princeton Seminary occupied such a formidable role in theological education, the influence of that misreading has been immense in the United States.

3. In response to the vigorous orthodoxy (of a scholastic kind) in the eighteenth century, a third habit of reading emerged with historical criticism, which wanted to resist absolutizing the text by situating each text "in context" so that it is located in time and place and not permitted a larger reach. The revolt against that powerful scholastic orthodoxy is commonly marked by the address of Johann Philipp Gabler, who dramatically proposed a "turn toward the historical" that signaled the deabsolutizing of the theological claims of the text. The work of historical criticism relativized everything in the text, including the God attested in the text, so that what we find in the text is a series of "religious construc-

---

6. Childs's more "creedal" reading is on exhibit in his study of the Suffering Servant Song of Isaiah 53. See Charles Shepherd, *Theological Interpretation and Isaiah 53: A Critical Comparison of Bernhard Duhm, Brevard Childs, and Alec Motyer*, Library of Hebrew Bible/Old Testament Studies 598 (New York: Bloomsbury T&T Clark, 2014); and Brevard S. Childs, *Isaiah*, Old Testament Library (Louisville: Westminster John Knox, 2001).

7. Jack B. Rogers and Donald K. McKim, *The Authority and Interpretation of the Bible: An Historical Approach* (San Francisco: Harper & Row, 1979; repr., Eugene, OR: Wipf & Stock, 1999).

tions" that yields a "history of religion."[8] The work of historical criticism, so much valued among us, was to accommodate the theological claims of the Bible to modern rationality and thus to explain away the "ontological embarrassment" of the text, most notably the agency of God and most particularly the "supernatural" performance of God. It is correct, I think, to conclude that the community of historical criticism (with the compelling liturgy of graduate study) now has developed into what is termed "progressive Christianity," which has successfully fended off the embarrassment of God-claims and left for us an urgent social-justice agenda. Thus, "history," as recently evidenced in the Jesus Seminar, has always been the escape hatch for liberals (progressives) who have found the theological claims of the text too much a violation of reason.

Each of these reading habits, each in its own community, enjoys a normative quality of certitude, and each looks deeply askance at the reading habits of other communities. The result, in each case, is an insular reading community that is not interrupted by or intruded upon by reading outside the preferred trajectory. The force of legitimacy, in each case, is so compelling that the particular reading community can imagine and accept that its reading is the best, right, and most faithful one to be accepted without questions. Indeed, alternatives tend not to be on the horizon.

III

So much for *the permit of the text* to all such communities of reading habits, a permit that has been exercised freely. In that regard, every reading community proceeds confidently and without doubt about its own habits and outcomes. To the contrary, however, the text exercises *long-term restraint* on such reading habits by way of the witness of the text itself, which sits there in front of us on its own terms.

- Thus in the face of creedal readings, there is simply so much text that will not accommodate itself so that the reading must be highly selective. After God is confessed in creedal cadences,

8. It turns out that the reconstruction of the "history of God" and the "history of Israelite religion" (which issued in an evolutionary scheme signaled by "JEDP") served the purpose of establishing Western (European) Christianity as the culmination of the evolutionary process of culture, thus asserting the superiority of that religion and culture. See Tomoko Masuzawa, *The Invention of World Religions: Or, How European Universalism Was Preserved in the Language of Pluralism* (Chicago: University of Chicago Press, 2005); and Walter Brueggemann and Davis Hankins, "The Invention and Persistence of Wellhausen's World," *Catholic Biblical Quarterly* 75 (2013): 15–31.

we still find in the text a quixotic, trickster God, or a God who remains hidden even from our best intellectual probes and formulations. It is for that reason that we have an insistent call for a "revision" of the lectionary to let the church read texts that do not readily fit our certitude. This subversive urge is to open the lectionary to texts that do not so readily conform to established creedal expectations. Everyone knows those texts are there, but we wonder whether it is proper (or necessary) to consider them. It is like a family secret that finally must be faced.

- The issue is the same with scholastic fundamentalist reading. The text itself readily challenges on two glaring counts. First is the testimony of the text that "God changes," so that we get a simmering about the question of an "open theism."[9] And, second, the "violence of God" constitutes an immense problem for our packaged certitudes, a problem that requires enormous agility that now evokes great interpretive energy for an issue that long, until recently, remained mostly unrecognized and unacknowledged.[10]

- As for historical criticism and its offspring, progressive Christianity, some texts refuse the dismissal of the agency of God, for when God is expelled from the text, there simply is no text remaining. John Cobb, in his recent winsome book, *Jesus' Abba: The God Who Has Not Failed*, has tried to soften the issue of divine agency, but softening finally is not very persuasive, at least to this reader.[11]

Thus, the text will not readily yield even to our best reading habits. I conclude that, as readers in any one of these reading communities with our convinced reading habits, we are required to be "selective fundamentalists" (all of us!). That is, we select carefully what texts will be read and heard, and we hope that we will not be summoned beyond our confines to other texts and other readings.

9. The best book on "God changes" is Terence E. Fretheim, *The Suffering of God: An Old Testament Perspective*, Overtures to Biblical Theology (Philadelphia: Fortress Press, 1984). On "open theism," see especially the discussion of Clark Pinnock, *Most Moved Mover: A Theology of God's Openness* (Grand Rapids: Baker Books, 2001).

10. For a fine and representative discussion of the problem of the violence of God in the biblical text, see Jerome F. D. Creach, *Violence in Scripture*, Interpretation (Louisville: Westminster John Knox, 2013).

11. John Cobb, *Jesus' Abba: The God Who Has Not Failed* (Minneapolis: Fortress Press, 2015).

IV

The great fresh awareness in Scripture reading is the recognition that the claims of the text cannot finally be contained within any of these "normative" reading communities. Thus the text summons readers

- well beyond the *creedal* to the *quixotic*

- well beyond the *scholastic* to *inexplicable dynamism*

- well beyond *historical-critical rationality* to *"The Holy One"* who is other than a "sacred idea"

As new readers join the conversation who refuse to submit to conventional communal habits, we witness the emergence of new reading communities, new perspectives, and new interpretive outcomes that are variously emancipatory for us or disconcerting to us. Thus, the various liberation trajectories (feminist, Hispanic, queer, Marxist) and the insistent discourse of postcolonial reading make clear over time the inadequacy of "normative readings." Characteristically but not surprisingly, such fresh readings come "from below" or from outside the zones of privilege and entitlement that normative readings are intended to support. It can be expected, surely, that these fresh perspectives place a check on uncritical readings done in "normative" communities and in fact are responses to the restraint of the text itself that often does not give in to our preferred reading. Thus, against creedalism, in recent readings the text attests the tricky restlessness of God. Against scholasticism, new readings require attention to the emancipatory impulse that breaks certitude. Against historical criticism, fresh readings insist upon the agency of God that tells against prideful human autonomy.

V

In this circumstance of *fresh permit for agency* in reading and *new restraints from the text* against established readings, the reality of biblical exposition is open and pluralistic. For the practitioners of any of the old trajectories, it is also unnerving. It is possible that this recognition of *the agency of the interpreter* and *nonnegotiable restraint of the text* will evolve into a series of disconnected sects, each of which reads in isolation and without responsibility to others. This it would seem is the direction of the Society of Biblical Literature in which our meeting is atomized into tiny interest groups, each of which operates with its own taken-for-granted assumptions.

It is also possible, however, that this rich pluralism in reading need not plunge us into fragmented sectarianism. It could, alternatively, lead to a fresh and intentional engagement whereby we pay careful heed to readings other than our own. Ziolkowski exhibits just such a rich pluralism, but it remains from his work to see about the field shared by these various renderings. There are no answers in the back of the book, not even our preferred answers, as we have been accustomed to think and trust. We may be, moreover, approaching a time when Jürgen Habermas's "ideal speech situation" becomes a prospect, in which all interpretive voices are heard by all of us. This would shake us out of our "dogmatic slumbers," out of our various normative (not to say objective) reading habits, perchance to stand face-to-face (see Exod 33:11) with the hidden God and the available neighbor. Such face-to-faceness would be an act of modesty appropriate to our task.

Index of Biblical Passages

Index of Names